Artist, Authorship & Legacy

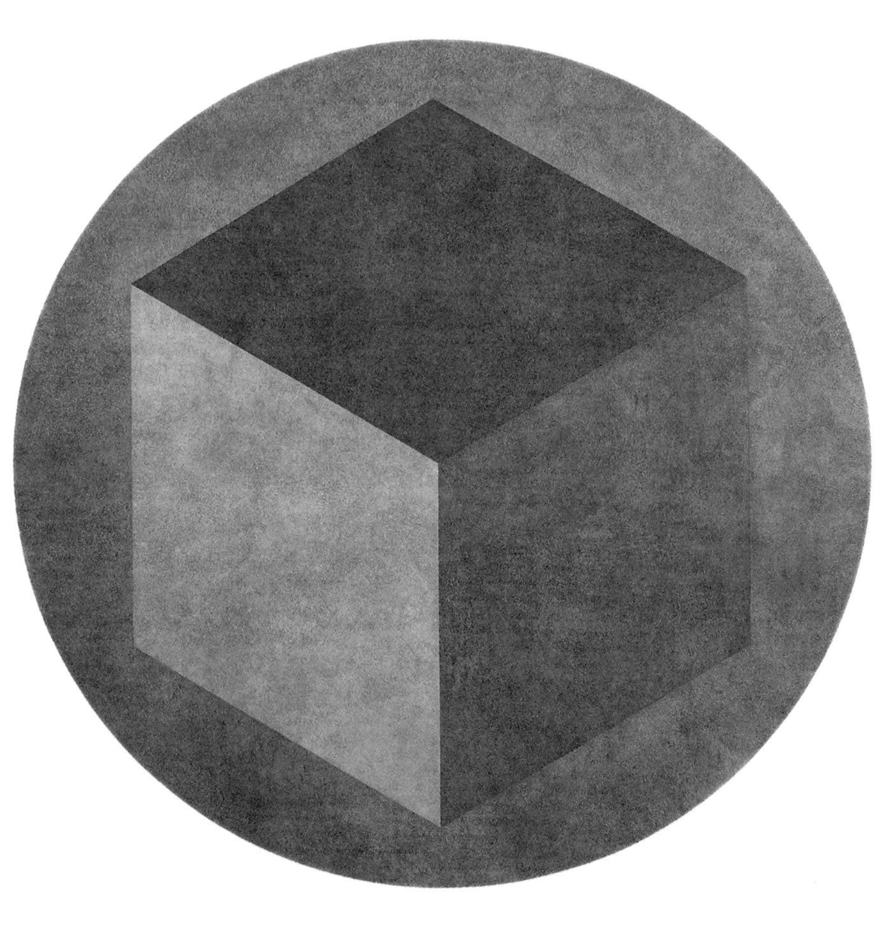

Artist, Authorship & Legacy
A Reader

Edited by Daniel McClean

Ridinghouse

Part Two: The Artwork, Aura, and Authentication

Part Three: Legacy and Its Stewards

Introduction

DANIEL McCLEAN

That a living artist has to defend the authorship of his own work should never have come to pass.
—Peter Doig

In 2016 the artist Peter Doig (b.1959) went on trial in a US federal district court. Doig, whose paintings can command significant sums in the contemporary art market, had surprisingly been sued for denying his authorship of a forty-year-old landscape painting signed in the name of "Peter Doige" not "Peter Doig."[1] The plaintiffs, a former Canadian corrections officer and a Chicago-based art dealer, claimed that Doig had been incarcerated as an adolescent at a correctional facility close to Toronto on drug-related charges: it was here, they claimed, that the officer had met Doig and had fallen in love with his painting, which he had bought from him. For refusing to positively authenticate the painting, and rejecting this improbable tale, Doig was sued in this surreal lawsuit for damages, caused by Doig's denial, to the work's commercial value. At trial, Doig was forced in his defense to prove a negative: that he had not created the painting. Though Doig was ultimately vindicated by establishing that a real "Peter Doige" had once been interned at the correctional center and most likely created the painting, it came at considerable personal and financial cost: the litigation was time-consuming and distressing, and though successful at trial, Doig could not (under US litigation rules) recover his hefty legal fees.

In 2015 it was publicly reported that the highly influential German painter Gerhard Richter (b.1932) had decided to exclude certain paintings from his comprehensive catalogue raisonné (also available online).[2] Richter had created these paintings early on in his artistic career, shortly after moving from the former East Germany (where he grew up) to West Germany in 1961. Richter reportedly decided to omit these early realist-style paintings from his catalogue raisonné because he disliked them so much and did not believe that they properly reflected his authorship. This was despite the fact that these paintings had apparently not changed from their original condition when created and released by the artist. Richter's meticulously ordered catalogue raisonné of his complete works (from 1962 onwards) is the medium through which the authenticity of Richter's works, his art market, and his artistic legacy are controlled. By excluding these now-orphaned early works from his catalogue raisonné, Richter had effectively withdrawn his authorship from them.

It is appropriate to begin with these two extreme expressions of contemporary artistic authorship in the context of this collection of essays. Both illustrate themes essential to the book: on the one hand, the importance of artistic authorship (in particular, the identity of a valorized, individual artist-creator) to how we value artworks as artifacts both symbolically and monetarily within the art system; on the other hand, the contingent and often conflicting relationship between artists and owners of artworks—a relationship regulated by law that in extreme instances may be played out in the courts. Within Doig's and Richter's narratives of artistic authorship, the figure of the artist-author emerges at opposite ends. First, there is the artist as a commodity, sued by an owner for denying that he created a particular artwork (which he did not in fact create) because this undermines the artwork's commercial value. Second, there is the artist as a sovereign subject, free to retract the artwork's authorship even after it has been released into the world and remains unaltered. It is within these contradictory and yet deeply intertwined configurations of authorship that much of this book unfolds. This is seen, for example, in *Kreuk v. Vō*, the trial of the Danish artist Danh Vō (b.1975), sued by the collector Bert Kreuk in the Dutch courts (2013–15) for failing to deliver "commissioned" artworks that the collector could capitalize on by quickly reselling.[3] *Kreuk v. Vō* was echoed in the legal dispute in 2016 between the LA collector/investor Stefan Simchowitz and Dublin-based art dealer Jonathan Ellis King, and the Ghanaian-born artist Ibrahim Mahama (b.1987), who disavowed of a group of three hundred works put up for sale by the collector and dealer, works that the artist alleged had been wrongfully spliced from a single large installation of jute sacks.[4] The complex push and pull between the artist as commodity and the artist as sovereign subject is further articulated in the legal disputes of the American artist Cady Noland (b.1956) with collectors and dealers of her work.[5] Noland, by withdrawing authorship from successive artworks owners have sought to sell, has arguably adopted a position of authorial retraction close to that of Gerhard Richter.

This anthology of interdisciplinary essays critically examines the interlocking themes of artistic authorship, authenticity, and legacy from legal, art market, and art historical perspectives and is structured in three sections: Part One: Authorship and Artists' Rights; Part Two: The Artwork, Aura, and Authentication; and Part Three: Legacy and Its Stewards. The book addresses how artistic authorship is iterated over time by different actors, from the artist to the artist's heirs to art experts. It is through the law that artists' rights of authorship are articulated and tested against collectors, dealers, museums, and even against other artists and photographers. It is increasingly through the law that conflicts are being resolved in the art market as it expands (at least at the high end) despite short-term dips across the world and as artistic production dramatically increases to meet demand often leading to legal disputes particularly between artists and collectors.[6]

The law provides artists with a bundle of authorial rights—including intellectual property rights, such as copyright, moral rights of authorship, and the artist's resale royalty right—as well as contractually conferred rights. Although legal protection varies between jurisdictions, these rights enable artists as authors to control, to differing degrees, the reproduction, exhibition, resale, and authentication of their works even once legal ownership has been transferred.

Artists' rights, along with artworks and archival materials, are often passed on after the artist's death to heirs or foundations, who exercise many of the artist's authorship functions posthumously on the artist's behalf.

At the same time, however, as this volume also demonstrates, the law only partially explains how artistic authorship is structured and negotiated. On the one hand, artistic authorship is mediated through art world practices and conventions: the artist's signature and certification of unique or limited-edition works, exhibitions in galleries and museums, art market and art historical discourses, and the artist's catalogue raisonné. On the other hand, artistic authorship is mediated through the art market's unique ecology of relationships. In the upper echelons of the international art market, for instance, artists and their primary galleries often assert control over the resale of artists' works by "blacklisting" collectors and their advisers who resell artworks for short-term speculative gain (particularly at auction).[7] This is commonly done alongside purporting to impose resale restrictions on artworks sold to these parties in sale contracts. This type of "soft power," which is dependent upon the artist's market position and the relative scarcity of work, is arguably more important than reliance on the law for this group of privileged artists.

PART ONE: AUTHORSHIP AND ARTISTS' RIGHTS

In Part One, we see how artists' rights have developed from the 1960s to today.[8] At the center of this trajectory is the paradigm of the "Artist's Reserved Rights Transfer and Sale Agreement" (1971), also known as the "Artist's Contract," co-drafted by the seminal Conceptual-art dealer and curator Seth Siegelaub and lawyer Robert Projansky. Through the Artist's Contract, Siegelaub and Projansky sought to address the economic inequalities of the art world, providing a template by which artists could seek to protect the fruits of their labor and benefit from the future resale of their work as well as control of the work's exhibition and reproduction.[9] As much a manifesto of artists' rights as a legal document, the Artist's Contract was in practice adopted by only a handful of artists, most notably by Hans Haacke, because of the stringent covenants it imposes on collectors.[10] Nevertheless, the Artist's Contract anticipated future legal developments in the protection of artists' rights. The artist's resale royalty right, guaranteeing qualifying artists set royalties on the resale of their artwork, would be adopted throughout European Union member states in 2006, for instance.[11] In 1990 the United States implemented the Visual Artists Rights Act (VARA), paralleling earlier legislation in Europe, to protect the moral rights of artists, including the rights of attribution (to be publicly credited as the author of the artwork and to object to false attribution) and integrity (to object to the derogatory treatment of the artwork, through its modification or destruction).[12]

This trajectory in the development of artists' rights continued with the notorious dispute between the artist Christoph Büchel (b.1966) and the Massachusetts Museum of Contemporary Art (MASS MoCA, North Adams)—a dispute that went on from 2007 to 2010 and involved the unauthorized display by MASS MoCA of Büchel's abandoned, sprawling, unfinished installation, *Training Ground For Democracy* (2007).[13] In asserting his moral rights as an artist under VARA against MASS MoCA in successive trials, Büchel tested the limits of the museum's authority as a commissioning institution to determine when and in what form an artist's work can be displayed.[14] In doing so, Büchel also arguably transformed the law, and specifically VARA, into an artistic medium in its own right, using the trial as the ultimate conduit, perhaps, of "institutional critique." Büchel's assertion of his legal rights as an artist-author under VARA are echoed in the legal battles of Cady Noland, who in several cases has fought to retract her authorship from artworks she considers to have been materially damaged since being created.[15] In one ongoing dispute, Noland has objected to the refabrication in 2010 of part of her wooden installation *Log Cabin* (1990). Like Büchel, Noland has tested the limits of VARA, and now also US copyright law, with the defendants contending that

Log Cabin lacks protection as a Conceptual artwork under US copyright law.

It would be misleading to suggest that all artists have unambiguously aligned themselves with values of sovereign authorship. Part One also reveals that many artists have been committed in their practices to questioning and destabilizing the figure of the artist as solitary genius, recognizing that the meaning of the artwork is formed through its context and interpretation, and that the figure of the author, just like the self, is contingent and unstable. Artist Mike Kelley (1954–2012) explored such matters through his labyrinthine project *Timeless/Authorless*, which questions the artist's own authorship as well as selfhood.[16] In a separate vein, other artists have even tried to complicate the notion of sovereign authorship by creating artist collectives, such as General Idea and Claire Fontaine, in which multiple creators collaboratively perform the functions of the artist-author anonymously under the guise of a fictitious name.[17]

Yet despite these assaults on the authority of sovereign authorship, the Romantic figure of the individual genius appears ineluctably fundamental to the construction of artistic authorship, including within the art market, the museum, and art historical discourse. These hierarchical assumptions are reflected in the copyright infringement dispute in the US courts (2009–13) involving the "appropriation artist" Richard Prince (b.1949) and the photographer Patrick Cariou (b.1963).[18] In this dispute, Cariou sued Prince for the unauthorized reproduction of black-and-white photographs of Rastafarians from Cariou's book *Yes Rasta*, used in Prince's series of collages *Canal Zone* (2008). In defending the lawsuit, Prince was ultimately able to successfully rely on an expanded copyright defense of "transformative" fair use. While welcome in expanding the boundaries of artistic freedom of expression, Prince's defense also betrayed at times hierarchical assumptions about the priority of his authorship as a celebrated fine artist over that of Cariou—the photographer—treating the latter's photographs as authorless "facts of nature" amenable to Prince's authorial appropriation and creative transformation.[19]

PART TWO: THE ARTWORK, AURA, AND AUTHENTICATION

Part Two reflects first on how a lot of contemporary artistic production complicates artistic authorship, testing the boundaries of the "unique," original artwork, and undermining the ascription of a singular creator to the artwork. This in turn leads to difficulties with authentication, which can become even more complex after the artist's death, when third parties (including artists' estates and art experts) come to speak on the deceased artist's behalf.

In contemporary art practice, the artwork, like artistic authorship, is complicated because not only does the artwork exist within diverse, nontraditional media (from performance to film, from instructions to installation), but artistic production is often "delegated" by the artist to his or her assistants (as seen in much Pop and Minimalist art), and artistic performance is delegated to collectors of the artwork, who are authorized to activate it. Collectors and collecting institutions take on this active role for many Conceptual artworks, for example, the wall drawings of Sol LeWitt (1928–2007), which are executed by owners according to the artist's textual and visual instructions, and Hélio Oiticica's *Parangolés* (1937–1980), which are literally habitable paintings composed of layers of painted fabrics, to be worn or carried while dancing to samba rhythms.[20]

Within this context, the unique "auratic" artwork, as famously described by the German philosopher Walter Benjamin (1892–1940), often exists, paradoxically, in multiple, replicated forms (as seen particularly with sculpture, video art, and photography), coexisting in different places and times. Yet this paradox of authorship—which is widely accepted in the art world and defines much contemporary artistic practice—has been arguably present throughout the course of modernism.[21] It is seen notably in Auguste Rodin's (1840–1917) bronze sculptures, which were cast in multiple copies both during the artist's life and after his death from plasters made by the artist. As Rodin's practice illustrates, the question of what is an "original copy," and who has the authority to decide this, is at times as much a legal question as an aesthetic one.[22] When Rodin died in 1917, the French state inherited, along with Rodin's studio and sculptural casts, the artist's moral rights of authorship and, in particular, the right to sanction the use of the artist's name in relation to "authorized" copies of his sculpture. Invoking these moral rights in 1993, the French state passed a decree limiting the number of permitted first editions taken from Rodin's casts to twelve. In 2014 the French authorities sought unsuccessfully to criminally prosecute the American Gary Snell for producing through his company, Gruppo Mondiale, counterfeit copies of Rodin's sculpture in violation of this decree.[23] Disputes over the scope of artists' editions have also surfaced between artists and collectors—specifically, disputes over the artist's right to later remake, or reprint in a modified from, earlier works, brought on by the ever-increasing demand for supply of work in the contemporary art market.[24] In 2012 the collector Jonathan Sobel sought to unsuccessfully sue the artist William Eggleston (b.1939) for producing subsequent prints (in a different size and edition run) of earlier limited-edition photographic works created by the artist, which Sobel had purchased. The New York federal district court rejected Sobel's argument that Eggleston had breached express and implied representations in creating the later edition and had thereby diluted the value of the earlier edition.[25]

It is perhaps unsurprising that the legal-style regime of signed artists' certificates of authenticity has also come to assume such a vital role (as opposed to the signed artwork) within the contemporary art market in regulating the artistic authorship and ownership of artworks.[26] Attesting to the work's authenticity, and in some instances authorizing the work's owner to activate the artwork (as in Sol LeWitt's wall drawings) and sometimes the work's lender (as seen in the reactivation of the happenings of Allan Kaprow), the certificate also confirms ownership of an authentic artwork for which the otherwise conventional indicia of artistic authorship (the signed painting, drawing, or print) are not present. Without an accompanying certificate, it is often impossible for owners to sell their artworks. Some artists and their estates refuse to reissue certificates for artworks, where the certificate has been lost, stolen, or damaged, as with Sol LeWitt's estate. Loss of a certificate for Sol LeWitt's *Wall Drawing #448* (1985) by the Rhona Hoffman Gallery, in Chicago, where the artwork had been consigned for sale, led the collector Roderick Steinkamp to sue the gallery in 2012 for the value of the artwork in the New York courts (though the gallery retained possession of the accompanying maquette created by Sol LeWitt to visually represent what this wall drawing should look like).[27] Within this legal-style regime, some artists (including Carl Andre and Lawrence Weiner) operate archival systems recording the ownership and the transfer of ownership of these certificates.[28]

Part Two further addresses some of the recent legal conflicts between collectors and authenticators involving the disputed authentication of particular artworks. Authenticators—whether artists' estates, the appointed authentication committees of foundations, or independent art experts—play a key role in protecting an artist's legacy and market by positively identifying the artist's work (principally by issuing certificates for works and including them in the artist's catalogue raisonné) and by eliminating fakes and misattributions. Yet fear of litigation by dissatisfied collectors—who can potentially bring claims against authenticators under a wide variety of legal theories, including breach of contract, negligence, misrepresentation, product disparagement, and antitrust—has caused many authenticators to withdraw from this vital role, even though these legal claims are often difficult to establish in practice.[29] At the heart of this section is the legal dispute between the collector Joe Simon-Whelan and the Andy Warhol Foundation for the Visual Arts and Andy Warhol Authentication Board (2007–10). The board controversially denied Warhol's authorship of *Red Self-Portrait* (1965), one of an edition of ten silkscreen paintings, which led to a legal battle that revolved around Warhol's industrial methods of artistic production and his delegation to his studio assistants.[30] Despite strong evidence that Warhol himself had considered the series to be authentic, the board twice refused to grant Simon-Whelan a certificate for the work, even stamping the back of his painting with the word "DENIED."[31] The board's perceived lack of transparency and consistency in its decision-making, coupled with perceived conflict of interest (Vincent Froment, who sat on the board, was also a dealer in Warhol's work), led Simon-Whelan along with other claimants to commence an improbable antitrust action against the board and foundation. Though Simon-Whelan later settled his claim in the wake of escalating legal costs, the fact that it survived the defendants' motion to dismiss, coupled with substantial legal costs, encouraged the foundation to voluntarily dissolve its board in 2011. This was followed by the closures of the authentication committees of the Keith Haring Foundation and Jean Michel Basquiat estate in 2012.

The closure of the Warhol board and other artists' authentication boards in the United States has led to difficulties in the art market: owners of genuine artworks who lack requisite certificates find it difficult to sell their works (or at least for their full market value), and an important mechanism for removing fakes and misattributions has been removed from the market. The conflict over authentications has shown no sign of abating, with other high-profile legal disputes in the United States, including between the collector Gerald Cramer and the Calder Foundation (2014) over the foundation's refusal to provide an inventory number officially confirming Alexander Calder's authorship of the mobile, *Eight Black Leaves* (1948).[32]

The conflict between collectors and authenticators has also been played out in other jurisdictions.[33] In 2014 Bozena Nikiel, a leading expert on the Cubist artist Jean Metzinger (1883–1956) and also holder of the artist's moral rights, was sued by Laurent Alexandre, a collector in France, for disparaging goods by refusing to positively certify the painting *Maisonblanche* as an authentic work by Metzinger.[34] After being ordered to pay damages by the lower French court, which determined that the work was likely authentic on the balance of probabilities, Nikiel was eventually vindicated by the Cour de cassation (the highest French court). The final verdict determined that she was entitled to her opinion as an expert (her "intimate conviction") based on her right to freedom of expression as protected under article 10 of the European Convention on Human Rights, which trumped the collector's rights.

As all these instances reveal, it is difficult for the law to strike a balance between the rights of art experts and authentication bodies to issue opinions free from the unwarranted fear of litigation, and the rights of owners not to have their otherwise valuable property wrongly maligned.[35] In late 2015 the New York Senate passed a Bill (yet to be passed by the New York Assembly) addressing this problem for the New York art market. The draft Bill makes the standard of pleading and proof much higher when bringing claims against authenticators while allowing defendant experts to recover their attorneys' fees and legal expenses if successful in their defense. If passed, this legislation would provide greater protection to authentication bodies and experts and might encourage artists' foundations such as the Warhol and Haring foundations to reopen their authentication boards.[36]

PART THREE: LEGACY AND ITS STEWARDS

Part Three addresses artists' legacy planning and the stewarding of artistic legacy; in short, who shapes the narrative of the artist's legacy and his or her place in art history? At the core of the section are complex questions concerning how an artist wants their oeuvre and authorship to be seen over time; who should be entrusted by the artist as stewards; and, importantly, how legacy should be stewarded.[37] In most instances, it is the artist's heirs who are the immediate guardians, though artist-endowed foundations, stewarding the artist's legacy for the public benefit, have become (at least for wealthy artists) an increasingly common artists' legacy model, particularly in the United States.

Artists' estates and foundations play a key role in conserving and exhibiting the artist's work; undertaking and encouraging research and scholarship on the artist; bringing artworks to the market; authenticating artworks (through the preparation of a catalogue raisonné and by issuing certificates of authenticity); and authorizing the posthumous production, installation, performance, and exhibition of the deceased artist's work. These vital authorship functions are often underwritten by the estate's ownership of an inventory of the artist's work and archival materials, as well as control over their intellectual-property rights (including copyright and moral rights of authorship, which in most jurisdictions last for the lifetime of the artist and seventy years post mortem). The artist's estate or foundation is often also recognized within the art market as being the authoritative source of authentication on the artist's work, which is also frequently underwritten, particularly in civil-law countries, by inheritance of the artist's moral right of attribution.

Artists' estates and foundations have assumed increasing importance in today's contemporary art world, exercising authorship on behalf of the deceased artist. As "blue chip" contemporary art galleries compete aggressively to represent artists' estates and foundations alongside living artists, it has become fashionable for curators to include work of deceased artists within the framework of exhibitions and biennials traditionally dedicated to showcasing the work of the living.[38] Within this ecology, specialist platforms and entities have developed in Europe and the United States dedicated to assisting artists with legacy planning and to helping artists' estates navigate relationships with the art market and museums.[39] In an unprecedented step, in late 2016 Sotheby's advisory arm, Art Agency, Partners, New York even hired Christy MacLear (former director of the Robert Rauschenberg Foundation) in a move designed for the auction house to work directly with artists and their estates on legacy planning.

As Part Three discusses, artists' legacy planning is shaped by many factors—personal, legal, and financial—as well as by the artist's consideration as to what should happen to his or her work after death. Two important factors that might influence a legacy plan are whether the artist has heirs (and wishes to bequeath their work and archival materials to these heirs or to an independent foundation, for example) and the value of the artworks and intellectual-property rights left behind, which can determine if an estate or foundation is financially viable.[40] For many artists, legacy planning is an anathema, as exemplified by Pablo Picasso (1881–1973) who, haunted by fear of his own death, refused to make a will. Yet the consequences for artists who fail to legacy-plan are clear, as the example of Picasso shows. On his death, Picasso left hundreds of thousands of paintings, drawings, sculptures, and prints with no direction as to how they should be divided, leading to a bitter, six-year legal dispute among family members in France and a settlement that reportedly cost $30 million.[41]

Tax reliefs in many countries incentivize artists and heirs to place artworks and other assets into not-for-profit foundations (created both during and after the artist's life), enabling the artist and heirs to minimize tax duties on death and allowing the artist's estate, through the foundation, to operate tax-free.[42] In the United States, the tax-favorable model of the private operating foundation (Section 501(c)(3) of the Internal Revenue Code) has been particularly important for artists' estates, notably those of Joan Mitchell, Andy Warhol, Robert Rauschenberg, Keith Haring, and Robert Mapplethorpe, supported by substantial endowments from these financially highly successful artists.
As well as promoting the work of these artists, all of the above private foundations were established with broad philanthropic aims, including supporting other artists and art institutions through grants (including grants for research and exhibition), thereby securing the artist's legacy in an expansive sense.

As Part Three also examines, failure by an artist to appoint suitable executors can frustrate and taint his or her legacy. This is illustrated in the infamous litigation in the New York state courts during the 1970s between the heirs of Mark Rothko (1903–1970) and the executors of his estate and Rothko's gallery, Marlborough Fine Art to release the estate from a highly disadvantageous agreement entered into with the Marlborough Gallery group by the estate's executors immediately following the artist's death.[43] The executors of Rothko's estate (one of whom was a Marlborough Gallery director [44] had sold and consigned all of the 798 Rothko paintings left to his estate upon death to Marlborough. The court found that one hundred of these works were sold to Marlborough significantly under value (at $1.8 million) and that the remaining 698 were consigned on highly unfavorable (50 percent as opposed to 30 percent or lower net commission) terms resulting in huge profit for the gallery. Ultimately, the New York State Court of Appeals found breach of trust, self-dealing and fraud by the estate's executors and Marlborough in a manner "manifestly wrong and indeed shocking". The court upheld the lower court's cancellation of the contract, its ousting of the executors and orders that Marlborough return the remaining unsold Rothko's paintings to the artist's estate [45] as well as pay (with the estate's executors) the Rothko heirs $9.2 million in damages and costs.

Other artists' legacies have been afflicted by similar high-profile legal conflicts caused by failed legacy planning.[46] When the Austrian artist Franz West (1947–2012) died, his children, the Franz West Archive (a not-for-profit organization established by the artist in 1997), and Franz West Private Foundation (established only days before the artist's death) became locked into bitter litigation over ownership of West's estate.[47] In 2016 the Austrian Supreme Court of Justice found that the copyright in West's photographs and furniture had not been lawfully transferred from the archive to the foundation, and in 2017 a regional Viennese court declared that West's other assets, including his artworks, were to go to his children and not to the foundation (which the court determined had not been formed validly).

An artist's failure to provide proper guidance as to how their legacy should be managed by their stewards can also taint an artist's legacy. Using its authority negatively, an artists' estate or foundation can prevent an artist's works from being copied by other artists, accessed by scholars, exhibited in museums, reproduced in exhibition catalogues and monographs, and even from being sold in the art market. The management of the estate of the leading Brazilian Neo-concrete artist, Lygia Clark (1920–1988), by the artist's sons has been widely criticized for its perceived negative impact on Clark's legacy.[48] Clark's heirs have threatened legal action against public art institutions exhibiting works that are widely recognized as genuine, but that the estate nevertheless refused to authenticate (wrongfully, it is alleged). The Clark estate has also been criticized for refusing to provide copyright licenses for photographs of disputed works to be featured in exhibition catalogues.

As Part Three demonstrates, an artist's legacy—their influence on the language and history of art, the art market, and society and culture more generally—can assume myriad forms. Some artists wish to obsessively control the conditions in which their work is made visible after death. Here, the artist's desire for a museum or a public site dedicated to the preservation and display of their work is the apotheosis of this process. A striking example is the Chinati Foundation, in Marfa, Texas. In 1979 Donald Judd (1928–1994) acquired a vast tract of land in the remote town of Marfa with the aid of the Dia Foundation (now managed by the Chinati Foundation), to permanently exhibit the work of Judd and his peers, including Dan Flavin and John Chamberlain, in the context of a very specific landscape and architecture.[49] By contrast, other artists wish to control their legacy by rewriting their own history so that certain works disappear. In extreme instances, this has led artists, including Georgia O'Keeffe (1887–1986), to destroy their early works. Agnes Martin (1912–2004) reportedly sought to do so too, but her friends, who were entrusted with this task, fortunately ignored her instructions. Other artists, like Gerhard Richter, have withdrawn their authorship from earlier work, as discussed above.

Just as artistic authorship is often contested, the importance of artists' authorial legacies will continue to be revised as new art historical narratives emerge.[50] The last two decades have been characterized by a rewriting of the modernist (predominantly white, Western, male) canon, in which a heterogeneous array of artists from Africa, Asia, the Middle East, and Latin America as well as female artists and artists of color in the United States and Europe have been art historically repositioned.[51] Despite the enormous symbolic and monetary value attached to it, artistic authorship is not constant and stable. Instead, as this book shows, artistic authorship is fluid, iterated by different protagonists (including the artist) through different structures and practices over time. If the artist's role within these practices is often the most prominent, an artist's relationship to his or her work is subject to change and revision. For these reasons, artistic authorship and legacy will likely remain both valued and contested.

In addition to being an exploration of current practices of artistic authorship in contemporary art, this book can be read as an investigation into how the law intersects with and regulates the art world. For although art world custom often appears blind to the machinery of the law (with high-value art deals regularly concluded on the basis of a telephone call or email exchange followed by a sale invoice), and although the art market is not regulated like other markets, when disputes arise in the art world that cannot be resolved through internal mediation, the parties involved often turn to the law as a means for resolving disputes.[52]

Yet it is important to remember that although the law is integral to the construction of artistic authorship and legacy, just as it is to other aspects of the art market, legal criteria and judgments regarding the authorship and authenticity of artworks can be at variance with those adopted in the art world. Nowhere is this disparity more starkly witnessed than in the dispute fought out in a federal district court in 1993 over the authenticity of *Rio Nero* (1959), a mobile attributed to Alexander Calder.[53] In this dispute, the judge rejected the plaintiff owner's claim against the sellers to cancel the sale because the leading expert on Calder, Klaus Perls, had declared the work to be a forgery based on his connoisseurship. Instead, the judge (taking the work's provenance, signature, and other expert testimony into consideration) ruled that on the balance of probabilities the sculpture was likely an authentic work by Calder—a lower standard of "proof" than that used in the art market. Despite the court's validation, the art market did not follow suit, and today the work remains reportedly unsold.[54]

Over the last decade or so, an increasing gap has sprung up between artistic practice—framed by postmodernity and digital technologies—and its legal codification—essentially still beholden to modernist and analogue terminology. The essays in this volume are an attempt to chart at least some of the developments and contradictions that have turned copyright and authorship (and by extension legacy) into such a minefield, and to suggest possible solutions to the most pressing issues. The law will always play catch-up with changing artistic and technological realities. The goal is not to close the gap—that is an impossibility—but to keep it as narrow as is feasible, for the sake of all parties involved.

Part One: Authorship and Artists' Rights

Artists' Rights in the United States; or, A Remembrance of Claims Occasionally Checked

JOAN KEE

On a cold January day in 1969, the artist Vassilakis Takis (b.1925) walked into the Museum of Modern Art (MoMA), in New York, grabbed his work *Tele-sculpture* (1960), which he had sold to the museum six years before, and left. More than a performance or a gimmick, the act was meant to protest the museum's decision to include his work in a show without his permission.[1] Yet this act—vividly described by art historian Julia Bryan-Wilson as a "kidnapping"—was also a crime. For although *Tele-sculpture* was Takis's work, the artist no longer had any legal rights over what was done to or with it; the work belonged to the museum.

Compare Takis's response to that of Giorgio de Chirico (1888–1978). In 1950 the venerable Italian painter filed a lawsuit against the organizers of an exhibition of his work at the Venice Biennale, claiming that they had included too much early work without his consent. Although he eventually lost the case, the Italian court initially found in de Chirico's favor, stating that his rights had indeed been violated.[2] Both Takis and de Chirico sought to assert what they considered their authorial rights. Yet the case in Italy turned on the legal doctrine of moral rights, a concept widely accepted in many Western European countries, which grants the creators of most copyrighted works a wide array of "inalienable" rights, among them attribution, or the right to claim authorship of a work, as well as the right to prevent its alteration, mutilation, or destruction without the creator's consent. In contrast, artists' demands for moral rights in the United States have encountered ambivalence from jurists and lawmakers deeply skeptical of any claim of exceptionalism for artists and their works. Moral rights did not exist in the United States when Takis removed his work from the walls of MoMA.

EXPANDING DEFINITIONS OF LABOR AND THE ART WORKERS' COALITION

For centuries, artists have fought for what they feel is rightfully theirs, whether it be proper attribution or compensation due.[3] But the concept of identifying and claiming legal rights specifically for artists is a late twentieth-century phenomenon—one radicalized in the wake of a general reconsideration of the social purpose and function of art. Actions like Takis's "kidnapping" fell under "artists' rights," an umbrella term widely used in lockstep with numerous campaigns for social and legal reform that took place in the United States during the 1960s. Artists' rights included not only moral rights but also the more general right to make a living from creating and selling work, which, in the context of an expanding market, gained increasing urgency, particularly given the distinct lack of legal oversight concerning dealers' activities.[4]

"Artists' rights" was initially a battle cry for US artists seeking to correct what they saw as a fundamental imbalance of power between themselves and institutions, namely museums, but the concept came to assume a central role in the power struggle between artist and collector. Unsurprisingly, perhaps the first organization to systematically use the term "artists' rights" was the Art Workers' Coalition (AWC), founded in New York in 1969 after Takis abducted his work from its institutional home. A loose coalition of artists, writers, filmmakers, museum staff, and others associated with the art world, the AWC petitioned museums to be more expansive and inclusive in their admission and exhibition policies. Part of its campaign lay in getting the public to recognize artworks—or, more broadly, what artists do—as output, the value of which should be based in part on the amount and quality of labor necessary for production. Here, labor included both physical and intellectual effort, and it is unsurprising that many of the AWC's members were artists associated with Conceptualism, for whom labor included more than the physical production of objects. The AWC tried to work around a key aspect of the Copyright Act, which, prior to its amendment by Congress in 1976, permitted the owner of an artwork to do as they pleased with their property, including, even, acts of destruction.[5] The AWC also tried to get institutions to recognize moral rights–related claims, including "copyright, reproduction rights, exhibition rights, and maintenance responsibilities."[6] Eventually artists' rights operated as a platform for artists to work politically, allowing them to more effectively ask "for whom" artworks were shown, bought, and created.

Economic rights were a priority, especially given the expansion of the contemporary art market in the United States and Western Europe from roughly 1966 to 1973. Artists found themselves having to grapple with the sale and transfer of their works. Even former AWC member Carl Andre (b.1935), who had once declared that buyers should not be allowed to profit from a sale of a work, recognized as much: capital letters hardly conveyed his "DESPAIR at being the kept artist of an imperialist class."[7]

THE MATTER OF THE MARKET

A few years before Takis dramatically liberated his work from institutional clutches, Los Angeles–based artist Edward Kienholz (1927–1994) —who had previously embraced the barter system by successfully exchanging sheets of paper bearing the name of a product or service he wanted for just that—took up the language and form of the contract. Intended to accompany the sale of his *Concept Tableaux* (1965–66), which consisted of descriptions of artworks not yet made, the contract specified the terms under which these unmade works would be executed. Kienholz drew a parallel between Conceptual art and physical labor by requiring buyers to compensate him at an hourly wage "equal to" the hourly wages of "plumbers, electricians and carpenters."[8] His contract dispelled the misconception that artists work for love and that personal gratification should be adequate compensation. It also tried to banish the suspicion many viewers harbored toward Conceptualism, which one US critic described as a "fraud" even as late as 1993.[9]

Kienholz's contract counts among the more notable examples of how artists have turned to the ideas, structures, and protocols of the law to claim and enforce what they have regarded as their just due. The 1970s saw increasing numbers of artists using contracts and canvassing lawmakers, a move that was as timely as it was assertive in its concurrence with the gradual recognition of art law as a distinct subfield in legal studies.[10] If the engagement with legal institutions and practices had a newfound directness, it may have been due to a transactional environment that frequently pitted artists against buyers and buyers against sellers. What artists saw as a justified extension of their authorial rights sometimes ran counter to those that buyers claimed for themselves.

Consider Robert Rauschenberg's (1925–2008) famous outburst to the collector Robert Scull. In 1973 Sotheby Parke Bernet held the first auction dedicated exclusively to contemporary art, at which Rauschenberg's *Double Feature* (1959) sold for the astronomical sum, at that time, of $90,000.[11] The irate artist confronted Scull, who had originally paid $2,500 for the work: "I've been working my ass off for you to make all this profit!" The collector retorted: "Well, I've been working for you too."[12] The Scull sale underscored how the accumulation of capital preempted other forms of value creation. It set a new benchmark for art prices, consequently renewing interest in the potential of art as a form of investment whose rate of return could compete with more conventional forms of investment—a phenomenon others tried to monetize by establishing various financial schemes, ranging from mutual funds based on art investment to borderline cons rooted in dubious buyback schemes.[13]

The Scull auction played a decisive role in reframing artists' rights as a call for a general redistribution of wealth. Several artists, Rauschenberg included, championed resale rights granting royalties to artists whose works were sold at a profit.[14] Their efforts recalled those of both the Society of Artists, a Paris-based organization of mostly painters that in 1909 tried to have a law passed in France that would allow an artist to receive 20 percent of any profit realized on the sale of his or her work, and of Grant Wood, the US painter who, following the swift price hike of one of his paintings around 1940, announced that he would sell new work on the condition that he could subsequently collect half of its appreciated value.[15] Unlike Wood, however, artists like Rauschenberg actively lobbied lawmakers to create legislation protecting artists as an occupational class—a campaign that became front-page fodder and eventually helped bring about the passing of the 1976 California Resale Royalty Act, which grants artists who meet certain criteria the right to receive a share of any profits realized from the resale of their works.[16]

Rauschenberg's campaign underscored how the art world seemed to revolve around systematic asymmetries of power—a view shared by courts and legislatures. Already wary of what they perceived as an imbalance of knowledge between savvy dealers and naive buyers, many courts and legislatures were already predisposed to decide in favor of buyers rather than sellers of artworks. Indeed, judges and lawmakers immediately took the side of buyers, insisting on numerous provisions intended to safeguard what they, as agents of the law, saw as unsophisticated, entry-level buyers operating in an industry lacking any oversight committees or regulatory bodies "comparable to those in the medical or legal professions."[17]

Lawyers experienced in dealing with artists' concerns called their presumptive clients to defend themselves against common seller abuses, whether it be a dealer's refusal to pay an artist or the return of unsold works.[18] Few artists knew how to negotiate with galleries and institutions; fewer still had recourse to legal assistance, which was expensive and time-consuming despite the creation of organizations like Volunteer Lawyers for the Arts, the first of which was established in New York in 1969 to provide free or low-cost legal aid to artists. In many cases, artists shouldered the burden of having to puzzle out the law for themselves, a particularly heavy burden for a class of professionals later described by Robert Projansky in 1974 as "amazingly ignorant of their legal rights."[19] Agreements were often exploitative; consider, for example, how the Multiples Gallery in New York City sent a contract to numerous artists participating in the important 1970 group show *Artists and Photographs* curated by the eminent critic Lawrence Alloway, including Jan Dibbets,

Douglas Huebler, Sol LeWitt, Joseph Kosuth, and Robert Smithson, offering $100 in exchange for "all rights including copyright for the material you have sent to us."[20] Condemning the arrangement as "pure bullshit," curator and artists' rights advocate Seth Siegelaub was particularly upset by how much profit the gallery would make (the gallery, which, having invested just $2,000, would net roughly $30,000 for the sale of the editions produced for the show), not to mention the participating artists willing to agree to such unequal terms. Even in transactions involving public institutions, artists faced considerable disadvantages.[21]

Faced with numerous structural disadvantages in the course of producing, showing, and selling their works, artists increasingly called for the law to recognize the uniqueness of their occupation as deserving of certain forms of protection. Many cited the example of moral-rights regimes in civil law countries like Germany, where the Supreme Court declared in 1971 that "art is unconditionally guaranteed its independence and its own inherent laws."[22] And, contrary to the experience of former AWC member Jean Toche, who was forced by court order in 1974 to undergo psychiatric counseling for simply suggesting the kidnapping of museum officials as part of his work, French judges have defended Noël Godin's right to throw cream pies at public figures, observing that his actions (undertaken since 1969, when he threw a pie in the face of the novelist Marguerite Duras) were but examples of Surrealism.[23] Notable in these decisions is the question of whether society as a whole should be automatically willing to grant legal protection to such forms of expression irrespective of the labor involved—whether, as a "receptacle for personality," such expression is unquestionably entitled to protection.

Since the Customs Court expanded legal definitions of art to include nonrepresentational works in its landmark 1928 decision *Brancusi v. United States*, US law has recognized the existence of legal problems unique to visual art.[24] Courts and legislatures have been much slower, however, to recognize as legitimate the specific concerns of artists as a distinct occupational class.[25] Moral rights claims, in particular, have been met with almost uniform rejection; a key example is *Crimi v.*

Rutgers Presbyterian Church, a 1949 case that barred well-known muralist Alfred Crimi (1900–1994) from claiming damages from a church that destroyed his work without his consent, which existed as a lasting reminder of just how reluctant US law was to accept any moral-rights argument.[26] Only the state of California entertained moral-rights claims in any substantial way; by the early 1980s it had passed more laws designed to protect artists' rights than any other state, including the unprecedented, in the United States, California Resale Royalties Act of 1976 (intended to protect the reserve rights of an artist) and the California Artist-Dealer Relations Act of 1976 (passed to regulate the working relationship between artists and dealers).

THE TURN TO CONTRACTS

The lack of legislation helps explain why artists in the 1970s turned to common law, namely, the law of contract, to claim what they saw as their rights. Among the best known was the conception and publication of "The Artist's Reserved Rights Transfer and Sale Agreement," first published in 1971 and coauthored by Seth Siegelaub and Robert Projansky. A collage of parts taken from many different forms and contracts—including those used by artists Daniel Buren and Edward Kienholz, as well as standard contracts developed by professional organizations or legislatures, under titles such as the Artists' Equity Contract, the Sale of Photograph Contract, and terms from New York State Fine Print Legislation—the Agreement was conceived as "a legal tool that you can use yourself to establish ongoing rights when you transfer your work."[27] To be used for the first sale of a work and also to bind subsequent purchasers, it was intended to "remedy" what Siegelaub pronounced was the "artist's lack of control over the use of their work and participation in its economics after they no longer own it."[28] But as well as being structurally problematic, the Agreement proved to be of limited practical use. Collectors were irked by what they saw as an unjustified encumbrance on their property rights, frequently threatening to boycott dealers who used it. Artists, for their part, feared both the potential impact on sales and the record-keeping costs incurred upon each sale of a work; very few artists, with the notable exception of Hans Haacke (b.1936), consistently used it.[29]

The failure of the Agreement highlighted the power of what might be called art-world law, or the unwritten but commonly accepted practices of the constellation of galleries, institutions, critics, curators, and collectors to which artists are also subject. Some gallerists, in fact, were more receptive to using contracts in the early 1970s than they had been previously. The New York gallerist John Weber observed how he sold the works of Daniel Buren, Sol LeWitt, and Carl Andre on a royalty basis with hardly any impact on total sales.[30] But other influential dealers, for example Leo Castelli, dismissed contracts as not even "worth the paper they're written on."[31] Contracts could only work if the federal law required them, a point attorney Robert Rie argued in response to a questionnaire Siegelaub circulated in connection to the Agreement.[32]

Although the Agreement remained more as a theoretical exercise and even a Conceptual artwork than a practical tool used in the course of everyday transactions, it still ranked among the most prominent efforts to secure the financial and intellectual interests of artists, which in part explains its significance today. Moreover, the Agreement's visibility in art-world circles has encouraged others to be more proactive in issuing and even drafting their own contracts.

Artists committed to feminism, for example, have often regarded contracts as an important tool in their struggle against an economic system that has institutionalized unequal pay between the sexes. In their view, artists' rights are inseparable from larger commitments to women's rights. In the heated political context of the proposed Equal Rights Amendment, debated by US lawmakers in Congress from 1977 to 1982, the artist Laurace James, for example, argued in the *Women Artists Newsletter* that contracts gave unknown "defenseless" artists rights and status.[33] Former AWC member Poppy Johnson instituted an "Art Transfer Agreement" (1977) for all artwork sales related to her $100 Gallery, so named for its policy of thus pricing any work sold from this commercial gallery, regardless of the maker's status. The "Art Transfer Agreement" "documents the authenticity of the work and protects certain rights of the buyer and the artist" while requiring the buyer to cede the "liberty" of altering a work for any reason, such as painting a sculpture white to match the decor of a room.[34]

Still there were occasions when contracts failed to accomplish what artists wanted. In 1985 Athena Tacha (b.1936) completed a sculpture for the University of South Florida in Fort Myers pursuant to a contract. In 1999 the university sold the land on which the sculpture was built to Edison Community College (ECC), which then informed Tacha that her work was a dangerous structure that would have to be taken down. Although she had a contract with the University of South Florida guaranteeing that her work would remain in perpetuity, it was made before the passing of the Visual Artists Rights Act (VARA) in 1990, and a new contract had not been made with ECC.[35] Tacha has noted how difficult it is for artists to successfully secure the rights they want even with a contract and VARA, mainly because the parties with whom they would enter into such agreements (institutions, dealers, and collectors) insist that artists waive their claims.[36]

In 1990 lawyer Tim Cone wrote of a transactional environment that leaned more on "shared visions, trust, and goodwill than on economic needs."[37] He pointed out that without the presence of these attributes, not even "the threat of a lawsuit" will "keep either side from breaking its promises."[38] Cone further added that the difficulty in introducing contracts as a standard feature of business between artists and gallerists lay with the former and their demands for a percentage of an artwork's resale price. From the perspective of either buyer or seller, such demands encumbered the potential liquidity of the work, thus making a "meeting of the minds" difficult, if not altogether impossible. For artists' rights to succeed, it had to be a collective effort.

ECONOMIC AND NONECONOMIC RIGHTS

The early 1980s saw the concept of "artists' rights" fracture between economic and noneconomic rights. Although artists continued to lobby for resale and other economic rights, the focus shifted to the definition and protection of noneconomic rights, especially those concerning what might be called the "life" of artworks: how and under what circumstances will an artwork exist after it is sold, or after the death of its creator? In 1983 the New York state legislature passed the New York Artists' Rights Preservation Act. The brainchild of New York state assemblymen Richard Gottfried and William Passannante with New York state senator Tarky Lombardi, Jr., it was passed thanks in large part to testimony given by artists like Crimi and Isamu Noguchi, whose work *Shinto* (1974) had been dismantled and removed by its owner, the Bank of Tokyo Trust Company.[39] More dramatic still was the hearing that took place before a Congressional subcommittee formed in 1987 to review the Visual Artists Rights Act, which considered, among other issues, whether artists should receive proceeds from the resale of their work. The artist Robert Mangold (b.1937), one of the most consistent advocates of artists' rights legislation, characterized the resale provision as a state-mandated subsidy of the arts. In a letter to Senator Ted Kennedy of Massachusetts, a supporter of the act, Mangold insinuated that it was a means for the government to correct gross inequities in the commercial art market, where younger or less-established artists had no choice but to sell work at lower prices.[40] Making the act federal law would give these artists a chance to recover some of the fair market value.

The turn to noneconomic rights as the barometer by which to gauge the state of artists' rights was vividly underscored by the infamous removal in 1989 of *Tilted Arc*, the large-scale sculpture Richard Serra (b.1938) created at the behest of the US government. Few incidents have offered a clearer view of the skepticism with which the law has treated artists' perspectives regarding the definition and nature of art.[41] Indeed, it was a judge who began a grassroots campaign to have the sculpture removed from its location in Federal Plaza in downtown Manhattan.

The hearing, which did result in the physical removal of *Tilted Arc*, indicated that conventions so well entrenched in the art world as to themselves constitute a virtual law, like site specificity, had almost no currency in the legal realm.

Ironically, the removal of Serra's work came only a year before the US Congress passed the Visual Artists Rights Act (1990), arguably the single most important piece of legislation to directly affect visual artists as a specific class. An amendment of the US federal Copyright Act passed in order to conform US law to international standards, the new law gave an artist the legal right to claim authorship of a work and also to disclaim authorship if he or she did not make the work or if it had been changed in ways "prejudicial to the artist's honor or reputation."[42] It thus represented a major benchmark in what had been, since the 1960s, the especially difficult struggle of artists to determine what became of their works, including after they were sold.

But as many legal commentators have pointed out, the scope of VARA is far more limited than comparable legislation in Europe that has tended to grant broad protection even without being certain of the final outcome. Conversely, US legislatures have been more sparing in their willingness to pass laws, only doing so to address specific problems.[43] VARA protects only certain forms of visual art, including paintings, drawings, prints, sculptures, and still photographs existing in single copies or in limited editions of two hundred or fewer copies. It explicitly omits architecture and, perhaps to remain consistent with US copyright law (infringements of which incur similar penalties or remedies as violations of VARA), is distinctly silent on the matter of Conceptual art. Another conspicuous omission are the resale rights for which artists battled for many years and continue to do so.

The limitations of VARA, in the years after its passing, reminded artists of the need to understand the system in which they were inextricably embedded. Relying on legislatures to enact laws to protect various rights specific to the circulation of artworks, namely those concerning authorship and resale royalties, proved ill-fated. Existing law was therefore less than effective as a means of remedying wrongs done to artists or even as a means of regulating the sale and circulation of artworks generally. Nowhere was this more apparent than in the first half of the 1990s, during the "culture wars" so indelibly marked by deep judiciary and legislative suspicion toward art and artists generally. Government arts funding was cut or eliminated altogether, and often on ideological grounds, as abundantly illustrated not only by the highly publicized cases brought against the photographer Robert Mapplethorpe and the "NEA Four" (the four performance artists denied government funds on the basis of their works' content), but also by the notoriety surrounding works such as Sally Mann's photographs of her children (against whom lawsuits were threatened, but never filed).[44] Practically speaking, artists seeking redress under VARA had to defend themselves under conditions that were hardly fair or favorable.

ARTISTS' RIGHTS AFTER 1990

During the 1970s and 80s, the concept of artists' rights was suspended between a growing legal recognition of moral rights, on the one hand, and an expanded sense of discontentment with a legal system that sometimes acted as if artists were excluded from its protection, on the other. Artists seeking certain rights had to first understand and work within a legal system riddled with particular biases. In 1980, after numerous attempts to legally rent exhibition space from the New York City government, the artists associated with the *Real Estate Show* illegally occupied an unused storefront in lower Manhattan. They claimed that their actions were "extra-legal" and "calls for no 'rights,'" descriptions that suggest profound skepticism in rights-based models of civic participation.[45] In the 1980s and 90s, questions of artists' rights continued to revolve around narratives of opposition; some artists rationalized claims of moral probity or social relevance by characterizing their works as challenges to a moribund status quo.

Yet the rapid pace at which artistic strategies changed and multiplied thanks to new technologies in the 1990s and 2000s ushered in a new set of questions concerning the limits of what artists could do. An increasingly significant part of the ongoing debate surrounding artists' rights was the artistic strategy of appropriation. When can artists "borrow" visual material for their works, and how much? At what point does appropriation become theft? In the United States, the question has been argued in relation to a variety of work, perhaps most famously in connection to that of Jeff Koons (b.1955), and more recently, Richard Prince (b.1949). By the second half of the 2000s, the law demonstrated greater sympathy toward artist perspectives than previously, especially in cases involving alleged copyright infringement or violations of freedom of expression. In the 1990s, the US Court of Appeals for the Second Circuit ruled against Koons, who had made a colored sculpture based on a black-and-white image taken by a professional photographer.[46] In 2006 the same court affirmed a decision in Koons's favor, concurring that the artist's use of a copyrighted photographic advertisement in his work was an example of fair use, a legal doctrine that allows copyrighted material to be used under certain circumstances.[47] The Second Circuit, which has perhaps overseen more cases pertaining to artists and artworks than any other US court, also ruled in favor of Prince, who was sued by another professional photographer, Patrick Cariou, for using his photographs without his permission. In 2013 the court asserted that Prince's works presented a "new aesthetic" and thus met the "transformative" standard established for deciding fair use (the material used resulted in the creation of something new rather than a verbatim copy).[48]

Courts have also become more receptive to claims made under VARA. Witness, for instance, the decision concerning the treatment of Christoph Büchel (b.1966) by the Massachusetts Museum of Contemporary Art (MASS MoCA, North Adams). Arguably the highest profile legal case to explicitly and successfully invoke VARA, *Massachusetts Museum of Contemporary Art Foundation v. Büchel* turned on an unwritten agreement between the Swiss installation artist—who may have been more accustomed to the generous moral-rights laws of continental Western Europe—and the museum to install one of his works at the latter's expense. After communication between the artist and the museum broke down, the museum sued the artist, claiming that it was entitled to publicly display the unfinished artwork. Following a lengthy battle in the courts and the media, in 2010 the First Circuit decided partly in favor of Büchel in an opinion that recognized artists' rights in unfinished works.[49]

Yet the Büchel case, which involved a work whose production costs ran into the hundreds of thousands of dollars, also implied how legal concern over "artists' rights" is commensurate to the monetary amount at stake. Unsurprisingly, richer and established artists are better able compel others to honor their rights as individual economic actors. Exemplified by artists like Koons, with his penchant for Wall Street–worthy suits, artistic labor now falls within the ambit of white-collar work. The blue-collar ethos to which so many AWC members aspired has given way completely to what the artist Hans Haacke had noticed as a "remarkable demographic resemblance between the art professionals [and] the art public at large," both sides belonging to an "embarrassing and embarrassed class" somewhere "between the owners of the means of production and the 'proletariat.'"[50] As a distinct occupational group, however, artists have even less political or legal clout than they did before. Lawmakers, for example, continue to resist any expansion of artists' rights, as demonstrated in the recent "death" of the American Royalties Too ("ART") Act of 2015, a bill introduced in US Congress that would have granted artists 5 percent of every secondary market sale exceeding $5,000.[51] Contrary to its earlier history, then, the term "artists' rights" has become a synonym for the asymmetry of power underpinning the art world, a reality underscored by how discussions now take place via a judicial system largely inaccessible to all save those able to afford prohibitively expensive legal fees, or whose works involve such large amounts of money as to render them comparable to other forms of large-scale investment.[52]

Today, the issue of artists' rights remains as polarizing as ever, continuously reminding us of the separation between the presumptive art world and the supposed world "outside." The most effective attempts to secure rights unacknowledged or unenforced by prevailing legislation have been those aimed at reconciling different sets of claims, such as the interests of both creators and owners. Beginning in 1989, Félix González-Torres (1957–1996) issued certificates of authenticity for many of his installations, which range from interactive pieces that allow viewers to take individual sheets of paper to words painted directly onto walls in a particular typeface. Containing general terms guiding owners as to the installation of these works, González-Torres's certificates reallocate rights associated with the creation of a work so that its execution becomes a set of potentially endless duties to be fulfilled in accordance with the artist's wishes. Owning a work means more than buying a material object or the rights to create it; it also means having to perpetually consider various choices, risks, or responsibilities from the moment of acquisition to when the work is sold (if it ever is). The certificates are issued by the Félix González-Torres Foundation, and while that entity does not seek to apprehend wrongdoers, it provides, upon request, assistance in clarifying the certificates' terms. The owner becomes a collaborator, entrusted with realizing the work and also preserving his, her or its financial investment. Small wonder, then, that collectors of González-Torres's works are unusually vigilant in ensuring that the artist's intentions are honored; loan agreements tend to be highly specific in content and approach.

But rather than consider artists' rights as an either-or proposition, whereby securing the rights of the artist means infringing upon the rights of the owner or seller, a more productive step is to identify where and how the interests of those involved in an artwork's creation, circulation, and display converge. The case of González-Torres paradoxically implies how artists' rights, however defined, might be more readily preserved if authorship is reconfigured as a form of social redistribution, where artworks are regarded not as inert objects but as opportunities for negotiation among and between artists and their audiences. This entails a rethinking of artists' rights around the act of obligation and custodianship, and calls on us to think of the intersections between art and the law.

Training Ground for Moral Rights: *MASS MoCA v. Christoph Büchel*

DONN ZARETSKY

In 2006 the Massachusetts Museum of Contemporary Art (MASS MoCA), in North Adams, Massachusetts, invited Swiss artist Christoph Büchel (b.1966) to create a work of art for its massive Building 5—a space for which the museum had a history of commissioning new work from artists. The work was never finished. Instead, we were treated to one of the saddest imaginable art-world spectacles: a museum suing an artist in an attempt to gain permission to show the unfinished work to the public over his objections. In the end, the litigation clarified one important aspect of moral-rights law in the US (that unfinished works are as worthy of protection as any other), but missed an opportunity to strengthen the law even further (by affirming that only an artist can say when his work is ready to be presented to the public).

THE DISPUTE

The work Büchel conceived for the space was to be called *Training Ground for Democracy*. It would be:

> essentially a village, . . . containing several major architectural and structural elements integrated into a whole, through which a visitor could walk (and climb). It was to adopt the role-play of U.S. military training for its visitors, who would be given the opportunity to "virtually" change their own various identities in relation to the collective project called "democracy": training to be an immigrant, training to vote, protest, and revolt, training to loot, training

> iconoclasm, training to join a political rally, training to be the objects of propaganda, training to be interrogated and detained and to be tried or to judge, training to reconstruct a disaster, training to be in conditions of suspended law, and training various other social and political behavior.[1]

The vast installation was to include, among other elements, a vintage movie theater, a two-story house, an old bar from a tavern, a mobile home, several full-size sea cargo shipping containers, various vehicles (a bus, a truck, etc.), an aircraft fuselage, and a leaflet-bomb carousel. There would be a re-creation of the famous "spider hole" where Saddam Hussein was captured. The museum's director, Joe Thompson, called the proposed work "the *Guernica* of our times." (He would later call it "the best unfinished work of art of the century."[2])

Things did not go well from the start. Büchel came to believe that the project was beyond the museum's ability to manage, the announced opening date was postponed, and, eventually, the show would have to be scrapped. Or would it? Büchel had estimated the work was approximately 40 percent complete when he last left North Adams.[3] In his absence, the museum had continued to work on its own—in an email Thompson suggested that the museum staff do "anything else [the curators] feel is known with 80% certainty."[4] Finally, in May 2007, Büchel's show was canceled, but in its place the museum announced the opening of a new exhibition entitled *Made at MASS MoCA*, which visitors could only reach by passing through Building 5, where the unfinished *Training Ground for Democracy* remained.[5] When Büchel would not consent to have his unfinished work—including all of the museum staff's 80 percent–certain guesswork—shown to the public in this way, MASS MoCA took the extraordinary step of suing him in the United States District Court for the District of Massachusetts.

THE DISTRICT COURT DECISION

The crux of the lawsuit was a statutory provision called the Visual Artists Rights Act, or VARA. Passed in 1990 by the US Congress as an amendment to the Copyright Act, it protects the "moral rights" of visual artists in the works they create. The two most important rights it protects are the rights of "attribution"—the right to be identified as the author of his work and (more importantly for this dispute) the right *not* to have his name used in connection with work created by others—and "integrity"—the right to prevent any distortion or modification of his work. As the appellate court in the case later put it:

> VARA's passage reflected Congress's belief that the art covered by the Act "meet[s] a special societal need, and [its] protection and preservation serve an important public interest." To encourage the creation of such art, VARA protects the "moral rights" of its creators. These are "rights of a spiritual, non-economic and personal nature" that exist "independently of an artist's copyright in his or her work" and "spring from a belief that an artist in the process of creation injects his spirit into the work and that the artist's personality, as well as the integrity of the work, should therefore be protected and preserved." The recognition of moral rights fosters a "climate of artistic worth and honor that encourages the author in the arduous act of creation."[6]

The District Court ruled in favor of the museum on its motion for summary judgment. Although the judge never explicitly ruled that unfinished works were not protected by the statute, that belief clearly informed his decision. He began by noting that "unfinished art may not be covered by VARA at all" and, therefore, "to the extent that an artist seeks protection for an uncompleted work," the violation of his rights "must be demonstrated with special clarity."[7] Call that the "special clarity" rule. Later in his opinion, however, he went beyond even his newly invented special clarity rule. After once again stating that "it is doubtful that VARA even covered" Büchel's unfinished work, he held that "nothing in MASS MoCA's planned display of the unfinished installation would have violated Büchel's right of integrity, for the simple reason that *no completed work of art ever existed* . . . for the museum to distort, mutilate or modify."[8] He found that the case "simply fell outside the boundary of VARA," and so he gave the museum the green light to publicly display the unfinished work, 80 percent guesses and all.[9]

THE APPEAL

But the museum did not take that green light. Bowing to the clear weight of opinion within the art world—right before the District Court hearing, for example, influential *New York Times* art critic Roberta Smith wrote a scathing piece for the Sunday paper that began: "When a museum behaves badly, it's never pretty. But few examples top the depressing spectacle at the Massachusetts Museum of Contemporary Art"—they decided, just days after their District Court victory, to dismantle the work.[10]

Nevertheless, Büchel, as a matter of principle, appealed the District Court decision, in part to correct what would have been, if left standing, a very damaging precedent for artists' rights. To that extent, he succeeded: the First Circuit Court of Appeals made it crystal clear that unfinished works are entitled to the same moral rights protection as finished works. There is no special clarity rule, or any other meaningful distinction between finished and unfinished works under VARA. On the other hand, the Court of Appeals declined to strengthen artists' rights even further by reading the statute to give an artist the right to determine when his work is ready to be presented to the public.

i. The holding. Unlike the District Court, which seemed so troubled by the notion that unfinished works could be protected by VARA, the Court of Appeals easily concluded, as a matter of statutory interpretation, that they were:

> The text of VARA itself does not state when an artistic project becomes a work of visual art subject to its protections. However, VARA is part of the Copyright Act, and that Act's definition section, which defines "work of visual art," specifies that its definitions, unless otherwise provided, control throughout Title 17. That general definitional section of the Copyright Act states that a work is "created" when it "is fixed in a copy . . . for the first time." Further, "where a work is prepared over a period of time, *the portion of it that has been fixed at any particular time constitutes the work as of that time*." A work is "fixed" when it has been formed, "by or under the authority of the author," in a way that is "sufficiently permanent or stable to permit it to be perceived, reproduced, or otherwise communicated for a period of more than transitory duration."[11]

Beyond pure statutory interpretation, the Court of Appeals also determined that equal protection for unfinished works was simple common sense: "Moral rights protect the personality and creative energy that an artist contributes to his or her work. That convergence between artist and artwork does not await the final brush stroke or the placement of the last element in a complex installation."[12] And so, after nearly three years of litigation, the Court of Appeals concluded: "We thus hold that VARA protects the moral rights of artists who have created works of art within the meaning of the Copyright Act even if those works are not yet complete."[13]

ii. The missed opportunity. So the main mischief of the District Court decision was eliminated. There should be no doubt now that VARA applies to unfinished works as well as completed ones. There is no need for a special clarity rule. But all this really means is that unfinished works are *eligible* for protection under VARA. An artist would still have to show that his rights under the statute were, in fact, violated—for example, because the unfinished work was distorted or modified, which in my view, had the Büchel case continued rather than settled, would have been easy to do because of the museum's "Plan B" and its 80 percent–certainty standard.[14]

But imagine a different case, one in which it is undisputed that the work has not been touched by anyone but the artist, where there is no question of (physical) distortion or modification. Would it be a VARA violation for a museum (or other third party) to publicly display *that* work despite the artist's objections? The Court of Appeals says "no":

> Büchel maintains that, even aside from the alleged modifications to "Training Ground," merely exhibiting the work of art in its unfinished state, without the artist's consent, constitutes a distortion. We reject this claim. A separate moral right of disclosure (also known as the right of divulgation) protects an author's authority to prevent third parties from disclosing [his or her] work to the public without the author's consent, and is not covered by VARA. Although Büchel proffered an expert who opined that showing an unfinished work without the artist's permission is inherently a distortion, we decline to interpret VARA to include such a claim where a separate moral right of disclosure is widely recognized in other jurisdictions and Congress explicitly limited the statute's coverage to the rights of attribution and integrity.[15]

This is very formalistic reasoning: some other jurisdictions (in particular, France, where the right originated) provide an express right of divulgation, and Congress could have done so here when it passed VARA. Therefore Congress did not intend for VARA to include such a right. But it strikes me as incorrect.

Suppose an artist is commissioned to create a sculpture for a children's playground in a city park. The artist conceives of a work to fit the site—a large, colorful piece made up of three sculpted letters:

FUN

Now suppose that, for some reason, the project is not finished—the city runs out of money, the new mayor does not believe in public art, the parties cannot get along, whatever. And suppose, at this point, the artist had completed and installed two-thirds of the work, that is:

F U

This is a very different piece, with a very different meaning, perhaps more appropriate for Quentin Tarantino's new house than for a children's playground. Is it not clear that *merely to show* that work is a distortion? One need not believe that VARA contains a general right of divulgation in order to believe that, at least in some cases, to show a work before the artist thinks it is ready is necessarily a distortion of the work. That is true of our hypothetical children's playground artist, and it was, I submit, true of *Training Ground for Democracy*.

So in the final analysis, *Training Ground for Democracy* provided an opportunity for the courts to continue their training in the moral rights of artists. The District Court flunked the test, but, by affirming in no uncertain terms that unfinished works are indeed protected by VARA, the Court of Appeals reversed the damage. The Court of Appeals, in turn, missed its own chance to further strengthen artists' rights in the United States by giving them the right to say when their work is ready to be shared with the public. That will just have to wait for a future training session.

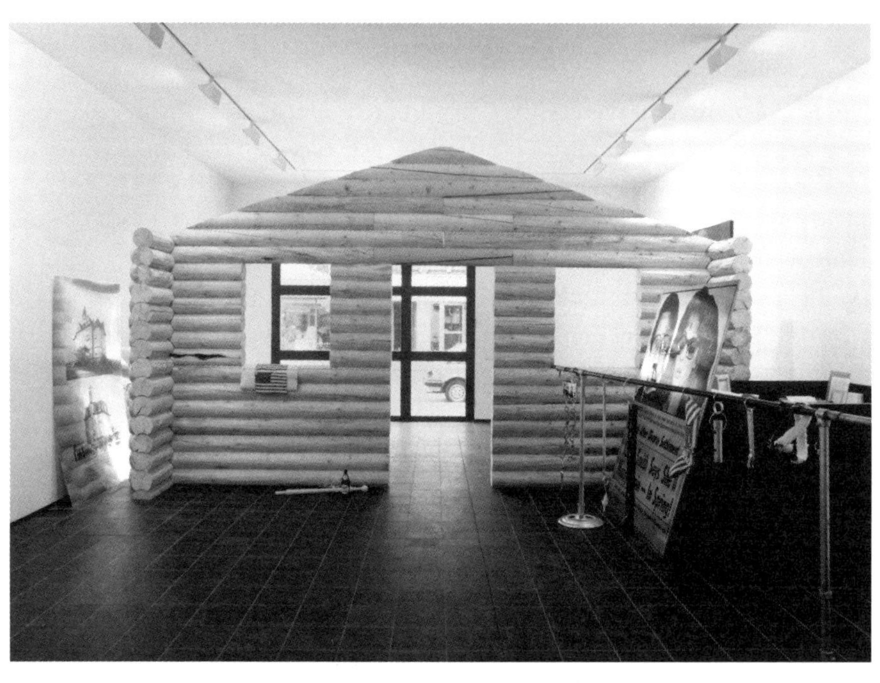

Cady Noland (contested)
Log Cabin Blank with Screw Eyes and Café Door (Memorial to John Caldwell), 1990
Mixed media, dimensions variable

Retraction

MARTHA BUSKIRK

When exactly does a work actually become art? A great many things made or manipulated by artists do not achieve that status. In relation to traditional forms of production, the artist's signature or the moment when an object emerges from the studio can be good indicators. For art that has the potential to remain in flux, based on shifting arrangements or installation requirements as well as potentially replaceable elements, the point of sale is often when a work's identity is clearly defined. Works that are actually made by an artist are distinct in many respects from the readymade paradigm initiated by Marcel Duchamp (1887–1968) in 1913, with his provocative gesture of creating solely through an act of designation. Yet the readymade helps emphasize the significance of the artist's declarative act for all forms of artistic production—both in the initial moment when something becomes a work and, far less often, when the artist is involved in a gesture of renunciation.

It has also been obvious for some time that the artist's name functions as a form of branding—carrying a value in the art market and beyond that can sometimes appear rather arbitrary in how it attaches to individual works. Perhaps it should be possible to enjoy art, or any object, without regard for who made or designed it. But the name is a form of categorization that allows for comparisons with other examples emanating from the same source, and it has become a fundamental marker that extends beyond quality to every aspect of how art is valued.[1] Even as many contemporary forms do not show direct, internal evidence of authenticity, external forms of validation, including artists' certificates, have become increasingly central to the contemporary art market. Names are controlled by a particular person only up to a point, however.

The world of business presents numerous examples of individuals who have lost the right to their name in specific realms, whether through the willing sale of a company they have founded or via hostile takeover.

So far no artist has been divested of his or her artistic license, but conflicts about posthumous authentication raise the specter of the artist's act of declaration being usurped by committee or legal authority. In a particularly notorious case, the since-disbanded Andy Warhol Art Authentication Board denied the authenticity of a 1965 Warhol (1928–1987) self-portrait that, although made through a more distant process of delegation than Warhol generally employed up to that point, had been dedicated by the artist to Bruno Bischofberger, a dealer with whom he had worked. The letter sent by the board included the remarkable line: "It is the opinion of the authentication board that said work is NOT the work of Andy Warhol, but that said work was signed, dedicated, and dated by him."[2] Although Joe Simon-Whelan, who sued the board over their denial of a different work from the same series, was eventually forced to abandon his legal quest, the court documents and attendant publicity revealed a great deal about the operation of the secretive authentication board and precipitated its dissolution.

CADY NOLAND AND THE RIGHTS OF THE ARTIST

Other issues come into play when it is the artist who issues the repudiation. A 2012 lawsuit by dealer Marc Jancou against the auction house Sotheby's and artist Cady Noland (b.1956) was brought in response to Noland's denial of a damaged work, and Sotheby's attendant decision to remove the piece from a 2011 auction to which it had been consigned by Jancou. Although the case itself ultimately turned on matters of contract law, the underlying issue was the right of the artist to exercise ongoing control over her creation long after it had left her hands—and in particular, her prerogative to remove her name, and hence its status as a work, from an object that had already been in circulation for a couple of decades.

The piece in question was Noland's *Cowboys Milking* (1990), consisting of imagery screenprinted on aluminum that depicted two cowboys who seem to be struggling to milk a cow juxtaposed with a bit of Montana promotional copy celebrating Robbers' Roost, a historic site associated with a violent gang of nineteenth-century outlaws. Jancou consigned *Cowboys Milking* to Sotheby's, and the auction house made plans to offer it in their November 10, 2011, afternoon sale. The catalogue had already been printed when Noland inspected the work, found it damaged, and had her lawyer write to Sotheby's asserting, per the Visual Artists Rights Act, or VARA, "that her honor and reputation will be prejudiced as a result of offering *Cowboys Milking* for sale with her name associated with it, in light of the material and detrimental changes to the work that have occurred since its creation."[3] Sotheby's withdrew the work based on their contractual right to do so in the face of doubts about authenticity or attribution. Jancou sued Sotheby's as well as Noland for "breach of contract and for tortious interference with contractual relations," claiming that there was actually no doubt that the work was authentic.[4]

VARA, cited in the letter from Noland's lawyer to Sotheby's, is the somewhat circumscribed version of moral-rights legislation enacted at the federal level in the United States in 1990. Limitations include the types of creative work it covers (visual arts, but not movies, for example), the fact that it pertains only during the artist's lifetime, and a controversial provision allowing artists to waive its protections. It also applies only to work created or sold by artists after June 1, 1991, so a substantial part of Noland's oeuvre would not fall under its purview (though much of her work would be covered by New York State's Artists' Authorship Rights Act of 1984, or AARA).

The more extensive rights artists might wish to claim are suggested by attorney Robert Projansky and curator Seth Siegelaub's 1971 "Artist's Reserved Rights Transfer and Sale Agreement," or so-called Artist's Contract, which envisioned far-reaching control over a work's future context, including where it can be shown or reproduced, the right to borrow the work back from the owner, and consultation on repairs, as well as a 15 percent resale royalty provision. The contract emerged from activism initiated by the Art Workers' Coalition in 1969, which grew to include a fairly extensive critique of the lack of diversity in museum programming and related issues of access, but was precipitated by the artist Vassilakis Takis's (b.1925) physical removal of his work from an exhibition at the Museum of Modern Art (MoMA), in New York, where he did not want it shown (a largely symbolic gesture nevertheless, since he only took it as far as the MoMA courtyard).[5] Even though Hans Haacke (b.1936) seems to be alone in his consistent use of a version of the Artist's Contract, many artists and dealers do sell works accompanied by extensive instructions and stipulations, and the open-ended nature of contemporary forms, where installations and other components need to be adjusted or even remade for different spaces, means that artists or their representatives are often closely involved in a work's long-term fortunes. It is also common for artists to use reproduction permissions to exercise control over exhibition and publication projects.

Even in the context of extensive artistic prerogative, however, Noland's willingness to say "no" has become the stuff of legend, from her total repudiation of altered or damaged works to her denunciation of exhibitions of her work where she was not consulted.[6] A renewed wave of interest in Noland's work has also raised the stakes: when her 1989 *Oozewald* sold for $6.6 million during Sotheby's November 9, 2011, evening sale, it set a new record for the highest price paid for the work of a living female artist (broken in 2014, by a Yayoi Kusama painting).[7] The sculpture *Oozewald*—the first in an edition of four plus one artist's proof—achieved its record price despite being a multiple.

The hot market for Noland's work is all the more striking given her bleak take on American history, including an iconography of violence driven by her interest in the interplay between celebrity and psychopathology. *Oozewald*, a 72-inch-high cutout (made from silkscreen on aluminum), presented a depiction of Lee Harvey Oswald taken from an infamous photograph capturing the moment, two days after the assassination of President John F. Kennedy, when Oswald was in turn shot to death by Jack Ruby (whose hand and gun appear within the contours of the figure). Eight golf-ball-sized perforations suggest enlarged bullet holes, including one, where Oswald's mouth would be, that is stuffed with an American flag. *Cowboys Milking* incorporates less well-known references, but there is a similar reorientation of iconic as well as disquieting imagery.

Jancou's suit against Sotheby's and Noland (filed February 1, 2012, and amended April 9, 2012) demanded $6 million in actual damages from Sotheby's, along with the same amount plus $20 million in punitive damages from Noland (adding $20 million in punitive damages against Sotheby's to the amended complaint). It is not clear where those numbers came from, given that Jancou paid $106,500 for the work during the same year that he put it up for auction, and Sotheby's planned to offer it with a $250,000–350,000 estimate. (Although *Oozewald* sold for substantially more than anticipated, it carried a much higher estimate of $2–3 million.)

Attorneys for Sotheby's and Noland both responded with motions for summary judgment dismissing Jancou's suit, together with their own counterclaims. The Sotheby's motion was granted November 14, 2012, Jancou appealed, and the New York State appellate court affirmed the lower court ruling on June 27, 2013. Noland's motion to dismiss was granted on May 3, 2013, and at that point Noland withdrew her counterclaim. But Sotheby's continued to pursue its counterclaim, and the discovery process revealed additional information about the work's ownership and sales history—including documentation related to the fact that it had been consigned to Christie's earlier that same year, when it was likewise withdrawn after Noland objected to its condition.[8]

There were other complicating factors as well. Court documents revealed that Jancou had actually owned the work twice, selling it at an earlier date and then repurchasing it five days after it was withdrawn from an April 2011 sale at Christie's (where it had been consigned by a private collector identified in court documents as William J. Hokin). There was also a June 30, 2011, condition report from conservator Christian Scheidemann that Jancou failed to disclose to Sotheby's until after Noland lodged her objection. Jancou chose to emphasize the aspect of the report that referred to the overall condition of the work as "very good", but Scheidemann had also noted damage to all four corners, concluding that, despite restoration attempts, "some deformations ... will always be noticeable."[9]

Part of Jancou's dismay clearly related to what he viewed as disparate treatment. *Oozewald* achieved its record price during the same auction cycle despite the fact that it was missing its original stand. Sotheby's specified that the buyer "will be provided with a new stand, which will be in accordance with Ms. Noland's copyrighted stand design for this lot, and which will be an integral part of the complete work."[10] Evidently Noland determined that *Oozewald* could be returned to its intended condition with a replacement stand, in contrast to the arguably minor but nonetheless permanent damage to Jancou's piece. And she could hardly have been pleased to see a work that she had already denounced once that same year suddenly reappear.

Although VARA does not articulate a general right of withdrawal equivalent to French moral-rights law, under VARA attribution and integrity are closely linked. The first concerns the right to claim authorship as well as prevent attribution for works the artist did not create; the second allows an artist to prevent the use of his or her name in the event of distortion or mutilation. Jancou's lawyer attempted to separate the two, arguing that attribution was not in question despite the damages. In a certain sense, Jancou was right: there is now ample confirmation from the artist's own representatives that the object Jancou was contesting was made by Noland as a work of art in 1990. But her demand that her name be removed has left the piece in limbo.

It should also be noted that the case did not determine whether Noland was acting within the scope of VARA, which specifies that distortion does not include modification based on the passage of time or the inherent nature of materials (an emphasis on intentional distortion that might very well not have been found to apply to this case, given the fragility of the thin and unprotected aluminum support Noland had used as the surface for her screenprint). In relation to the contract that Jancou signed with the auction house, it was merely enough that Noland had asserted her demand to have her name removed from the work. In dismissing Jancou's claim against Sotheby's, the New York State Supreme Court found that "Absent the author's name, the print was not the 'Property' listed on the Property Schedule."[11]

Noland's counterclaim asked for "an injunction preliminarily and permanently prohibiting Jancou from using Ms. Noland's name in conjunction with marketing the Work, or from offering the Work for sale, or from selling the Work, at auction or by private sale."[12] But the New York State court was not the right jurisdiction to make an argument based on VARA (a federal statute), and the countersuit was withdrawn, without prejudice, with the option of filing in federal court. Since Noland did not pursue federal action, there is no specific court order that would prohibit Jancou from using Noland's name in relation to the work. But it does not require a legal ruling for Noland's denunciation to have a sharp impact on Jancou's ability to sell his purported example of her work within the rarified segment of the market where her art now circulates.

ARTISTIC WITHDRAWAL

In a well-known ironic gesture, Robert Morris (b.1931) employed a notary public to certify his "Statement of Esthetic Withdrawal" for inclusion in his 1963 *Document*, through which he purported to withdraw "all esthetic quality and content" from another work, his earlier *Litanies* (1963). In this case, the legalistic document actually served to increase interest through the pairing of the statement and the slightly earlier construction consisting of a combination of readymade elements and a series of keys inscribed with text from one of the notes in Duchamp's *Green Box* (1934). But many other artists have issued entirely serious renunciations.[13]

It is also interesting to think about Noland's disclaimers in relation to attempts by artists to shape their histories. Richard Prince (b.1949) has systematically pushed to suppress evidence of the collage-based work that he did before 1977—despite the fact that examples were exhibited and sold—such that the catalogue for an exhibition of early work that Michael Lobel organized in 2007 for the Neuberger Museum of Art, Purchase, New York, was published with empty boxes appearing where the works would have been reproduced.[14] Félix González-Torres (1957–1996) also demoted a number of examples of his production to "non-work" status, a fact recorded in the 1997 catalogue raisonné of his oeuvre published after his death. In fact, the González-Torres catalogue includes two categories in addition to the official listing: "Catalogue of additional material," which details various items given to or traded with friends, sometimes even signed, but not specified by the artist as works; and "Catalogue of registered non-works," which includes pieces that may even have been exhibited, but which were later stricken by the artist from his oeuvre.[15] Gerhard Richter (b.1932) is also well known for having excluded early figurative canvases from his catalogue raisonné, even though he acknowledges having painted them.[16]

Noland's career is unusual because of her fairly abrupt shift from a prolific studio practice that was accompanied by extensive interest in her work through the 1990s to a withdrawal from the art world largely accompanied by silence on her part. Sarah Thornton's interview with Noland, published in 2014, is a rare exception (and was tellingly accompanied by a disclaimer). Part of their conversation focused on auctions, with Noland criticizing the way that they throw works together, and suggesting that if she had "known that everything would be flipping at auction," she "would have made works that were impervious."[17] Given the market's willing embrace of many forms initially posited as uncommodifiable, it is not clear how such an inoculation might have worked. Noland also indicated to Thornton that she was too busy tracking past work to get back in the studio; but her general refusal to engage publicly with the art world, including her rejection of survey-type exhibition opportunities, means that auction records provide one of the few sources of ongoing information about her oeuvre.

What has been described as Noland's final new work was shown in

2000 at Team Gallery, New York, in the group exhibition *Hex Enduction Hour by the Fall*, curated by Bob Nickas. According to Steven Parrino, the work employed white, plastic, A-shaped supports, of the type that would normally be used to hold up either end of a plank-style barrier, but multiplied to create an entire row. "Cady instructed the Team Gallery to destroy the pieces after the show," Parrino would recall. "Like a serial killer disposing of a body, the gallery was ordered to take apart the work and to place the pieces into separate trash bins around the city."[18] Thus, readymade elements were shorn of their temporary art status by being removed decisively from any context where they could be connected with Noland (in contrast to a 1998 work using the same materials that was produced in an edition of twenty).[19]

The manifestations on display in the only version of a survey exhibition devoted to Noland's work since her withdrawal from the art world had an even more tenuous status. *Cady Noland Approximately*, organized in 2006 by the Triple Candie gallery, in New York, took the form of a strange homage: four artists (two of whom decided to remain anonymous) attempted to replicate Noland's work at a distance, based on reproductions and publicly available information. Perhaps Noland's silence in relation to this gesture derives from the fact that there was little danger of the objects on display being taken as her work, or even as art at all. Indeed, I encountered the remains of an example from the show during a studio visit with Taylor Davis (one of the participating artists)—a bench-like form built as part of her version of Noland's *Your Fucking Face* (1993–94) that had reverted to bench status as it kicked around her studio.

Various interesting questions arise within the continuum connecting unfinished, finished, and damaged works. A telling aspect of the legal conflict between Christoph Büchel (b.1966) and the Massachusetts Museum of Contemporary Art (MASS MoCA) concerned whether the artist could invoke VARA protections in relation to an unfinished installation that was therefore arguably not actually a work. The status of objects securely defined as art can also be altered by insurance payouts for damages designated as a total loss, based on determinations made by experts other than the artist.[20] In the case of *Tilted Arc* (1981), the artist Richard Serra (b.1938) defined the work as site specific, and therefore declared it destroyed once it was detached from its original location following a campaign against the work, and Serra's unsuccessful legal challenges contesting the removal decision. But for many years the General Services Administration, the US agency that removed it, held onto the metal plates in an apparent refusal to acknowledge that they no longer constituted a work.[21]

It is equally striking, however, when status and value are dramatically transformed by a reassessment that leaves the object largely unchanged. Banksy (b.1974) played up the emphasis on name-value during his 2013 New York residency by hiring an elderly man to sell his canvases anonymously as "spray art," from a street vendor's stall, for $60 each—to very few takers. When Banksy later claimed the work as his via a website announcement (his standard method for authenticating work otherwise presented anonymously), he effectively demonstrated how much the work is valued for its relationship to the Banksy phenomenon rather than internal evidence of a style that is recognizable but subject to imitation. For older works, changing attributions indicate how a consensus among recognized authorities can dramatically alter the value of an otherwise constant object. Sotheby's recently won a lawsuit regarding a Caravaggio sold as a copy that, to the seller's chagrin, was later reattributed to the artist himself (the distraught former owner was arguing that Sotheby's should have protected him from a lowball sale).[22] In that case, the work was cleaned by the new owner, which presumably helped facilitate reassessment, but it is only one of a great many examples where value has risen or fallen based on shifting estimations of authorship.

DELEGATED PRODUCTION AND ITS LIMITS

Occupying a different part of the spectrum are works defined to some degree as conceptual because their identity is framed in relation to an idea or plan rather than a singular physical object. While some artists have made this a focus of their practice (Sol LeWitt's wall drawings constitute a prime example), collectors sometimes make self-serving or strategic decisions about the degree to which an artist has delegated fabrication. Both Donald Judd (1928–1994) and Dan Flavin (1933–1996) complained vigorously about Giuseppe Panza's attempts to treat their work as conceptual, including the degree of latitude he assumed over works purchased on the basis of plans or requiring adjustments for different installation environments.[23] A similar misconception apparently guided the treatment of another Noland work that was the subject of more recent legal action.

For reasons that are not entirely clear, Wilhelm Schürmann, owner of Noland's *Log Cabin* (1990), placed it on long-term loan with the Suermondt-Ludwig-Museum, in Aachen, Germany, where it was displayed in an exterior courtyard for ten years. Not surprisingly, there was extensive deterioration. Rather than consult the artist, however, Schürmann authorized the remaking of the entire wooden structure (and therefore of most of the work), apparently thinking that it would be okay because he went back to the company that had fabricated the first version of the log-cabin facade and asked them to follow the original blueprints.[24]

Schürmann then decided to sell the work via Galerie Michael Janssen, Berlin, and art adviser Marisa Newman. But the sales agreement included provisions to unwind the sale if Noland refused the legitimacy of the work, disassociated her name from it, or claimed that her moral rights had been violated—which she did in a handwritten note faxed to would-be purchaser Scott Mueller, wherein she objected to the conservation done without consulting her and stated categorically: "This is not an artwork." The 2015 lawsuit itself was again a fairly straightforward matter: Mueller wanted his money back, and the gallery apparently did not have it (having refunded only $600,000 of the $1,400,000 purchase price over an extended period of time). The interesting aspect of this case is what it reveals about both the collector's assumptions—that it would be okay to replace most of the physical structure based on the plans strategically listed as constituting part of the work—and a wariness that led to a contract written with a strong escape clause.

Although Mueller's case against Janssen was ultimately dismissed due to the fact that his lawyer never served the German dealer with a complaint, the December 2016 decision by judge Naomi Reice Buchwald was still significant for her determination that Marisa Newman had not, as Mueller claimed, breached her fiduciary duty to him because no such relationship had been established via her service as independent art adviser to Mueller.[25] In July 2017, however, Noland initiated her own lawsuit against the cluster of individuals and galleries involved in the conservation decision as well as the exhibition and sale of the extensively refabricated object, asserting violation of her moral rights and, more broadly, that the replacement of all the wooden components of the work was a form of unauthorized replication that constituted copyright infringement.[26]

VICISSITUDES OF AUTHORSHIP

About the politics of value, Arjun Appadurai has stressed the importance of exchange, emphasizing how "things-in-motion" illuminate the social contexts through which objects are encoded with significance. He has also posited that commodity status is not necessarily a constant, referring to a "commodity phase" in the lifetime of things as well as certain situations, such as art auctions, that accentuate commodity dimensions that would be inappropriate in other settings.[27] For things that become works of art, one could also postulate an "authorship phase," initiated with the artist's assertion of the work's status as such, and potentially brought to an end if that declaration is rescinded.

Appadurai's related suggestion that it is important to examine the biography of a thing, including meanings and values that shift over time, and in different contexts, has an interesting inverse in Noland's refusal to divulge personal information about her own life. Because of her intense privacy, her role in relation to her work is almost pure author function. Her presence in the art world is something of a cipher: she demands control over not only the condition of her work but the context for its display, while nonetheless doing so from afar, and often through the intermediary of legal representatives.

The disposition of his case against Sotheby's and Noland left Jancou in possession of an object that Noland had silkscreened in 1990; whether it is still a work of art is an unresolved question. At the very least, its recent commodity phase has been suspended by publicity surrounding Noland's disclaimer. And one can certainly sympathize with Noland's desire to protect the integrity of her art. Yet it is important to consider the life of the work after it leaves the artist's hands, since assessments of value (both monetary and aesthetic) are dependent upon a broader consensus about cultural importance. Our museums are filled with historic objects that are esteemed despite irreversible damage, and in the contemporary realm it is quite common to encounter works that change dramatically from one installation to the next. Given that this material is collected, preserved, and displayed on the basis of a shared conception of its significance, an important question remains about whether the artist should have sole authority over a work's future. The premise at the heart of moral-rights legislation—that the work of art is more than a mere possession, embodying cultural value that exceeds the interests or priorities of any individual owner—also argues against an approach to such protection that disproportionately privileges the artist's personality rights.

The model of authorship around which the contemporary art world is organized is obviously a highly artificial construct. Dating at least as far back as Duchamp's readymades, and with increasing urgency during the last half century, artists have played against romantic ideals of individual agency through the incorporation of found objects, industrial methods, delegated production, and an emphasis on concept over physical skill. Yet rather than lessening the significance of authorship, these critical gestures have been absorbed into an extensive institutional apparatus devoted to the production, dissemination, and preservation of art that continues to be identified as the work of singular creators. Noland's renunciations, and the lawsuits that they have provoked, indicate a crucial tension in the center of this system, as the individuals whose names have been endowed with such important functions can find themselves at odds with other parties involved in a collective undertaking to distinguish and perpetuate art's cultural and economic value.

Up for Grabs; or, Artistic Authorship in the Age of the Flipper: *Kreuk v. Vō*

CHRISTIAN VIVEROS-FAUNÉ

Because art is seen as an asset class, the more rapid turnover is considered encouraging. There's a whole new generation of collectors who are playing the art market.

—Frances Beatty, President of Richard L. Feigen and Co.

If they only look at my work as a commodity, then that is something I am not interested in.

—Danh Vō, artist

CHECK OUT THE BILLBOARD

In early 2014 an undistinguished mid-range photography dealer in Los Angeles with financial experience started a popular website called sellyoulater.com. The site's distinguishing feature: it brazenly reduced artists and their artworks to four basic sales categories—"buy now," "early blue chip," "sell now," and "liquidate." On learning about the website, many in the art community were flummoxed. Some considered the platform a prank; others thought it was a particularly po-faced Conceptual artwork made in the vein of Andrea Fraser's *Untitled* (2003), a video that featured the artist engaging in hotel sex with a collector in exchange for $20,000. Despite its many detractors, the video was intended as a brutal commentary on the increasingly instrumentalized relationship between artists and their collectors.

Both groups, it turns out, were wrong—in fact and in spirit. Rechristened a year later as ArtRank, the website proved instead to be a digital billboard tailor-made for the internet. What it advertised was abundantly clear, at least to those not completely blinded by the web's false promises or the notion of an ever-expanding art market. Besides promoting services of dubious value, ArtRank explicitly shilled for art's ongoing transformation from a symbolic object or action into a fungible financial asset.

Launched somewhat ironically at first with a blingworthy Yves Saint Laurent–style "YSL" logo (reordered for "Sell You Later") but now much more corporate in appearance, the website displays sixty artists' names ranked under headings indicating their investment potential. Besides classifying artists' careers like stock options in spreadsheet-type columns —the categories are "buy under $10,000," "buy under $30,000," "buy under $100,000," "early blue chip," "undervalued blue chip," and "sell/ peaking"—the website also says it draws artists' data from "over three million historic data points." The site supposedly makes money through subscriptions (if it does so at all) by selling early access to quarterly rankings for $3,500 a pop.

ArtRank additionally claims to employ a carefully vetted if anonymous "network of experts" to "provide valuable clarity on previously opaque data." According to the platform, this data set includes "studio output, forthcoming representation, institutional acquisitions, private sales, etc." It also purports to use "machine-learning algorithms" to discover what it calls "prime collecting opportunities."

According to the site's FAQs section, its algorithm was "developed for an emerging art fund in 2012",which is entirely in keeping with the project's tenuous pretense of belonging to the financial industry. The site states that "the algorithm facilitated a 4,200 percent return on investment over a 16-month period." If true, this would make ArtRank's principals—whom the website describes generically as "a data scientist, a financial engineer, and an art professional"—among the art game's wealthiest players.

Among the artists listed as a steal at $30,000 or less on ArtRank in August 2016 were the emerging artists Josh Kline and Mira Dancy. At a higher if undisclosed price point were more established figures that the platform labels "undervalued blue chip" artists. This group included the well-known if currently unfashionable painters Carroll Dunham, Philip Guston, and Eric Fischl. The "sell/peaking" column contained an oddly mismatched group of artists, such as Nate Lowman, Alex Israel, Oscar Murillo, Tauba Auerbach, and Danh Võ.

In this purely transactional scheme, belonging to this last market category is the kiss of death. In the less professionalized, coolhunting lingo of Sell You Later, ArtRank's previous incarnation would have condemned these artists to the art market gallows—the "liquidate" column.

FINANCIAL CAPITALISM, OR SHORT-TERMISM

When asked about ArtRank by *Bloomberg Businessweek* in November 2015, at least one art adviser suggested the obvious—that the site naturally appeals to "flippers." That is to say, the site attracts buyers interested primarily in selling at a profit rather than in building a collection. The magazine also reported another reasonable finding—notably, that the artists listed on the platform were "less than pleased" with having their entire careers portrayed like hot or poorly performing stocks.[1]

Despite this unscientific consensus, *Bloomberg Businessweek* reporter Anna Altman found that not a single artist would agree to speak on the record about ArtRank, evidencing a typical art-world hedge against the pitfalls of sincerity (public opinions sometimes proving to be impediments to the smooth flow of private monies). But at least one unidentified artist was quoted as finding the site's premise preposterous, this despite being on the "early blue chip" list. His principal objection to the website's classifications: "Artists are not trying to meet sales goals."[2]

But if most artists today do not fully identify with ArtRank's transactional logic—despite the fact that a number of blue-chip artists, like Jeff Koons and Damien Hirst, have done so to the extent that they incorporate financial strategies into their artworks—a growing number of art buyers, dealers, and art institutions unthinkingly parrot ArtRank's financialized ethos. Essentially, they behave as if the evaluation and sale of artworks are activities indistinguishable from day trading. As illustrated by several high-profile legal cases and in various public forums, a large number of these players presently act as if the art market were primarily a winner-take-all global exchange that transacts primo examples of a high-performing asset class.

According to Mark C. Taylor, the author of several books about art and its culture, the relationship between art and money has undergone a drastic change in the last few decades. It has been transformed, Taylor says, "by the appearance of a new form of capitalism."[3] That new force has reshaped the globe. That juggernaut is, in a word, finance capitalism.

In an excerpt from his 2012 book *Refiguring the Spiritual: Beuys, Barney, Turrell, Goldsworthy*, Taylor lays out a brief history of art's breakneck financialization at the start of the new millennium:

> In previous forms of capitalism—agricultural, industrial and consumer—people made money by buying and selling labor and material goods; in finance capitalism, by contrast, wealth is created by circulating signs backed by nothing other than other signs. When investment becomes more speculative, the rate of circulation accelerates and the floating signifiers, which now constitute wealth, proliferate. The structure and development of financial markets and the art market mirror each other. As art becomes a progressively abstract play of non-referential signs, so increasingly abstract financial instruments become an autonomous sphere of circulation whose end is nothing other than itself. When the overall economy moves from industrial and consumer capitalism to finance capitalism, art undergoes parallel changes. There are three stages in this process: the commodification of art, the corporatization of art, and the financialization of art.[4]

In the same way mission creep once affected US military interventions in the 1990s, "finance creep" has shifted the basic structure of the art world in the first decades of the new millennium. This change has effectively transformed the strategies and goals of key art-world players—from guarantee-prone auction houses to art institutions undergoing constant expansions to museum boards that have become virtual VIP lounges for hedge-fund billionaires. A decade ago, Damien Hirst's and Richard Prince's get-rich-quick schemes shook up the playing field for artists. Today, the buying and selling habits of short-term buyers like Steve Cohen and activist-investors like Daniel S. Loeb have done the same for art collectors and art institutions.

Decried during the 2016 US presidential campaign by candidate Hillary Clinton as "quarterly capitalism," short-termism is exactly what it sounds like. As an economic model, it promotes the idea that companies—or other assets—should be managed for the short term, with decisions driven by the need to meet shareholder expectations regarding quarterly earnings and stock prices. As a corporate strategy it promotes the idea of a short-term lift in share price over long-term economic value, which can sometimes yield profitable results during periods of stagnation. Unfortunately, the model also has a marked tendency to destroy "brand value" in the medium and long term. Some economists argue that short-termism has been known to force companies to sell valuable assets "at fire sale prices during cyclical economic downturns."[5]

In certain circles, the terms "finance capitalism" and "short-termism" are used interchangeably. Critics of the current power of banks and other financial institutions argue that the economic ideology of short-termism was the root cause of the 2008 global financial crisis, and that finance capitalism remains the principal source of the globe's ongoing economic instability. These critics contend that finance capitalism, when applied to the largely unregulated arena of the art market, produces a microeconomy rife with unprecedented speculation. Some have taken to calling this development "global casino capitalism."

THE QUESTION OF AUTHORSHIP; OR, WHOSE ASSET IS IT ANYWAY?

Among ArtRank's FAQs, there is a question that establishes a fundamental baseline for art's redefinition as an aspirant to the status of asset class. That question is: "How do you quantify art?" The website provides the following illuminating answer: "Our algorithm is intent on assessing the *intrinsic* [emphasis added] value of an artwork, not its survival value. We do not judge any works' aesthetic or emotional value."

Unsurprisingly, ArtRank's definition fully echoes a similar statement issued by a principal in a prominent New York art-advisory firm. In the words of Artvest partner Jeff Rabin, art makes for an ideal financial investment vehicle when considered as an "unemotional" asset, or better yet, as part of what securities traders would call a "diversified portfolio." Put another way, what Rabin and others like him openly contend is that connoisseurship confounds investment potential where art is concerned. In such a scenario, art does not just constitute a tangible and measurable asset; its very distillation into financial value—its *intrinsic* value—makes it possible for "global wealth and the expansion of the art market to go hand in hand."[6]

Enter the Vietnamese-Danish artist Danh Vō (b.1975) and the wealthy Dutch collector Bert Kreuk. Together they enacted between 2014 and 2015 what is, to date, perhaps the most contentious showdown between finance capitalism's expansive new ethos—enshrined principally in the idea that art is an asset class—and the fundamental rights artists have exercised in the modern era to control their own production (rights that are based on a combination of copyright law, moral rights of authorship, and art-world custom regarding, in particular, the artist's ongoing authority to authenticate artworks). At issue, essentially, is the applicability of the model of finance capital to art, as well as basic notions of artistic authorship. These last include, but are not limited to, the following aspects of an artist's practice: the choice of materials the artist uses, the way in which an artwork is exhibited, the scale of an artwork and who gets to decide its potential size, the timeline of delivery, and ultimately the meaning of a specific work of art.

Previously, these issues were principally the domain of experts, among which the artist was deemed the foremost specialist—especially when speaking about his or her own art. Thanks to the manifest destiny-like expansion of finance capitalism, these creative decisions have recently come in for an unparalleled barrage of legal scrutiny. Such legal disputes predictably usher in their own existential and financial challenges. Because artworks by certain artists are openly considered to be the equivalent of tech stocks today, casual and open-ended conversations about sales or exhibitions have—especially in the case of *Kreuk v. Vō*—been construed by lawyers and even the legal system to constitute binding legal contracts outside the tight confines of the art world.

The financialization of certain artists' careers today carries with it the sort of expectations one associates with futures trading. To gauge the potential consequences of such a scenario consider this statement by Artvest's Rabin: "If you look at the big contemporary auctions at the major auction houses you realize that only approximately 300 artists are represented throughout the year."[7] Taking Rabin's information at face value, it stands to reason that the careers of the market's top artists would be dominated—as they surely are at present—by the one extraneous factor that estimates their so-called intrinsic worth most publicly: their auction prices.

In 2015 the total sales of Vō's works at auction rose to $2.37 million, up from $33,700 in 2012.[8] This put the young artist among an elite group of creators whose work is highly coveted by buyers who collect primarily to invest. Vō may be listed presently as "sell/peaking" on ArtRank, but—in pop-music terms—he is still one of the few artists whose resale value brings many of the big collectors to the yard. In his case, at least, they come running.

Vō and Kreuk's quarrel—a dispute between artist and collector, which is rare, though increasingly common in a financialized sales environment that often pits artists against flippers—began innocuously enough with an invitation to exhibit. In November 2012 Kreuk emailed Isabella Bortolozzi, Vō's former Berlin gallery, with the news that he wished to purchase one or several artworks to showcase in an exhibition he was curating at the prestigious Gemeentemuseum, in The Hague. The exhibition, titled *Transforming the Known*, was to be made up entirely of works from Kreuk's collection—an arrangement considered suspect by insiders who recognize the added value public institutions bestow on private collections, as well as the enhanced access it provides collectors to desired artists. "If I can have a major piece," the collector wrote Bortolozzi with typical deal-making aplomb, "I will give it a prominent space [in the museum]."[9]

Vō's highly Conceptual artworks and installations would not appear to be material for easy commodification, at least on first examination. They characteristically involve discarded documents, photographs, found objects, lettering, or other materials, which he fills with emotional or historical meaning to explore broader historical and political themes. In the past, his multimedia pieces have taken the form of altered photographs, planted flowers, and cardboard boxes covered in gold leaf. Unsurprisingly, perhaps, for an era that increasingly commodifies dissent and corporatizes rebellion—to borrow the parlance of cultural critic Thomas Frank—the fact that Vō's art is often made with non-archival materials has not dented the artist's appeal in either the retail or auction markets.

THE NITTY GRITTY: *KREUK V. VŌ*

In January 2013 Bortolozzi and Vō traveled to The Hague on what the artist's dealer called "a first visit with an exploratory nature."[10] They met Kreuk there, as well as the museum's director and chief curator. Subsequently, they toured the museum, discussed the exhibition, and eventually considered the nature of Vō's possible contribution. Then, depending on whose testimony you believe, the parties involved in the suit—artist Vō, collector Kreuk, and dealer Bortolozzi—either agreed or, alternately, did not agree to having the artist make "a room-filling installation" in exchange for €350,000. According to court testimony, it remains unclear whether the €350,000 sum was the price discussed for a finished work or the budget for the installation.

Several months went by and events intervened. Among other life-altering distractions, Vō's father—who often contributes to his son's artwork—suffered an aneurism. The artist also reportedly began having doubts about the collector. Vō asked around and heard back from friends and colleagues that many in the art world considered Kreuk to be an egregious flipper. According to his own account of the proceedings, Vō was less than thrilled to hear such information about Kreuk . Allowing a collector with a reputation for speculating on the careers of young artists to capitalize on his popularity was, he said, inimical to the essence of his creative process.[11]

The exhibition's June date approached and no new work materialized. Pressed by Kreuk, Vō loaned the exhibition a small existing work in lieu of creating a new installation for the collector. The work, a cardboard box with applied gold leaf, was titled *Fiat Veritas* (2013)—"Let There Be Truth," in Latin. *Fiat Veritas* was displayed at the Gemeentemuseum for the duration of Kreuk's show along with three gold-leaf letters by Vō, which the collector already owned.

The show closed in September 2013. When it did, Vō and Bortolozzi asked for *Fiat Veritas* to be returned. That is when they were informed that Kreuk, with the museum's help, had punitively requisitioned the artwork. Additionally, the artist and dealer learned, the collector planned to sue Vō and Bortolozzi for €1.2 million for failing to deliver an artwork for sale.

Transforming the Known turned out to be the perfect title for Kreuk's show, especially after he put thirteen of the artworks from the exhibition up for auction at Sotheby's London just two months after the show closed, including a Vō cardboard box with gold leaf similar to *Fiat Veritas.*[12] For many in the art world, the sale only reinforced Kreuk's dubious reputation as an active flipper (Kreuk has referred to his penchant for reselling recent purchases as "refining" his collection).[13]

The majority of the artworks the collector sold at Sotheby's had been made within two years of the auction date. Presumably, the judge presiding over the case did not consider this notable breach of art-world ethics to be legally significant.

As expected, Vō's works were among the pieces Kreuk transformed from modest objects into six-figure returns for Kreuk. There was the artist's 2011 work *Alphabet (M)*, which fetched $149,000, far more than its presale estimate of $60,000 to $90,000. Six months later—in the midst of the pair's bitter court battle—the collector auctioned off another work by Vō at Sotheby's. This was the gold-leaf box that resembled the one loaned for the Gemeentemuseum show. It sold for $700,000, or about fourteen times the value of a similar work in 2013. It bears repeating here that artists like Vō rarely benefit directly from a rise in the prices of their auction sales, as these are usually exponentially higher than their retail prices.

To add legal injury to insult, Kreuk won an initial judgment in a Rotterdam court against Vō and Bortolozzi in June 2014. In the ruling, Judge Pauline Adriana Maria van Schouwenburg-Laan found, incredibly, that the two parties had effectively agreed to have Vō deliver an artwork for Kreuk's brazenly commercial show, though even if this were correct, the content and form of such a work had not been agreed upon. Since no written confirmation of such an agreement exists, the judge relied almost entirely on a string of emails between Kreuk and Bortolozzi—which discussed possible works for the exhibition but no commission arrangement—as well as witness statements. The statements the judge found most convincing were—according to one contemporaneous report—provided by a Gemeentemuseum curator friendly to Kreuk, and by a relative and business partner of the collector.

Additionally, when Judge van Schouwenburg-Laan ruled on the contractual nature of the verbal and email exchanges between the parties, she also weighed in on the nature of the art Vō was to make. Astoundingly, she ordered him to produce a work the Dutch court defined as "large and experienced as impressive at first sight by the viewer."[14] The artwork would have to be finished within a year, the judge declared, or

Vō would have to pay daily fines of €10,000 ($11,000). The fines would be capped at €350,000 ($390,000). This figure matched the price (or budget) originally tendered to Vō for the commission Kreuk coveted—one that Vō felt perfectly within his rights as an artist not to deliver. As expected, Vō immediately filed an appeal. Van Schouwenburg-Laan's judgment held a small piece of good news: *Fiat Veritas*, still in The Hague after being seized as part of Kreuk's claim, was released by the museum.

According to Berlin-based writer and art adviser Marta Gnyp, the judge failed the case—and the art world—on a couple of key counts:

> Dictating the artist how to make an artwork is an adventurous undertaking for a judge. It shows how little she understands of contemporary artistic practice, in which autonomy of the artist and the subjectivity of the viewer are highly celebrated values. The big problem of this verdict is its verifiability. One viewer can find a golden balloon-dog impressive, while another might be impressed by a small coin lying on the floor in an exhibition space.[15]

But besides the issue of "verifiability," a much larger danger emanates from *Kreuk v. Vō* that makes this case a potential watershed in the ongoing financialization of art and the triumph of short-termism over art's historically longer-term goals. This is, simply, that courts of law like Judge van Schouwenburg-Laan's have become the next battleground in the expansion of finance capital at the expense of art and artists. Though it has to be said that the idea of a court ordering an artist to create and deliver an artwork to a collector (particularly when the subject matter of the contract was so uncertain) might seem to be problematic even from a legal perspective, conflicting, for example, with the artist's moral rights of authorship and freedom of expression. Furthermore, commercial courts, at least in the United States and England, have been historically unwilling to order the performance of so-called personal services contracts, regarding them difficult to monitor and enforce. Such a development could prove especially pernicious in the current legal environment, in which courts of law, such as Van Schouwenburg-Laan's, find themselves predisposed—whether out of greater familiarity with the realm of finance or simply in keeping with the expansion of this global transactional culture—to privilege one language, that of finance and financiers, over that of art and artists.

EPILOGUE

The denouement of *Kreuk v. Vō* was, as one might expect, not pretty. In July 2015 Vō proposed his own exasperated solution to Kreuk's court-ordered commission. In a letter sent to *Artnet News* and widely circulated on the internet, Vō offered to install, in both Kreuk's residence and at the Gemeentemuseum, a site-specific wall work tagged with a colorful line from the 1973 horror film *The Exorcist*. Vō's letter read: "To the extent it will become as impressive and large as you find fitting for the amount of $350,000: SHOVE IT UP YOUR ASS, YOU FAGGOT."[16]

Kreuk's reply also came in the form of a public letter. "This whole case is so bizarre it is unbelievable," he wrote. "It is like I landed in some kind of surreal world. . . . The court ruled that both parties should be in touch with each other in a 'professional way' and to 'normalize relations.' I do not think this type of behavior is what the courts meant by that."[17] It goes without saying that Kreuk's bafflement also defies belief, as it was the collector alone who filed a lawsuit that explicitly treated Vō, his career, and his artworks as one giant fungible commodity.

On December 1, 2015, Kreuk and Vō ended their legal quarrel at an appeals court in The Hague. The new ruling from that court declared simply that Vō would not have to create a large work that was "large and experienced as impressive at first sight by the viewer," as mandated by Judge van Schouwenburg-Laan. Concomitantly, Kreuk would also not have to disburse €350,000.

Kreuk's response to the verdict was downright Trumpian in its resistance to fact. Predictably, he lost no time in relaying his version of events to the *New York Times*: "I started the case about the principle that everybody has to abide by an agreement; I won my court case and made that point. Now it is time to move on and concentrate on the joys of collecting art."[18]

Vō, for his part, felt properly vindicated, describing the new agreement as an "unconditional withdrawal of [Kreuk's] claims."[19] In the aftermath of the appeal court's finding, the parties did manage to concur on one thing: both artist and collector said they would never have anything to do with each other again.

Like it or not, though, the Dutch collector-flipper may have the last word on this crucial matter. The ruling on appeal of *Kreuk v. Vō* cannot be considered to be a legal draw—not after Kreuk's speculative manipulations trumped the lack of a written contract between the affected parties in a court of law. The fact that Dutch courts, like US courts, recognize verbal agreements does not make the Dutch court's decision less bizarre or important. One principal consequence of this case appears clear: the precedent set by *Kreuk v. Vō* has opened the door for more such challenges. Consider, for instance, the ludicrous but nonetheless expensive 2016 authentication case involving the artist Peter Doig, in which the British painter was sued for $7.9 million for disavowing a canvas painted by a deceased Canadian man named—wait for it—Peter Doige.[20]

It remains, then, for artists and their allies to find a way to roll back such legal chicanery with strategies that explicitly protect artistic authorship. This may take, among other tools and tactics, recourse to ideas familiar to finance capital. Then, and only then, will artists and their active partners and defenders begin to confront the phenomenon of art's financialization directly.

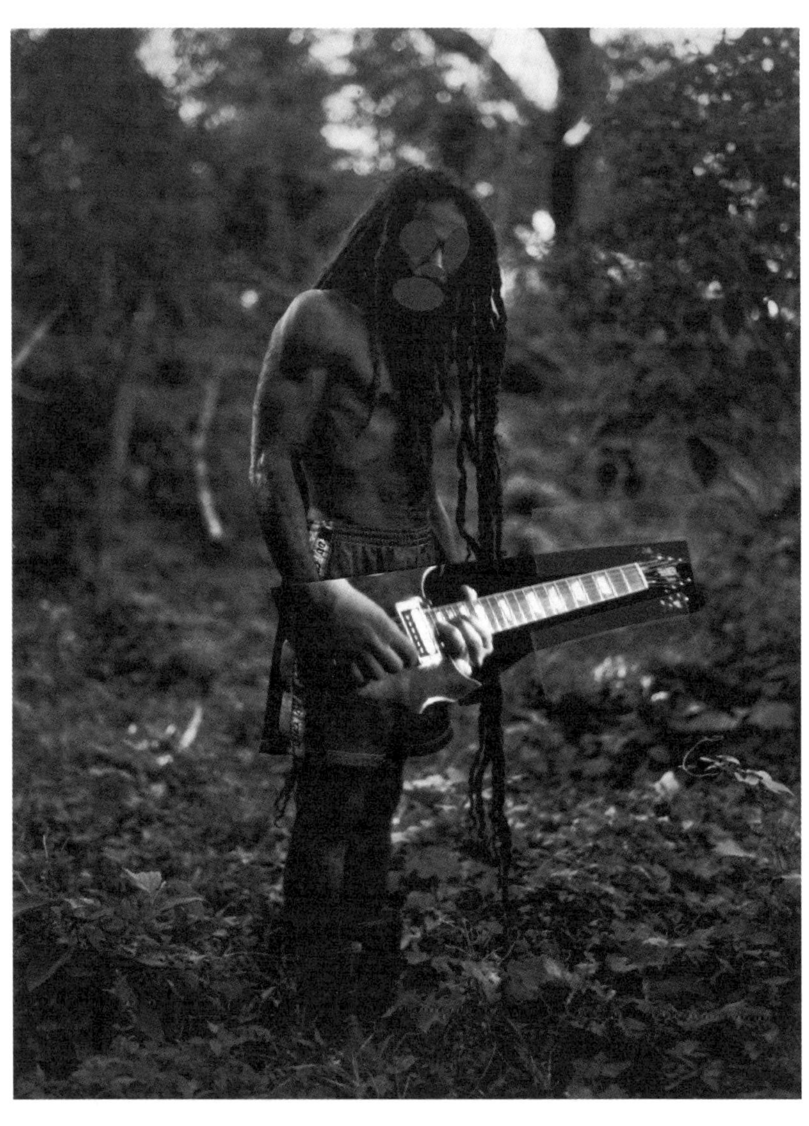

Richard Prince
Graduation, 2008 (from the *Canal Zone* series)
Collage, inkjet, and acrylic on canvas, 184.8 × 133 cm

Authoring Contradictions: Modern Appropriation Art and Postmodern Copyright Law in *Cariou v. Prince*

NATE HARRISON

And there was that essay by Roland Barthes called Death of an Author [sic] *. . . and I think I got caught up in it . . . you know, it's academic . . . it's something that takes place in October Magazine* [sic]*, which I don't particularly like. . . . I'm much more interested in trying to make art that stands up next to Picasso, de Kooning, and Warhol.*

—Richard Prince, 2009[1]

Is it simply the case that the "death of the author" and the general critique of authorial originality belong distinctly, yet solely, to the postmodern moment? "Distinctly," in that the incorporation of pre-existing photographs and moving images into works of art would develop in the late 1970s and early 80s in New York as de facto strategies striking at the very heart of modern individualism and the unique artistic gesture. "Yet solely," insofar as the initial, critical impulse essential to postmodernist appropriation art has now been overwhelmed by a broader culture of copying: given examples as far-reaching as "post-internet" art, the Google Book Project, and pharmaceuticals, an uncritical, "redistributed" authorship abounds. Thus, questions surrounding the *purpose* of the copy—and *who* copies what—become urgent.

Any discourse taking up contemporary approaches to artistic appropriation begins with the acknowledgment that alternative formulations of the relationship between authorship and the copy were already addressing the shifts apparent in practices over the past four decades. Writing at the turn of the millennium, art historian John Welchman would unpack the notion of appropriation both transhistorically and geopolitically, seeking to release it from the clutches of a certain post-structuralist strain of 1980s criticism.[2] Even further back in time, in an essay less well known than Douglas Crimp's influential "Pictures" (*October*, 1979) but written at around the same time about another New York exhibition, Leo Steinberg described appropriating artists as those who "clear cobwebs away and impart freshness to things that were moldering in neglect or . . . had grown banal through false familiarity. . . . A latter-day artist can lend moribund image a new lease on life."[3] Both Welchman and Steinberg rejuvenated, if indirectly, the centrality of the author-subject, and the importance of artistic intent in the realization of the work of art. Literary theorist Linda Hutcheon, in proposing an expanded notion of parody as the essential embodiment of postmodernism's preoccupation with copying, placed even greater emphasis on the producer of the cultural text. "The Romantic creator," she stated, "as originating and original source of meaning, may well be dead, as Barthes argued years ago, but the creator's *position*—a position of discursive authority—remains, and increasingly is the self-conscious focus of much contemporary art."[4]

Writing in 1985, Hutcheon sought to push back on theories of representation prevalent at the time, which attenuated authorial intent in the production of meaning. Hutcheon's description of an artist's "discursive authority" points to the status and power of an enunciating agent in the act of appropriating primary content. This essay addresses both artistic intent and the artist's position within the social and economic regimes of contemporary art as viewed through the prism of copyright litigation involving *Canal Zone* (2008), a series of works by artist Richard Prince (b.1949). Courtroom battles waged over the legal status of appropriated images provide unique windows of opportunity into the creative mind, if for no other reason than that they often entail artists having to articulate, for the public record, their philosophies of art. At the same time, legal disputes reveal the ways in which other social and cultural authorities outside of the art world—here, the law—interpret and even regulate it, ultimately controlling the distribution and likewise visibility of images. *Cariou v. Prince* (District Court ruling

2011, appellate court ruling 2013) is all the more significant insofar as it set a precedent in US copyright jurisprudence as it applies to so-called appropriation art, and marked a kind of "official" conclusion to a way of thinking about appropriation art as a critique of the authorial subject.

CARIOU V. PRINCE, PART I

The legal controversies surrounding appropriation art in the late 1980s reemerged when, in late 2008, Prince found himself at the center of a copyright infringement lawsuit brought against him by French photographer Patrick Cariou.[5] A month prior, Prince had exhibited his series *Canal Zone*. He produced the thirty large-scale collage works by applying paint and collage elements to inkjet enlargements of appropriated photographs that had been scanned and printed onto canvas. The photos were culled from "German nudist books, classic erotic magazines, music magazines, [and] anatomy books"; portraits of Rastafarians amid leafy Jamaican landscapes comprised the bulk of the collaging.[6] Across twenty-nine of the paintings, Prince reproduced at least forty-one images from Cariou's book of photographs *Yes Rasta*, published in 2000.[7] Several of the photos in the *Canal Zone* series were heavily abstracted as a result of the artist's layered painting technique, while others appeared virtually identical to the reproductions in *Yes Rasta*. None of the images were used with Cariou's permission.

Prince did not attempt a settlement. Rather, he chose to defend his appropriations by claiming they constituted "fair use" according to the doctrine within US copyright law recognizing that, in some circumstances, the unauthorized use of protected materials is allowable. Federally codified for the first time in the Copyright Act of 1976, fair use delineates "four factors" that judges may use in order to determine whether or not the expression in question infringes. They are: "(1) the purpose and character of the use, including whether such use is of a commercial nature or is for nonprofit educational purposes; (2) the nature of the copyrighted work; (3) the amount and substantiality of the portion used in relation to the copyrighted work as a whole; and (4) the effect of the use upon the potential market for or value of the copyrighted work."[8] Courts have interpreted the four factors in different, and sometimes contradictory, ways, with the effect that, even with them, consistent interpretations of fair-use cases have been rare. Eventually, this inconsistency led to federal judge Pierre Leval writing a treatise, titled "Toward a Fair Use Standard," in 1990, in which he sought to bring courts across the United States into better alignment, so that they might adhere more faithfully to copyright's constitutional mandate "to promote the Progress of Science and useful Arts."[9]

Ever since Judge Leval's work and subsequently the Supreme Court's 1994 ruling in *Campbell v. Acuff-Rose Music*, which found that rap group 2 Live Crew's remake of Roy Orbison's song *Pretty Woman* did not infringe the latter's copyright, the central issue determining whether appropriating expressions are legally permissible has come to revolve around the extent to which they are *transformative*, "altering," as Leval stated, "the original with new expression, meaning, or message."[10] Future rulings significant for appropriation art, *Mattel Inc. v. Walking Mountain Productions* (2003) and *Blanch v. Koons* (2006), found in favor of the artist-defendants who, judges ruled, had sufficiently transformed their source materials toward parodic or other critical purposes.[11] In *Mattel*, judges opined that when artist Tom Forsythe (b.1958) used Barbie dolls in his photographic series *Food Chain Barbie* (1997), he effectively parodied the toy company's product and the stereotypical values Barbie represents. And in *Blanch*, Jeff Koons (b.1955) was able to successfully articulate his rationale for appropriating photographer Andrea Blanch's advertising image for Gucci sandals. Yet, in later defending the fair use of Cariou's photographs for his paintings, Prince attempted an altogether different reading of transformative fair use. Rather than argue parody, or a type of commentary that assumes an intertextual and dialogic relationship between primary and secondary works, Prince claimed that it was his unique, creative vision alone—bearing no consideration for the original intent of Cariou's photographs—that signaled the transformative nature of his paintings.

According to Prince, *Canal Zone* evolved principally from two moments: a trip in 2005 to his birthplace, the region of Panama that in 1949 was an unorganized US territory called the Panama Canal Zone; and his work in 2007 on a film treatment recounting the tale of nuclear-holocaust survivors stranded in a tropical setting. Court documents state that Prince drew from these inspirations, as well as from his love of punk rock, in order to imagine "a make-believe, post-apocalyptic enclave, the Canal Zone, in which bands and music are the only things to survive."[12] Additionally, the artist's stylistic innovations in this body of work extended to another that he completed between 2006 and 2007, his *de Kooning* paintings, tributes to the Abstract Expressionist painter. Prince also aspired to pay homage to past masters such as Pablo Picasso and Andy Warhol by painting "primitive masks" over many of the Rastas' faces, as well as by introducing serial repetition as an aesthetic trope throughout the series.[13] Taking on these artistic techniques and influences, Prince argued that his paintings were undeniably transformative in that they "create[d] a fictionalized world that transforms the individual raw elements used . . . into a completely new expression and a different message that has nothing to do with capturing . . . Rastafarian culture in native landscapes in Jamaica."[14] Prince's "new expression," then, did not supplant Cariou's originals, but instead endowed them with a novel meaning or message, in alignment with the transformative model of fair use.

The rationale behind Prince's appropriations marks a paradigm shift in fair-use defenses of appropriation art. In past cases based on claims to transformative use such as *Campbell*, *Walking Mountain*, and *Blanch*, defendants had sought to meet the burden of justifying their use of specific materials over other available options. In cases involving parody, this is straightforward. Secondary users appropriate particular images and other cultural materials precisely in order to expose their highfalutin aspects. By definition, parody is not effective without the direct use of an original (and its context)—no other is adequate.[15] And even in *Blanch*, although it is arguable that any number of images other than Andrea Blanch's could have achieved an effect similar to the one artist Jeff Koons sought, the picture of sandaled feet Koons ultimately appropriated from Blanch stood as an archetype of glamorous advertising. According to Koons, such use formed part of an overall "commentary" on contemporary consumer culture; it was important to the artist's concept that his source material come from the pages of fashion magazines, even if parody in the strict sense was not the objective. This was not the case in *Cariou v. Prince,* where Prince could have chosen from a plethora of available Rastafarian images to realize the *Canal Zone* paintings; commenting on Cariou's images specifically was of no concern. In retrospect, it is clear that Koons's use of Blanch's sandaled-feet photo as part of a larger collage with a vague meaning paved the way for Prince's defense. Prince employed similar collage techniques in the *Canal Zone* works, if toward even more ambiguous effects and readings.

Besides authorial intent, there is another, related lens through which to analyze *Cariou v. Prince*: the hierarchical relationship between appropriating authors and those from whom they appropriate. This hierarchy among authors played out previously with dramatic effect in *Rogers v. Koons* (1992). In that case, Koons appropriated a postcard image from photographer Art Rogers in the creation of a life-size wood sculpture without Rogers's permission. Koons claimed that he took an otherwise banal photograph and endowed it with "higher meaning" in the creation of a work of art. Courts eventually found Koons's work to be satire, not parody, and therefore not a fair use.[16] The tension that played out between two authorial modes in *Rogers* was echoed in *Cariou v. Prince*: well-known, controversial artist appropriates the imagery of a relatively unknown lifestyle photographer, producing works of art that command high prices; photographer sues the artist for breach of copyright; artist defends his work on the grounds that it falls under copyright's fair-use doctrine in part because of its status as art. As in *Rogers,* there was a tendency in *Cariou v. Prince* for the defense to draw the distinction between an "artistic" author and a "mass" author, with the former, because of his stature in the contemporary art world, entitled to a creative license that superseded the authorial agency of the latter. Prince's defense strategy included belittling Cariou's artistic credentials, casting him as a second-rate author of cheap and disposable books, valuable only to the extent that they could serve as the "raw ingredients" in the creation of "unbelievably looking great [*sic*] painting."[17] It is from this elevated platform of the artist that Prince proclaimed his work as transformative. Yet Prince departed from Koons's defense in one key respect: Prince relied on his avoidance of any critical relationship with his source material; instead, his criteria for choosing certain images over others was simply whether or not he "love[d] the way they looked."[18] For Prince, it seems his unadulterated creative whims sufficiently justified the transformative claim.

Prince's court statements detail a view in which the sovereignty of the artist's disposition is presented as given. Such an individualistic—we might call it neomodernist—position stands in marked contrast to the ways in which postmodernist theory and criticism had tended to situate the author. Prince himself, as one of the central figures in the Pictures Generation of New York appropriation artists, gained critical and commercial success precisely from a discourse formed out of a rigorous critique of the modernist authorial mode. The epigraph that begins this essay, if it does not indicate a recentering of the author outright, at least reminds us of the degree to which the figure of the author was reinforced in the 1980s even as it was being deconstructed. Killing the author paradoxically also offered a new lease on authorship's life.

Yet such a rebirth would come at a price. In spring 2011, District Court Judge Deborah Batts found Prince liable for copyright infringement, ruling that his paintings were not transformative but rather derivative: they simply "recast, transformed or adapted" Cariou's original photographs.[19] Noting that the examples listed in the fair-use clause's preamble—"criticism, comment, news reporting, teaching . . . scholarship [and] research"—contain, at their core, "a focus on the original works or their historical context," Batts concluded that Prince's paintings could be transformative only if they "in some way comment on, relate to the historical context of, or critically refer back" to Cariou's images.[20] Since Prince emphatically rejected his works' correspondence with Cariou's images, arguing instead that they conveyed a fantastical, postapocalyptic tropical setting, the whole *Canal Zone* series constituted copyright infringement.

Prince's neomodernist brand of appropriation seemed, finally, to have caught up with him. But so did a postmodernist past. "Style," Hal Foster remarked in the mid-1980s, "is not created of free expression but is spoken through cultural codes."[21] Written as a polemic against neoconservative postmodernism, Foster's words could just as easily have appeared in Judge Batts's court opinion against Prince. Each in their own way—Foster in employing poststructuralist-inspired academic jargon and Batts in using the legal language of fair use—took artists to task for an irresponsible approach to the practice of appropriation. What for Foster marked the difference between neoconservative and critically engaged appropriation was, for Judge Batts, what distinguished "transformed" from "transformative" work: a recognition of and critical response to a received system of signification. Yet Prince used Cariou's Rasta photos neither to interrogate Cariou's method of representing the Jamaican communities he encountered nor to comment generally on the fetish (particularly ascribable to Western artists since the dawn of modern art) of imaging subaltern groups.[22] Rather, through Prince's amalgam of postapocalyptic landscapes, nude figures, and expressionist brushstrokes, Cariou's "classical" Rastas became "rock 'n' roll" Rastas. But "Rasta" as a representational category was never questioned; it (or at least Cariou's version) was taken "as is."[23] Prince merely re-presented the "code" initially extended by Cariou—the image of the exotic, mysterious, dark-skinned other—making it, in a word, derivative, in the most basic, and also legal, sense.

Yet the assumption in Judge Batts's reasoning—that works of art do not carry meanings when their makers do not intend them to (or, conversely, that they carry the meanings their makers intend for them to have)—is problematic, if perhaps understandable, given that artistic intention would be one of the few measures available to a judge otherwise reluctant to employ her own subjective readings of art. At least since US Supreme Court Justice Oliver Wendell Holmes proclaimed in 1903 that "it would be a dangerous undertaking for persons trained only to the law to constitute themselves final judges of the worth of pictorial illustrations," courts have attempted, however imperfectly, to separate legal from aesthetic judgements.[24] However, can determining whether or not a work is sufficiently transformative be accomplished solely through interrogating artistic intention? Are not the ways in which art is received and interpreted of great, if not equal, importance? This is exactly the line of questioning Prince introduced when he appealed the District Court's decision.

CARIOU V. PRINCE, PART II

In his 2011 appeal brief, Prince argued that Judge Batts's opinion misinterpreted the fair-use doctrine and the general judicial turn toward the transformative. The artist's appeal argument took two approaches. First, that nowhere in the wording of the Copyright Act does it require that authors refer back to the works they appropriate in order for their uses to be considered fair.[25] And second, that even if that were the case, Prince's works would still be fair use insofar as they may indeed comment on Cariou's photos, even if the artist did not intend them to. That is, commentary or criticism should be measured, Prince stressed, not merely through authorial intention as gathered from an artist's statements, but, in the final analysis, through audience reception.[26] The first point is more technical, while the second, though not without legal precedent, is nonetheless the more radical.

The appellate court concurred with Prince's assertions. "The law imposes no requirement," it ruled, "that a work comment on the original or its author in order to be considered transformative."[27] Rather, what qualify are uses that "employ the quoted matter in a different manner or for a different purpose from the original," as the court's own Judge Pierre Leval theorized at the outset of the "transformative fair use" discourse in the 1990s.[28] The opinion established a bright-line rule regarding how productive and different uses are identified. The court established that while Prince's testimony was important, "*What is critical is how the work . . . appears to the reasonable observer*, not simply what an artist might say about a particular . . . body of work. Prince's work could be transformative even without commenting on Cariou's work or on culture, and even without Prince's stated intention to do so."[29] Thus, analysis of the work itself, in comparison with its original source, should serve as the primary basis for evaluation. Judges then deemed Cariou's photos to be "serene and deliberately composed portraits and landscape photographs depict[ing] the natural beauty of Rastafarians and their surrounding environs," while Prince's "crude and jarring" paintings were interpreted as "hectic and provocative."[30] Given the comparison of the works, the court ruled that twenty-five of the *Canal Zone* paintings were transformative. The case was remanded to the District Court for further consideration of the remaining five canvases, and eventually Prince and Cariou settled.[31]

In light of the appellate court's decision, I contend that what we encounter in *Cariou v. Prince* is the ascendance of a "postmodern turn" in copyright law. At almost every opportunity, the court rescinded prior determinations, acknowledging legally what is increasingly understood across the cultural spectrum today: the derivative nature of creativity and, further, copying as a legitimate artistic technique. Of great significance in *Cariou v. Prince* is the appellate court's equivocal relationship with the Romantic authorial mode. On the one hand, the court validated the Romantic author (Prince), who treated the world of banal mass media as a field of open-ended possibility, extracting images at will in order to subject them to his alchemical, fine-art "transformation." This would seem to contradict the notion of aesthetic neutrality in copyright law and reinforce the high/low distinction in the valuation of cultural artifacts. On the other hand, the court subordinated artistic intent (or, in Prince's case, a professed lack of intent other than satisfying his own creative whims) to formal analysis. However Prince may have contextualized his work, it was the aesthetic differences between the paintings and Cariou's photographs that were of importance; this had the ultimate effect of diminishing authorial intent.

Yet, what marked an even more drastic change from the previous fair-use rulings was the court's reliance on the "reasonable viewer" to ascertain the transformative nature of the *Canal Zone* works. This was quite a divergence, given the ruling in *Rogers v. Koons* twenty years prior, in which the same court had rejected Koons's claim to a "higher" purpose, finding him liable for infringing Art Rogers's puppy image in large part because Koons's stated intent did not match his parody defense. It was even a shift from *Blanch*, in which the court had weighted Koons's explanations heavily in its determination in the artist's favor. With the concept of appropriation art's "transformative" nature now being given such wide latitude, and furthermore with the assessment performed with lessened regard for artistic intent and increased focus on viewer interpretation, twenty-first-century copyright jurisprudence may well be catching up to the sensibilities of late twentieth-century postmodernist appropriation art.

However, while we can understand the court's reliance on the "reasonable observer" as indication of the privileging of viewer reception over authorial intention, the final opinion in *Cariou v. Prince* should not be taken as an unproblematic, wholesale embrace of the agency of the receiver. As legal scholar Laura Heymann has noted, echoing Linda Hutcheon, "A reader-centric mode of interpretation cannot wholly free itself from the influence of the author: an implicit statement by Andy Warhol that 'this soup can is art' is likely to be reflected among readers to a greater extent than a similar statement by an unknown artist."[32] In its explication of fair use, the Circuit Court judges employed the "reasonable observer" measure to the economic factors in the case by recognizing that Prince's works catered to a "very different audience" than Cariou's: the celebrities and high-end art collectors who constitute the buyers of Prince's art have financial interest in the artist's paintings being understood as transformative. That Prince's reputation as a top-tier contemporary artist precedes any understanding of his work effectively serves to class the interpretive process. In the judges' estimation, Prince's works constituted fair use less because the artist (or, for that matter, academics well versed in the history and theory of appropriation art) claimed them as such, than because the rich and famous had validated them.[33]

Additionally, in casting themselves as "reasonable viewers," the Circuit Court judges mocked the process in which an actual interpretive community might have conceptualized Prince's transformations, and instead showed their willingness to ventriloquize an imaginary viewer. Restricted not only in their limited awareness of appropriation art's development but also to their duty as arbiters of the law—to "objective" evaluations—the judges' conclusions remained within simplistic, medium-specific aesthetic description (for example, describing Prince's large-scale paintings as "crude and jarring" and Cariou's smaller photographs as "serene"). This had the consequence of draping an otherwise postmodern turn in fair use with a type of analysis akin to formalist art criticism. A more robust assessment process could have involved expert testimony taken not only from museum officials and art collectors but also from art critics and historians (some of whom might well have described Prince's paintings as utterly banal and derivative in comparison to the history of critically engaged appropriation art).[34] Certainly, the participation of a wider range of "reasonable observers" might have brought about a different finding.

There is another, related problem with the judges' reliance on the "reasonable observer" test. Such a test attenuated the thought processes behind Prince's creative approach, instead establishing a precedent that deintellectualizes appropriation as a mode of artistic practice. While such an approach can be understood as consistent with copyright law's reticence to value some forms of creative labor over others, when courts assess a genre of art whose historical importance is so intimately tied into its own discursive formation—to its understanding as a largely conceptual and critical pursuit, in terms of aesthetics—they do a disservice to the very goal of copyright as inscribed in the US Constitution: the promotion of progress in the arts. The advancement of art occurs in tandem with the advancement of communication between artists and the public—when works enter into dialogue and debate with one another. Much of that dialogue rides on artistic intent, concept, and criticism. By granting that Prince's paintings were fair use, the court effectively cast appropriation as a type of practice that merely reshuffles the deck of an already glutted mediascape in aesthetically seductive but ultimately inconsequential ways apart from market valuation. The precedent set in *Cariou v. Prince* goes some way toward absolving cultural producers of their responsibility to the images they appropriate, which is unfortunate insofar as the driving force for appropriation art throughout its history has been precisely the engagement of images through critique. Richard Prince would not be who he is today were it not for that history.

At the very least, Prince's win is ultimately a loss for the legacy of the Pictures Generation and postmodern appropriation. Any embers of criticality still glowing within the postmodern project of appropriation art have been extinguished. Whereas Prince's works were once heralded as radical commentaries on authorship, originality, and commodity fetishism, they now simply parrot both modern and postmodern appropriation art. The artist's paintings have been deemed viable by one of the highest courts in the United States. Their monetary value is now augmented by their status as legally sanctioned art. They are safe. As if to prove this point himself, Prince in essence agreed to pay "licensing fees" for Cariou's images when he settled the case over the five remaining *Canal Zone* paintings, thus submitting to the intellectual-property regime he has treated with disdain for so long. It is not known whether Prince settled of his own volition or on his attorney's advice, but the effect is the same: Prince paid for his images.

It may be that *Cariou v. Prince* will help forge a new judicial tolerance for artistic appropriation. Slowly but surely, the stigmas attached to it—that it is lazy, uncreative, and unoriginal—are being swept aside in favor of greater appreciation for appropriation and the reality that a culture of copying defines contemporary society. Yet the long-term effects on appropriation art as a critical project are uncertain. If *Cariou v. Prince* speaks to the contradictions of authorship in contemporary appropriation art, it is up to future practitioners to set the record straight in reclaiming the critical legacy so important to the genre's historical significance.

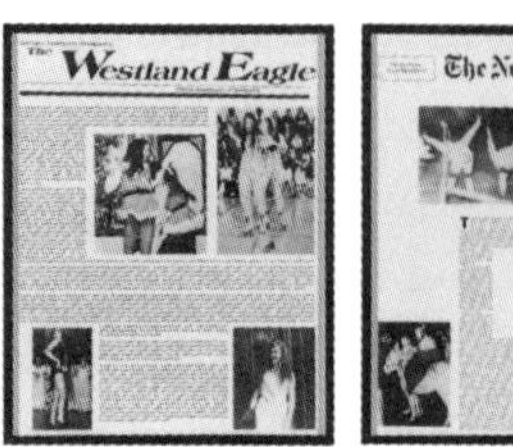

The Westland Eagle

The New York Times

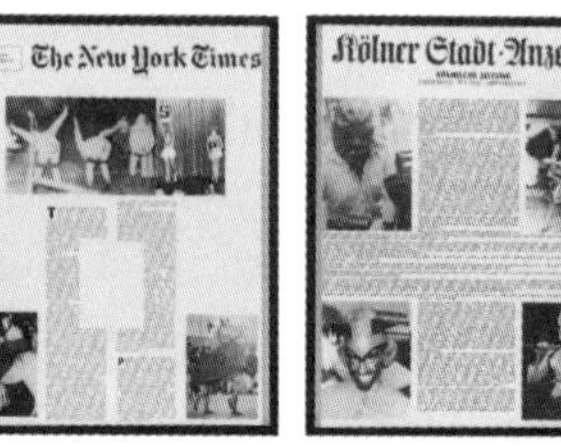

Kölner Stadt-Anzeiger

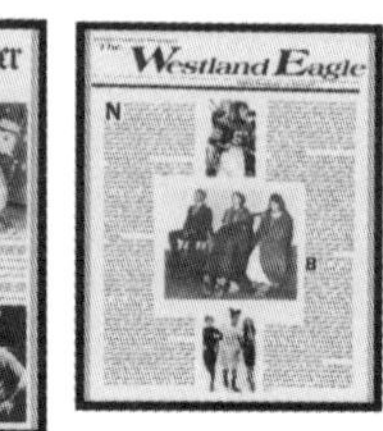

The Westland Eagle

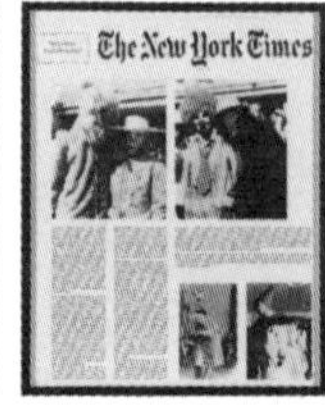

The New York Times

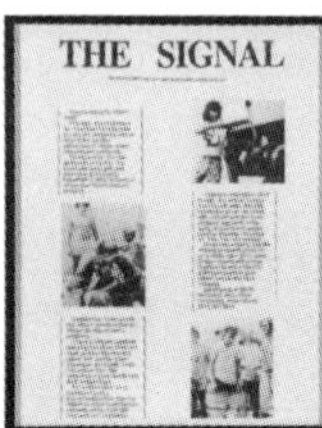

THE SIGNAL

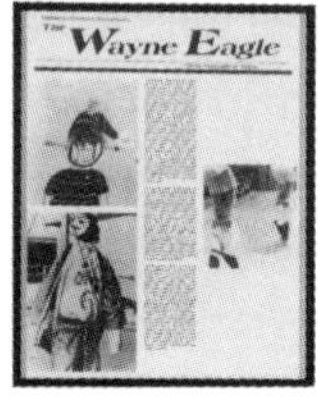

The Wayne Eagle

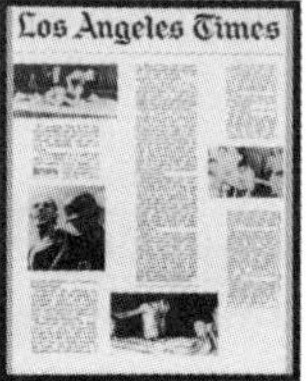

Los Angeles Times

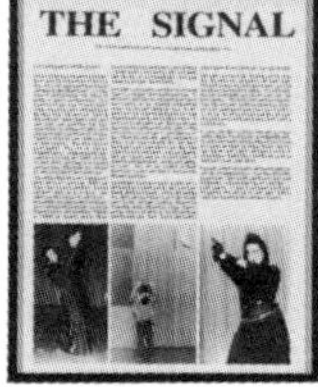

THE SIGNAL

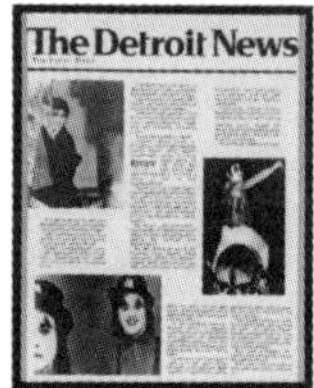

The Detroit News

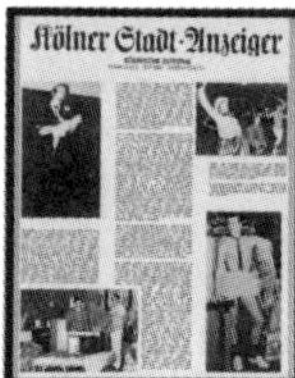

Kölner Stadt-Anzeiger

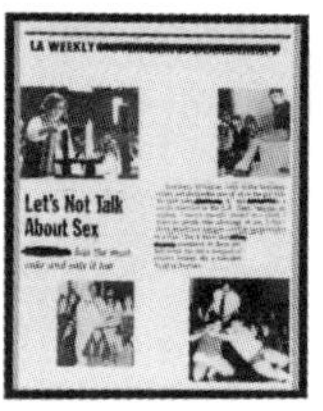

LA WEEKLY

Let's Not Talk About Sex

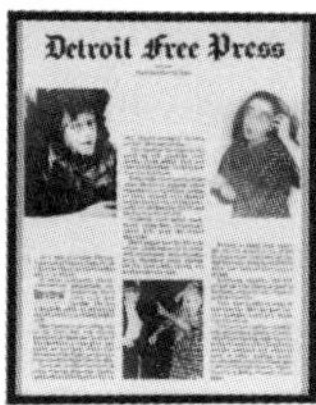

Detroit Free Press

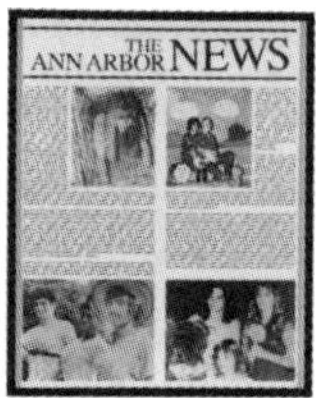

THE ANN ARBOR NEWS

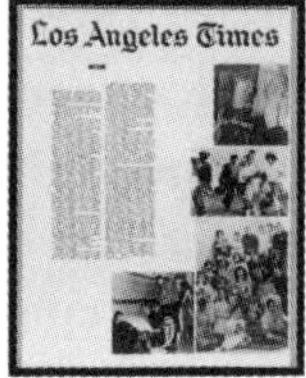

Los Angeles Times

Mike Kelley
Timeless/Authorless, 1995
Black-and-white photographs mounted on museum board in 15 parts,
79 × 61 cm (each)

Timeless/Authorless

JOHN C. WELCHMAN

Time softens, it stretches back.... For some reason my time is not yet. My true self is being shielded from me.... I somehow understand that this holding-back is in my best interest. Yet, I also know that my time is soon... the time when time collapses comes.

—Mike Kelley, "The Complex" (1995)

During the first part of his career, American artist Mike Kelley (1954–2012) battled hard, sometimes unfathomably, with the contested nature of selfhood, including his own—from the mesmeric monologues of his early performances between the late 1970s and mid-1980s, through his appropriation of stuffed animals, blankets, and thrift-store ephemera beginning in the later 1980s, to his work with memory, history, and repression made some half a decade later. Perhaps the central questions of his work converged on his interrogation of the very notion and implications of authorial making. The creative or authoring subject—beset and confined by social and political structures such as family, religion, education, and language, historically emergent only through the corroded fault lines of fitful recall, and caught up in futures that could only be obsessively desired or randomly predicted—was repeatedly besieged in Kelley's reckoning by intimations of its own impossibility. But rather than merely describe or diagnose the inevitable incompletion of the author-subject, Kelley fought back against its ruinous deflation by staging various experiences of the losses he associated with the creative subject: of certitude, position, and finality—of all, or most, of its anchoring agencies.

Kelley's early performances—monologues such as *My Space* (1979), *The Parasite Lily* (1980), *The Sublime* (1984), and *Plato's Cave, Rothko's Chapel, Lincoln's Profile* (1986)—deployed tactics of rhythmic iteration and punning allusion to explore how author-subjects are not so much produced by their contexts as overwritten—and overridden—by histories, concepts, and desires largely beyond their reach or comprehension. At the same time, he was compelled by the puns and percussion of language itself, and by the generation and dispersal of organized modes of accumulation and conceptualization. In *My Space* he meditates on the hard-won constitution of a personal or subjective space in which his "behavior is not influenced by another living thing."[1] The bio-Romantic soliloquy *The Parasite Lily* reflects on questions of decay and organic dissolution. *The Sublime* examines ideas of transcendence, sublimity, and exploration. And *Plato's Cave, Rothko's Chapel, Lincoln's Profile* grapples with the relationships among names, the possessive—and being "possessed." Kelley's interest in the constitution of subjectivity, the plurivocal conditions of language, ideas of sublimity and the beyond, and the conundrum of how things are named—while not specifically related to questions of authorship—creates a kind of potential energy for his more specific reflections. Perhaps this is clearest in the two performances given over most explicitly to the interrogation of order and logic: *Confusion: A Play in Seven Sets, Each Set More Spectacular and Elaborate Than the Last* (1982–83) is set out as a disquisition on rationality, sequence, and disorder, beginning with conjectures about the unraveling of "linear development" and "the limit of knowledge." In *Monkey Island* (1983), Kelley vented a high-energy discourse on corporeal and epistemological entropy centered on images of "bilateral symmetry" and "infinite multiplication" interspersed with figures notating "symmetrical sets" or various abstract "expansions."[2]

In one dimension, the author-subject is beleaguered in these early works by a tumultuous assault on volition and self-possession, but Kelley commenced in the performances a career-long struggle for the rehabilitation of authorship by other means. Armed with strategies of deterrence designed to avoid or circumvent the conditioning of a "normative" subject, he probed for access to authorial possibilities that arise outside the purview and formats of linguistic, social, philosophical, and visual "standardization."[3] This search is apparent in Kelley's earliest performances such as *Oracle at Delphi* (1978), in which sound, dance, rhythm, and "spirit" vocalities are combined with intimations of oracular knowledge and embodiment; *Perspectaphone* (1978), for which he used large and small megaphone prop-objects to collide notions of amplification and perspective; and *Tower of Babel* (1978), which relied on salient miscommunication. In work following on from the performances, he literalized his commitment to modes of subtraction and restraint intended to destabilize subjective particularity by taking up with the illustrational austerity of black-and-white acrylic paint (borrowing in part from traditions of diagramming). At around the same time, he further constrained what vestiges of authorial presence remained by privileging the medium of photography, which emerged as a matrix to adjudicate the conceptual disputes, memory-assisted recalibration, and negative dialectics around which much of his career developed. Photography would supply the deficits of recall, serving as a reservoir, or platform of potentials, for the production of work that allied with other material formats—such as video and multimedia installation—and gave rise to a range of both purposed and unpredictable reconfigurations.[4]

In addition to evasive action articulated by his choice of "diagrammatic" and photographic genres, Kelley also contended more directly with the conventional modes of representing and defining the artist. His illustrated text "Some Aesthetic High Points"—written, he noted, "in lieu of a biographical statement" for inclusion in a 1991 monograph—combines both tactics. Conceived as a purposeful contamination of the conventional format of artistic self-presentation, such as an annotated curriculum vitae or personal statement, Kelley's oddball sequence of captioned images joins several of the strategies he uses to deconstruct the idea of an author-subject. As in many of his "text-image" works (including *Timeless/Authorless*, which is discussed below), the seemingly random cluster of unlikely "high points" shuttles back and forth between the factual and the facetious, but does so in large part as a consequence of assumptions projected on it by readers or viewers. "Some Aesthetic High Points," Kelley observed, constituted "probably my most misunderstood text. It has often been cited as a serious commentary on my aesthetic concerns. In fact, it was designed as a humorous jab at the impossibly difficult assignment to write a thumbnail encapsulation of my artistic practice."[5] A significant segment of Kelley's ironic humor operates in the fitfully faulty space between presentation and expectation, which—as with the falsely imputed personal emotions projected onto his stuffed-animal and soft-toy pieces—the artist reincorporates in subsequent related work, including the series of "projective reconstructions" he commenced in 2000. The text of "Some Aesthetic High Points" was illustrated with found, mostly black-and-white, photographs sourced from newspapers and magazines from the 1940s through the 1980s, which he later subjected to a whole roster of subjective and period-specific projections. The gap Kelley exploited between the "common," snapshot, or documentary conditions of these images, and the molten forms of situational "reconstruction" he visited on them, resulted in prodigious amounts of potential comedic energy that simultaneously dismantles, supplements, and reroutes the attributes of the author-subject.

While Kelley was clearly committed to a complex rearbitration of the nature of the creative subject in many different aspects of his practice, I want to concentrate on his work as a writer. As I cannot offer a full survey of Kelley's views on authorship and the relation of subjects and their positions to the making and reception of texts, I will take on the more modest task of framing and contextualizing a signal shift in Kelley's thinking on these issues in the later part of his career, during the decade and a half following his exhibition *Toward a Utopian Arts Complex* (1995) at the Metro Pictures gallery, in New York.[6] The points of departure for *Timeless/Authorless: Four Recovered Memories* (1995), *Educational Complex* (1995), *Day Is Done (Extracurricular Activity Projective Reconstructions #2–32)* (2005), the later *Extracurricular Activity Projective Reconstructions* (EAPRs) *#33–36B* (2009–11), and the *Kandors* series (beginning in 2000) suggest something close to a form of development, even of progression, in the artist's reflection on the theory and practice of authorship, although conceiving this progression involves an act of straightening out that is somewhat inimical to the Kelleyean universe. A shift in the way he approaches authorship and the author-subject clearly emerges in his set-up protocol for the *Kandors* series, in which Kelley deliberately distanced himself from both the crypto-autobiographical markers established in *Toward a Utopian Arts Complex*, and in his move toward works that engaged generalizable regimens of leisure experience and social ritual (extracurricular activities, off-work down-time, religious observances) organized around community and work-place types—and stereotypes (boss, administrator, coworker)—culminating in *Day Is Done* and the *EAPR*s.

TIMELESS/AUTHORLESS: FOUR RECOVERED MEMORIES

Kelley's series of fifteen black-and-white photo-text works, *Timeless/ Authorless: Four Recovered Memories*, represents a moment of consolidation, concentration, and defining negativity in his engagement with the author function.[7] Topped by the masthead of a local newspaper published in a city in which Kelley either lived, attended school, or regularly exhibited his artwork—including Detroit, Wayne, Westland, and Ann Arbor, in Michigan; the Santa Clarita Valley and Los Angeles, in California; New York City; and Cologne, Germany—each component of *Timeless/Authorless* mimics the appearance of a blown-up newspaper clipping.[8] The text includes a combination of actual newspaper restaurant reviews and "recovered memories" of apparently personal childhood abuse. They are illustrated by photographs lifted from high school yearbooks depicting extracurricular activities—such as sporting events, school plays, and carnivalesque productions (for example, a dance related to the maenad, a figure from Greek mythology)—designed to break the monotony of general institutional order through symbolic reversals of power and displays of nonsensical action. The narratives of the recovered memories are apportioned between multiple photo-texts: the text for "Recovered Memory 1" spans *Timeless/Authorless* photo-texts nos. 4, 7, and 11; "Recovered Memory 2" is used for photo-text 2; "Recovered Memory 3," for photo-text 13; while "Recovered Memory 4" spans nos. 9 and 15. The texts used in *Timeless/Authorless* nos. 1, 3, 6, 8, 12, and 14 consist of restaurant reviews, while the newspaper items in *Timeless/Authorless* nos. 5 and 10 are more psycho-sexual in nature. Kelley chose the format of the newspaper clipping because of the sense of truthful reportage it often signifies; he appropriated restaurant reviews because they are the newspaper excerpts we experience most commonly, appended to restaurant walls or windows, in isolated and enlarged forms.

Shown in *Toward a Utopian Arts Complex* at Metro Pictures along with *Entry Way (Genealogical Chart)*, *Timeless Paintings*, and *Educational Complex* (all 1995), the *Timeless/Authorless* series is part of Kelley's larger project, *Missing Time* (1993–95), which addresses the concepts and implications of repressed memory syndrome (RMS)—a controversial postulate of modern psychology that claims the unconscious, traumatically induced, may block hypothetical memories.[9] Kelley took up with RMS—and the related notion of false memory syndrome—in several exhibitions and associated texts from the mid-1990s, including *Mike Kelley: The Thirteen Seasons (Heavy on the Winter)* (Jablonka Galerie, Cologne, 1995), *Mike Kelley: Missing Time, Works on Paper 1974–1976, Reconsidered* (Kestner-Gesellschaft, Hanover, 1995), and the experimental essay "Goin' Home, Goin' Home" (1995).[10] Written from the point of view of putatively fictive, possibly delusional, victims of abuse, the texts presented in *Timeless/Authorless* address primal scenes of "recalled abuse": gang rape and torture fuelled by religious bigotry; abduction and incarceration; and a scene of father-son incest and paternal tyranny.[11] Depending for their effect on subtle moments of believability and clearly drawing on the style of Kelley's scripts and monologues (though eschewing much of the fragmentation and allusive compounding of the early work), these pieces are among the most fantastical, provocative, and disturbing of all Kelley's writings. They reveal his dependence on the written word for the delivery, sustenance, and plausibility of imaginative extremism, for it would be almost impossible to deploy the contradictory impulses that play through these narratives—which are at once horrific, perverse, and darkly humorous—in any conventional visual media. Of course, all of this is rendered even more shocking—and effective—when one realizes that the four texts derive from a bout of auto-analysis, crossed with the "normative" schema for reports of social dysfunction; as Kelley revealed, "I used self-help books to determine what my 'pathological' psychology is. . . . I just plugged my own life story into the standardized scenarios for believable detail."[12]

The coupled negatives of temporality and authorship ("timeless" and "authorless") that govern this series create a force field of cancelations that converges on a characteristically Kelleyan scene of reduction, reversal, and blankness. Rather than staging events in controlled incremental sequences, Kelley summons a title that points to the project's subtraction or unraveling of accumulated, successive time. Paradoxically ventured in a temporally and location-specific medium—the restaurant review, utterly dependent on the correlation between time, place, and opinion—Kelley's narratives are transacted as timeless recollections laced with fantasy and spiked by projected versions of the distortions, elisions, and fictions of traumatic recall. The timeless past thus engendered is a delusional space, in which becoming is fabricated by willful suspension of intentional logic. The corruption of time, of course, leads to and coproduces the dearticulation of authorship. In the four texts, not only are the identities of the narrating protagonists dissolved into the "unnatural" abstractions of excess they unfold, but any referential certainty about the other subjects who pass through the stories is also put into suspension. To borrow from—and cross-fertilize—an early collaboration between Kelley and Paul McCarthy, what eventuates here is a "family soup" permeated by "cultural tyranny"; a ménage of social and parental stereotypes is caught up in untrammeled manifestations of violence that shatter the stability of the victim-subject(s), whose beleaguered consciousness funds the four-part narrative.[13]

The collapse of subjectivity and concomitant ruin of authorial functionality in *Timeless/Authorless* is built into Kelley's use and modulation of language, which is braided with the inexorable deviance of the events and actions presented in the texts. In the first "Recovered Memory," for example, Kelley's narrator initiates an unremittingly prejudicial account of the licentiousness and general immorality of Protestant children by creating a distance between his putative subject-position as a Catholic schoolboy and the informal knowledge production of his religious community. "I was often warned of the dangers of chumming around with Protestant boys," he writes, "I was told of their warped views of our Lord's teachings." Within a few lines, however, the "warnings" and "tellings" that passed his way through gossip and hearsay have mutated into assertions of fact: "[Protestant] boys are unable to keep their hands off themselves, and as they get older this libidinal urge shifts to anything else they can get a hold of: inanimate objects, animals, whorish girls, and, worst of all, dead things." In the second paragraph of the text, the narrator reverts to, reiterates, and seems to redeem the external referentiality with which he had commenced: "I heard all of this," he notes, "yet I paid it no heed." The slippage between community-originated slander and its absorption into personal "belief" is then completed—though immediately deferred—by the narrator's observation that the story he will tell acts as an exemplum that will prove the viability of a wholesale defamation of the Protestant ethos: "Religious prejudice, as I was to find out," he ventures with a touch too much conviction and pseudo-objectivity, "is the norm."

Couched as a crescendo of ever-more damaging abuse, the first narrative layers an account of extreme corporeal violence with the calculated mindlessness of male group dynamics, in which physical and psychological torture are ramped up by the infectious suspension of individual volition. What transpires in and around the gang's garage headquarters is organized, therefore, through the erasure of personality, individualization, and the constructs of self-possession through which author functions are transacted. The narrator is reduced to meat-like objectivity as his body is ravaged and invaded. But the abusers are also abstracted from their positions as individual subjects, becoming a kind of mass-perpetrator of unconscionable actions. The framing device of the recovered memory—apparently buried, repressed, and later recalled—offers another form of distantiation as its details and the syntax between, and succession of, various actions are inflected by unknowable quotients of distortion, exaggeration, and omission. Normative temporality is thus broken down not only by the trans-temporal coordinates of durational intensity, or the stretching out of small increments of time, but equally by flashbacks and fragmented highlights, which collide and interact with paranoid projections and fantasies. In a crumpled and fractured temporality that finally becomes "timeless," authorship is likewise collapsed into a pure effect of authority fueled by manic volition (on the part of the abusers) and the virtual suspension of selfhood at the threshold of death (by the victim, who, nearing the "zenith" of his abuse, recalls that he "would have rather died").[14]

The religious denomination of the first recovered memory adds another frame within which time and authorship are contested. The denouement of the story, turns, in fact, on the Catholic theology of timeless affirmation and corporeal renewal engendered by the transubstantiation of the host. Forced to purloin a communion wafer from a Mass at his local church, the narrator bears witness to numerous attempts by members of the gang to destroy the Host by throwing knives at it or flushing it down the toilet. "At the first bull's-eye," he noted, "the host began to miraculously bleed and cry, alternating between shedding blood and tears. Despite the bullies' best attempts, the miracle could not be stopped. When the host was chopped to pieces, it reassembled itself. When it was flushed down the toilet, it floated again and again back to the surface." The story ends with a vision of hell accompanied by "a fluctuating image of Christ the Judge, and the wondrous bread that is also He, [that] appeared in the sky."[15] The mystical affirmation and reparative absurdity of this final vision, and the subjection of the now terrified and repentant gang first to the law of the state and later to the judgment of God ("their fate according to the laws of Heaven, I will discover only at the time of my own death"), underscores yet another formation in which subjects are bound over by forces and terms beyond themselves. Thus the miraculous counter-temporality of religious envisioning and the codes of secular law are added to and merge with the contextual formation—and determination—of the self proffered in other dimensions of the text.

Through his religious allegory, Kelley reveals a shredding of time and collapse of rationally variegated selfhood that have parallels in clinical diagnoses of personality disorders, and in the psychological and psychoanalytical discourse that sustains them. Thomas Fuchs, for example, points specifically to the "temporal fragmentation" or "splitting" of the self in borderline personality disorder.[16] He refers to Paul Ricoeur's identification of personhood itself with "the temporal relationship that we have toward ourselves"—the "ipse identity"—that "opens up the sphere of responsibility and faithfulness, of the values and norms we adhere to, and thus establishes the historical continuity . . . essential for personal identity."[17] In contrast to the wittily parodic terms Kelley set out in the fake psychological analyses of children's drawings made under the artist's tutelage in *We Communicate Only through Our Shared Dismissal of the Pre-linguistic* (1995), he has not, of course, created a series of case studies in *Timeless/Authorless*. Kelley was aware of the challenges, underlined by Fuchs, to the Freudian conception of repression and neurosis as the cost of civilization's stability and order represented by "early or ego-structural disorders, . . . the rapid dissolution of traditional family structures and role patterns in post-industrial society, resulting in fragmented biographies," as well as various critiques of the artificial construction of the self "under the rule of an authoritarian rationality."[18] But Kelley works here with an almost desperately corrupted text that meshes performative simulation and fictional projection with rounds of unstable impersonation and implicit and contextually enfeebled critique.

"THE COMPLEX" AND *DAY IS DONE*

Nowhere are the elisions between the corruption and loss of time and the degradation of authorial selfhood better exemplified than in Kelley's "The Complex" (1995), a crypto-fictional written introduction to the institutional space that informs his works *Educational Complex* (an architectural model with miniature versions of every school he attended, along with representations of the parts he could not recall) and *Day Is Done* (thirty-one "projective reconstructions" of episodes and activities transacted in the "complex" based on found photographs). Kelley's brief text stakes out the erosion of its author's basic capacity to remember and record: while he notes that the (imaginary) full manuscript delineating the myriad aspects of "The Complex" purportedly ran to "thousands of pages—or more," the artist's introduction is a preface to just forty abbreviated and willingly censored extracts. In what seems to be an ironic reversal of the prurience of *Timeless/Authorless*, Kelley wrote that "entries of a particularly horrid nature have been deleted so as to not offend the reader"—a claim that is ironic all over again as the list of spaces where abuse is transacted and the abuses themselves are already extreme and horrific. In the introduction, the authorial probity of the writing subject is undermined in multiple dimensions. Kelley deliberately collides chance ("happenstance"), deceptive appearance, and "dim memories," and he offers further obfuscation by referring to the "secrecy" surrounding the circumstances of the recall as well as the "intermittent" and disorienting "dream"-like state to which he succumbed as he attempted to remember details. The loss of the subject's self-possession correlates with a "softening" and "stretching" of time that sets in as the author is escorted on a Dantesque, otherworldly journey through the "ether" of an afterlife suffused with "previous incarnations" that leads to a loss of "racial" and self-identity. "For some reason," the text suggests, "my time is not yet. My true self is being shielded from me by these folk. I somehow understand that this holding-back is in my best interest. Yet, I also know that my time is soon, . . . the time when time collapses comes."[19]

Exiled from terrestrial time, the author is made over through self-alienation by way of a process that somehow converts him into an actual alien—the only apparently viable strategy by which the subject can sever, or utterly repress, the ties of blood and family and escape the confines of the symbolic order. One of the entries in the list that follows points to this "remote" or exterior position, but at the same time implicates alien actors as the perpetrators of the itemized abuses: entry number seventeen describes one space in the complex as "a remote satellite outpost where sage aliens perform genital operations and anal probings." We are left with the imagined possibility that the loss of self in a timeless zone inhabited by torrents of fear and loathing begets only the prospect that subjects are made over as the phantom authors of their own abuse.

The forty cells, chambers, offices, stages, cloakrooms, research centers, stalls, and stands described in "The Complex," each associated with a particular perversion or atrocity, meet with their anodyne antitheses in *Day Is Done*, a video installation composed of thirty-one musical-cum-vaudeville "numbers," called *Extracurricular Activity Projective Reconstructions* (EAPRs). The thirty-one videos are distributed across a series of twenty-five sculptural viewing stations. The variegated abuses of "The Complex" are answered in the video installation, a decade later, by scenes based on images from high school yearbook and newspaper photographs of musical and dance performances, dress-up days, meetings and mixers, workplace gatherings, and other putatively benign group events. As with the contact zone between alien formations that connects the introduction to "The Complex" and the list redacted from the wider manuscript, Kelley has built-in an overlay between the list and the methodological underpinnings of *Day Is Done*. Two of the locales described in "The Complex" (nos. 29 and 31) refer to photographic activities—the former to "the cock-sucking research center with film and photo archive," the latter to "a photo hut where photographs of a deviant nature are immediately projected onto the exterior as soon as they are developed." The deviant manifestations referred to in the list from "The Complex" not only represent the carnal and repressed obverse of the permissible leisure activities of *Day Is Done*, but also are products of the same protocol: the amassing of an "archive" that forms the basis for different modes of "projection"—a literal "screening" or projection in "The Complex," and imaginative "projective reconstructions" in the episodes of *Day Is Done*. Typically, Kelley's language presses further and more subtly in his text than in the physical installation of *Educational Complex*, as the temporal "immediacy" of the photographic "development" of images in the hut glimpses unmistakably at the erosion of time in normal developmental cycles, such as the growth from childhood through adolescence to maturity. This elision also forecloses on creative time, as images strung together in "The Complex" are not so much produced but passed on in a relay of reflexes that moves in an instant from a deviant action to its photographic representation, development, and public projection.

The sheer referential range and giddy overcoding of the projective reconstructions in *Day Is Done* deliver Kelley's version of appropriation into a creative dimension quite different from the "critical" pretensions of New York postmodernism. Kelley launched a scintillating retort to the rephotographic practices of Sherrie Levine (b.1947), Richard Prince, and others that so gripped the New York art world from the late 1970s through the 1980s. While subscribing to the proposition that, as he put it, "all life is quotation; nothing is new, things are only recontextualized," Kelley engaged with the question of authorship in a radically different way than the New York postmodernists, who he viewed as preoccupied with ideas of commodification and the art market, or American readings of Walter Benjamin.[20] Both Kelley and Levine begin with a photograph—one ultravernacular (for example, a photograph from a school play), the other "high" or "fine" (a reproduction of an iconic documentary photograph). Levine's gestures of singular appropriation provoke questions of originality and authorship that are elaborated upon by viewers and critics; they are effective only through the critical context that underwrites their reception. Kelley, on the other hand, subjects his found photographs to social and formal extrapolation, overloading them with a vertiginous combination of faux-logical implication and situational projection. Levine inters the photograph in the coffin of its authorship; Kelley resurrects its anonymous protagonists into a voracious afterlife of apocryphal dimensions—quite literally in *EAPR #23: Joseph Supplicates*, in which Kelley makes recourse to the *History of Joseph the Carpenter*, an extra-biblical manuscript probably written in Egypt in the fourth or fifth century A.D.[21]

KANDORS

The point of origin for Kelley's *Kandors* series was not in common photography or newspaper reportage, but in popular graphics—specifically, in depictions of Kandor, onetime capital of the planet Krypton and the city of Superman's birth, which was shrunk by a villain and placed in a bell jar. While researching for the project, Kelley realized that, from its first presentation (in *Action Comics*, vol. 1, no. 242, 1958), images of the miniaturized city encased in a bell jar were radically unstable and lacked almost all measures of consistency—whether defined by scale, urbanistic continuity, immediate context, formal concentration, building type, architectural style, or even systematic modes of abbreviation. The horizontal city, tucked under Superman's arm as he deposits it in his Fortress of Solitude in the concluding panes of the comic strip, is thus rendered as a faint, utterly retiring confection of hatch marks and one-liners that is overwhelmed by the reflection creases on the glass itself, but also identical with the forms that constitute the reflection marks themselves. This is premonitory, of course, as the most formally radical of Kelley's representations of the city return to the short circuit between light and metropolis by staging their architectonic structures with analogously—but now effusively colorized—dissolution.

The city as point—and line—initiated the key extrapolation of the *Kandors*, as Kelley sought to extend these faint suggestions into planes, then monochrome models, then shimmering polychromatic redoubts, and finally the charred survivalist lump of the black-hole-cum-cave of

Kandor 10B (Exploded Fortress of Solitude) (2011). Another way to approach the progression of Kelley's reckoning with the author function is to narrow our focus momentarily to consider the question of how authorship is staged, as it were, from point and line to plane. For unlike the *EAPRs*—clearly anchored in Kelley's personal formation and, reading out, on the social and cultural pressures exerted by his domestic and educational milieu—*Kandors* starts with the issues of third-party authorship and interpretation, beginning with the pencilers, inkers, and colorists who, along with a letterist, produced the text, and created, filled-in, detailed, or abstracted the city of Kandor in their particular ways. While the Superman comics also furnish a context of sorts that aligns, even coincides, with Kelley's own formation—he was three years old when the first issue of *Action Comics* was published in 1958—comics per se were never such a prominent part of his childhood and adolescence as they were for his friend Jim Shaw, for example, and rarely defined his subject choices or conceptual orientations. In his 2010 essay on *Kandors*, Kelley italicizes this distance and points to the social extension for which he sought: "I was not personally interested in the Superman mythos," he notes, "but I felt the popularity of the narrative would lead me to a large number of people who have a common interest."[22]

The radical variegation manifest in the imaging of Kandor was a prompt, then, for a signal reinflection of Kelley's long-standing preoccupation with projective reconstruction and authorship, which correlates not only with a move from the horizons of personal experience to those of community or collective memory, but also with questions of medium specificity. This is vested not so much in the media that constitute the works' triggers or launching pads—the found photographs of *Day Is Done* and the later *EAPRs* and the comic-book images of *Kandors*—but rather in the media through which congregations of these images are collected, analyzed, reordered, and socially diffused. For the *EAPRs*, this "medium" was bound up with the innovative format of their exhibition—notably, the complexly interactive video-sculptural-performance gallery appearance of *Day Is Done*, which

Kelley later reworked into a feature-length "narrative" film musical as well as an ambitiously scaled publication. While *Kandors* also eventuated in a series of exhibitions, at its inception the project was yoked to a wider field of media organization and presentation. Building on the more modestly "interactive" precedent of *We Communicate Only through Our Shared Dismissal of the Pre-linguistic*, for which he employed a computer and monitor so that viewers could browse the children's paintings and the spoof psychological analyses that occasioned this work, Kelley's initial "project proposal" for *Kandor-Con 2000* "called for the construction of a website" that would be used to gather "information regarding Kandor . . . from fans of Superman comic books via the internet." This material would form the basis for the construction and museum presentation of both "physical and digital versions of the city." Kelley rounded out his journey from concrete to virtual and then back again to the domain of physical communities with the idea of throwing a party, to which he wanted the host institution to invite all those who had contributed to the website. As Kelley noted, sardonically as ever, none of this came to pass as "there was not even enough money in the museum's budget to set up the website," let alone to ferry in legions of Superman aficionados from far and wide.[23]

The new-media dispensation that might have organized *Kandor-Con 2000* helps us to frame the different temporalities of the *Kandors* and *EAPRs*. While both are predicated on what Kelley referred to as "missing time," the memorial absence or insufficiency of the *EAPRs* is directed toward the past—marked out as Kelley's formative school and college years, though apprehended through a kind of sampled spectrum of contemporary instances—and the *Kandors* series, although drawing on a "historical" lineage of comic-book illustration, filters and reanimates the original images by committing to the technologies of the (then) present (as Kelley specifically notes, "the internet . . . at that time was just beginning to come into popular usage"). Both "then" and "now" are directed toward an image of the future emblematized in Kelley's *Kandors* as multiply imagined, would-be utopian forms. As Kelley puts it, "an interactive computer program that would allow the city to be changed continuously, based on fan's [*sic*] input, would have been a perfect reflection of the ambiguous nature of the city and an appropriate model of memory's elusive nature."[24]

For Kelley, of course, media are never simple delivery vehicles. So while interested in soliciting the "input of a broader public," the materials that would have been generated were also "responses to a culturally shared fantasy space."[25] The miniature exemplum of the city of Kandor thus functions in a synecdochical relationship to the World Wide Web—a contested, futuristic fragment standing in for an unimaginably huge communal space that makes possible a new order of fantasy and projection. In a sense, this is Kelley's version of Marshall McLuhan's adage that the "medium is the message," for media are seldom inert, never merely modes of realization and circulation: instead they are caught up almost authorially in historical constructions and imaginative projection that seemingly have a life outside of the lives of their users. For Kelley, the internet in its earlier years was defined by a kind of utopian techno-positivism, on the one hand, but could be understood as the labyrinthine retreat of a hoard of social isolates hunkered down in "disembodied fantasy role-playing," on the other. In one of Kelley's signature cross-hatchings, the social alienation of the internet mirrored the metaphorically obdurate alienation symbolized by Superman's city in a bottle, whose vitrinous entrapment he also likened to Sylvia Plath's "use of the bell jar as a symbol of psychic disconnection."[26] As often, the points on Kelley's tilting planes of consistency light up like a neural network triggered only by analogy.

THE INVISIBLE AUTHOR

What would have become of the complexly materialized dialectic between the *EAPR*s and the *Kandors* series, the organizing principle of most of Kelley's exhibitions in the years leading up to his death in 2012, will never fully be known. But the consequential shift away from the pseudo-autobiographic investigation that animated the earlier works gave rise to his renewed emphasis on forms of authorship—mostly originating in popular or countercultures—that were marginalized, anonymous, or virtually "invisible." Kelley's interest in invisible forms of authorship was anticipated by his "general working methodology," established in the late 1970s and early 1980s, which was based on the "somewhat random" selection of "a limited number of word or image pairings" that would direct his "research" into "associated topics." As Kelley notes, "this yielded a vast amount of disconnected information that I would then attempt to organize mythopoetically into what, on the surface at least, resembled a coherent belief system."[27] The results of this method are most apparent, perhaps, in his investigation of cave formations—and the repertoire of names ascribed to them—in the form of black-and-white photographs shot from books and pamphlets in 1984 and 1985. The subterranean subject matter of these images fed into *Plato's Cave, Rothko's Chapel, Lincoln's Profile* (1986), and the photographs were regrouped a decade later for the photo series *The Poetry of Form: Part of an Ongoing Attempt to Develop an Auteur Theory of Naming* (1984–96). The recursive emergence of his thinking on authorship is underlined by the relation of the rephotographed caves to a network of polarizations through which they circulate—the relation of image to text; of color to monochromatic images; of conceptual to formal modes of art-making; and of high art to mass culture. For it was actually the production of seemingly unremarkable linguistic descriptors—"commercial paint chips" represented by "sample cards, with rows of titled colors, given away at paint stores"—that prompted Kelley to attend to the ways that things are named in popular and commercial cultures, how the names stick, and what forms of unattributed authorial agency might have been involved.[28]

Kelley's emphasis on forms of making and authorship that have been overlooked is present, too, in his decision to write about artists he felt had been neglected by the mainstream art world (including Paul Thek, Öyvind Fahlström, Douglas Huebler, David Askevold, and John Miller), and in his motivation for *The Uncanny*, an exhibition he curated in 1993 and revised in 2004.[29] Kelley begins his essay, "Playing with

Dead Things: On the Uncanny," with a citation from the critic Jack Burnham, who laments the marginalization, by an art history suffused with a Greek-oriented view of the body, of a whole world of "anthropological forms," such as "fetishes, idols, amulets, funeral images, dolls, waxworks, manikins, puppets, and, most dramatically, automata."[30] Following what could be seen as a long detour—accelerated by the misassociation of Kelley's soft-toy works with his own autobiography, the emphasis on repressed and dissociated memory in the mid-1990s, and the overlay of his personal formation on the images of social and leisure activities in the *EAPRs*—Kelley renewed his attention to authors and subjects that were all but invisible to dominant cultures, whether aesthetic, social, or political.

In 2008 he provided the preface to an anthology of *Sex to Sexty*, a smutty magazine referred to as the bible of hick erotica, published in Texas between 1965 and 1983. In contrast to more "classy" skin magazines such as *Playboy*, *Sex to Sexty* was, according to Kelley's preface, "unapologetically low, silly, and most importantly . . . geared toward lower-class rural Americans living far away from the sophisticated urban sin-centers."[31] Describing itself as guardian of "the True Jokelore of America," *Sex to Sexty* furnished its prurient, generally non-metropolitan, readership with "page after page of politically-incorrect quips and moronic men's magazine-style sex gag cartoons (many focusing on hillbilly and farm themes)," much of it reader contributed.[32] Kelley's preface was the culmination of a long-standing interest in the magazine that self-consciously elided many of the issues I have examined here, including the relationships between color, time, and form. Two series of paintings, *Missing Time Color Exercises* and *Missing Time Color Exercises (Reversed)* (both 1998), used the covers of *Sex to Sexty* that Kelley had collected over the years to form chronological (and reverse chronological) grids, with the missing issues filled in by colors precisely mixed to fit the existing chromatic sequence.

The more extreme outcomes of Kelley's analysis of authorial subjectivity and autobiography—an utter loss of selfhood and its temporal anchorage behind a miasma of allegorical alienation—are answered by a similarly radical move in relation to the questions around third-party authorship, both amateur and professional, that came to the fore in the *Kandors* works. In the last decade of his life, he reflected with growing urgency and intensity on forms of authorship that were "culturally invisible" and gave rise to what he termed "a quality being hidden."[33] He wanted, for example, "to develop an auteur theory of pan and scan" (the process used to adjust widescreen film images so that they can be shown within the proportions of a standard-definition 4:3 aspect-ratio television screen).[34] Reviewing the film *Mondo Cane* (Paolo Cavara, Gualtiero Jacopetti, and Franco E. Prosperi, 1962) and its spin-offs, he was compelled by questions of documentary authorship and the notion of "the invisible documentary voice," issues that in the work of artists such as Cameron Jamie were interleaved with the autobiographical.[35] Kelley even conceived of a vast general project (the pair, perhaps, of his gargantuan conception of 365 *EAPRs*, one for each day of the year) that was to address the totality of "anonymous mass culture" and was based on interviews with "auteurs in various fields."[36] In the end, the project's disconnect from the values of the high-art world, and the overweening scale and probable impossibility of such an enterprise, combined with the artist's only partial transformation of the guilt he accrued from his Catholic upbringing into guilt about the egregious relegation of so many scenes of making and doing in the wider culture. At some point, unable to find himself again, Kelley was preoccupied, and then tragically overwhelmed, by the failure to transfer a sense of loss of selfhood into the duties and pleasures of making contact with the wider sphere of popular or marginalized auteurship.

The Author Stripped Bare by Its Employees: Artistic Authorship in the Twenty-First Century and Beyond

LISA ROSENDAHL

The commissioning of this text started with a question: why have all critiques of artistic authorship ultimately ended up reinforcing authorship as a category? Despite all the subversive antics played out over the course of twentieth-century art production, artists cannot seem to rid themselves of the authorship function—why not? The simple answer is that, if they did, their efforts would no longer be considered art. Although the Romantic figure of the author-as-individual-genius was dethroned long ago, the compulsive rule-breaking that has characterized the visual arts for the past hundred years seems incapable of relinquishing the function of authorship as one of its main framing devices. Like in a game of musical chairs in which all other supporting conventions have been pulled away, one after the other, we are left with one seat in the middle when the music stops playing: demonstratively left empty or occupied by several persons at once, the last remaining chair reminds us that, should it be removed altogether, the game (of art as we know it) would definitely be over.

Hence, it is more interesting to ask how artists' relationship to authorship has changed over time and what these shifts can tell us about the cultural environments that produced them. This essay looks at a selection of contemporary artists operating out of a European-American context, all of whom take the question of authorship as a central theme for their practice, to discuss how artists keep rearticulating their relationship to the notion of the author as a way to comment on art as a symptom of the society that supports it. Although the scope of this essay can offer only a grossly abbreviated account of how the author function has evolved into the twenty-first century, it is my hope that the greater question lurking beneath the limited narrative outlined herein will nevertheless make its presence felt: is art as a category based on historically specific power relations without which it would not be able to continue to exist, or can it indeed function as a training ground for overthrowing the mechanisms that have been foundational for its own coming into being?

THE AUTHOR FUNCTION

As Michel Foucault so eloquently explained in his seminal text *What Is an Author?* (1969), the author function is not universal, constant, or equivalent in all fields or discourses.[1] Highly contingent, the notion of the author takes on different meanings in relation to different historical times and contexts. In seventeenth- and eighteenth-century Europe, the author function emerged at different times and in different ways concurrently with the gradual development of the idea of an autonomous rights-bearing individual, which in turn arose as a response to the notion of the nation as a territorial state. In eighteenth-century England, the idea of an individuated originary author was formed by the fields of law and literature as a way to control the number of copies of literary texts that would be allowed to circulate publicly. It was in this cultural environment that the concepts of possessive individualism and original genius intersected to create the idea of the Romantic author, embodying both legal and literary "originality." From that moment on, authorship in law and literature became determined through the relationship between the categories of "idea," "expression," and "work," in the sense that an idea is transformed by an author into an expression, which becomes the work. Thus, the trope of individual authorship is bound historically to the understanding in eighteenth-century England of the concepts of "property," the "individual," and the act of "expression": whereas ideas were seen as something common to all and circulating freely, the way they were expressed became a matter governed by the rights accredited to morally autonomous individuals.

Although individual authorship within visual art was recognized both legally and intellectually in various ways well before the eighteenth century, Foucault's narrative of how the authorship function was consolidated in dialogue with the ideals of modernity will serve as a reference point for my argument in this essay. With the onset of modernity, the idea of the individual as the center of things reached its apotheosis; it was believed that ways of knowing and acting in the world were no longer derived from traditional norms, but established autonomously.[2] The human self was granted with the status of subject, and the figure of the artist became the ultimate symbol and bearer of this idea. The modern artist appeared as the ideal sovereign subject through his ability to authentically express his innermost self. In the words of art historian Cornelia Klinger:

> Authenticity is the pure expression, the expressivity, of the artist, whose soul is mirrored in the work of art. . . . Consequently, the degree to which an artist gave expression to his true self, to his intuitions, visions, ideas and sensations, became a criterion of judging the quality of high art. . . . Only in the person of the artist does the self achieve in full measure the status of subject suggested by the modernity process.[3]

In the twentieth century, the idea of individual expression was repeatedly attacked and reinvented by a succession of artists. Marcel Duchamp's (1887–1968) "readymades," the first of which dates from 1913, are often cited as early obliterations of subjective gesture, soon to be followed by artists defined as Minimalist or Conceptual, or those using strategies of appropriation. Gradually undoing its ties to specific traditional skills and media, twentieth-century art eventually became increasingly nebulous and difficult to define as a category beyond the generic claim of "being art." As art won the right to be anything and take any form—not to mention the right to not even be made[4]—artistic output paradoxically became increasingly reliant on authorship as the last remaining recognizable framing device validating its circulation as art. The accelerating importance of certificates of authenticity from the 1960s on bears witness to this, as does the art-industry standard of presenting biographical details and exhibition history to accredit an artist's work with cultural and capital value. When Sol LeWitt (1928–2007) declared that "Conceptual art is good only when the idea is good," that "the idea becomes a machine that makes the art," and that "the idea itself, even if not made visual, is as much a work of art as any finished product," it was still understood that the idea had to come from an identifiable source.[5] Although LeWitt maintained that Conceptual art was not dependent on the skill of the artist as craftsperson, he continued to place great importance on human traits such as "intuition" and "all types of mental processes." Were *the idea* for a work generated by a machine as well, the work would most likely have been considered irrelevant in terms of social, economic, and art-historical value.

If the figure of the author was consolidated in the eighteenth century as a way to control the circulation of literary texts, in the twentieth century the trope of the author seems to have taken on the reverse function, meaning that nothing will become visible *without* an author. To be recognized as art, a work needs to be made public according to the rules of art's particular discourse, which invariably means through authorship. As Alain Badiou has pointed out with reference to the twentieth century, when the entire world starts to be viewed in terms of a global market, "Everything that circulates falls under the unity of the count, while inversely, only what lets itself be counted in this way can circulate."[6] The tendency toward thinking in these terms is so strong that although the idea of the individual and originary author is repeatedly killed off by successions of radical art practices—through work experimenting with audience participation, performance, and collectivity attempting to undo the division of labor set up by the holy trinity of "author," "work," and "audience"—the function of authorship as a framing device seems impossible to abandon.[7] Even George Maciunas, the New York–based artist and founder of Fluxus who in his work and the seminal *Fluxus Manifesto* (1963) promoted "collective spirit, anonymity and Anti-individualism" so that "eventually we would destroy the authorship of pieces and make them totally anonymous—

thus eliminating the artists' 'ego,'" cannot let go of authorship as a vehicle for becoming visible, declaring: "author would be Fluxus." To make a work of art public—to *publicize* it in the words of Maciunas's manifesto—it needs to have a name, a sender, and a locatable origin attached to it.

CONTEMPORARY DECONSTRUCTIONS

Bernadette Corporation

Toward the end of the twentieth century, this split in the authorial function between the name and those laboring behind it became the focus of several art practices, one of the more famous ones being Bernadette Corporation, formed in New York in 1994, thirty years after the founding of Fluxus. Comparing the meaning at the root of the two collectives' names—*flux* ("continuous change; instability"[8]) and *corporation* ("a group of people authorized by law to act as a legal personality and having its own powers, duties, and liabilities")—one gets an immediate sense of the ideological shift that occurred in the three decades that separate them. The propensity in the 1960s toward radical change had by the 1990s been replaced with a more defeatist outlook that seemed to say: if there is no way to escape capitalism, then let us emulate the beast and beat it at its own game. By emphasizing the split between the name and the person(s) behind it, Bernadette Corporation not only evoked the historical use of pseudonyms, but also exemplified how this should be understood in twentieth-century terms—that is, with the creation of a brand.

Set up with the premise that a corporation was "the perfect alibi for not having to fix an identity," Bernadette Corporation simultaneously inflated and deflated the art world's need for marketable identity.[9] Working across fashion, art, and publishing to produce catwalk shows as well as video works with political ambitions (such as *Get Rid of Yourself*, a film about the Black Bloc made in 2002) and a collective novel (*Reena Spaulings*, published in 2004), the moniker functions as a way to allow a diversity of approaches to cultural production, while still being a recognizable entity, enabling the accumulation of cultural capital. In the foreword to the novel *Reena Spaulings*—allegedly written by 150 people in a process modeled upon the Hollywood screenwriting system, in which a studio boss has a stable of writers at their disposal—Bernadette Corporation notes that an author "is a routine," explaining: "Not only is an author a person who writes, but also a role that is negotiated and trained by those who choose the books one can read today. Becoming an author is a process of subjectivation, and so is becoming a soldier, becoming a cashier, becoming a potted plant."[10] This passage suggests that a book is authored by its context—that is, the system that has the power to make the text visible as a book—just as much as by the people who write it. Furthermore, by equalizing the process of becoming an author with that of becoming a soldier, a cashier, or a potted plant, Bernadette Corporation emphasizes the generic nature of assuming any predefined role, effectively short-circuiting any potential leftover expectations of individual expression that could still be haunting the field of art. In the words of the book's main protagonist, Reena Spaulings: "Our lack of uniqueness is the only thing we share today."[11]

Claire Fontaine

Indeed, the responses of many twenty-first-century artists to the legacy of Duchamp's readymades are manifestations of the generic. The Paris-based Claire Fontaine, which was started in 2004 by Fulvia Carnevale and James Thornhill and takes its name from a French stationery supplier, goes as far as describing herself as a "readymade artist" who makes art that "looks a lot like other people's work."[12] In addition, Carnevale and Thornhill refer to themselves as "assistants," maintaining that "Claire Fontaine is composed only of assistants, its management is an empty center."[13] In this case, the use of a pseudonym is not a way to appear mysterious or render the artists behind the name invisible. Neither is it a front behind which a changing multiplicity of identities and artistic strategies may momentarily come together to then disband and reform in other configurations; Claire Fontaine remains the vehicle of Carnevale and Thornhill and has a well-articulated and documented political position that continually defines her practice. Rather, the use of "Claire Fontaine"—a preexisting brand name—coupled with the reference to the readymades is a way to address the standardization of subjectivity in contemporary society by revealing the artist as a subject that is as "exchangeable as the products she produces."

It is well established that the principal consequence of Duchamp's readymades was the collapse of the difference between art and the commodity. What Claire Fontaine seems to be suggesting is that this collapse also led to the implosion of subject and object in the artist: to be an artist after Duchamp's readymades is to inhabit a generic function.[14] Duchamp's gesture testified to a shift in the understanding of the creative act—from being determined by specific skills (such as painting or sculpting) to existing independently of any aesthetic ability or judgment. After the readymades, one is an artist because one is an artist, and not because one sculpts or paints. Artistic practice has been reoriented from the specific to the generic; the subject has become an object. When Claire Fontaine takes an existing brand name as her own, she is not inventing a fictional character. Rather, she is redirecting our attention from the fictitious belief in and promises of individual subjectivity, as represented by the figure of the originary author, to the reality of the objectified existence of all subjects under the regime of capitalism.

Goldin+Senneby

In the project *Headless*, begun by Swedish artists Goldin+Senneby in 2007, the trope of authorship is similarly used as a vehicle for exploring the fictitious machinations of capitalism. The project sees the artists entering the world of offshore finance and appropriating its methods, language, and strategies for the purpose of producing a novel—allegedly ghostwritten by an author named John Barlow—while continuously displacing their own subject position. Taking its cue from Acéphale, the secret society formed by the French literary figure Georges Bataille in the 1930s, *Headless* was initiated as an investigation into the existence of any possible connection between its historical precedent and the contemporary offshore company Headless Ltd., registered in the Bahamas by the Sovereign Trust. The undertaking of the investigation as well as the generation of content for the novel was predominantly outsourced; a cast of collaborators and paid contractors "whose actions would be at times generated by the novel and at times cannibalized by it" were enlisted as protagonists.[15] The reader is taken through a labyrinth of plotlines, in which each character might just as easily become an author, and vice versa. The result is a vertiginously oscillating relationship between the real world and the fictional realm, where fictive constructs create real-life events—not unlike the way money exercises its influence over our everyday lives.

The porous boundaries in *Headless*—between "reality" and "fiction," and "author" and "character"—can be understood as a performative enactment of the contemporary dissolution of the historical concepts of "property" and "sovereignty" that underpinned the formation of the notion of the individual author in the eighteenth century. The Western vision of individual autonomy and liberty articulated by the Enlightenment thinkers developed in close connection to ideas of property and sovereignty. But by the mid-twentieth century, property was no longer tied to physical entities, and both individual and public sovereignty had become challenged by supranational structures of power and finance. The contemporary renegotiation by artists of the authorship function as transient, and not bound to fixed entities such as a biological body or legal personality, can be read as a response to the erosion of national and territorial sovereignty by multinational companies and international legal frameworks. In *Headless*, the destabilizing of the relationship between reality and fiction serves to remind us that the figure of the autonomous individual is as much a cultural construct as a character in a book.

Pierre Huyghe and Philippe Parreno

The project *No Ghost Just a Shell*, by French artists Pierre Huyghe and Philippe Parreno, interrogates the relationships between character, authorship, and autonomy, as well as the parallels that can be drawn to how the ideas of the autonomous subject and individual property are linked in capitalist society. The body of work was initiated in 1999, when Huyghe and Parreno bought the copyright in a female Manga-style figure developed by the Japanese company Kworks and decided to call her AnnLee. Over the next three years, the project engaged artists such as Liam Gillick, Douglas Gordon, and Dominique Gonzalez-Foerster to make work of, with, and in response to AnnLee, resulting in films, posters, and other objects, which were brought together in an exhibition at Kunsthalle Zürich in 2002. After three years of intense activity, Huyghe and Parreno decided to end the project and transferred the copyright in AnnLee to a foundation, which at least symbolically owned the copyright on behalf of AnnLee as a beneficiary, finally granting the character her independence. Was this a Romantic gesture born out of the belief that property is the basis of personal liberty, or an insightful act of authorial hara-kiri triggered by the master-and-slave-like dialectic between a vacant subject and its exhausted managers? Alluding to the fact that the only possibility of sovereignty is in the realm of (legal) fiction, AnnLee stands testimony to the shift that has occurred in the understanding of authorship and the use of the author function from the eighteenth century to today, whereby an ideology of individual authorship based on property, originality, and personality has been replaced with a multitude of strategies for the mobilization of zombie-like empty vessels. Worth noting, however, is that although the "liberation" of AnnLee into an autonomous entity could be seen as a kind of victory over the system that created her, it also short-circuited any further potential generation of artworks in her name. In this instance, the insurrection against authority inevitably entailed a permanent exit from the discourse of art.

FROM AUTHOR TO PRACTITIONER?

The examples of contemporary art practice discussed above reveal the treasured figure of the artist-as-individual-genius to be an impersonator of the authentic subject promoted by the ideology of modernity. Through actively avoiding originary individual authorship on the level of production as well as representation, these artists suggest that the author is not only dead, but also that he never existed (beyond the realm of law). Instead of upholding the image of the artist as an ideal sovereign *subject*, the work of Bernadette Corporation, Claire Fontaine, Goldin+Senneby, and Huyghe/Parreno displays how humanity has been affected by the modernity process through being *subjected to* commodification, standardization, and fragmentation, including the divisions of labor and mechanisms of control produced by the function of the author. To what extent the strategies of these artists, which some might call cynical, are impersonations of contemporary constructs of subjectivity that can only become visible with the passing of time, remains to be seen.

As art holds up its mirror to the world, the subject is revealed to have become an object. Is there then no way for art to exit the logic of production and circulation that has so thoroughly dominated the twentieth century and continues to do so today? To rid ourselves of the author function, as I pointed out at the beginning of this text, is a futile gesture as long as the art discourse remains tied to the concept of art as the circulation of ideas expressed as artworks, however immaterial they might prove to be. But if the focus of the discourse (and its ensuing value system) would shift from the production of definable "works" towards the ongoing and immeasurable acts of "practice" that precede them, the game might change.

Practice, in this sense of the word, involves the cultivation of agency —the doing rather than the final result. Whereas works of art are the symbolic residue of this process, practice is the act of agency itself. As every artist knows, practice is that which comes *before* the work; it is the search while it is still ongoing and inconclusive. Practice might result in various forms of output, but it does not hinge solely on its public dissemination and reception to be of value to those who are engaged in it. It is not something you publicize and circulate, but still it can be shared. As British artist Emma Smith has pointed out: "practice is not exclusive to art, it takes many forms and belongs to everyone, making the role of the artist simply to draw our attention to the existence of these practices and the growth of agency they potentially entail."[16] As practice does not abide by the division of labor among artists, artworks, and audiences, it does not have authors—it has practitioners. Looked at in this way, art could most certainly be understood as a training ground for overthrowing the mechanisms that have been foundational for its current state of being.

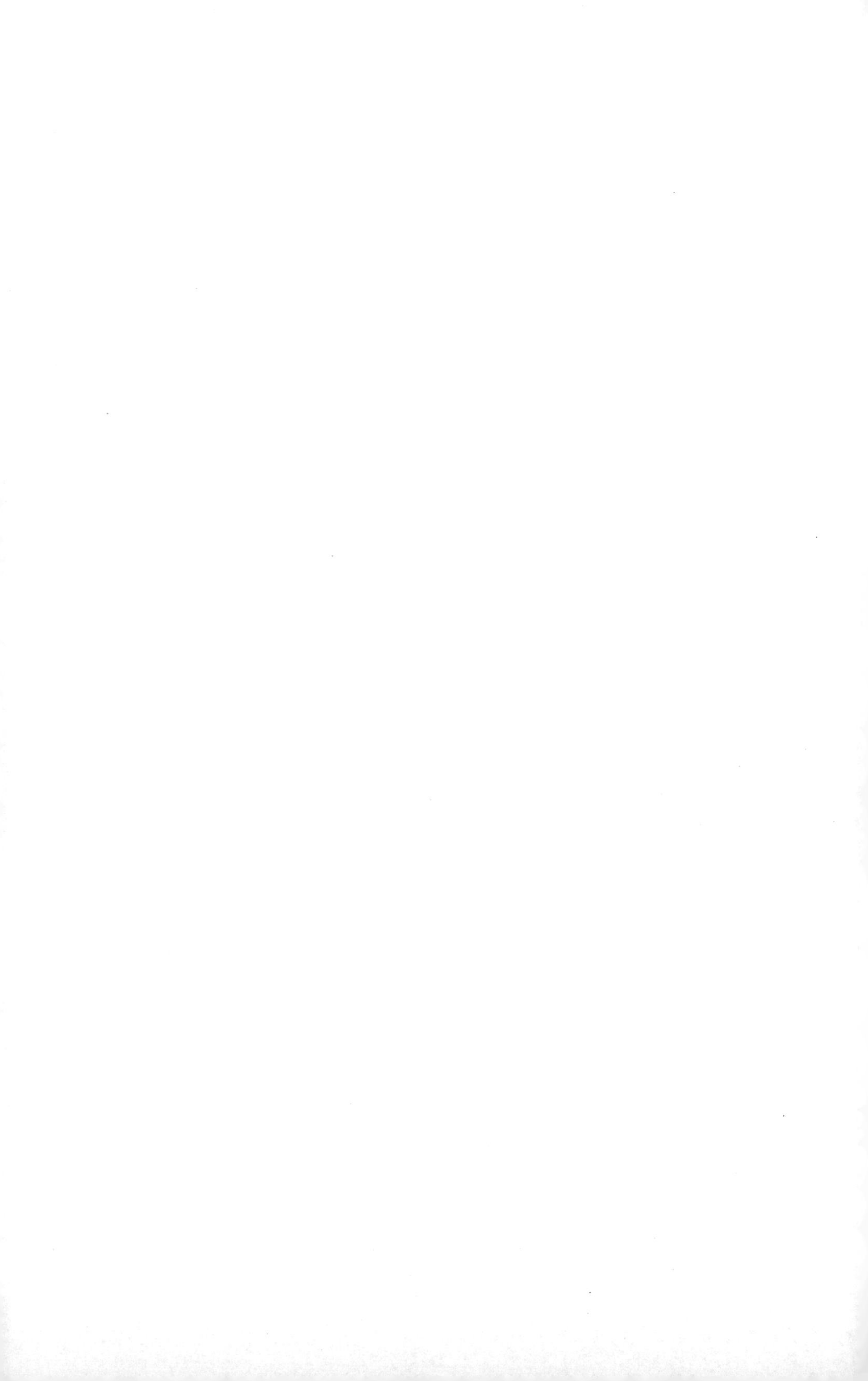

Part Two: The Artwork, Aura, and Authentication

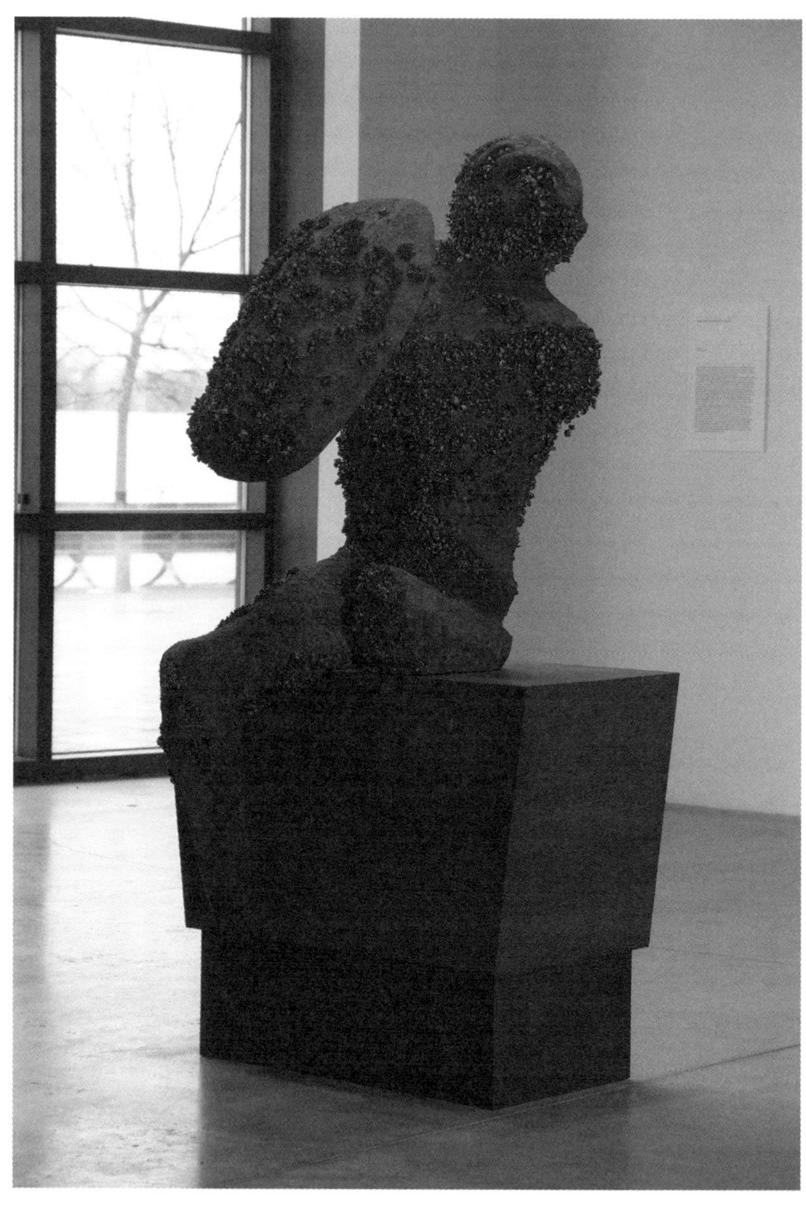

Simon Starling
Infestation Piece (Musselled Moore), 2006–8
Steel replica of Henry Moore's *Warrior with Shield* (1957)
Steel and Zebra mussels, 162.6 × 76.2 × 76.2 cm (with base)
Installation view at The Power Plant, Toronto, 2007

Demonstrable Legacy; or, What Sculptors Leave Behind

PENELOPE CURTIS

This essay considers the question of artistic legacy through the lens of the sculptor, and of sculpture—a lens that gives us a specific view, but one that is telling for artistic legacy more generally. It argues that Auguste Rodin (1840–1917) provides a case study that is relevant more widely and suggests, too, that his museum (the Musée Rodin, in Paris) is an example that holds good in considering how museums in general may handle issues of legacy.

Authorship has long been a central criterion of art appreciation and value. Protecting an artist's right to authorship—and to the fruits of authorship—is the business of galleries, agencies, and lawyers. It is similarly in the interests of museums. Authenticating works after the artist's death is also the business of the same experts, and of the artist's executors (and foundations). As the protection of authorship becomes more important for the artist, and as the artist becomes more successful, so it becomes more important for all those who have invested in the artist. And yet, and as this essay shows, the investiture of authorship within the single body of the artist runs increasingly counter to the way in which art is made, and in which it is understood, at least by its primary audiences. By this I mean that art historians, artists, and curators have come to embrace the plurality and seriality of the art product, deeming these attributes as interesting as, or even more interesting than, the uniqueness of a work.

As we finally learn to embrace pluralistic or collaborative authorship in fine art (as it has been in other areas), and as contemporary artists often deliberately complicate the authorship category (just as workshops always complicated it in the past), it is odd that we still find ourselves focusing on the protection of single-name authorship, and thus on the preservation of legacies that become oddly (and misleadingly) monolithic. In this the actual and intellectual content of many artworks is disguised in the interests of preserving the perceived benefits of the lone author.

This essay considers questions of authorship and legacy primarily in relation to modern sculpture. This is not merely incidental: sculptors leave behind substantial material reserves that are not easy to look after, and they also leave behind the means to replication, from casts or instructions. More than other artists, perhaps even more than photographers, their working methodology lays their production open to abuse: the creation of unauthorized copies. The problem, however, is that their own output has often been based on the very edges of "proper use," and sculptors such as Rodin, Aristide Maillol, Wilhelm Lehmbruck, and Henry Moore (1898–1986) found and established their creativity in the use and reuse of the same parts differently arranged. Moreover, many of the artists who have recently been most interested in reusing the legacy of their predecessors have not only been sculpturally inclined, but also used the works of these very artists. There is, it seems, a sculptural bias at the heart of an examination of artistic legacy.

MULTIPLYING RODIN

While sculpture is particularly interesting for those who study it because the "same piece" can be in several or even many places at the same time, this very aspect is so poorly understood by the larger public that it causes upset, recrimination, and even litigation. This may, of course, be justified. Rodin's remarkable position around 1900 depended at one and the same time on a consistent and plentiful supply of sculptures for clients, and on the Romantic cult of the unique, in inspiration, conception, and execution. Rodin had a huge team of assistants, on and off the studio site, and although bronze was perhaps known to be cast by technicians, there was a widespread notion that Rodin carved his own works, when in fact they were mostly carved by his assistants. The Romantic mythology of the artist-genius is precarious, but despite momentary upsets—as in the period just after the First World War when a cartel of interested parties was found to be turning out Rodins on a semi-industrial scale in the environs of Paris—it can endure. To a degree, many artists depend on their public's willing suspension of disbelief, but Rodin had benefited more than most. He had weathered various storms, but when Charles Émile Jonchéry was discovered in 1919, after Rodin's death, to be making fake Rodins, something snapped in the public's perception. In many ways it was (and is) easier to perpetrate illusions when the supposed author is alive. When the linkage to the artist's "touch" as the index of his authorship was questioned, the whole enterprise was jeopardized, and many existing owners worried about the authorship of works that they had not previously questioned.

The "faux Rodin" affair of 1919 is a telling amalgam: the recent death of the artist, the creation of the Musée Rodin, its dependence on the market for its survival, the involvement of those who had worked for Rodin (like Jonchéry and the Montagutellis) and of those who had been close to him. Rodin had been connected with court cases during his lifetime, but the stakes became much higher after his death, not least because his museum, despite being the artist's heir and a national institution, depended (and still depends) on selling new casts for a substantial part of its running costs.[1] This is a very difficult situation to be in. The museum's first director, Léonce Bénédite, quickly discovered how hard it was to promote reputation and control production at the same time.

Rodin's example brings to the fore very relevant distinctions between lifetime and posthumous casting, counterfeits and forgeries, authorship and copyright, the edition and the reproduction, and the use of the signature versus the founder's mark. All these issues are with us still. And yet all these art-world conventions and legal niceties are regularly, and interestingly, upset and even nullified by the actions of artists (Rodin himself, and others since), who re-create, replicate, and recast works according to their own criteria of value. The right of artists to work as they wish has made the posthumous task of authentication and guardianship much harder.

CONSOLIDATING A LEGACY

Legacies are as much immaterial as material; finding the balance between protection and dissemination is delicate. The Musée Rodin has long managed a subtle strategy that combines the creation of exhibitions with the creation of market interest. The recent—exceptional—sale of *The Gates of Hell* (modeled 1880–1917, cast 2014) to a Mexican buyer allowed for the refurbishment of the museum itself. Although the Henry Moore Foundation does not cast, it does, occasionally, sell works from the founding collection, doing so recently, for example, to help fund a new visitor center at the artist's home. In each case, it might be argued, legacy is as much about creating the "proper" conditions for viewing the artist's works as about the works themselves. The balance between the discreet preservation of the works, the promotion of scholarship, and the popularization of the artist is mobile and discursive. Very often one will depend, if only implicitly, on the other. Opening Rodin up to new markets in Central America and China has paid dividends in Paris. The popularity of Moores on American golf courses has, arguably, funded research on Moore and on other sculptors.

Rodin made the French state his heir; Moore set up a foundation before he died and worked for it as an employee. Successful contemporary sculptors—Tony Cragg, Thomas Schütte, Andy Goldsworthy—are similarly finding it most useful to create foundations within their lifetimes to deal with the demand for loans without recourse to either public or private collections, to facilitate and manage exhibitions more generally, and to show large and semi-permanent works to advantage on their own sites, and in this way to consolidate their own legacies. Increasingly, at least at this level (if suitable lifetime planning has taken place), the artist, rather than the executor or legatee, is the agent of legacy.

Rodin's case is partly symptomatic because his estate has been governed by a legal framework that he did not define (or follow) himself, but more strongly so in that the notion of a "false" Rodin was (and is) very often created by a combination of ignorance and determined misinterpretation on the part of Rodin owners, who would rather think that the artist himself made their work. This is where his story starts to accord so interestingly with those of contemporary collectors, who similarly want to believe that the artist was closer to the work than was or is the case, and that the object, in its material realization, bears the mark not only of the artist's hand but of the artist's engagement. Many owners of works by Rodin who suddenly feared that they had been duped had not, in fact, but had instead been confronted by the reality of production, in which the final product, whether cast or carving, was largely executed by other artists. That some of these same artists and technicians had also been deliberately involved in making additional works for profit shows how complex the situation is, and how much it depends on belief. Even the usual benchmark—the "lifetime" cast—is not necessarily a watertight criterion. (Most Rodin casts are posthumous, whereas Moore's are not.) On consideration we find that we have the "good" copy and the "bad" copy, looking similar or indeed identical, but defined differently according to the reasons that lay behind its creation, rather than its final appearance.

This "good" or "bad" copy is very much a question in museums today, where curators and conservators, habituated to being responsible for troublesome objects, make exhibition copies and even substitute copies surprisingly regularly for works that are fragile or damaged. (Again, this is a practice more common with sculpture; though it can exist with photography, it does not, to my knowledge, happen with painting or drawing.) The phrase "inherent vice" is the term used in fine-art conservation to describe the inevitable degradation of material. It was particularly apt for the case of Naum Gabo (1890–1977), whose use of early plastics has severely compromised the preservation of his sculptures, which have softened, discolored, and lost their original form, meaning that his estate has had to confront the problem of alternatives. With the estate's involvement, the Andrew W. Mellon Foundation sponsored a series of small workshops followed by a larger conference in 2007 under the name *Inherent Vice: The Replica and Its Implications in Modern Sculpture*. The conference was held at Tate Modern, in London, which holds much of Gabo's (problematic) work, largely because of the generosity of the artist and his family. These discussions made clear that even if replicas are still an exception to the rule, most museums have examples, and that their status as such is imperfectly known to many of the institution's own curators. Time has a way of allowing copies to become bona fide works, from which we have learned key parts of twentieth-century art history; examples include the confusing partial reconstruction of Kurt Schwitters's lost work *Merzbau* (ca. 1923–27) at the Sprengel Museum, in Hanover, Germany, and exhibition copies of various Russian Constructivist works at the Van Abbemuseum, in Eindhoven, the Netherlands. We may indeed become more accustomed to the exhibition copy than to the degraded original, knowingly or unknowingly.

The immediate and concrete result of the conference was the effective public approbation given the Tate and the Gabo Estate to proceed with the replication project. The first replica, accordingly approved and duly labeled (and the need for full disclosure was, perhaps, the single key conclusion from the conference), was exhibited in 2010 at Tate Britain, in London, in *Prototypes for Sculpture*, a special display that also highlighted the cataloguing project undertaken on the Gabo archive, sponsored by the Getty Foundation.[2] Significant as the replication project was, the remarkable archive in a sense superseded it. Assembled by the artist himself, the archive made clear that Gabo had always seen his work as something that could be reconstructed by others, and that he was open to material improvements. The fact that an itinerant artist had made the archive function in tandem with his own methodology in many ways rendered redundant the moral questions raised by the replication project. His archive contains "flat-pack" sculptures, with scalable templates, which demonstrated Gabo's understanding of legacy in a remarkably rich way. The replica, good as it was, was conceptually overshadowed by the archive.[3] The replication project will continue as long as new staff at the Tate have the confidence of the Gabo Estate, and as long as the Tate is ready to put acquisition funds toward replicas (so far two have been funded). The replication project is inherently fragile, based as it is on personal connections, but the archive will outlive this fragility. The Gabo projects became paradigmatic, foreshadowing the increasingly dominant role of the archive in under standing or defining the potential of the artist's legacy, and in the proper documenting of the artist's "intent."

WHO OWNS THE LEGACY?

By and large artists like to be copied (at least by good artists), and if institutions tend to protect their master works, it is perhaps the archive that allows the next generation of artists in on more generous terms. Besides, copying now is rarely simply copying, if it is that at all. The archive is the terrain where we find the legacy in a more malleable form, at once purer and more impure, and where we find imagery that allows for re-presentation by younger artists attuned to the image and its manipulation. The readiness of institutions, at the present time, to open up the archive to artists, contrasts markedly with their interest in capitalizing on the image rights and reproductive permissions that they own and sell.[4]

Artists very often have a lightness of touch (or unexpected angle) that confounds the institutions charged with looking after their works. One might cite senior artists, such as John Latham and Richard Hamilton (1922–2011), who became famous for reworking or repairing works that were no longer in their ownership, concerned that they were ageing poorly, or could have simply been better; or consider younger artists, who display an insouciance that allows them to play around with other artists' works, with or without their complicity. (The Tate had to set up a special project to deal with Hamilton's concern, so as to marshal his interest within a negotiated terrain that allowed early works to remain early works, and had to protect its collection from Latham's intervention.) But other works, and other artists, have benefited from the intervention of fellow artists, who have rescued, remade, and restored older works to public view, and interest.

Hamilton's 1965–66 reworking of Marcel Duchamp's *The Bride Stripped Bare by Her Bachelors, Even (The Large Glass)* (1915–23) is a prime example, but is not alone. Damien Hirst has paid for much of the restoration of the Cumbrian barn where Kurt Schwitters made his last *merz* work (which had previously been rescued by Hamilton and is now in Newcastle). Anthony Caro's (1924–2013) response to Charles Ray's (b.1953) interest in *Early One Morning* (1962) was pragmatic: he understood Ray's point, but all too well, asserting that Ray's wish to sit on the horizontal beam would give the mistaken impression that the work was load-bearing. (Ray's work ultimately found life as a catalogue cover; he was pictured beside the sculpture rather than on it.[5]) As an artist speaking (literally) to another (living) artist, sculptor Keith Wilson found it permissible to remake *an exhibit* (1957), a collaborative work by Hamilton and Victor Pasmore, in a way that was utterly different from the painstaking academic remake to be found in the subsequent posthumous Hamilton exhibition.[6]

Simon Starling's (b.1967) request to the Henry Moore Foundation to put a new cast of Moore's *Warrior with Shield* (1953–54) on the floor of Lake Ontario was also well understood, and therefore granted. This cast was the same as earlier versions, but would become clearly different, a "mother" or "home" for the lake-dwelling mussel, just like a mother form for a new generation or colony. Starling's piece, *Infestation Piece (Musselled Moore)* (2006–8), speaks very directly about the fostering and adoption of the second generation, and thus about the legacy of the sculptural parent. British sculpture has long been described in Oedipal terms, and in some ways this expresses its form and content as well as its teacher-student lineage. If Caro's early 1960s work refers to Moore's only slightly earlier reclining figures, so we find, and still today, artists such as Starling, and Mark Wilsher and Eric Bainbridge, discovering the nooks and crannies of dis/respect that allow them space to deal with the weight of this legacy.

While Starling has focused heavily on Moore, and Bainbridge on Caro, other projects have taken for their subject the sculpture collection more generally, rather than individual oeuvres in particular. It is notable how a number of these, by Starling again, but also by Dominique Gonzalez-Foerster (b.1965), Pierre Huyghe, and others, are based on a disaster situation in which the sculptures are "survivors," signs of life, maybe, but perhaps rather of death. These stage sets, as in the central halls of Tate Modern, or Tate Britain, or at Kassel, allow sculpture a center-stage position, but within a deeply compromised and implosive wider environment. Such projects require permission to use the sculptures held in collections, and these requests may well be granted, as they were for these projects, because, on balance, the museums and foundations responsible for preserving the works and the artist's integrity are inclined to let artists use the works of other artists.[7] Indeed, one might say, this has become something of a trope, and one of which some curators are wary.

Individual projects may well prove, at worst, harmless, and at best, inspiring in relation to the legacy of earlier artists. It is only later, as patterns develop, that we might perceive a broader urge to characterize the work of previous generations, and notably of a handful of sculptors: Constantin Brancusi, Alberto Giacometti, Barbara Hepworth, Moore, and Rodin. Their works have become a kind of shorthand, arguably a shortcut to the immediate post-war era, providing a fixed set of human gestures and of humanistic positions, which is then staged in ways that might be read as deeply undermining. (To what extent the works themselves are in fact undermined is, however, another question.) Projects that reference works by the earlier artists in this way take legacy as their subject. Violence and destruction is fundamental to many of these projects, which seem to test the very endurance of modernism under conditions of fire, flood, and nuclear meltdown. A long timeline is also more or less explicit, especially with Gonzalez-Foerster, who increasingly titles her shows and installations with future end dates (for example 1887–2058), thereby suggesting a semi-familiar but somehow reduced world in which elements of art just about persist. In 2058, she suggested in 2008, the museum will have been flooded and looted, but some sculpture will remain. These bronze relics will represent our artistic legacy.

From the Object to the Archive: Guaranteeing Authorship and Ownership in Contemporary Art

ALESSANDRA DONATI

Protecting and managing the identity and authenticity of an artist's oeuvre, particularly in light of the transitory and ephemeral modes of expression used in much of contemporary art, is a complicated business. Contemporary artworks are often complex: art objects may decompose easily, or sometimes completely dematerialize; many installations need to be reactivated and are made using degradable materials; and many works need to be adapted to the requirements of each exhibition site, which could involve not only spacing adjustments but also changes in the material components of the work, thus leading to modification in both structure and identity over time. Unlike works of traditional sculpture and painting, contemporary artworks have taken on a temporal dimension that is often intermittent, or in the process of "becoming": works may even never acquire definitiveness, and, sometimes, this may be the explicit intention of the artist who, in this way, also exposes an artwork to random modifications over time.

In other words, contemporary art has demonstrated a decline in the idea that the durability of the artwork as an object is one of its intrinsic features. In addition, it has expanded the very concept of what art is: not only is art realized with all kinds of materials (often fragile or frail, and highly degradable and perishable) but also at times the artist does not even actually make the work, but delegates this to others. Some classic examples of work by American and European Minimalist and Conceptual artists were (and are) made and installed by artist' assistants or, in some cases, by the collector. The same is true for work by Italian Arte Povera artists and, today, for almost all complex works such as installations. Michelangelo Pistoletto's iconic *Venus of Rags* (1967/74) is an emblematic example. The sculpture comprises a large marble statue of the Roman goddess Venus, installed facing away from the viewer, along with a pile of bright clothing, or rags. The rags (which are often replaced for new installations of Pistoletto's work) are always the same because they are decontextualized through the process of delocalization; they are always the same everywhere in the world, but they are always different. As conservator Antonio Rava puts it, "Replacing perishable serial material not made by hand or noticeably developed by the artist makes it possible to reactivate the work indefinitely in the future."

Many artists identify the creative act purely with the conceptual/planning stage or, in other cases, determine that the creative stage continues after the work has been put into circulation. As a result, the artwork is no longer clearly defined and immutable, and is not necessarily in need of protection from material degradation. Instead, the artwork becomes the manifestation of an artist's idea through ephemeral media, which is also capable of being conceptually renewed. The artwork thus requires a complex accompaniment of documented information so its identity remains intact over time and its authenticity lasts.

Moreover, and almost in contradiction with, or perhaps in compensation for, the intrinsic ephemeral nature of many artworks, the era of the "contingent object" of art has exalted interest in the substance or consistency of art objects and in the particular characteristics, laid down in minute detail, of the material used. It becomes essential for an artist to provide information relating to possible future replacement of parts of works (as with installations) or of materials that easily degrade. At the same time, such forms of expression of contemporary art have led to a corresponding shift in attention from the work itself—as a material object produced and marked with the artist's personal "imprint"—toward the documentation of instructions provided by the artist that define the artwork-idea or object-to-be.

In these cases, obsessive interest in material or exclusive interest in information, we are presented with a complex work, not exclusively perceivable through observation of the object or its completed form, but also defined and delineated through reconstruction of the artist's intentions. In this way, the artist maintains a close link to his or her creation, and consequently the collector is increasingly often, as will be seen below in more depth, personally bound, at least symbolically, by a contractual type of relationship with the artist.

Increasingly, whether a collector or museum will be able to preserve the original form of a contemporary artwork, and hence maintain its authenticity, depends on the quality and completeness of documentation of the artist's creative process, of the original creative action, and of subsequent interventions carried out to conserve or to reactivate the artwork, or, later still, to restore it. Broadly speaking, then, written information now provides value and a binding, essential function. The documentation that follows an artwork—traditionally, "scripta"—is no longer only historical and cultural information, as is the case with traditional paintings and sculpture, which have objectively definitive materiality, and for which both historian and curator play a role in interpreting meaning. The documentation accompanying artwork that is conceptual, ephemeral, or to be reactivated has value as documentation of the artist's intention and of the process of his or her creative act; artwork is systematically accompanied by its manifesto of instructions—an integral part of the work itself and of its identity.

Even taking into account the difference between civil-law and common-law systems in principles regarding contracts—and the broader area of categories of contract and of juridical act (*negozio giuridico*) in civil-law systems—art has come to take on a strongly contractual connotation. The relationship between artist and collector is thus partly legal, and, as such, binding in terms of contractual obligation, and in part metaphorical, that is programmatic in mutual declaration of intent, and, hence, important also for the purpose of evaluation of good faith in performance. This is the case not only when it is the artist who requires a personal relationship with the owner of the work (as in the systems organized by Carl Andre (b.1935) or Daniel Buren (b.1938), where each change in ownership of the work must be registered with the artist), but also because, according to market practice, the owner may need to sign up to the artist's system of authentication to ensure that the work is validated as authentic. Definition of the identity and preservation of the authenticity of the object-work is made possible by a succession of agreements between the artist (and the artist's successors) and the owner of the work—agreements that may relate to continual transformations, modifications, and variations of the work and of its reactivations. The reactivated work is reproduced in other works, forms of the original, and all originals in their turn. As a result, it becomes especially important for collectors and museums to preserve any documentation of the artist's intention and idea for an artwork, and this documentation is often crucial in terms of both the material conservation of the work and the work's reactivation for display. Artists' certificates and documentation and artists' archives now play an essential role for collectors, helping them to define what it is they actually own.

SYSTEMS OF AUTHORSHIP RECOGNITION

What does authenticity mean in relation to art objects, and how can it be protected? One of the greatest challenges in contemporary art relates to the complexity of systems of authorship recognition. Once authorship is formally recognized, and authenticity certified in some way, it is difficult to guarantee that the claim of authenticity will last. The enormous transformation in visual art has prompted, or perhaps compelled, artists to invent original systems of authentication and traceability for their creations that no longer find adequate protection in the institution of copyright or authors' rights because it has no effective means of recognizing ephemeral and easily reproducible forms of artistic expression.

It is worth looking at some sophisticated mechanisms of authentication adopted by Conceptual artists to enable them to achieve control over the dealing and collecting of their works. Conceptual artists have cast aside the principle on which the rationale for copyright and moral rights for authors (including artists) is based: tied to both legal regimes for protecting authorship is the notion of the work as fruit of the artist's action, or the material making of an object as personal expression of its creator. Conceptual works situate the originality of the work not in its concrete materialization but in the idea it manifests. Especially in countries that today require fixation as an essential condition for protection of artistic expression, and in countries where an original form of the work is necessary in order to meet the requirement of originality, artists themselves have developed a complex system of objectification and traceability of nonmaterial works and have made it their own through tools provided by the law—specifically, through the contract and the certificate of authenticity. Examining these practices is important because it provides insight into the possible functioning of a different approach to authentication and to the control of authenticity.

In the 1960s important artists such as Daniel Buren, Sol LeWitt (1928–2007), and Lawrence Weiner (b.1942), gallery owners, and curators such as Seth Siegelaub began to come up with complex contract models for selling Conceptual works (for example, the Artist's Reserved Rights Transfer and Sale Agreement, conceived by Siegelaub and lawyer Robert Projansky in 1971). These new contract models enabled them to track circulation and guarantee authenticity, in the sense of authorial control, even after the artist's death. They developed some innovative and original rules in terms of assertion of absolute intellectual ownership of their work. The contractual model proposed by Siegelaub at the beginning of the 1970s—introduced in the US legal context, in which moral rights for artists were not recognized or enforceable at this stage (prior to the enactment of the Visual Artists Rights Act 1990)—turned out to be more restrictive than copyright-law regulations set out in the Berne Convention. Buren used a similar system of strict regulation regarding the exploitation rights and resale right, as will be seen below.

Having introduced the idea of nonmaterial artwork, often presented as a plan, Conceptual artists then had to come up with an instrument that created a link between the artwork and the document providing a description of the idea of the artwork, which is given value by the artist's name and signature as expressed through the certificate of authenticity. The connection between the work and the document became indissoluble because authentication and ownership of the work was nonexistent without the certificate that identified it. For Sol LeWitt or Félix González-Torres (1957–1996) the certificate of authenticity takes on the configuration of a contract, as the requirements contained in the certificate are tacitly accepted by the purchaser on completion of the purchase. The contract, in the case of a work by Donald Judd, or the juridical act (*negozio giuridico*), in the case of a unilateral undertaking such as Buren's, became an integral part of the artwork, and so did a complex ritual endorsed by the artist for circulation of the work.

The system of certification of authenticity is thus dependent on the material conservation and authentic archiving of the original certificate, an often unique and irreplaceable document. Andre, Buren, González-Torres, Weiner, and Ian Wilson have created special archives for the purpose of certifying their own works, sometimes also requiring the intervention of an official certifier (notary) to document the existence and circulatory history of works, recorded in special registries. Generally, unusual procedures are also adopted today for the circulation and the sale of some complex typologies of artworks, such as installations, process artworks, ephemeral works, and works that can be reactivated.

SYSTEMS OF OWNERSHIP

It is worth focusing here on the value and effectiveness of these documents (contracts and certificates) in terms of correct identification of the work. The work does not survive without the document, because the document is an integral part of the work itself. If collectors lose the certificate, they also lose the work (as property that can be transferred and sold), since they have lost one of its components, which the artist has defined as essential to its constitution. Moreover, the certificate is often a specific, personal document: each time the work changes hands, a new and personalized certificate must be registered, as for example for works by Andre, Buren, and González-Torres. It is significant that insurance providers Crystal & Company and AIG Private Client Group have recently offered collectors an innovative, specific product for the loss or destruction of certificates of authenticity of Conceptual artworks. It is also significant that, as will be seen below, artists control and manage the future of the work, and of the certificate, even after their death.

Sol LeWitt, for example, invented a complex system of authentication for his wall drawings. The artwork owned by a collector is not the large drawing realized on a material medium (in this case, a wall), but it is a plan coupled with the exclusive right, or license, from the artist to enact the plan. The document containing the plan or instructions for the work—which consists of a detailed description of how it must be made, usually accompanied by a drawn diagram—is signed by the artist, which also certifies its authenticity. The document states clearly that it constitutes the signature of the wall drawing and that, if ownership is transferred, the document must always accompany the work for the drawing to be considered authentic.

When ownership of a LeWitt wall drawing is transferred, only the document containing the instructions for how to make the work is present, not the material form of the work. Indeed, upon transfer of ownership, the physical manifestation of the work must be destroyed by the work's former owner. The artist succeeds in maintaining the work's aura in the documentation of the work (which contains the description of the idea) coupled with the work's certificate of authenticity, without having to materially create it. If a material work does not exist, if only the idea expressed exists, copyright or author's right, the system of rules requiring a work to be in material form for protection to be activated, no longer has an object-artwork; there is only a document or certificate, which is complementary to the work, and which does not substitute it. Here, it is the document that takes on a specific aesthetic meaning.

Furthermore, the work circulates and is identified by means of the document or certificate, which acts as and contains the artist's signature, and thus constitutes a certain indicator of the work's relationship with the artist. Each LeWitt wall drawing is assigned a particular number, which must correspond to the number in the register held by the Sol LeWitt Estate, the organization that has catalogued, numbered, and then renumbered these works. Possession of the document alone does not suffice to prove authenticity; title to the document must also be recorded in the LeWitt registry, and, therefore, confirmation of the authenticity of the work depends for validity on this formality, which, however, is always unilateral.

Superflex, a Danish artist collective founded in 1993 by Bjørnstjerne Christiansen, Jakob Fenger, and Rasmus Nielsen, effectively explored and recorded the tension in the contractual relationship (in the widest sense of juridical act that produces contractual effects) between the artist, public, and collector through a project called *Free Sol LeWitt* (2010), conceived for an exhibition at the Van Abbemuseum in Eindhoven, the Netherlands. It is a complex work, consisting of various phases and forms, and it is explicitly appropriationist. The work aims to reproduce the system of art-making proposed by LeWitt and other Conceptual and Minimalist artists—a system founded, as described above, on the greater importance of the idea of a work described by the artist in a certificate of authenticity, as opposed to a material work that anyone can realize by following the instructions provided by the artist. Superflex (in collaboration with Daniel McClean) organized an exhibition in 2010 at the Van Abbemuseum dedicated to Minimalist artists; works, certificates, and instructions were displayed in a special "Information Room." They also set up, as part of the show itself, a workshop that produced copies of an artwork on display, specifically of LeWitt's *(Untitled) Wall Structure* (1976). The workshop functioned as a kind of photocopier of this work, of which not even the original had been made by the artist's hand. Skilled fabricators worked for the duration of the exhibition, reproducing a considerable number of copies of the work. Each copy was then offered, free of charge, to randomly selected visitors to the exhibition; these members of the public had been previously asked to sign a special form to participate, in which it was expressly stated that, naturally, this artwork produced by Superflex could not be attributed to LeWitt.

Here, the contract performs the same function as the certificate of instructions in a Conceptual work: it is able to shift attention from the "fetish of the original, auratic art object" produced by the artist, to the more important idea realized through the complexity of the Superflex work—exhibition, work of reproduction, selection by lottery of recipients, and gift of object, thereby assigning to the museum the function of "platform for the exchange of ideas." Using this complex system, Superflex puts into concrete effect one of the main ideas inspiring LeWitt himself: "the idea becomes a machine that makes the art," implementing through this procedure the idea of the "value machine, the information machine or the distribution machine being as important as the production machine." At the same time, the work is allowed to escape from the museum in which it is enclosed, by means of a random and extensive distribution system that forms a challenge to the collectors' way of thinking, which is attracted by the exclusivity of a unique and original object.

Through the formula of homage, in this case homage to LeWitt, the Superflex artists' relationship with museums and with collectors is modified and distorts their respective functions and roles, setting up the conditions for testing also the strength of copyright or authors' rights. This system, of creation of a work through copying, and distribution through random selection, appears to assign to the Conceptual artist's idea the status of common property, which the public can take freely and at no charge for their own use. This matches what LeWitt himself stated: "ideas once expressed become the common property of all." Gaining access to information takes on primary and fundamental importance over possession of material property, and hence expository value in practice takes the place of cultural value, as Walter Benjamin had hypothesized. This is the significance of the Superflex works and the role of the contract as their medium but it also highlights the shifting role of the museum, from archives of works to a now more literally archival function, as a place of safekeeping of the creative, reproductive, or reactivating phases of artworks.

In such a context, the documentation system of artworks and their cataloguing and conservation are clearly gaining greater importance, including economic importance. Consequently, museums have acquired an increasingly significant number of artists' archives, and archives of documents of various and other types. The artist's archive has acquired a new function: it not only possesses cultural value but also is the exclusive authority for certification and verification of the authenticity of the artist's work. Indeed and especially to prevent widespread reproduction, Conceptual artists stipulate that to purchase an "original" work of their creation, the collector is required to enter a more advanced level of contractual relationship with the artist: in addition to possession of the certificate with its information, each title must also be registered in the artist's archive.

The archive plays an important role in the many "statement works" by Lawrence Weiner. Each of these works—normally a short sentence or phrase expressed for and in a specific expository context—is initially pure information, is open to all for use, and belongs to anyone who knows it (though it is embellished with visual elements and the text is specifically set in Margaret Seaworthy Gothic, a typeface created by Weiner). Nevertheless, the status of each statement work as an artwork highlights the exclusive nature of certain experiences, such as that of ownership, when the work is acquired by a collector. In order to certify the transfer of title and the new ownership of the work, Weiner sends a letter to his archive manager. The letter is handwritten and signed by the artist and contains a description of the work: the statement. The sale is then registered in the archive, and an invoice is sent to the new owner. This document also specifies that the purchaser assumes responsibility for the work; that is to say, he or she becomes responsible for participating in the notion of art propounded by the artist.

The work of Daniel Buren is characterized by a constant style: vertical monochrome lines, 8.7 centimeters in width, alternate with white lines of the same width. Since his style is easily recognizable and above all easily reproducible, he manages authorship of all his artworks in a highly sophisticated way. Ever since he first began to produce work, the artist has sought to closely link certification of authenticity of his mark as an artist to a document, an *avertissement*, which he drafts with the assistance of a lawyer. However, unlike the procedure adopted by LeWitt, the identity of the work is not fixed and finalized in the document: to complete the formal validity of the certificate, a ritual exchange of means of proof is required as well as compliance with the conditions imposed by the artist, enabling the purchaser to access the work and assume ownership. In other words an extremely complex mechanism is created; the artist, as he himself explicitly asserts in paragraph 5 of the *avertissement*, has come up with this mechanism in order to "éviter tout abus du nom de l'auteur auquel est attribuée l'oeuvre qui est attachée audit avertissement" (to prevent any abusive use of the name of the author of the work to which the notice is attached).

The contract of sale is, in reality, a unilateral deed signed only by the purchaser. The procedure is particularly significant in terms of Buren's position regarding the role of the market and the system of assigning value to art. There is a total disregard for the system of authentication that the market—or the law—recognizes as the area of expertise also of gallery owners or art experts. The *avertissement* states: "Notamment, aucun marchand, ni intermédiaire ou tiers quelconque n'a jamais été et ne sera habilité à authentifier de quelque façon que ce soit une ouvre qui serait attribuée à Daniel Buren" (No dealer, middleman, or any third person has ever been or will be entitled to certify the authenticity of a work attributed to Daniel Buren). As the artist himself states:

> When I delved a little more deeply into the problem of making a work and launching it outside my orbit—into the market, the world, etc.—I felt that something must be done to maintain a kind of control over the work. I had already studied this problem, and found, more intuitively in the early stages of my career, that, then at least, I was doing something which was—somewhat, let's say—close to a painted object. All objects—painting, sculpture and later on any kind of object made

> by artists—are open to incredible forms of manipulation. And I found this manipulation very damaging, very bad for the work most of the time. So my first notion was to protect what I thought was the basic idea of the work—something that was, and still is, much more important than the protection of its monetary value.

The *avertissement* lists a series of duties and obligations that the purchaser and "possessor" of the work takes on, and only full compliance with all of the conditions stipulated in the *avertissement* certifies the work's authenticity: the artist requires the collector to inform him and submit for his approval any images of the work to be published.

Even partial nonperformance of the duties undertaken by the purchaser (for example, reproducing, displaying, or selling the work without the artist's approval) strips the work of its aura and, consequently, of its connection with the artist: a special clause provides that Buren will no longer recognize the work as his own, since one of its constituent parts is lacking, that is to say, an essential element of what the purchaser has undertaken according to the agreement. Thus the work is not only the object created by the artist: it also includes informative and legal material, as well as the formal procedure through which it is identified and according to which it circulates. Loss or destruction of the certificate results in the irremediable loss of the work, since it is clearly stated in the certificate itself that it is impossible to obtain an authenticated copy or a second version (section h of the *avertissement*). Procedures and practices are applicable even after the artist's death.

Siegelaub's complex "Artist's Reserved Rights Transfer and Sale Agreement" is similar: the existence of the agreement must be communicated by means of a notice that is physically attached to the work. If a collector does not perform the duties specified in the agreement, the authenticity of the work sold is compromised (clause 16). The contract has effect for fifty years after the death of the artist; the collector also undertakes to pass on these terms and conditions to his or her heirs or assignees (clause 17), which has made the contract largely unenforceable in practice as it places heavy burdens on collectors (only the artists

Hans Haacke and Jackie Winsor have consistently used the agreement). Another example is Ben Kinmont's contract for the management of his constantly evolving work.

To a certain extent, this is an inevitable corollary to Walter Benjamin's theory: to protect against loss of aura of an individual work, its aura is fortified by means of procedures that are an integral part of the work itself. As a consequence of the ease with which Conceptual artwork can be reproduced and in a sense faked, and in order to preserve the aura and the uniqueness of the work, the artist makes every effort, for every work created, to establish an individual relationship with the collector-purchaser; this relationship becomes part of the work, as it is the primary guarantor of the work's uniqueness and authenticity. The work's aura shifts to the documentation attesting the exclusive and personalized relationship between the artist and the collector. By and large, the same applies for ephemeral works and installations that can be reactivated. These may also comprise material elements, which can be reinstalled according to precise instructions (for example, the installations of Jason Rhoades) or, in the case of ephemeral works (like those by Mario Merz), remade. Performative works (such as those by Marina Abramović, Fabio Mauri, or Tino Sehgal) may be documented through instructions, so the work can be re-performed, but only according to precise rules and, at times, by "interpreters" officially supervised by the artist.

THE ASCENDANCY OF THE ARCHIVE

These complex systems for managing the authenticity and circulation of artworks demonstrate the existence of a desire for records—the *mal d'archive*, or "archive fever"—described by the philosopher Jacques Derrida in 1995. For many types of contemporary artwork, archives also hold a record of a work's aura, of the artist's idea, and of the information and documentation required to re-realize the artwork. In contemporary art, the role and function of artists' archives is crucial.

As artists know, and as the market has already understood and accepted, the purpose of an artist's archive is not only to collect and organize the most complete documentation possible of the figure and work of an artist. Its purpose is also to take on, in many instances, the role of official, or at least authoritative, certifier of the authorship and authenticity of the artist's work, and act as guarantor of the permanence of the identity of the work, all of which has important repercussions on the market. This is demonstrated by the fact that today collectors reveal a keen interest in having any work they purchase registered in the artist's archive and inserted in or added to the artist's catalogue raisonné; that is to say, they want "authentic archiving." Certification by archives can be both direct, through granting of a certificate of authenticity, and indirect—but with equal validity for the market—through inclusion of the work record in the artist's archive, or through inclusion of the artwork in the artist's catalogue raisonné.

In the international contemporary art market, it is now common practice for the authenticity of an artwork to be only considered conclusive if the work is included in the artist's archive (that is, if the work is certified) and/or catalogue raisonné, both in terms of assigning authorship and controlling identity. This process of authentication is especially important in relation to the monetary value of the work, and it has come about apart from and regardless of any specific legislation in the area. Moreover, it is worth noting that legislation recognizes certificates of authenticity as proof of identity (although not absolute), whereas, in legal terms, no specific value is given to accreditation and registration of an artwork in an artist's archive, just as no specific legal value is given to inclusion of artworks in catalogues raisonnés. The art world and the art market operate, however, according to the opposite line of reasoning: they give greater importance to catalogues raisonnés and to registration of an artwork in the artist's archive, and less importance to certificates of authenticity granted by other bodies or individuals, such as a gallery owner, even when this is a legal authority.

Today, authentication by artists' archives is an activity based on de facto practice and not regulated by any particular legal provisions.

It is imperative that such activity, to acquire authoritativeness, be consolidated and organized according to ethically well-grounded practices, such as those adopted by the Associazione Italiana degli Archivi d'Artista (AitArt). The association brings together independent Italian artists' archives and museums that own Italian artists' archives with the aims of safeguarding the conservation of existing archives, promoting the establishment and consolidation of common interests, and fostering and encouraging the establishment of living artists' new archives. Good practices promoted by AitArt include: complying with principles of transparency and collegiality in evaluations and decisions (for example, a collegial approach in assessments of authenticity), justifying assessments, and keeping clear records of justifications.

In reality, especially in continental European jurisdictions—where authors' rights and, in particular, moral rights are widely protected and are inalienable—the managing of rights and legacy after the death of an artist is often dangerously fragmented, which is harmful to authentic conservation of the artist's legacy. The Italian situation is a significant example: under the legislation protecting authors' rights (Law 633/1944), as consistently interpreted by the courts, artists do not have the right to bequeath their own moral right—a personal right—in their wills. They are not entitled to identify those most qualified to protect their work after death; this exclusive right is assigned, aside from any inheritance provisions, to certain categories of family members (wife, children, and ascendants), by right.[47] Thus it appears that artists are considered not fit to decide the fate of their own intellectual property, of their own cultural legacy, as they are not permitted to identify the appropriate person or persons to safeguard their work in the future. Such a restriction seems to be in conflict with the current urgent need to promote and encourage artists themselves to set up institutions, such as official artists' archives or foundations, that are able to guarantee their cultural memory and what they bequeath to the future.

Lastly it is important to mention a practice that is becoming established in the complex maze of economic interests and cultural claims that relate to art in general and, more directly, to modern and contemporary art: through a "third market," influential galleries sometimes purchase the legacies and archives of deceased artists.[48] For example, in 2015 the Gagosian Gallery acquired the works and representation of the estate of Korean American artist Nam June Paik (1932–2006), and Hauser & Wirth took on representation of the estates of Italian artists Fausto Melotti (1901–1986) and Piero Manzoni (1933–1963), which were previously with Gagosian Gallery, among many others. A new order of relations, and sometimes of possible competing prerogatives, is forming between artists' archives and gallery owners.[49] A market is emerging where once again autonomous practices are taking root—ones that do not necessarily follow the rules relating to authors' rights written in positive law systems. Clearly, those who by virtue of these new practices hold and manage exclusive title to such cultural legacies and archives must base their consequent and collateral management of these assets on best ethical practices. AitArt, as mentioned above, adheres to the highest ethical standard in its management of artists' archives, in particular in regard to management and protection of cultural property, and to procedures used for assessment and certification of authenticity. When an artist's archive coexists with a gallery's exclusive management of the artist's legacy, there is a need for mutually agreed practices to be established in carrying out these activities, which are parallel and potentially conflicting. For example, the artist's archive and the gallery must agree on the role of each party in the authentication process, and on the management of the archive. Furthermore, in order to provide greater protection, there is an urgent need for legal recognition of the cultural value of artists' archives as artistic heritage, so as to prevent them from being uprooted or from becoming inaccessible to the public, especially when the purchaser is from another country.

EPILOGUE

Artists themselves express the need for appropriate principles in the management and valorization of artists' archives and legacies. *Woman with Sombrero* (2013), a work exhibited by Jill Magid (b.1973) at New York's Art in General gallery, is a relevant case. In the work, the artist draws attention to the difficult question of what happens to archives and their accessibility through a look at the legacy of Pritzker Prize–winning Mexican architect Luis Barragán (1902–1988). Barragán's professional archive, together with ownership of the author's rights and an important part of his legacy, was acquired in 1994 by Rolf Fehlbaum, head of the Vitra Design Museum in Birsfelden, near Basel, Switzerland, and the architect Frederica Zanco, his wife.[50] Zanco, who has devoted her life to promoting Barragán's legacy, set up the Barragán Foundation and purchased the official professional archive of the architect's works. She arranged for everything to be moved to Switzerland and made access to the archive rather more difficult for the public, often denying visits.[51] Jill Magid's work is revealing of the archive management methods used by Zanco: Magid used the archive to imagine and construct a kind of morbid relationship between Zanco and the architect. Challenging the rules of authors' rights to the limits of plagiarism, a form of expression Magid frequently uses, she created an exhibition of Barragán's work. She copied design pieces (enlarging small models made by the Vitra factory) and plans by the architect, she used catalogues edited by Zanco as readymades that were framed and hung on the gallery walls, and she exhibited images of documents found in Barragán's personal archive, still located in Mexico.

"What does it mean for an artist or architect's legacy to be owned by a corporation?" Magid asked. One might also ask: "What does it mean for an artist's legacy to be owned by a gallery?" Jill Magid's reply: "This opens onto larger issues of copyright, and then aura and place."[52]

Score, Performance, and the Posthumous Conductor

SHANE BURKE

Conceptual artists have consciously sought to renegotiate orthodoxies of authorship. In the wake of philosopher Richard Rorty's "linguistic turn," these artists have privileged language and idea as means of achieving a more direct cognitive engagement with the viewer.[1] They have interrogated modernist ontological assertions and undertaken a more political project concerning the dematerialization of the traditional art object.[2] Law has been integral to this project of dematerialization. Art historian Benjamin Buchloh has written of how works of art are increasingly defined by legal language and institutional validation, the result of which is that traditional notions of aesthetic judgment and taste have been displaced by legal endorsement and institutional discourse.[3] He further argued that, consequently, the art world has developed its own "administrative aesthetics," in which authorization of the work by the artist and/or their estate is fundamental.[4] This system of administration is evidenced by the use of certificates of authenticity and registries of works by artists and their estates.

In the context of such strategies, the role of language and the form and degree of engagement of the artist's hand in the final realization of works become increasingly volatile and complex. This essay argues that Conceptual works that rely on certificates and systems of authorization require a new authorial analogy, one in which the artist is seen more as the composer of a score, to be performed by others under the guidance of a conductor, but that the law of copyright may struggle to accommodate this analogy in the visual-art context. The art market, on the other hand, facilitates alternative conceptions of authorship and ownership resulting from the dematerialization of the art object by virtue of the fact that that market relies on the certificate to give solidity to the artwork as commodity.

The wall drawings of Sol LeWitt (1928–2007) are instructional works, sometimes involving both text instructions and diagrams, sometimes solely text instructions (particularly his earlier works). When a collector or museum purchases a LeWitt wall drawing, what they are buying is a sheet of paper with instructions on how the work is to be drawn, painted, or applied to a wall.[5] The instructions encompass a varying degree of indeterminacy: his earlier works allowed for a greater degree of interpretation by the installer, and many of his later instructions became more detailed and specific.[6] While LeWitt famously made statements indicating that the idea is the foremost element in such works, he also averred, "If the artist carries through his idea and makes it into visible form, then all the steps in the process are of importance."[7] In the context of Minimalism, art historian Martha Buskirk has referenced the kind of dichotomic tension that may be at play here with the veiling of the artist's hand to a degree yet also the desire for a level of ongoing control in relation to the work.[8]

Notwithstanding such frictions, the continuing authorship role undertaken by artists in relation to instruction-based works has often been equated to that of the composer, providing a notation—a score—for others to perform the work.[9] Yet the conceptual shift from autonomous art object to a multilayered process of realization and its subsequent musical analogy needs the addition of a further layer of abstraction in order to satisfy the realities of the creative process. The artist may, and in many cases does, still exercise a degree of control over the execution of the work. In this regard, the artist may be said to also perform a conductorial role, acting as an interpretive conduit between the instructions and their performance. The artist composes a score, and that score is later performed by others, with guidance from a conductor.

It is after the death of the artist that the musical analogy and certification/authorization practices become perhaps even more conceptually challenging, as then the estate will often fulfill the conductorial role. The certification/authorization process has thus become a site of intersection between notions of authorship, artifact, aura, conservation, and legacy. We have seen this play out in recent years through the posthumous realization of the works of LeWitt and others. In 2013 the estate of Dan Flavin (1933–1996) reversed its earlier decision not to produce new works by the artist posthumously, despite seemingly dismissive statements in relation to such practices by the artist when he was alive.[10] Félix González-Torres (1957–1996) posthumously represented the United States at the Venice Biennale in 2007, and included in that show was a previously unrealized piece, *Untitled* (1992–95), based on sketches by the artist. The continuing role of estates in the realization of new works postmortem, especially for instructional works that involve high levels of indeterminacy in their execution, raises questions not only of authenticity and value but also of authorship and legacy, as well as questions of who has the authority to make determinations in relation to such matters. The estate's role may be characterized as that of a "posthumous conductor," directing the execution of new visual works on the basis of the artist's instructions. Particularly in the realm of the works of LeWitt, it may be argued that such an approach is ideal for ensuring that the integrity of the idea is respected through the interpretation and execution of the artist's instructions (as overseen by the artist's estate), thereby making certain that the artist's intentions are heeded and their ongoing legacy is protected.

Yet how does the law—particularly copyright law, the traditional historical mechanism by which authors' rights are protected—accommodate this model of authorship? The score/performance/conductor model in the context of LeWitt's text-based instructional works is one that cannot be readily accommodated within the current framework of copyright law. As we shall see, copyright law desires certainty of subject matter and demands certain forms of medium-specific authorship in order for protection to be forthcoming. The law struggles with visual interpretations of textual content and therefore has difficulties in protecting the artistic authorship that is inherent in written instructions. This is particularly true for works by LeWitt because there may be a high degree of choice left to those who execute the instructions. The law also has difficulties protecting these works because copyright's central tenet of originality, often cited as the sine qua non for protection,[11] is interpreted with an increasing focus on personal creative contributions to the work,[12] with the result that appropriate attribution of authorship in the legal context and art world are frequently in conflict. How, then, is the continued operation of the score/performance/conductor model ensured in practice? The answer may be in what art lawyer and curator Daniel McClean has termed the "self-validating authority of the art system,"[13] an authority perhaps best illustrated by the effectiveness of certificates of authority in underpinning the economy of much of the art market.

Sol LeWitt's wall drawings are transferred and realized through a combined system in which the collector must not only obtain a certificate of authenticity for a work but also involve the artist/estate in the realization of the work.[14] If owners of wall drawings install a work without the guidance and approval of the LeWitt estate, they risk the potential withdrawal of approval of authorship. The certificate of authenticity combined with the step of contacting the artist's estate provide the collector with the "right to complete the visualization process," or what perhaps may be viewed as a "license" to create.[15] Such an approach produces a saleable artifact in the form of the certificate and also maintains a degree of control while protecting the ongoing integrity of the work/idea. While copyright is generally blind to any distinctions between forgeries and other infringing reproductions, this license system can arguably work as it is tied to the economy of the unique art object rather than to the wider reproduction and dissemination of the work.[16]

This essay, based on an interview with the installations director for the LeWitt estate, considers the wall drawings of LeWitt that are communicated primarily by text instructions. The essay argues that in light of copyright's struggle to accommodate this model of authorship, the score/performance/conductor model employed by the art world provides a more appropriate method of protecting the ongoing legacy of an artist, effectively granting perpetual rights akin to the moral rights of integrity, disclosure, and repentance/withdrawal, thereby superseding the level of copyright protection generally available to art works in both the United Kingdom and United States. The essay also explores how this system functions in terms of what underpins its effectiveness and safeguards the role of the "conductor" in the protection of the artist's legacy postmortem. It examines how art-world norms and institutional conventions dictate that, even though certificates of authenticity may constitute part of a contract, collectors who face a potential withdrawal of authorship rarely take legal action, at least in the context of Conceptual art.[17]

COPYRIGHT AND PERFORMANCE OF THE ARTWORK AS SCORE

Copyright law has been decidedly reluctant to commit to precise definitions of authorship[18] and what may be regarded as artistic; it has simultaneously struggled with situations in which "ideas" are provided by one party and the execution by another.[19] In the United Kingdom, the legislative framework traditionally does not attempt to conceptualize artistic works, but copyright law does enumerate a definitive "closed" list of works that are considered to be "artistic."[20] US copyright law proceeds with a similar approach, but the list used is an "open," nonexhaustive set of examples.

The categorization of a "work" as one type or another has implications for the nature of the protection offered under copyright law. In the United Kingdom, a three-dimensional reproduction of a two-dimensional drawing constitutes infringement.[21] However, despite the fact that the law prohibits reproduction in "any material form,"[22] the unauthorized representation of a work that is disclosed through a description or set of instructions has traditionally not been considered to constitute infringement in copyright law. This is due to the principle that copyright does not protect ideas and also the fact that any resultant visual work would generally not be seen as sufficiently objectively similar to the underlying literary instructions in order to constitute an infringement.[23] It could also be the case that such works could be seen as exhibiting the wrong type of creativity, as courts on occasion have previously taken a very medium-specific approach to authorship.[24]

In terms of an accommodation of the score/performance/conductor model, textual instructions that form the basis for visual artworks face another challenge: while they may gain very limited protection under copyright law as literary works, certain provisions of current UK copyright law are grounded in an assumption that artistic works are synonymous with their documentation.[25] Under that logic, sketches or other forms of instructions or notations would only gain copyright protection if they are held to be artistic works in their own right.[26]

The philosopher Nelson Goodman deemed a work "autographic" if the most precise reproduction of it was not seen as genuine—painting, for example; on the other hand, he regarded literature and music as nonautographic or "allographic."[27] It may be argued that, prima facie, copyright law does not recognize such distinctions, and infringing production is just that, regardless of whether it is a forgery or not. In this regard, artistic works are not treated differently from literary, musical, or artistic works.[28] However, David Booton cites this autographic/allographic framework as central to current taxonomic considerations, stating, "the categorization of works as either allographic or autographic is not only consistent with the rules on subsistence of copyright but is implied by them."[29] He argues that there is a distinction in the logic of UK law: while literature, music, and drama may be seen as conceptually separate from their recordings, for artistic works no such conceptual separation is contemplated.[30]

However, a number of UK cases have evidenced a more expansive notion of an artistic work.[31] In *Abraham Moon v. Thornber and Ors*, Judge Colin Birss, who is now a High Court judge, held that a weaving "ticket stamp"—essentially instructions comprising two pages of words, letters, and numbers used for setting up a loom to produce a fabric design—could constitute a graphic work on the basis that an experienced fabric designer would find that "the ticket has real visual significance."[32] In the case, the defense had argued that such a person "could look at a weaving ticket and visualise what the fabric looks like."[33] Although they had also argued that terms like "graphic work" should be given their "ordinary meaning,"[34] the judge stated that it is not "doing violence to the language to regard the ticket as a graphic work. It may be of an unusual sort but it is a record of a visual image."[35]

In one sense, the judgment suggests that it may be possible to protect a work with the score/performance/conductor model under existing UK law. However, the judgment only relates to a very specific example—fabric production—in which the weaving instructions must be followed exactly to yield a particular pattern. LeWitt's instructions often allow for a greater level of indeterminacy and a varying degree of interpretation; such works may thus be beyond the reach of the interpretation employed in *Abraham Moon*. It remains to be seen how this approach, which has implications for works in the score/performance/conductor model, develops in the UK courts.

In the United States, several cases involving visual representations of literary characters raise interesting authorial parallels with the works of LeWitt, since both a work by LeWitt and a literary description of a character entail a text description of something that may be realized in visual form. In several cases, the US courts have examined whether or not copyright in a literary work could be infringed by someone visually reproducing a character described in text. While the US courts have not sought to introduce an unbreakable distinction between literary and visual characters, they have noted that the crucial issue is one of sufficient "delineation," and they have acknowledged that it is significantly harder for a literary character to achieve this as opposed to a visual comic character that, for example, has physical and conceptual qualities that are more likely to contain elements of copyrightable expression.[36] In practice it may be very difficult to secure a finding of infringement in relation to a visual reproduction of a literary character. The cases referred to above reveal judicial assumptions in relation to the nature of, and incompatibility between, specific media.[37]

DELEGATED INSTRUCTIONS AND JOINT AUTHORSHIP

When the artistic authorship inherent in text instructions is not protected through artistic or literary copyright, it could still be protected under copyright law as a contribution to a work of joint authorship in the United Kingdom and United States. Joint authorship protects authorship in a work created by two or more individuals and, in the case of LeWitt's works, could protect the contributions of the author of the instructions and those who physically execute the visual work, as well as the artist's or estate's input when acting in a conductorial role, maintaining a degree of control over the work's execution. It may also be argued, however, that the law in relation to joint authorship demonstrates how copyright law does not facilitate the score/performance/conductor model. As scholars Lionel Bently and Laura Biron have noted, the law often fundamentally "misattributes" authorship when viewed against the backdrop of art-world conventions.[38]

In terms of UK law, during his lifetime, LeWitt's contribution of the written instructions could have given rise to a claim of joint authorship, but this would depend on the level of indeterminacy built into those instructions and may also be influenced by any control that was exercised over the final execution of the work, in other words, the nature of the input from the conductor.[39] Relevant contributions must also exhibit "joint labouring in furtherance of a common design."[40] It has also been held that the concept of "common design" does not necessarily involve an intention that there will be joint authorship but rather a common design to produce the work.[41]

Thus, any instructions or guidance by the artist or subsequently the estate, even verbal instructions, could constitute authorship in certain circumstances, the essential factor being the presence of "something which approximates to penmanship, . . . a direct responsibility for what actually appears on the paper."[42] If the level of control over the execution of the instructions were of a high order, then a case for even sole authorship may not be out of the question.[43] While copyright law does not regard the "performance or interpretation"[44] of a work as a contribution sufficient to give rise to joint authorship of that work, the performers in the score/performance/conductor model may well be regarded separately as legal authors (depending on the nature and scope of their interpretive contribution) under copyright law because they physically execute the work, and authorship is ascribed on the basis of who "creates" the work.[45]

The idea that the performer of the work could be classified as a legal author is often fundamentally at odds with art-world conventions that tend not to recognize performers or audience participants as making authorial contributions to the work. LeWitt himself, and now his estate (and collectors and art institutions), view it as extremely important that those who physically execute the works do not put any of their own personality into those works, and that they act merely in service of the idea. Indeed, it is seen as a paradox that those who intend to create "a LeWitt" authored by themselves have, in fact, by definition, created a work by themselves.[46] LeWitt's approach and that of his estate rules out the possibility of joint authorship under US law, because the law requires both parties to demonstrate the intention to be joint authors. The interviews that underpin this essay also indicate that draftspersons who "perform" the works do not generally seek to claim authorship, as they see their role as that of apprentice to the master—a model that may have been more prevalent in previous periods of art history.[47]

Copyright's attribution of authorship is fundamentally at odds with art-world norms, with copyright potentially seeing the performers or the conductor as authors, perhaps at the expense of the author of the score. About LeWitt's artistic authorship in the postmortem context, it has been noted that "it is almost unthinkable that copyright law would treat LeWitt as an author of the wall drawings, as there could be no relevant 'collaboration' between the living and the dead."[48] As we will see in the next section, the estate sees the nature of its conductorial role as one that involves the protection of the integrity of the idea as communicated by LeWitt's instructions, rather than any element of authorship. Bently and Biron have stated that the competing copyright-law and art-world convention perspectives of the type cited above are "not merely 'out of sync,' but outright contradictions."[49]

THE ART WORLD AND THE SCORE/PERFORMANCE/CONDUCTOR MODEL

The artistic authorship inherent in LeWitt's written instructions is not easily accommodated by current copyright law because the law does not allow for the complexities of the score/performance/conductor model. However, this model does function effectively in the art world, largely outside the traditional context of intellectual-property law, and ensures a continuing active role for the conductor—a role taken on by the artist, while he or she is alive, and subsequently the artist's estate or foundation. As the "conductor," the estate or foundation protects the integrity of the work and the artist's legacy.

When works such as LeWitt's wall drawings enter the art market, they do so by the means of instructions contained within certificates of authenticity. When a certificate is sold and resold, the purchaser generally has a conditional right to create the work, with the restriction that only one copy of the work may exist at any time. John Hogan, the Mary Jo and Ted Shen Installation Director and Archivist of Sol LeWitt Wall Drawings at the Yale University Art Gallery, who worked as the principal draftsperson at the LeWitt Studio while the artist was alive and was made the installation director for LeWitt's estate after the artist died, has spoken about how such transactions concern intellectual property:

> With LeWitt's work it is exactly that existence, it is IP; he created the idea and it enters the marketplace or a collection, and the people who legally own that own the right to complete the visualization process with the involvement of the LeWitt Studio as may be required to varying degrees dependent on the individual work. That is then

> the artwork, but if somebody read it in a book and then followed the instructions, then . . . it is parody, it is perhaps a nice compliment that somebody wants to copy the work but it is not ownership.[50]

After collectors or museums buy a LeWitt wall drawing, they are notified that they are required to consult the artist/estate before attempting to execute the work. Each time a wall drawing is installed, the owner must contact the estate to receive guidance on how to install the work correctly, in order to respect the integrity of the idea and the intent of the artist. This might be seen as somewhat at odds with the position that the owner of the instructions to and certificate to a LeWitt wall drawing is free as owner to simply execute them. When LeWitt was still alive, the artist himself might also have been involved. Now the estate, as the conductor, plays a supervisory function, but Hogan says the artist was, and now the estate is, concerned expressly with maintaining the integrity of the work rather than any assertion of authorship. Hogan adds that LeWitt's estate makes no financial gain from this conductorial/supervisory role. The supervision may take a number of forms dependent on the complexity of the instructions. The estate's oversight may range from a simple phone call to sending someone to oversee the installation. For more complex works, the estate first assesses the dimensions of a wall to decide if it is appropriate for the work. Subsequently the estate may send someone "who understands the specific aspects of the work" to oversee the installation and thereby protect the integrity of the idea. The actual execution of the work is often conducted by local artists, as had been LeWitt's desire.[51] Hogan gives an example of the type of considerations that may arise in relation to protecting the integrity of the work:

> If you are drawing a line with a marker [you ensure] that it is done in a certain way, just so that ultimately there is not a misconception of what the intent of the work is. There is a certain . . . aspect to the work [in that the instructions] may say black crayons, so, . . . what does black crayons mean? There is a narrower one or a wider one.[52]

Although there have been instances in which works were executed without the oversight of the artist/estate, there is generally respect for the role of the conductor. The art world would be made aware if a work were completed without the appropriate consultation and guidance of the estate. Hogan indicates that there is widespread acceptance of the artist's/estate's position once it is communicated to purchasers, stating: "I think generally that there is the perception that this should be respected and ultimately that the artist's intention is: . . . the value of the work is the integrity of the work. If you don't respect, then all bets are off."[53] In the interview, Hogan made it clear that the art world would be made aware if a work had been completed without the appropriate input of the artist/estate.[54]

On this point, John ffrench, Director of Visual Resources at the Yale University Art Gallery, acknowledges that the gallery would react in such a situation, stating, "If we became aware of it, we would make the foundation aware of it, [that] this piece is being reproduced and not going through the appropriate channels."[55] Because auction houses and galleries make every effort to respect the wishes of artists and their estates, such as that of LeWitt, a communication that the estate is questioning the integrity of a work would in effect constitute a withdrawal of authorship and thereby render the physical work an unapproved and inauthentic reproduction.

The role of the conductor in LeWitt's works is widely accepted in the art world. It must be noted that there are not yet any cases in which a purchaser, faced with an effective withdrawal of authorship by the conductor, has taken legal action against the artist or estate.[56] This indicates that art-world norms ensure that what could otherwise be potentially conflictive situations are resolved without legal interventions. Daniel McClean has stated that the purchase of such works operates on the basis of a "convention of the art world; there is an understanding, or a trust relationship, that the collector, the owner, can iterate or speak in the name of the author."[57]

THE POSTHUMOUS CONDUCTOR AND LEGACY

When the artist has passed, his estate is responsible for the protection of the artist's legacy. The LeWitt estate, through its conductorial role, is now primarily concerned with the conservation of the artist's work. This conservation role, however, is very much tied to a particular notion of intellectual property. Hogan states:

> So in a very particular way, conservation comes to apply in this situation, but it is conservation of intellectual property.... A responsible conservator does their homework and respects the integrity of [the] underlying concept of the work, doesn't make assumptions, does the history, does the homework, and if the materials are readily available, it is irresponsible not to contact and use it. That is how I see my job, and how we hope the work would be perceived going forward.

The art world has, in effect, developed its own system of intellectual-property protection that, while proceeding on the basis of broader conceptions of intellectual property and authorship, serves as an ideal method of protecting the ongoing legacy of the artist postmortem. The score/performance/conductor model protects the artist's idea, grants restrictions in relation to reproduction through the use of certificates and associated instructions, and allows the conductor the right to protect the integrity of the work. The right of the artist and estate to protect the integrity of the work is effectively a perpetual right and is in substance located somewhere between the right of disclosure and the right of revocation. The protection of the integrity of the idea/work, and the possibility of controlling the disclosure or allowing for revocation thereof, mirrors, and perhaps even supersedes, moral-rights protections under intellectual-property law regimes.

PROTECTION UNDER MORAL RIGHTS

Moral rights are defined as the ostensibly noneconomic, personal rights that protect the bond between authors (including artists) and their work.[58] Moral-rights laws provide artists with a means of protecting the integrity of their work and ensuring correct attribution. In certain jurisdictions, these laws allow authors to revoke authorship of a work if it no longer represents his or her artistic sentiments. However, because of the number of restrictions on the exercise of moral rights, and the difficulties associated with their assertion in relation to Conceptual works, the nonlegal approach may have significant advantages for those seeking to protect the conductor role.

The duration of moral rights may be fundamentally problematic for the protection of an artist's legacy. In some cases, moral rights may not apply posthumously, or the possibility of exercising those rights may terminate on the expiration of economic rights.[59] Conceptual works such as LeWitt's may not even qualify for moral-rights protections, for the same reason such works are not covered by copyright law; the existence of moral rights is generally dependent on the work being protected under copyright law.[60] In some instances, artists may find it even more difficult to qualify for moral rights than copyright's economic rights. In the United States, for example, moral rights as introduced through the Visual Artist's Rights Act (VARA) of 1990 provide protection to a narrowly defined closed list of traditional art forms, such as painting and sculpture, produced in limited editions. The courts have confirmed this more traditional view of authorship by excluding the possibility of Conceptual art receiving moral-rights protection.[61]

Even if Conceptual works could qualify for protection under moral rights, the limitations on the duration of these rights serve to make them a less-than-ideal way to protect the ongoing legacy of a Conceptual artist. In the United Kingdom, the moral rights of attribution and integrity last for as long as copyright.[62] The right against false attribution only lasts for the life of the alleged author plus twenty years.[63] These rights may be exercised postmortem but are not perpetual.[64]

In the United States, an artist may prevent the use of his or her name as the author of a work they did not create or a work that has been distorted, mutilated, or subjected to other modification in a way that would be prejudicial to the artist's honor or reputation.[65] While the length of protection may vary depending on when the work was created, the longest these rights could exist is for the duration of copyright.[66] It should also be noted that while VARA generally terminates the possibility of moral rights on the artist's death,[67] preemption in this area is prospective only and it does not apply to state laws that may confer postmortem moral rights.[68] Moral-rights laws in individual states may become relevant after the terms of federal VARA protection expire. State laws such as the California Art Preservation Act 1980, which protects the integrity right and a right to disclaim authorship "for a just and valid reason," allow for rights to exist for fifty years after the death of the artist.[69]

The integrity right—the right of an author to object to the distortion, mutilation, other unauthorized modification of a work, and in some cases any other derogatory action—thus enables the author to preserve the form in which the work was originally created. In the United Kingdom, for art forms that use a notation and performance model such as musical or dramatic works, the integrity right may be infringed by the person who publishes, performs in public, or communicates to the public a derogatory treatment of the work.[70] In other words, there may be infringement through the performance of a work. But this protection is not available for instruction-based artistic works. For the reasons cited above, it is likely this right under US federal law would not be available to these works, as the text instructions would not qualify as artistic works under VARA. Also, given that artists working in the score/performance/conductor model do not generally demonstrate the necessary intention for joint authorship to arise, the integrity right as it applies to joint authors under US law would be irrelevant.

BEYOND MORAL RIGHTS

In contrast to the limitations of the legal models, the art-world approach to instruction-based Conceptual works in effect grants those in the conductorial role a perpetual moral right, and after an artist's death the estate is able to maintain the integrity of the artist's idea as expressed through the written instructions. In the art world, the score/performance/conductor model is underpinned by the potential that the artist or estate could let it be known that they are unhappy about an unauthorized execution of the instructions. Given the nature of the art market and the nature of the artworks in question, such an approach would effectively constitute a perpetual right located somewhere between the moral rights of disclosure and withdrawal. Yet, as we will see, there are limitations attached to those two rights, which make the art-world version convention a far more attractive option.

THE RIGHT OF DISCLOSURE

Arguably the most fundamental of all moral rights, the right of disclosure "allows the author, and those deriving title from the author, to choose when and under what circumstances the work should be made publically available."[71] In France it has been recognized since the middle of the nineteenth century, the Court of Appeal in Lyon in 1845 stating, "the author remains judge of the opportunity of publication of his work."[72] In perhaps the most famous exercise of the right, the painter James Abbott McNeill Whistler refused to deliver a painting, despite the fact that he was contractually bound to do so, on the basis that it was not in a sufficiently completed state. The court in that instance held that Whistler was justified in his exercise of this right, but that the artist had to return the purchase sum and meet other conditions.[73]

By analogy, it may be suggested that the disclosure to the public of a LeWitt wall drawing is controlled by the fact that authorization of authorship may be withheld, and, depending on when disapproval is expressed by the artist/estate, an inauthentic work is what is in effect being displayed. In this instance, it is the delivery of authorial authorization rather than the physical work that is in question rather than a lack of completion of the work. It is an incorrect completion that activates the right.

The legal right of disclosure has the limitation that it generally relates only to the first disclosure and not subsequent ones. There is division, however, among courts and commentators as to whether a disclosure of a different type (for example, different form or different medium) could constitute first disclosure for the purposes of the right.[74] Whether each necessarily slightly different visual iteration of a text-based LeWitt work could constitute such a different disclosure is a moot point.

The right of disclosure may be exercised postmortem.[75] It has been stated that perhaps its duration should be regarded as indefinite rather than perpetual.[76] But there are special, complex rules that apply, and courts may well scrutinize the exercise of the right more rigorously for abuse after the artist's death, when "the moral right becomes a right with duties ('droit-fonction') and it must be exercised in the sole interest of the deceased author, according to his perceived convictions."[77]

THE RIGHT OF WITHDRAWAL

An artist/estate expressing disapproval over the installation of an instruction-based work could also be characterized as a withdrawal of the work post-disclosure. Adolf Dietz has defined the right as one that: "conditionally entitles an author to revoke contractual engagements so as to protect his personal and intellectual interests. In a way, this right is an extension of the public right of disclosure, in cases where disclosure or publication has already taken place but the author would now rather have the work withdrawn from circulation."[78] In Italy, Spain, Brazil, Germany, and France, for example, there exists such a right of withdrawal. Under this right in France, the artist, notwithstanding the assignment of exploitation rights, may exercise the right to retract or withdraw the work ("droit de retrait et de repentir") as long as the transferee is indemnified for any prejudice that the withdrawal may cause him.[79] But perhaps due to this latter stipulation, it has been argued that this right is largely theoretical, as the lack of case law would appear to indicate.[80] Whether this right is perpetual in France is a matter of dispute, but Elizabeth Adeney argues that since the right only subsists in relation to the exploitation rights granted by the artists, it may be reasonable to assume that it does not outlive those rights.[81]

While the preservation of art is an integral element of moral-rights laws and a motivating factor in their adoption, this essay has attempted to illustrate that they are perhaps not the ideal method of protecting the legacy of artists, particularly the legacy of those whose works struggle with attaining copyright protection in the first instance.[82] However, the art world has in effect ensured a perpetual nonlegal right located somewhere between that of disclosure and withdrawal. In the art world, the score/performer/conductor model does not face difficulties in relation to copyright protection, and does not encounter the inherent limitations of legal moral rights, which in any event have weak protection in non–civil law jurisdictions.[83]

PROTECTING THE LEGACY OF CONCEPTUAL ARTISTS

This essay has sought to demonstrate that the score/performance/conductor model, as it functions in the art world, provides a flexible and effective means of protecting the integrity of certain Conceptual artworks and the legacy of artists who make such works. Based on a broader notion of intellectual property that is less concerned with aspects such as personal execution, this model enables protection for a wider conception of artistic authorship: the model allows language to serve as sufficient conduit for the idea in question, and it enables the conductor to maintain the integrity of the work by controlling the performance. This model also provides an effective, potentially perpetual, and more flexible facsimile of those protections that moral-rights law intends for artists.

Given the aforementioned inherent tensions between the privileging of the idea in Conceptual art on the one hand and the artist's desire for a continuing role in the physical execution of the work on the other, Sol LeWitt's use of written instructions and certificates reveals an authorial approach that is located perhaps somewhere between Buchloh's "aesthetic of administration" and Walter Benjamin's concerns in relation to the "auratic" qualities of the work.[84] The score/performance/conductor model provides a framework that allows for a varying level of input in the execution, thereby accommodating such tensions. It may also allow for artists to "play" with such dynamics as part of their artistic practice, as seen in the work of Félix González-Torres and Tino Sehgal.[85]

It is arguable that the law, in principle, should be capable of recognizing Conceptual artworks and their heretofore regarded as "non-artistic" notation, particularly in light of the nature of much contemporary artistic practice. However, it is also clear that the level of choice left to those who may execute the work would still pose significant issues for copyright law. Yet, it is valuable to note that the art-world model described above is not over-sensitive to such indeterminacy; the choices made by the draftsperson have no effect on the attribution of authorship. Works that do specifically allow for a large degree of indeterminacy are still generally regarded as looking like a "LeWitt." On this issue, John Hogan has stated, "It's intriguing in that every time the drawing is done, it is a little different, but you know it is that drawing. No matter how badly someone plays Bach, you generally know it is Bach. So it is that."[86]

Copyright has proved to be incapable of identifying authorship in a manner that runs concurrent with many contemporary art-world conventions, and this has rendered it fundamentally out of step with many art-world practices, particularly in the postmortem situation. John ffrench reinforces this disconnect rhetorically, stating: "To what extent are we going to look at Sol LeWitt's death date and truly say that seventy years after that anybody could get a set of instructions and start executing them all over the world? Or is it when it is executed then that becomes copyrightable?"[87]

In conclusion, it must be said that the success of the score/performance/conductor model is dependent on an appropriate husbandry of authorship, where the intentions of the artist have been sufficiently and accurately documented and appropriately communicated to those who execute the works. In this regard, the LeWitt estate has provided a functional model that will allow the intentions of Sol LeWitt to live on through performances carefully directed by the posthumous conductor.

Hélio Oiticica: A Principle of Renewal

GUY BRETT

At a very general level the question cannot be answered. It depends on specific circumstances and specific proposals.
—Noam Chomsky

The question of the replication, reproduction, and re-creation of artwork becomes particularly poignant in relation to the Brazilian artist Hélio Oiticica (1937–1980), because he himself was very concerned with the life and afterlife of his works. Not only the existence they might have posthumously, but also how they would continue to live, and to retain their vitality and efficacy during his lifetime. Certain later works are devices designed to rescue, in a sense, an earlier concept—or what he would probably have called a "life-act"—from appropriation and acculturation by the art institution and art market. A clear example is the *Contra-Bólide (Devolver a Terra à Terra)* (Counter-Bolide [To Return Earth to the Earth]), enacted in 1978, two years before Oiticica's death. The work was "counter" in the sense of its reversal of the original *Bólides*, in which a material—earth, pigment, and so on—was withdrawn from the world and placed into a container to become an energy center, or "fireball," as the Portuguese word denotes. The *Contra-Bólide* was part of an event Oiticica organized on a site in the Rio de Janeiro district of Caju—a forlorn lot and rubbish dump near the port, in what used to be the Portuguese imperial quarter. Rich black earth was brought in and poured within a small rectangular enclosure; when the wood frame was removed, the earth stayed on the earth. It was a kind of burial of the *Bólide* as an object and its rebirth as an "act"—a renewal, in fact, of the original intention to make "manifest the presence of some earth as a piece of the earth."[1]

Another example is the made-on-the-body *Parangolé* participatory events, undertaken on several occasions between 1964 and 1979 in different cities and countries. Out of a plain, 3-meter length of brightly colored fabric, "each person must build on the body a structure, uniting the edges and extremes with safety pins."[2] Oiticica stressed that each cape should be removable without disturbing the pins, so that it can be handed on to someone else to "wear" and activate in a different way. He emphasized the desirability of participation by a heterogeneous public. Recently, a set of capes surviving from a made-on-the-body event at Recife, the capital of the Brazilian state of Pernambuco, in 1979—capes improvised by participants on their own bodies and those of others—were shown like chichi fashion items on specially designed hangers in a commercial gallery in São Paulo. I can imagine Oiticica's total freak-out at such a development.

Oiticica was radical in his adherence to a principle of renewal. The *Contra-Bólide*, he said, could be repeated whenever circumstances demanded it (and during the 1992–94 traveling retrospective *Hélio Oiticica*, for which I was a member of the curatorial committee, we did repeat it in the environs of each museum that the exhibition traveled to).[3] On the other hand, the whole elaborate scenario of the 1969 exhibition of the artist's work at the Whitechapel Gallery, in London, which he called the *Whitechapel Experience*, was not to be repeated. The artist wrote: "It would be a mystification to 'repeat' through Europe the same show, unless those works or propositions could take a new sense, which I doubt. The London show is a unique experience as such."[4]

In a practical sense, however, Oiticica did allow for some reconstruction or replication of certain works during his lifetime. In 1968 I accidentally broke *B 31 Bólide vidro 14 "Estar"* (B 31 Glass Bolide 14 "Being"; 1965–66), a loose mass of seashells in a glass container, which I had in my flat at a time when I was searching for possibilities of exhibiting Oiticica's work in London. The artist sent me detailed instructions of how to cut off the top of a large glass flask, smooth the edges, and transfer the shells into the new container. In England, we were not able to find the same flask he had used in Brazil, and my memory is hazy as to whether we substituted an available bottle or not. Nevertheless, his letter shows that he wanted to reconstruct the work. It was eventually posthumously remade in Rotterdam for the 1992 retrospective, but such versions can never be *exactly* the same as the original.

The huge growth of interest in Oiticica after his death brought requests to exhibit his work, which confronted the Projeto Hélio Oiticica, the foundation established after the artist's death to oversee his legacy, with a dilemma: how to allow the public to physically participate in the work—essential to its nature—while ensuring the preservation of its material and aesthetic qualities?[5] The solution adopted was to make a number of copies, of the *Parangolé Capes* (1964–79) and *Penetrables* (1960–78, 1980), including the "environment" *Tropicália* (1967). Later, they also made a replica of a key work, *Bed Bolide 1* (1968). Luciano Figueiredo, artist and director of the Centro Cultural Hélio Oiticica, wrote:

> The first replicas to be made were in 1985, when we (myself, Lygia Pape, Mauricio Cyrne, Thomas Valentin, and other members of the Advisory Board for Projeto HO) were asked to lend works by Hélio for an exhibition organized by the Brazilian art critic Frederico Morais called Opinião 65. The exhibition was an attempt to revive the historical show of the same name that had taken place in [the] Museum of Modern Art in Rio in 1965. It was precisely in this show that Hélio had made the first public presentation of his *Parangolés*.[6]

He continued:

> I personally [researched the] fabrics and other materials and I painted myself the parts that were to be hand-painted and I recall that we presented the two or three replicas in the street outside the art gallery at Copacabana beach with live music playing. We considered the presentation very effective and this was how the posthumous existence of these works began.

In 1986 we made the first reconstruction of *Tropicália*, to be presented in an event in São Paulo. This reconstruction involved a special problem because either Hélio did not design a drawing-plan for the construction or the drawings had been lost. So, the re-assembling of panels that make the cabins was done by studying all the photographic material in the archives: photos of the first installation of 1967 at MAM—Rio de Janeiro [the Museum of Modern Art], photos from publications and photos from the Whitechapel exhibition. Other materials and aspects of *Tropicália* were found in Hélio's texts and also in his letters.

In the same year (1986) we organized in São Paulo an exhibition including many of Hélio's works (*Bilateral* [1959], *Spatial Relief* [1960], *Bolide*, *Parangolé*, and *Tropicália*). This show took place at Galeria São Paulo and it drew very strong attention from the public, the artists, art critics, and the Brazilian press. It was the first major presentation of Hélio's works in Brazil since the late 1960s and again we made replicas of *Parangolés*, which were worn by the public in a very satisfactory way. We also supervised the making of one replica of a *Spatial Relief* and an edition of approximately 150 copies of the banner "Be a Marginal Be a Hero" was made, based on an original copy made and signed by Hélio. This exhibition marked the beginning of a new discussion about Hélio's work in Brazil.[7]

Ariane Figueiredo, who looks after the Projeto Hélio Oiticica archive and actually made the *Parangolé* replicas that the public have been permitted to wear in some exhibitions of Oiticica's work, pointed out that some of the capes are extremely difficult or impossible to replicate while others are simpler. She wrote of her frustration at not being able to find the exact materials to make a satisfactory copy:

> Oiticica used a great variety of fabrics, plastics, canvases, sponges, straw, charcoal, nylon mesh, and bags which are no longer available. Looking for the right material involves much research and long walks [that are] not always rewarding. At times I could find the right material but with

> a different color or the right color but the material is not the same, so a question always challenged me: should I be more faithful to the color or to the texture, as in the case of the works of Hélio Oiticica both values are extremely important?
>
> I suppose this conflict will always exist and maybe there will never be an answer to it. But, without the copies, how could we show today and in the future a work that is sensorial by its nature and that demands the participation of the spectator?[8]

Works actually constructed for the first time from plans, notes, and drawings left by Oiticica and carried out or supervised by Luciano Figueiredo for the Projeto include two of the *Cosmococa* installations in New York (planned in1973; constructed in 1991) and the *Penetrable* known as *A Invencao da Luz* (The Invention of Light; 1978–80). The latter work existed as a small maquette (indeed, Oiticica referred to it as a "transformable maquette-work") and was later enlarged to become five translucent screens set in sockets in an earthen or crushed brick ground. The screens could be moved or removed in "strong light (not very close to the pieces) for light effects."[9] For the 1992 retrospective, this was enlarged to a scale where people could walk into it and, with some difficulty, move the screens.

The last reconstructions, or replications, Luciano Figueiredo made were of the *Penetrable* called *Nas Quebradas*. The original work, made in 1979, was destroyed while Oiticica was still alive; there was one reconstruction in 2002 and another in 2003. For his reconstructions, Figueiredo used the artist's original drawing plans, which included a detailed list of all materials as well as photographs of the original installation.

The construction of the *Cosmococa* series is a special case because the plans evolved in New York with Oiticica's friend, the filmmaker Neville d'Almeida, who quite naturally interpreted them in the light of his own experiences and memories. In the case of *The Invention of Light*, I felt the simple enlargement of a maquette did not work well. I felt sure Oiticica would have carefully considered the problem of scale and made changes (his term "maquette-work" seems to establish this). Such judgments, though, are inevitably subjective. The reconstruction of *Nas Quebradas* (The Gullies) was criticized by some people who remembered the original. Having never seen it, I can say that I liked the reconstruction, and in fact was deeply moved by it. I recognize it as in the same lineage as the *Grand Nucleus* (1960): a strange meeting of the lucidity and compression of geometric abstraction with the lived experience of the hillside favela.

There are notebooks filled with detailed plans for complex *Penetrables* that Oiticica invented while in New York but lacked the support and means to build. My instinct is that they should be left as they are—or perhaps three-dimensional models could be made from the drawings—but I am ready to be proven wrong. I think we have to approach these questions in the spirit of these words by Noam Chomsky: "At a very general level the question cannot be answered. It depends on specific circumstances and specific proposals."[10] Luciano Figueiredo seemed to concur with Chomsky's view:

> Having had the experience of studying and handling the works of Hélio Oiticica for so long, and by showing his works in many museums in Brazil and abroad, I must confess that after all these occasions and giving thoughts today to these matters, I think that the making of replicas or reconstruction of works can be more complex in the case of some artists than others. I think that due to the originality of each artist, the values, qualities, and problems vary from one to the other and each artist can provoke a different point of view of what is in question.
>
> When I participated in and encouraged the decisions about making replicas of works of Hélio Oiticica, I did so under the belief that the role of the replica would effectively contain the meaning of the original work. It was always clear to me that a duplication of *Parangolé*, for example, when faithful to the original, can offer to the public the essence of the original piece.
>
> [Even] if I have today disappointment and criticism to express about some aspects of showing *Parangolés* (either originals or replicas) in the

spaces of institutions, how could these works be part of the discussions of contemporary art if it was not [for their] presence made possible by replicas? It would not be possible to experience what is a *Parangolé* just by looking at documents and photographs or by looking at motionless originals as in a museum of costumes.[11]

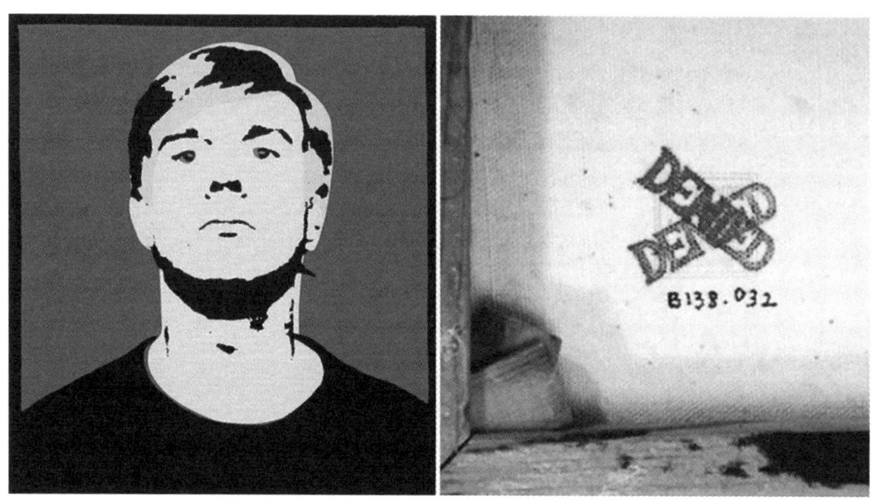

Andy Warhol (contested)
Red Self-Portrait, 1964
Synthetic polymer and silkscreen ink on canvas, 60 × 50 cm

Artists' Legacies, Authentication, and the Art Market: Not Always a Happy Ménage

GEORGINA ADAM

The art market is riven with conflicts regarding the authentication of artworks after the artist has died, and even occasionally during the artist's lifetime. Nowhere is this more visible than in the relationship between the art market and artists' estates and foundations. At issue is who has the right to speak in the name of the artist and to maintain the artist's legacy once he or she is no longer around. Heirs and those who own the moral rights of deceased artists often become paid authenticators of the work, and they sometimes also benefit from artists' resale rights and copyright royalties. These potentially juicy revenues have led to some extraordinary battles, sometimes escalating into decades-long vicious wars, between rival members of the family, often fanned by self-interest, personal animosity, and entrenched positions.

The problem for the art market is that it needs a reliable source for authentication, and when these battles arise, they impact the market negatively. Conversely, the concentration of power in the hands of a single artist's estate or foundation can lead to abuses, which can also be a problem for the art market. One heir might authenticate a work, the other not. More than one catalogue raisonné might appear. Some perfectly genuine Modiglianis, for instance, are drastically undervalued because they were not listed in the "right" catalogue raisonné. In several cases, the art trade has had to seek more than one certificate, to cover all eventualities. Then there is the thorny issue of posthumous editions: Did the artist want them produced? Can they be modified, in size or material, from the original work? In the absence of clear guidance during the artist's lifetime, what should an estate or foundation do if it needs to raise money to continue to protect an artist's legacy? These questions have become most crucial in the field of modern and contemporary art, where prices have exploded, the artist is often no longer present to make decisions, and a number of heirs are still alive, determined to defend their illustrious forebears' legacy—and sometimes also determined to defend their rights to make a living out of this heritage.

In the following pages, I outline the dominant legacy models, and I look at the various issues that arise when works of art must be authenticated, usually before a sale. I consider the involvement of artists' heirs, lawsuits targeting foundations, the compilation of catalogues raisonnés, rival authenticators, and the problems that may emerge once the artist is no longer alive, such as posthumous editions or the re-creation of deteriorated artworks.

LEGACY MODELS

It is necessary to make a distinction between the legacy models or models of estate management in the United States and Europe, particularly in France, where many of the highest-priced modern artists lived at the beginning of the twentieth century. A lot of the estates of these artists—for example, Pablo Picasso or Marc Chagall—are now run by the artists' heirs. In France, and in a number of other European countries where the "Latin" system of law prevails, the moral right is inalienable, perpetual, and inviolable; it allows heirs to assert authority over the works of the artist long after his or her death. Consequently, authorship is normally exercised posthumously by a deceased artist's heirs. And while these rights do not include authentication, in practice the two often overlap, as the moral rights include the right to attribute the artwork, the right to object to the false attribution of the artwork, and the right to object to the derogatory treatment of the artwork. Moral rights cannot be sold, but are left either to heirs or to the executors of a will, or another designated person, and do not expire with time, although their enforcement over time tends to gradually disappear once the work is in the public domain.

In the United States, by contrast, an artist's legacy is more often managed by a foundation, which tends to act independently of the artist's estate. However, estate members may sit on the board of the foundation (for example, Alexander S. C. Rower, grandson of Alexander Calder and the chairman and president of the Calder Foundation). The protection of moral rights of authorship in the United States is more circumscribed than in European civil-law countries. The Visual Artists Rights Act (VARA), passed by the US Congress in 1990, protects some moral rights postmortem, but not all. It is worth noting that the provisions are messy. In essence: for artworks made after VARA was enacted, moral rights only last for the lifetime of the artist, but for pre-VARA works, they generally last for the period of copyright in the artwork (as protected under the US Copyright Act of 1976), which is the lifetime of the author plus seventy years after death.

Perhaps as a result of the need to protect legacy, many artist-endowed foundations have been established in the United States: up to three hundred, according to the Aspen Institute.[1] The United States has some tax incentives for the creation and funding of private foundations, which is one means to accomplish the reduction of nonliquid, taxable assets held in an estate. In France, it is so difficult to set up these institutions that only ten are devoted to a single artist, including Jean (Hans) Arp, Victor Vasarely, Le Corbusier, and Georges Rouault.

AUTHENTICATION BY EXPERTS AND HEIRS

When the authenticity of a work of art is in question, or its authenticity just needs to be confirmed officially before a sale, the seller may go to the artist's heirs or foundation, or to an expert on the artist (particularly, where there is no estate to turn to), to seek authentication. But this is not always a clear process. In some cases, the market itself may turn out to be the ultimate arbiter of authenticity, independent of an issued certificate or expert's opinion that may accompany a particular work of art.

Art experts (including scholars, auction houses, and dealers) have historically played a critical role in authenticating artworks, particularly works by Old Masters. Yet the authentication opinions of art experts are often subsequently contested, leading in some instances to disappointed sellers and buyers bringing legal proceedings against them. Not all legal systems offer great protection for sellers, or for experts who give an opinion. The English courts in particular have been wary of enforcing legal claims when artworks are determined to be forgeries or misattributions. Under English law, risk (and the need for due diligence) has been allocated onto buyers in art transactions as expressed in the maxim "caveat emptor," or buyer beware.

In one prominent recent case, a seller, Lancelot William Thwaytes, took Sotheby's, London, to court after the auction house described a work he owned—*The Cardsharps*, a version of the well-known painting by Caravaggio in the Kimbell Art Museum, in Fort Worth, Texas—as by a follower of Caravaggio and sold it for just £42,000. The work was bought by a friend of Sir Denis Mahon, reportedly for him. Mahon, the leading specialist on Caravaggio, later declared the painting to be an authentic Caravaggio and worth £10 million. Thwaytes sued and, during the court case, brought in two experts to testify that the painting was by Caravaggio. He accused Sotheby's of negligence (as his agent in the sale) in not exploring this possibility more thoroughly before the sale. However, Sotheby's prevailed in the case, and was cleared of Thwaytes's accusations. Note that the court did not pronounce on authenticity itself, but on possible negligence.[2] Significantly, the market's belief that the painting was not autograph was reinforced by the low price it fetched when put up for public auction; none of the bidders went over £42,000, showing that they did not accept a potential attribution to Caravaggio. The market decided that the work was not authentic.

Dealers, who invest their own money when they buy works of art to sell, are often highly experienced specialists themselves, but they need to be able to defend their opinion vis-à-vis their clients and conform to trading laws. Auction houses have to stand behind their catalogue descriptions, and risk very public opprobrium if they get anything wrong, not to speak of lawsuits both from disappointed buyers or sellers, as in the Caravaggio example. This means that dealers and auction houses must exercise due diligence, contact the "right" specialists, and consult the "right" catalogue raisonné before selling a work. Even if auction houses do everything they can to cover their bases, things do not always go their way. In an interesting contrast to the Caravaggio case, Christie's was forced to reimburse the Russian oligarch Victor Vekselberg £1.7 million plus legal costs after he bought *Odalisque* (1919), a work listed as by Boris Kustodiev, at auction in 2012. Importantly, here it was found that Christie's had a legal duty to describe and value the property accurately to the buyer as well as to the seller as its agent in the sale, which it failed to discharge. While Christie's maintains, to this day, that its specialists were correct in attributing the work to Kustodiev, the buyer brought in other experts who doubted it, and won his case and the refund. In this instance a number of other bidders had forced up the price of the painting to ten times estimate, so Christie's was not alone in believing in the authenticity of the work.[3]

It is also worth mentioning the issue of paid expertise. Many heirs and specialists earn a living through delivering certificates of authenticity, for which they are paid, and by compiling catalogues raisonnés. A number of them are also dealers, which can give the impression of a conflict of interest. Accusations have long been bandied about—often without any actual proof—that some compilers will only accept a work of art if it is also confided for sale. Further rumors hold that sometimes the reigning expert on an artist's work, given a sufficiently large inducement, might be prepared to deliver a certificate or a favorable opinion.

Even perfectly upright heirs can make some quirky decisions. Widows have been known to refuse to authenticate perfectly genuine works when they depicted the dear departed's mistress, as was the case with Alice Derain, wife of André Derain, according to the French authors Hervé Le Boterf and Emmanuel David.[4] Marc Chagall's estate once refused to give a certificate of authenticity to the buyer of a drawing, *Moses and the Angel*, on the basis that it had been given to friends by the artist as a gift. His widow decreed that it should not have ended up on the commercial circuit, and she refused to sign the certificate.[5]

AUTHENTICATION, FOUNDATIONS, AND MARKET MANIPULATION?

The authentication boards of artists' foundations can wield enormous power in the art market, particularly in the United States. There have been several attempts to assert, in the United States, that artists' committees linked to foundations with significant holdings of an artist's works and materials deliberately interfere with the market by limiting the number of works available in order to boost the value of works owned by their members, or other linked bodies. This was one of the allegations in the case with the Warhol Foundation for the Visual Arts and its authentication board, which was attacked under US antitrust laws by the collector, Joe Simon-Whelan. The case was eventually dropped by Simon-Whelan, but he managed to inflict enormous financial (with estimated legal fees of $7 million) and reputational damage on the Warhol Foundation and set an ominous legal precedent (as his antitrust case survived in part the foundation's motion to dismiss).

Another example in which this argument was put forward was the case of Elizabeth Bilinski and others against the Keith Haring Foundation, filed in the US Southern District of New York in 2014. Bilinski and her eight co-plaintiffs own a group of 111 artworks that they tried, and mainly failed, to get authenticated by the foundation. When they put them on display in Miami, the foundation brought a lawsuit, saying they were inauthentic.[6] The owners then sued, alleging that the foundation had wrecked the collective $40 million value of the pieces. The owners' complaint stated:

> An authentic Haring artwork can be worth millions of dollars in today's art market. However, without a certificate of authenticity from the Foundation (or at least its tacit approval), no major auction house is willing to sell a Haring artwork. . . . By rejecting authentic Haring artworks, the Foundation has inflated the value of works owned by the Foundation and its representatives, all of which bear the Foundation's certificate of approval. . . . [Between 2008 and 2011], the Foundation sold more than $4.5 million of Haring artworks that it owns. The Foundation has also used its authentication powers to carefully cultivate Haring's image, . . . which has benefited the Foundation and its representatives.[7]

Plaintiffs described the conspiracy as being between "defendants and their allies," specifically art galleries, dealers, and major auction houses who "severely restrict the supply of Haring artwork in the marketplace."[8]

This and other allegations were dismissed in a decision on March 6, 2015, by district judge Denise Cote, who closed the case. "The complaint's allegations regarding the refusals of auction houses and others to accept plaintiffs' works can be explained by unilateral decisions motivated by entirely lawful goals," she wrote. "The decision by any individual entity not to sell artwork that may not be authentic is an act consistent with lawful, independent action." And she pointed out that, as in the Warhol case, the foundation had ceased its authentication activities in 2012: "The defendants . . . could not be plausibly alleged to control authentication of Haring's work."[9]

Does this decision, coupled with that in the Warhol case, mean the end of such lawsuits? The judge pointed out that the two cases were dissimilar, as in the Haring case there was no catalogue raisonné. Commenting on the case, art lawyer Nicholas O'Donnell said: "If anything, the case will likely accelerate the trend of foundations declining to issue opinions at all, since this matter was surely more trouble than it was worth for the Foundation."[10]

While the Warhol and Bilinski cases attempted—and failed—to prove antitrust practices, the whole issue of authentication and the legal costs incurred by foundations and estates in defending their opinions (which in the US legal system are essentially nonrecoverable costs) have led to many of these institutions closing their authentication arms. The Warhol Board disbanded in 2011. Other examples of closures were the Krasner-Pollock Board, which disbanded in 1996; the boards of Roy Lichtenstein and Robert Rauschenberg in 2011; and then Keith Haring, Jean-Michel Basquiat, and the Noguchi Museum in 2012. While it is understandable that money spent fighting time-wasting and costly lawsuits could be better spent on promoting artists' legacies, it is also true that the lack of a proper authentication body makes it easier for fakes to circulate and places owners who may own perfectly valid artworks by an artist in limbo if they wish to sell their works for their true market value.

RIVAL FOUNDATIONS AND DIVERGENT AUTHENTICATION

The problem of warring artists' foundations (which can lead to divergent bodies of authentication for a particular artist's work) and their relationship with the market can be illustrated by the case of Alberto Giacometti (1901–1966). This example is also certainly the one in which the stakes are highest: Giacometti holds the record for the most expensive sculpture ever sold at auction: his *L'homme au doigt* (1947) made $141 million at Christie's New York in 2015.[11] Other pieces regularly fetch tens of millions of dollars.

Until 2014 there were two rival bodies in France—an association and a foundation—plus the privately funded Alberto Giacometti-Stiftung (Foundation) in Zurich. Giacometti died without having made a will, and under Swiss law his art and money were divided between his Paris-based widow, Annette, and his younger siblings. Annette received seven hundred artworks, and over two hundred plasters were left undivided, with revenues from castings to be shared between the heirs, including two younger brothers, a nephew, and great-nephews.[12]

Annette set about tackling the forgeries and unauthorized castings that were already on the market, and started a catalogue raisonné. She created an association, which was the first step to establishing a foundation. And this is where major problems began. After Annette's death a foundation did finally materialize, but her trusted secretary, Mary Lisa Palmer, continued to run the association, while a lawyer, Véronique Wiesinger, ran the separate foundation. During all these years, auction houses and dealers habitually asked for certificates of authenticity from both the association and the foundation before a sale, just to cover all eventualities. "It was very difficult situation, and their rivalry didn't help," comments one very well-respected London dealer.[13] Any move by one tended to be followed by contrarian retaliation by the other.

The two women, who detested each other, also fought bitterly in the courts. In 2002, in the teeth of Palmer's opposition, the foundation offered forty posthumous bronzes for auction at Drouot, in Paris. "Mrs Palmer never wanted us to sell anything. But how was the estate supposed to continue surviving without any money?" asked the administrator for the estate at the time.[14] Palmer failed to stop the auction, but when the running total reached €6 million the sale was stopped by the auctioneer. This was because the Ministry of Culture had granted permission for the sale to raise exactly that sum. Potential bidders for the remaining sixteen lots left empty handed, and some who had made a special trip to the sale were furious.

The lawsuits did not end there. After 2005 the Swiss stiftung started systematically opposing the production of posthumous casts by the foundation, in the name of protecting the artist's legacy. The foundation accused the Stiftung of taking an abusive position, but lost the case, so was not able to sell any new casts. Finally peace broke out in 2014: Wiesinger left the foundation, and a new president, Catherine Grenier, ended all the lawsuits. A few sales per year, with the agreement of all concerned, are now planned via two commercial galleries, and proceeds from these disposals will help pay for acquisitions.[15] In 2015 the foundation bought *Homme (Apollon)* (1929) for £782,500 at auction.[16] The foundation collaborated with the Chinese-Indonesian collector Budi Tek to hold the first exhibition of Giacometti's work in Tek's Yuz

Museum in Shanghai in 2016—a decision that could certainly also boost the market for the sculptor's work, even though the exhibition itself was noncommercial. The foundation is now the sole body that issues certificates and makes posthumous editions.

CATALOGUES RAISONNÉS

Producing a catalogue raisonné gives the author, usually an art expert or someone involved with the artist's estate or foundation, great power over the artist's work. When carried out seriously, the catalogue becomes the authoritative reference work for determining authenticity, and the value of a work of art can be destroyed if it is not included in the catalogue. This has led to abuses, with owners of works sometimes resorting to bribery and even threats to ensure inclusion. Indeed there have been court cases, notably in France, where owners have gone to the courts, sometimes forcing the author to list a work that he or she does not endorse.

A recent case in France concerned a work by Jean Metzinger (1883–1956). Bozena Nikiel, author of the catalogue raisonné, refused to include a work, and the owner went to court. The wrangle went all the way to the Cour de Cassation, France's highest court. In the end the Cour decided that the painting was authentic, based on other experts' opinions, but that the catalogue raisonné's author had the "liberty of expression" to refuse it since the catalogue was her "personal work."[17] The case certainly highlights the possible impact of such a decision on the market value of a work. In the Metzinger case, the author of the catalogue is an acknowledged specialist, and the fact that she considered it inauthentic, whatever the court said, could certainly put some doubt into the minds of potential buyers.

There have been a number of cases, mainly in France, where more than one author has worked on an artist, but the poster boy for multiple catalogues raisonnés is Amedeo Modigliani (1884–1920), whose portraits and sculptures are among the most sought-after works of art from the early twentieth century. His chaotic life and tragic death from the Spanish flu in 1920, followed by the suicide of his pregnant mistress Jeanne Hébuterne, turned him into the iconic *artiste maudit*—one whose works are prone to frequent forgery.

He was already successful at his death, and according to his biographer Meryle Secrest, during the week of his death, his studio was cleared of canvases and sculptures: "There was nothing left for Modigliani's heirs to claim," she writes.[18] What happened to them? This is unclear, but the artist's friends and dealers may have been responsible for taking them.[19] The artist's daughter, also named Jeanne, was heir to the *droit moral*—which does not give the legal right to authenticate, but which does confer some authority through the right of attribution. But she was just a year old when her father died, so her experience of his work was severely limited. This did not stop her from giving her opinion: according to art dealer Marc Blondeau, "Jeanne was impossible because she signed authentication certificates in a very subjective way, without doing serious research. She even authorized people to produce bronze reproductions of her father's work, despite the fact that he only worked in stone."[20] While she had the legal right to reproduce his sculptures, changing the medium is considered borderline acceptable.

"Nowadays certificates from Jeanne Modigliani have been thoroughly discredited," writes Secrest.[21] Also disregarded are catalogues by convicted forger Christian Parisot (who inherited the moral right from Jeanne), Joseph Lanthemann, Osvaldo Patani, and Arthur Pfannstiel. The only catalogue that auction houses and dealers trust is the three-part work by Italian appraiser and critic Ambrogio Ceroni. If a work is not in Ceroni, it loses a substantial chunk of its value and would not be accepted for sale by the major auction houses. As for Modigliani's works on paper, for which there is no reliable catalogue, the auction houses generally will only accept those with a Paul Alexandre provenance—the collector who acquired some 450 of his drawings. The Paris-based art historian Marc Restellini has for some time been working on a catalogue of Modigliani's works, but despite announcing that it would be released online at the end of 2016, at the time of writing in late 2017 it had still not been published. Prices are now so high, and fakes so rife, that many in the trade believe that the long-awaited work will never appear: "There are just too many interests at play," said one dealer who did not want to be identified.

"Where there is no recognized expertise or a respected catalogue raisonné for an artist's work, this can have an impact on the market, because it reduces the number of works that can be sold to only those that have impeccable provenance," says Philip Hook, Senior International Specialist of Impressionist and Modern Art at Sotheby's, who also mentions the situation with Fernand Léger (1881–1955).[22] Léger's works on paper, in the absence of a complete catalogue by the specialist Georges Bauquier, who died in 1997, are generally only accepted for auction if the provenance can be traced back to the dealer Daniel-Henry Kahnweiler, which may mean that some perfectly good works are ignored by the market.

WHEN THE FAMILY FALLS OUT— WHO OWNS THE ARTIST'S MORAL RIGHTS?

In the 1960s and 70s, the Op art practitioner Victor Vasarely (1906–1997) was the height of fashion—an "official" artist of the Pompidou era. His eye-bending compositions were enthusiastically reproduced and soon widely graced hotel receptions and boardrooms. Interest in his work fell dramatically in the late twentieth century, and only revived in the mid-2000s, boosted a fascination with the period and other Op art creators. Today his most sought-after works are the often black-and-white pieces from the 1950s, with one selling at auction in 2010 for £565,250.[23]

Vasarely's death was followed by a quite extraordinarily bitter battle between his heirs. Vasarely's daughter-in-law Michèle and his grandson Pierre fought with endless lawsuits against each other as to who should have the *droit moral* over his work. At one point Michèle was president and sold works to pay taxes; she was followed by the controversial Pierre Debbasch, who also sold off works, and the foundation almost went into liquidation. Michèle decamped to the United States, taking other works by Vasarely with her, and she still runs an "official artist's website." Pierre saved the foundation *in extremis* and is rebuilding it. He was finally declared, after decades of litigation, the sole owner of the *droit moral* and is compiling a catalogue raisonné. Today his certificates are accepted as authentication.

In another recent case, the heirs to Lygia Clark (1920–1988), Brazil's best-known and most expensive artist, have had a bitter falling-out, and authentication of her work has been halted. Alvaro Clark, one of the artist's two sons, has filed a lawsuit against his brother, Eduardo, seeking the return of works of art he claims were inappropriately taken.[24] Both ran "The World of Lygia Clark," the institution that manages her legacy and fights forgeries; at the time of writing, the issuing of authentication certificates had been stopped, and the organization was no longer functioning.

However, according to art adviser Allan Schwartzman, the impact on the market might not be as negative as some expect. In a suggestive comment, he said: "Perhaps the absence of a family, which might at times be perceived as having its own goals, might open the door for more Clarks to appear in exhibitions, publications and the marketplace that can be validated through other tried and true tests of authentication and proven provenance."[25] That is to say, experts not linked to the family could authenticate works by Clark, just as other specialists do for many artists with no living heirs and no foundation.

THE QUESTION OF POSTHUMOUS EDITIONS

In addition to the problems faced by artists' estates and foundations when authenticating works of art, they can run into trouble when making decisions about posthumous editions—decisions that can have a major impact on the market. One specific question is whether heirs should be allowed to change the materials or size of posthumous editions.

One case in France, involving the production of sculptures in different materials from the original, rumbled on for over fifteen years. The case concerned nine posthumous casts based on Camille Claudel's *La vague* (1897–1903), a sculpture now at the Musée Rodin, in Paris, and one of *La valse* (1889–1893). Claudel's great-niece, Reine-Marie Paris, who is the recognized specialist of the artist's work and has the reproduction rights, made and sold nine copies of *La vague*—but in bronze, not in the original onyx marble with bronze figures—and a *La valse* twice the size of the original. The sculptures were accompanied by certificates of authenticity and a Claudel signature. Part of Claudel's family took Paris to court for counterfeiting, and a Belgian buyer, who had paid €800,000 for an example of each work, accused her of deception. Finally, the judge dismissed the charge of counterfeiting, stating: "Nothing proved that the artist wanted the sculptures to be made only in the same size or with the same materials."[26] As for the charge of deception, the court ruled that the period in which the action could be brought had expired.[27]

ISSUES WITH TODAY'S MATERIALS

Estates that manage the legacy of artists who worked with unconventional materials, or in media that are inherently reproducible, deal with a range of medium-specific issues. Such works may depend on particular technologies that become obsolete and are no longer produced, or on materials that deteriorate rapidly. For example, Damien Hirst's *The Physical Impossibility of Death in the Mind of Someone Living* (1991) involved a shark in a tank of formaldehyde, and the whole work had to be remade after the first fish rotted. In this case, the artist was alive to endorse the re-creation. Once an artist is no longer living, these types of decisions become more complicated: what is to be done when ephemeral materials decompose or stop working? The conservation problems of the Hirst shark will become a legacy issue once the creator is no longer alive, and there are cases of now deceased artists where such issues have already come to the fore.

In the case of Dan Flavin (1933–1996), for example, the light bulbs in his illuminated works were discontinued in the mid-1990s. This should not have displeased the artist himself, as he stated in 1982 that once worn out, the light bulbs should not be replaced. But in a curious contradiction to this avowed intention to make something ephemeral, the Flavin estate found two US manufacturers to make copies of the bulbs and fixtures, which the estate sells to owners of Flavin's works. Interestingly, Flavin's espousal of the ephemeral contrasts with his rigid documentation process, which he established in his lifetime: a one-off certificate is made for each work. Without the certificate, a Flavin sculpture is unsalable today, and you need it when applying to the estate to buy a replacement light bulb or fixture.

In another example, the American photographer William Eggleston (b.1939) reprinted images and was landed with a lawsuit brought by collector Jonathan Sobel. Sobel claimed that the new printing diminished the value of his own collection of dye-transfer prints, estimated as being worth up to $5 million. That court case was thrown out by the judge, who ruled that even though they were of the same images, the reprints were in a different size, medium, and date, and so did not diminish the value of Sobel's collection. And the collector was not allowed to appeal the ruling.

This case, coupled with increasingly sophisticated technology allowing rapid and faithful reproductions, must surely be worrying for owners. They might have bought what they thought were original works, but if these can be replicated later, they could face a loss in value. And some media are so new that accepted practices, such as releasing works in limited editions, are not yet in place. *Der Lauf Der Dinge* (The Way Things Go; 1987), a video work by Peter Fischli (b.1952) and David Weiss (1946–2012), was originally shot on 16 mm film, transferred to color video, and sold as a signed and numbered tape cassette. A few years later, an unlimited edition of the same work was sold for just CHF 45, and then more recently Artspace released a "limited edition" DVD of 150 copies at $7,500.[28]

From all of the above, it is clear that issues surrounding expertise, authentication, reproduction, estates, foundations, and the market are complex, difficult to resolve, and often not clear-cut. Experts may disagree about a work; conflicts of interest may arise in foundations; the artists' own instructions may be confusing or evolve over time. When authenticating works of art, the art market has to take account of all these variables, and dealers, auctioneers, and collectors have to make the best decisions they can in the light of the information that they have at a given time. But there is always the danger that elements informing an authenticity opinion may change, be it progress in forensic testing, advances in connoisseurship, or new information about provenance and ownership.

Brave New Art Market: Unsilencing the Authenticators

JUDITH BRESLER

The art market is peculiarly vulnerable. While art can fetch stratospheric prices, its value is dependent on its authenticity—and authenticity of works can be notoriously difficult and slippery to determine. Authenticity, which is tied to the artistic authorship of an artwork as well as to its uniqueness and condition, is a major driver in art transactions. When a party spends a sum of six, seven, eight, or even nine figures on a work of art—for example a painting by Andy Warhol—the buyer wants confirmation that he or she is buying a genuine work, whether the object in question is being acquired from a private individual, a gallery, or an auction house. Whatever the source of the sale, a buyer is unlikely to have any interest in the artwork if there is no reliable opinion regarding the work's authenticity. Similarly, when a work is lent to a museum (a nonprofit institution essentially educational and aesthetic in purpose), the museum requires assurance that what it will be exhibiting is, in terms of authorship, what it is described to be. When a US resident donates a work of art to a museum, the donor, in order to be able to take an appropriate tax deduction for the charitable donation, must obtain a qualified appraisal from a qualified appraiser, which is predicated on a reliable authenticity opinion to justify the amount of the deduction. Estates that include works of art are also required to obtain authenticity determinations to affix a dollar value to each work.

Authenticity opinions encompass more than uncovering fakes and forgeries. Often, disputes over authenticity arise because a legitimate work of art (that is, an artwork not created with the intent to deceive) has been misattributed to a particular artist. For example, the question of whether a painting was authored by Sir Joshua Reynolds, the distinguished eighteenth-century English portrait painter, or by Tilly Kettle, a lesser-known contemporary of Reynolds, was the subject of the 1980s lawsuit *Travis v. Sotheby Parke Bernet*.[1]

Artworks are generally authenticated by three separate modes of analysis, sometimes used in combination—documentation, stylistic inquiry, and scientific verification—but each of these methods has its drawbacks. Documentation of the history of ownership and public exhibition of a work of art is sometimes unavailable, inasmuch as documentation itself is, on occasion, either forged or missing entirely. Stylistic inquiry is inherently subjective: an expert examines the work and, on the basis of his or her knowledge, experience, and intuition, determines its authenticity. The results of stylistic inquiry may vary from expert to expert. For example, in November 2016, a set of sixty-five newly revealed drawings by Vincent van Gogh, verified as authentic and collated by two renowned Van Gogh scholars, was published internationally in *Vincent van Gogh: The Lost Arles Sketchbook*. However, in what has been termed by a number of Van Gogh experts an "unprecedented" faceoff among scholars, the Van Gogh Museum—which has the sole power to officially authenticate works attributed to the artist, and which has repeatedly dismissed the sketches as "imitations"—released, on the same day publication of the book was announced, a detailed statement disputing the drawings' attribution (based on both stylistic analysis and ownership history).[2] To further complicate matters, any given expert may change their opinion on stylistic determinations over time. Scientific verification can assist in authentication, but even this has limitations. Scientific techniques used to analyze art include radiocarbon dating, thermoluminescent analysis, x-ray technologies, and high-resolution digital photography. All of these processes are objective, and the accuracy of the results can be tested by other scientists. However, scientific verification, which can be effective in detecting the age of art objects, is often more useful in uncovering a fake, rather than in positively confirming authorship. In one recent example, Sotheby's New York brokered a private sale to an art collector in 2011 for about

$10.8 million dollars of *Portrait of a Man*, which was considered by leading scholars to be an undiscovered masterwork by Frans Hals (1582/83–1666), then declared the painting a "modern forgery" in October 2016, rescinded the sale, and reimbursed the buyer.[3] The Sotheby's opinion was based on an in-depth scientific analysis of the "Hals" that determined it contained traces of twentieth-century materials, and therefore could not have been painted in the seventeenth century. Yet, even with all the limitations of the various authentication techniques, authenticators have a crucial role in the art market, and it is essential that they are able to do their work with scholarly integrity and in good faith without the threat of being sued.

THE PROBLEM

In the art market, authentication plays a vital role, yet authenticators must practice their profession at their own risk (a risk compounded by the imperfections of the authentication process), including incurring potential legal liability for their authenticity opinions. Over the course of rendering opinions in good faith, they have been sued by buyers, owners, and sellers about the authenticity, attribution, or authorship of artworks on a variety of legal theories, namely: negligence, negligent misrepresentation, fraud, product disparagement, and defamation, as well as on antitrust grounds.[4] Although usually the law, whether state or federal, is on the side of art experts, and they have prevailed in the courts, the costs of vindication have been too great: thousands of hours and dollars spent on legal defense rather than on the practice of their profession has increasingly forced experts to withdraw from offering their opinions. This is particularly a problem in the United States, where legal costs are high and are rarely recoverable by the successful defendant (in contrast, for example, to the jurisdiction of England and Wales). The result of this silence has been detrimental to the art market, causing fakes and forgeries of a valuable commodity to flood the marketplace.

Examples of lawsuits that have been brought against individual art experts—and ultimately dismissed—include *Kirby v. Wildenstein* and *Ravenna v. Christie's*. In *Kirby v. Wildenstein*, an owner of a painting by the artist Jean Béraud (1848–1935) sued Daniel Wildenstein on a theory of product disparagement after the owner's painting, evaluated by Wildenstein, failed to sell at auction at Christie's in New York.[5] In dismissing the suit, a New York federal district court held, among other points, that the owner of the artwork failed to demonstrate a requisite causal connection between Wildenstein's statements and any losses sustained by the owner. In *Ravenna v. Christie's*, a painting by Ludovico Carracci (1555–1619), a master of the Italian Baroque, was misattributed, on the basis of a photograph of the artwork, as being from the studio of a minor Italian artist and was consequently sold as such by the owner in a private sale.[6] When the painting, now owned by the buyer, was soon after offered for sale by Christie's New York as an authentic Carracci, the original owner sued James Bruce-Gardyne, the Old Master specialist at Christie's who had originally misidentified the painting. Bruce-Gardyne (along with Christie's) was sued on a theory of negligent misrepresentation. The New York State Supreme Court, affirmed by the appellate court, dismissed the case because a successful lawsuit in negligent misrepresentation requires a special relationship of trust and confidence between the parties—and Bruce-Gardyne's opinion was, in this instance, merely free advice based on a walk-in inquiry.

The temporal and financial hazards of authenticating art apply not only to the individual art expert, but to artists' foundations and authentication boards as well. If an artist has a resale market, the artist or his estate often creates a foundation to preserve the artist's legacy. That foundation will often publish a catalogue raisonné: a definitive text of the artist's work, which is a primary reference for the art market. Inclusion of a work in a catalogue raisonné—particularly one affiliated with the artist's foundation—generally constitutes an imprimatur of the work's authenticity. If a work is excluded from such a catalogue raisonné, it may well be unsalable. If a work purportedly by an artist is *not* included in the artist's catalogue raisonné, an interested party may seek validation of the work's authenticity through an artist's authentication board, which is frequently created by the artist's foundation. An authentication board generally includes people with scholarly knowledge of the artist's work, people with direct experience of working with the artist, relatives of the artist, and/or people who are officers of the artist's foundation. Unlike the process of preparing a catalogue raisonné, an authentication board only reviews artwork submitted to it, and its process of evaluation is, of necessity, generally secretive, since transparency can enable art forgers to readily ascertain "hallmarks" of a work authored by the artist and incorporate them into fakes.

Perhaps predictably, artists' foundations and authentication boards have been sued on conspiracy theories in the course of rendering opinions about a work's authenticity, attribution, or authorship. The enormous impact on the marketplace of such expert opinions, coupled with the often intertwined relationships between an artist's foundation and the artist's authentication board, can provide fertile ground for accusations by the owner of a work. When the authenticity of a work is denied, the owner might claim that the artist's foundation and authentication board have colluded to exclude certain authentic pieces from the accepted canon of that artist's work, and thereby from the market, in an attempt to increase the value of that artist's work owned by the foundation and sold, generally, at auction.

One such artist foundation, the Pollock-Krasner Foundation, established an authentication board to examine and make authenticity determinations on works of art purportedly by the artist Jackson Pollock (1912–1956). In operation for six years (1990–96), a period during which it evaluated hundreds of hitherto unknown works and certified only a few for entry into the catalogue raisonné, the authentication board dissolved after the Pollock catalogue raisonné was completed. Prior to its dissolution, the foundation was sued in *Kramer v. Pollock-Krasner Foundation* for, among other claims, antitrust violations pursuant to Section 1 of the Sherman Antitrust Act, which prohibits conspiracies in restraint of trade, and Section 2 of the Sherman Act, which prohibits monopolization. In that case, one David Kramer, an art dealer, bought a painting privately for $15,000 that, he alleged, could be worth $10 million if it were authenticated as a Jackson Pollock and sold at auction.[7] Both Sotheby's and Christie's told Kramer that they would auction the painting if it were authenticated by the Pollock-Krasner Authentication Board. After a careful review, the board refused to authenticate the painting and Kramer brought suit. The New York federal district court dismissed all of Kramer's allegations for failure to state a cause of action. In doing so, the court, referring to the Sherman Act, noted that Kramer had reasonable alternatives to selling his painting through Sotheby's or Christie's (privately, for example, or through another auction house), and therefore no market restraint existed. Moreover, the court found that the complaint presented no coherent theory of participation by Sotheby's or Christie's in the alleged conspiracy, and that each house had an independent interest in not selling forgeries. The Pollock-Krasner Foundation, subsequent to dissolution of its authentication board, has continued to receive legal challenges based on its authenticity determinations.

More recently, in 2012, the Andy Warhol Foundation for the Visual Arts dissolved the Andy Warhol Art Authentication Board as announced in October 2011 following a series of controversial authenticity decisions, including the double denial of validation of a Warhol self-portrait prepared by a silkscreen factory that may or may not have been created at Andy Warhol's (1928–1987) direction.[8] This decision by the Warhol authentication board resulted in a lengthy lawsuit, *Simon-Whelan v. The Andy Warhol Foundation for the Visual Arts*, commenced in 2007, and involved an array of claims, including antitrust claims, lodged against the foundation by the owner of the purported Warhol.[9] The legal defense for this case alone cost the Warhol Foundation more than $6 million (legal costs that the foundation was unable to recover from the plaintiff Joe Simon-Whelan, despite the fact that the plaintiff eventually abandoned his claim against the foundation).

The artwork that was the subject of this lawsuit was a silkscreened Warhol self-portrait that was one of an edition of ten prepared by a silkscreen factory. There is a dispute over whether the series was created at Warhol's direction. This artwork was first sold in 1987 at a Christie's auction. Prior to the auction, Christie's sought and received authentication of the silkscreen from the Warhol estate. A trustee of the Warhol Foundation, Vincent Fremont, confirmed the authenticity by stamping the work with Warhol's signature. One year later, a dealer interested in buying the silkscreen sought and received additional confirmation of the work's authenticity: Fred Hughes, executor of Warhol's estate and Chairman of the Warhol Foundation, inscribed on the edge of the painting, "I certify that this is an original painting by Andy Warhol completed by him in 1964." The work changed hands again when Simon-Whelan purchased it in 1989 for $195,000. In 2001 he decided to sell it. He submitted the work to the Andy Warhol Art Authentication Board for authentication and for inclusion in the Warhol catalogue raisonné. The board rejected the authenticity of the work and stamped "DENIED" on the back of the work. Simon-Whelan subsequently amassed evidence for the authentication of the work and once again submitted the silkscreen to the board for approval. The board, however, denied the work's authenticity and once again stamped "DENIED" on the back.

Simon-Whelan then sued the Warhol Foundation, the Warhol Authentication Board, and the successor executor of the Warhol estate in a New York federal district court for failing to authenticate his silkscreen, alleging, among other claims, that they had violated Sections 1 and 2 of the Sherman Antitrust Act. More specifically, he alleged that the defendants had unlawfully conspired to refuse authentication of his and other works of art so that those rejected works would be eliminated from the marketplace, and thus to intentionally inflate the value of the Warhol works owned by the Warhol Foundation and the other defendants. He asserted that the authentication board was dominated and controlled by the foundation, which the board used as a tool to remove competing Warhols from the market in an attempt at "monopolization."

Although the defendants moved to dismiss the complaint for failure to state a claim (a defense asserting that even if all the factual allegations in a complaint are true, they are insufficient to establish a cause of action), the court denied the motion and permitted Simon-Whelan's antitrust claims to proceed. What was the court's line of reasoning? First, the court found that the complaint's antitrust claims under the Sherman Antitrust Act were sufficiently plausible in that the plaintiff had adequately alleged facts pointing to anticompetitive conduct with a specific objective to monopolize and a probability of achieving such monopoly power. Next, the court noted that the complaint had alleged that the anticompetitive activities took place within both a relevant product market and a relevant geographic market. Third, the court found that the plaintiff had successfully alleged antitrust injury: that is, he was prevented from competing as a seller in the lucrative market for Warhols because the authentication board had twice stamped "DENIED" on his artwork, which helped further the alleged antitrust conspiracy. Finally, the court found that Simon-Whelan's antitrust claims were timely because he had alleged sufficient facts to invoke the "continuing conspiracy exception" to the four-year statute of limitations for antitrust claims based on the board's second denial of authenticity. Consequently, after having evaluated approximately 6,000 pieces over a fifteen-year period, during which time the foundation and board found itself mired in a number of other authentication controversies, the foundation determined that, in the current legal climate, it should dissolve its authentication board and concentrate its resources on grant-making and other charitable activities.[10]

When authenticators are silenced, the results can be problematic. In 2011, the Knoedler Gallery, a distinguished art gallery in Manhattan that had been in business for 165 years, closed its doors. The gallery and its director, Ann Freedman, were subsequently sued in ten cases by collectors who had bought fakes through the gallery, including works purportedly by the artists Jackson Pollock, Clyfford Still, Willem de Kooning, and Mark Rothko.[11] The Knoedler Gallery had acquired the modernist "masterpieces" from a little-known art dealer on Long Island, New York, named Glafira Rosales, who apparently sold some sixty-three works to Knoedler and one other art dealer between 1994 and 2009. The works were all new to the market, and it is alleged that Rosales was not forthcoming about the ownership history of the cache of works. A number of art experts who authenticated some of the works were paid undisclosed consulting fees by Knoedler.[12] Other scholars privately identified a few of the works as being fakes, but were instructed by attorneys to remain silent to avoid being sued by Knoedler.[13] After many of the works had been sold, the FBI commenced an investigation based on the opinions of several experts who, when the works that were the subjects of lawsuits had been submitted for a determination of authenticity after they were sold, either questioned their authorship or denounced the works as fake. It is likely that the purchasers of such works from Knoedler would have agreed to indemnify such experts for any claims or causes of action asserted against such experts for their rendering of the authenticity opinions. Rosales allegedly was paid $33.2 million for the fakes, and the galleries allegedly sold them into the stream of commerce for $80.7 million.[14] She was arrested in May 2013, and later that year pleaded guilty to tax evasion and money laundering. She confessed that the paintings were created by Pei-Shen Qian, a Chinese immigrant artist living in Queens, New York. Qian was indicted but fled to China and is currently believed to be in Shanghai.[15] While Ann Freedman has settled the last of the ten lawsuits against her arising out of the forgery scandal, at the time of writing two lawsuits against the Knoedler Gallery are ongoing.[16]

WHAT ABOUT INSURANCE?

In today's litigious environment, the trend of many art foundations has been to entirely dissolve their authentication boards (some examples include the Pollock-Krasner Foundation, the Andy Warhol Foundation for the Visual Arts, the Roy Lichtenstein Foundation, the Estate of Jean-Michel Basquiat, and the Keith Haring Foundation) in the face of the risks of cost and time posed by litigation.[17] What possible solutions are there to this dilemma? Carrying liability insurance is one possible solution, but on its own it does not guarantee protection. For example, in the *Simon-Whelan* lawsuit, the Warhol Foundation's insurer, the Philadelphia Indemnity Insurance Company (PIIC), initially denied coverage but ultimately agreed to pay the full limit of $2 million of defense fees under its Errors and Omissions policy, but nothing under its Directors and Officers policy. This gave rise to further litigation by the foundation against the PIIC to recover the remaining balance of its defense costs: $4.6 million plus interest.[18] The lawsuit ultimately resulted in a settlement whereby six years after the foundation was sued by Simon-Whelan, PIIC reportedly paid the foundation the "lion's share" of the remaining cost.[19]

In addition to not guaranteeing protection, liability insurance can be particularly burdensome to an individual authenticator. An insurance provider can require the art professional to establish and maintain a loss-prevention program to help minimize the chance of a professional-liability claim being brought against the expert in the first place. Among elements of such a loss-prevention program would be the following: using engagement letters, contracts, and other means to precisely identify the scope of services to be performed; keeping written documentation of all activity, including telephone calls, billing calculations, and the like; participating in peer reviews, when feasible; and avoiding giving specific warranties and similar performance guarantees.[20]

Adherence to all of these elements can be burdensome to authenticators, particularly those with modest incomes, such as scholars, who practice their profession solo. Moreover, alleged noncompliance with even one of the above elements might cause an insurance carrier to "justify" withholding compensation payments from an authenticator who is sued. Therefore, while liability coverage for the art authenticator may be advisable (it can work well in conjunction with proposed legislation to be discussed below), it is unable to function as a stand-alone substitute for such legislation.

PROPOSED SOLUTION—THE NEW YORK LEGISLATION

To uphold and enhance the integrity of art market transactions, it is essential to foster an environment that allows art experts to render opinions about the authorship of artworks and "visual art multiples."[21] The New York City Bar (City Bar), through its Art Law Committee, of which this writer is a member, has proposed that an effective way to encourage art experts to practice their profession is through legislation designed to accord greater protection to art experts who render good faith authenticity opinions on works of art, including multiples. Yet, at the same time and in keeping with public policy, the City Bar recommends that the courts should be accessible to all parties so as not to deter meritorious lawsuits brought against such authenticators under New York state law.

Accordingly, the City Bar has approved legislation drafted by its Art Law Committee, which had been a Bill pending in the New York State Legislature in its 2017 session under bipartisan sponsorship. The Bill had sponsorship in both the New York State Assembly and the New York State Senate. This is the third time that the Bill had been introduced in the state legislature and, just as in the two preceding legislative sessions, the Bill once again passed the New York State Senate by a vote of 61 to 1, and remained stalled in committee in the Assembly, where it is still being analyzed. Although the 2017 legislative session, which runs from January through June, has effectively ended, the Bill can continue its legislative path in January 2018, where it will have to be voted on again in the Senate (where passage, as in the previous three sessions, seems certain). The challenge is moving the Bill out of committee in the Assembly. As of the time of writing, the Art Law Committee of the City Bar plans to regroup, perhaps do a touch of rethinking on the Bill, and at the same time continue to work to raise the volume of the Bill's already sizable industry support.

ELEMENTS OF THE BILL

The Bill addresses important deficiencies in the provisions of the New York Arts and Cultural Affairs Law (NYACAL), the state statute that governs art transactions in New York State. The key deficiency of the statute is the absence of protections under the law for the valuable work of authenticators who render independent, good-faith opinions about the authenticity, attribution, and authorship of works of art.

Who Is an Authenticator?

The Bill adds a broad definition of "authenticator" to Article 11 (the Definitions Article) of NYACAL to protect a wide range of experts. An "authenticator" includes authors of catalogues raisonnés or other scholarly texts as well as other persons or entities recognized in the visual-arts community as having expertise regarding the artist, work of fine art, or visual art multiple with respect to which the authenticator renders an opinion as to authenticity, attribution, or authorship. "Authenticator" also includes persons or entities recognized in the visual-arts or scientific communities who have expertise in uncovering facts (such as forensic scientists) that serve as a direct basis for an authenticity or authorship opinion about a work of art. The definition of "authenticator" expressly excludes any person or entity with a financial interest in the work being evaluated, other than to be compensated for the rendering of the opinion.

Requirement of the Claimant

The Bill adds a section to the law that would help prevent frivolous or meritless lawsuits. Section 15.12 to Article 15 of NYACAL would require a claimant, in any civil action brought against an authenticator for the expert's opinion or information concerning a work of art, to specify in the complaint facts sufficient to support each element of each claim. This requirement would effectively expose a frivolous or meritless lawsuit, such as the earlier-noted case of *Ravenna v. Christie's*—the case in which the New York state courts dismissed a complaint alleging "negligent misrepresentation" in the misattribution by Christie's and its expert of a work by Carracci on the grounds that the plaintiff was unable to set forth any special relationship of trust and confidence requisite to sustain an action under that theory of liability.[22]

Cost/Fee-Shifting in Favor of the Art Expert:
Finally, the Bill amends Subdivision 4 of Section 15.15 to create Subdivisions 4(a), (b), and (c). Subdivision 4(a) refers to the already existing discretion of the court to award court costs and fees to a prevailing purchaser of visual art multiples. Subdivision 4(b) permits this same discretion to the court with respect to a prevailing authenticator in an action arising from an authenticator's authenticity opinion about a work, subject to the proviso that such costs and fees may only be awarded if the court finds good and just cause for the award, as specified in a written finding. Subdivision 4(c) merely makes it clear that the already existing discretion of the court to award court costs and fees to an art merchant does not extend to actions brought against an art authenticator with respect to the authenticator's opinion or information regarding a visual art multiple or work of fine art.

UNSILENCING THE AUTHENTICATORS

The Bill has the support of an array of art-market constituents, among them museums of both regional and international stature, multiple trade associations involving appraisers, and art dealers and the International Foundation for Art Research. The passage of this legislation would be unique in the United States. It is fitting that New York, the art capital of the United States and a leading center of the worldwide art market, should be a pioneer in creating incentives for art experts to render authenticity opinions without fear, thereby enhancing the integrity of art transactions conducted in New York State and perhaps serving as a model for other states to enact similar legislation.

Artistic Authorship, Legacy, and Expert Liability in the French Art Market

CORINNE HERSHKOVITCH

Authentication of a work of art by an expert entails respecting the artist's right of attribution by crediting the artist as being the author of his or her work when the author is no longer alive or able to perform this role. When experts accept this task, they become potentially legally liable, as their authentication or certification can drastically impact a work's artistic and economic value. The value of the authorship or authenticity of works of art—the idea that a work of art was created by the artist under whose name it is presented—is of growing importance as the global art market becomes broader and increasingly financialized.

Certification of a work's authenticity—the official warrant that a work is authentic—is indeed often one of the necessary conditions for it to be traded on the market, and for it to reach its best price. For example, after buying a work in 1965 attributed to Jean-Michel Atlan from the Parisian dealer Abel Rosenberg, the new owner sued the artist's authentication committee for refusing to issue a certificate, claiming, accurately, that this refusal significantly reduced the work's market value. The French court did not order the committee to issue a certificate on the grounds that the refusal was not abusive as there was no malice, but it did not contest the fact that the work's value had suffered as a result.[1] In a more recent yet similar case that is discussed in detail below, the court condemned the authenticity certificate issuer to a fine, unless it delivered the said certificate, thus confirming the idea that a certificate does have an impact on market value and salability.[2]

Those responsible for stating whether deceased artists' works are authentic or not (including sellers, experts, and artists' authentication committees) must therefore respond to both this increase in the market for certification and to legal actions brought by traders or collectors who are disappointed, or who consider that they have been misled. Yet who prevails in such legal disputes: the expert or the collector? Furthermore, in such disputes, what protection do moral rights of authorship provide for the artists' estates and experts authenticating artworks? To understand the legal environment surrounding art authentication in France today, we must, first, examine the criteria that enable authenticity to be assessed; second, determine the "experts" qualified to state whether particular works are authentic; third, assess the legal liabilities authenticators may incur; and fourth, consider the latitude given to the holder of the moral rights of an artist or the author of the artist's catalogue raisonné in an expert's assessment of authenticity.

THE AUTHENTICATION PROCESS

To reach a judgment concerning an artwork's authenticity, an expert must undertake a stylistic analysis of the work. Traditionally, the expert does a close visual examination of the work, seeking to discover, through his or her deep knowledge of the artist's practice, signs of the artist's hand or expressions of the artist's personality by comparing it to other certified works or sketches by the same artist and analyzing elements such as brushstrokes and the use of color, light, and contrast. However, for contemporary artworks in which production and performance are delegated by the artist to others, or for works that can in theory be replicated endlessly without individuation (for example, Andy Warhol's *Brillo Boxes* or Dan Flavin's light works), the notion of "authorization" is often much more important and meaningful for authentication than any stylistic analysis.

In addition to a stylistic evaluation, techniques of scientific analysis —such as an analysis of the pigments used by the artist in the paint, a search for clues to date the work, or x-radiography, in particular—can contribute decisive elements in assessing the authenticity of a work.

For example, if in a paint layer a pigment is found that did not exist on the date an artwork was supposed to have been produced, or if any other dating clue reveals a production date after the claimed date of the work, its authenticity can be called into doubt. Conversely, an x-ray of a painting that shows a drawing under the paint layer—a pentimento—could confirm the work's authenticity.

Finally, the expert must search for clues in the provenance (or history of ownership) of the work that may reveal something about its history, enabling its authenticity to be accredited or, on the contrary, to be discredited. For example, if the work can be traced back as far as the atelier of the artist, or if one of its identified owners had a close personal link with the artist, an expert might be able to conclude more easily that the work is indeed by the artist. To support an opinion on authenticity, the expert must analyze these various elements and justify the way in which he or she came to a conclusion.

WHO IS AN ART EXPERT?

Art experts are individuals, usually professionals, who specialize in a certain artist, historic period, or technique and analyze works of art, providing insight on them. They can volunteer authenticity opinions and, in some cases, certify the authorship of specific works. Museums, commercial galleries, auction houses, and courts of law rely on art experts to provide analysis of a work of art, and to present a professional opinion on whether a work was made by a particular artist—that is, on the work's authenticity. These experts generally practice their profession alongside auctioneers and gallerists, and they help produce sales catalogues, which often include a stylistic analysis, provenance, exhibition history, and a list of published references for each work of art, in addition to the basic information such as attribution and date. Despite various legislative attempts, the profession of "art expert" is not regulated in France.[3] There are three main categories of art experts: art historians, the holders of the artist's moral rights, and authentication committees. All three of these groups have formed self-regulating bodies to protect the title of "expert," which they attempt to do by imposing on their members conditions of age, professional experience, ethical conduct, and knowledge.

An art historian who has an extensive knowledge of the work of an artist can be recognized by the market and by colleagues as the most qualified specialist on an artist and, consequently, can often be the only "legitimate" person to express an authoritative type of opinion concerning the authenticity of works attributed to that artist. This type of specialist may also be the author of the artist's catalogue raisonné, which is a book that lists all of an artist's known works, with details such as title, date, description, and, when possible, a photograph.

The second type of expert—the person who holds the artist's moral rights—can also be considered a legitimate authenticator, or might claim the power to authenticate the work of the artist. Once an artist has passed, his or her will might name someone as the moral-rights holder; in the absence of such a designation, the moral rights are held by the artist's inheritors as specified by law. Holders of moral rights frequently maintain the artist's archives and assert that they are the persons best able to recognize the signs of the artist's personality, due to their intimate acquaintance with the artist. They often claim a discretionary right to state whether or not a work is authentic. Artist's moral rights of authorship are very strong in France. They are perpetual, inalienable, imprescriptible, and transferable upon death to the author's inheritors. The right of attribution, one of the four types of moral rights granted to artists by the French Intellectual Property Code, is the right for an artist to be credited as the work's author.[4] This right is inalienable, which means that however harmful for the vendor or owner of an artwork, authenticity certificates that were issued by anyone other than the artist can be invalidated if the works are proven to be by another hand.

The third category of expert—the authentication committee, or authentication board—entered the scene more recently. Set up to ensure that an analysis and attribution for a work will stand the test of time, and in an attempt at professionalization, authentication committees are made up of professionals from the various disciplines related to the authentication process, such as art historians, art-restoration specialists, and conservation scientists. The beneficiaries of the artist, and holders of moral rights, can also be associated with authentication boards, contribute the artist's archives to them, and give them their moral approval.

Some of the experts who assist auctioneers in producing sales catalogues also choose to use their knowledge to serve justice as a court-appointed expert.[5] When a dispute concerning the authenticity of a work is referred to a court, it may appoint someone from a list of court experts, in the specialty related to the work in dispute, and ask them to issue an opinion on the work's authenticity. Because such a wide range of people may be responsible for declaring whether or not works are authentic, inevitably there are contradictory opinions on the authenticity of a work, and the courts must manage these contradictions, as will be shown below through recent case-law examples.

THE EXPERT'S LEGAL LIABILITY

An expert's legal liability depends on whether the opinion of authenticity is stated with a view to a sale or by an expert outside of any trial, or alternatively in the context of a legal action. In France all vendors of works of art, whether a professional or an occasional vendor, are subject to the provisions of decree no. 81-255 of March 3, 1981.[6] The provisions of this decree grant the purchaser a guarantee concerning the name of the work, its epoch, and its authorship as expressed through the artist's signature. The vendor assumes statutory liability in relation to the authenticity and the elements comprising it, both with regard to its buyer and to third parties, on the basis of liability in tort, and contractual liability with regard to the seller.[7] Most court cases are initiated by purchasers, who consider themselves to have been misled about one of the claimed qualities of a work, and who thus bring an action to declare the sale invalid due to an error relating to one of the work's essential qualities.[8] If the court declares that the sale is invalid, the work must be returned to the vendor and the sale price returned to the purchaser. When the object has been sold in a public auction, liability is assumed by the auctioneer and any expert whose services the auction house has enlisted in producing the sales catalogue, and they will therefore be ordered to repay, at minimum, the commissions received when the auction sale took place.[9] To summarize, French law favors the buyer over the seller of the artwork, and over the expert, if the buyer is relying on the expert's judgment. Conversely, if the seller is relying upon an expert to authenticate an artwork, then the law clearly states that the seller can also bring an action for failure to authenticate properly when the work was sold in a public auction, and presumably also when the sale occurred in another context.[10]

It is interesting to note that in France the term "expert" covers all those who, due to their extensive knowledge of the work or their link with the artist, issue certificates of authenticity. When a certificate of authenticity is issued in this manner, its author therefore assumes liability, whether or not they are professionals. The Paris Appeal Court thus judged, in a ruling of March 22, 2005, that in the absence of regulation on the "expert" title, any person who certifies without reserve the authenticity of a work of art assumes liability on the basis of this assertion alone.[11]

In a trial, the court-appointed expert must inform the judge about any factual aspects of the dispute that require a technician's knowledge. Because judges are not art experts, they are not capable of forming a judgment concerning the authenticity of a work, despite the essential role played by authenticity (or lack thereof) in the outcome of the dispute. It is only after having acquired a degree of certainty regarding the authenticity of the work in dispute that a judge will adjudicate the application to declare a sale invalid. The role of the court expert is therefore very important in the context of legal proceedings, even though the judge is not bound by the expert's conclusions and may disregard his or her opinion. The expert's liability in the law of tort can be engaged if he makes any professional mistakes in analyzing a work of art.[12]

THE EXPERT, THE CATALOGUE RAISONNÉ, AND FREEDOM OF EXPRESSION

The liability of authors of catalogues raisonnés is more complex, because they are protected as authors by the right of freedom of expression, as recent developments in French case law have confirmed. The Court of Cassation (the supreme court in France) noted, in two judgments issued respectively on March 13, 2008, and December 1, 2011, that requiring an author of a catalogue raisonné to include a work that he or she judged inauthentic did not inhibit freedom of expression nor prejudice the moral rights of the author of the catalogue, since the author was able to stipulate that this insertion was dictated to them by a legal ruling and "did not therefore imply that the author agreed with this view."[13] The court therefore considered "that such a measure is necessary and in proportion to the outcome sought," that is, the comprehensiveness of the catalogue raisonné.[14] This meant that the market for an artist's work could not be ruled by just one expert, as he would have to accept the court's ruling on authenticity by integrating works he may not consider authentic, enabling said work's value not to plummet automatically. However, the author of the catalogue could voice his or her opinion, as the expert was authorized to mention that he or she was obliged to include the work in the catalogue. The market could then decide whether to trust the catalogue's author or the judge's ruling.

THE MAX ERNST CASE

Werner Spies, author of the Max Ernst catalogue raisonné, is considered to be the leading specialist on the artist's work. In July 2002 he was consulted about *Earthquake* (1925), a painting attributed to Ernst (1891–1976). He wrote on the back of the painting's photo: "The reproduced work, *Earthquake*, . . . will appear in the catalogue raisonné to be published under my direction."[15]

The painting was acquired two years later through a Parisian gallery by Monte Carlo Art, which sold the work at auction through Sotheby's New York in 2009. An investigation conducted by the German police revealed that the painting was a forgery made by a German painter, Wolfang Beltracchi. Monte Carlo Art sued the Parisian gallery and Werner Spies to obtain a reimbursement for the painting. The Tribunal of Grande Instance of Nanterre ruled that since Spies is seen as the leading specialist on Ernst's work, he is responsible for the authenticity opinion he issued on the painting, which had an influence on the buyer's decision to acquire the painting.[16] The tribunal condemned Spies to reimburse the buyer for its loss. The French Court of Appeal overturned the judgment issued by the Tribunal and released Spies of its liability.[17] The appeals court decided that, since Werner Spies's authenticity opinion was issued two years before and was not linked to the sale of the painting to Monte Carlo Art, his opinion cannot be considered as a certificate issued at the occasion of a sale.

THE METZINGER LITIGATION

In a recent case concerning an authenticity opinion given by Bozena Nikiel, the holder of the moral rights for the Cubist artist Jean Metzinger (1883–1956) and the author of his catalogue raisonné, the Court of Cassation ruled to protect the freedom of expression of catalogue raisonné authors further. As the holder of the artist's moral rights, Nikiel is responsible for authenticating works by Metzinger and holds the right to prevent false attribution. The case was in relation to *Maison blanche*, a work that belonged to Laurent Alexandre. Alexandre had inherited this painting from a collector and claimed that it had been purchased on the advice of a museum curator, who was a great expert on the artist, which supposedly accredited its authenticity. Alexandre decided to sell the painting, and it was submitted to an expert by the auction house, who concluded the work was authentic before its presentation in a public auction. It was purchased for a closing bid of €60,000, on the buyer's condition that the author of the catalogue raisonné and holder of the artist's moral rights issue a certificate of authenticity for it.

Nikiel examined the work and refused to issue such a certificate, judging that it was a forgery. Alexandre and his expert were furious to have been denied the opportunity of selling the painting for the above sale price and applied to the court to appoint a court expert with the assignment of providing a judgment concerning the work's authenticity. The court expert produced a report, in which he concluded that the work *Maison blanche* was most likely authentic, justifying his opinion by the comparison he had made between the work in dispute and a painting owned by a Parisian gallery, which was deemed to be authentic. Nikiel maintained her position, noting that the museum curator who had supposedly recommended the purchase of the work had died ten years before the purchase, and, in any event, that a comparison with a single work by a particular artist deemed to be authentic was not evidentially sufficient to demonstrate that the work in dispute was authentic. Following this, the vendor and the expert summoned Nikiel before the Paris High Court for liability, seeking damages. In a judgment of May 27, 2011, the court ordered Nikiel to pay Alexandre the sum of €10,000 in damages for his loss of opportunity to sell his painting as an authentic work by Metzinger and ordered publication of the judgment.[18]

On appeal, the Paris Appeal Court (in a judgment given on October 12, 2012) found that the work was on balance authentic, as a consequence of the clues and corroborating opinions obtained by the court expert tending toward this conclusion.[19] Applying prior case law of the Court of Cassation in this field (the above-mentioned judgments of March 13, 2008, and December 1, 2011), the Paris Appeal Court held that since the authenticity of the painting *Maison blanche* has been legally acknowledged, Alexandre was economically prejudiced by the work's omission from Nikiel's catalogue raisonné of Metzintger's work. The court assessed damages to Laurent Alexandre at €30,000, to be payable by Bozena Nikiel, unless she issued to Alexandre, within one month following notification of the judgment, the required certificate of authenticity, coupled with an undertaking to have the painting included in the catalogue raisonné of the works of Jean Metzinger, as specifically requested.[20] Though Nikiel was the author of the catalogue raisonné and furthermore the holder of the moral rights in Metzinger's work, and, as such, responsible for defending the integrity of the artist's work and for opposing forgeries, she was ordered by the legal ruling, and under penalty of paying the owner a sum of €30,000, to insert the disputed work in her catalogue, and to issue Alexandre with a certificate of authenticity intended to enable the work to be traded on the market and reach its best price.

Nikiel appealed against the ruling. She asked the Court of Cassation to acknowledge her right to freedom of expression and, consequently, her right not to be compelled to issue a certificate, and therefore not to be obligated to insert the disputed painting in her catalogue raisonné of Metzinger's work. On January 22, 2014, the first civil division of the Court of Cassation, applying article 10 of the European Convention on Human Rights (ECHR), reversed and quashed the appeal judgment. The new ruling held that the exercise of the right of freedom of speech can only be considered abusive in cases specifically determined by law and decided consequently that the Paris Appeal Court had breached the ECHR "by ruling in this manner when the refusal of the author of a catalogue raisonné to insert a work in it, even if it is authentic, may not, in the absence of a specific piece of legislation, be considered to be wrongful."[21]

Why did the court reverse its earlier ruling? Commenting on the court's judgment, Christophe Caron, a prominent intellectual-property law professor, argues that the basis for the reversal is not to be found in the fact that Nikiel held the artist's moral rights: "It is true that the author of the catalogue raisonné was also the holder of the postmortem moral right. But case law has already found that the moral right held by beneficiaries in order to defend the work does not give them discretionary power over its authentication."[22] Instead, Caron explains the ruling by the Court of Cassation's application of the right of freedom of expression, as both enshrined in article 10 of the ECHR and independently in the French constitution (see article 11 of the Declaration of Human and Civic Rights of 1789, and the preamble of the constitution of the 5th Republic of 1958).[23] In prior rulings, the supreme court had considered it to be a proportionate interference with freedom of expression, by requiring the author of the catalogue to include a disputed work in a catalogue raisonné, yet granting her the possibility of stipulating that this insertion was the consequence of a legal ruling with which she was not in agreement. By contrast, the court was careful to stress in its judgment of January 22, 2014, that, according to the provisions of article 10 of the ECHR, only a specific piece of legislation could limit the freedom of the author of the catalogue (and such legislation does not exist in France).

Whereas in its earlier decisions the Court of Cassation had applied the rules of tort liability strictly (based on the general provisions of article 1382 of the French civil code), and so allowed itself to limit the freedom of the author of the catalogue raisonné, the court in January 2014 made a literal interpretation of article 10 of the ECHR, considering that only a specific legislation could limit freedom of expression.[24] Art experts must still act with professional and ethical responsibility: they must remain aware of the judgment of their peers and of the art market and take care to maintain the credibility of the catalogue, while staying neutral in their assessment of the authenticity of the works attributed to the artist and seeking to achieve comprehensiveness by a compromise of their own standards and that of the experts' majority opinion. Following this ruling of the supreme court, the Versailles Appeal Court, ruling pursuant to referral after partial reversal of the appeal judgment of October 12, 2012, followed the position of the supreme court and set aside the judgment given by the Paris High Court on May 27, 2011, dismissing all Laurent Alexandre's applications for compensation with regard to Bozena Nikiel.[25]

As French law currently stands, the author of a catalogue raisonné on an artist's work has, by virtue of freedom of expression, a discretionary power over the contents of his or her book. It remains to be seen whether this important precedent will be followed outside of France, in other countries where freedom of expression is protected. In particular, it will be interesting to see how things unfold in other European states that are signatories to the European Convention on Human Rights and its protection of freedom of expression as outlined in article 10, and in the United States, which also protects freedom of expression by virtue of the First Amendment of the Constitution.

Authentication and the Italian Art Market

GIUSEPPE CALABI

Disputes over the authenticity of artworks are becoming increasingly frequent in the international modern and contemporary art market today. Because of ever-increasing financial stakes, the market arguably demands greater reliability and certainty regarding opinions on authenticity. The Italian art market is no different and has also been subject to high-profile authenticity controversies.

In July 2017 the Italian Carabinieri spectacularly closed an exhibition dedicated to Amedeo Modigliani (1884–1920) held at the Palazzo Ducale, in Genoa, on the grounds that a staggering twenty-one of the sixty "Modigliani" paintings featured in the show were believed by the Italian authorities to be fakes. The legal grounds of the criminal investigation included grand larceny, money laundering, and art forgery. The Court of Genoa ordered the seizure of the paintings and appointed an expert to comment on their authenticity. In January 2018 the court-appointed expert confirmed that all of the seized paintings are fake, but legal proceedings are still pending and the private lenders are expected to file counter-claims. In short, this hotly debated matter is far from being resolved.

Authenticity issues are addressed differently depending on the laws of the country where disputes arise. This essay gives an overview of the legal issues that are commonly faced by private collectors and art-market professionals in Italy in relation to the authentication of artworks. It first deals with the rights of heirs and foundations to authenticate; second, it assesses the role of experts and certificates of authenticity; finally, it provides analysis of three specific cases.

MORAL RIGHTS

Under Italian law, when an artist dies, the artist's moral rights of authorship may only be exercised by that deceased artist's relatives and descendants, and not by third parties such as galleries or foundations. This has important consequences for the authentication of artworks. Foundations and third parties may also authenticate, yet their authentication is not based on moral rights, but on the authority and prestige of the authenticator, as well as on the principle of freedom of expression as enshrined in article 21 of the Italian Constitution. Moral rights of authorship are protected under the Berne Convention (1888), which provides that "independently of the author's economic rights, and even after the transfer of the said rights, the author shall have the right to claim authorship of the work and to object to any distortion, mutilation or other modification of, or other derogatory action in relation to, the said work, which would be prejudicial to his honor or reputation."[1] Moral rights are recognized in Italy by copyright law enacted in 1941.[2]

Moral rights give recognition to the artist's personality as expressed in his or her work and accrue to the artist, rather than to the artwork itself. In short, instead of monopolizing the monetary gain arising from a work, moral rights are meant to protect the artist's reputation. Since moral rights protect the personality of the creator of a work, under Italian law they can neither be transferred to a third party while the artist is alive (inter vivos), nor be bequeathed; they are indeed personal to the author. This inalienability is probably the most controversial feature of the law of moral rights in Italy.

Moral rights include: the right of attribution, the right to integrity, and the right of first publication. The "right of attribution," is the authors' right to claim authorship of their works; in other words, it is the artist's right to have his/her name associated with his/her creation. It also includes the author's right to object to the false attribution of authorship.[3] The "right to integrity" is the right to prevent any deformation, mutilation, or alteration of the work, and any act that may damage the work itself and thereby diminish the artist's reputation and honor. The artist is entitled to challenge any physical alteration that may affect the work, as well as any representation of the work that might falsify its perception from the public. Since a work of art is an expression of the artist's personality, any alteration, mutilation, or misrepresentation of the work negatively affects the artist's personality in itself, as well as his/her artistic identity, personality, and honor.[4] The "right to first publication" of the work includes the right to decide when and where to publish it, and the right to disclose the author's identity or to publish the work under a pseudonym.

Under Italian law, unlike copyright, moral rights are perpetual in duration. Consequently, there is no statute of limitation for the protection of such rights. Under article 23 of Italian copyright law, moral rights may be invoked by the descendants and any living next of kin of the author without time limits. In the name of "public interest," the Ministry of Cultural Heritage is entitled to invoke moral rights on behalf of deceased artists and in theory could exercise rights on behalf of artists going back to the Renaissance. Descendants and any of the author's next of kin are entitled to exercise the deceased author's moral rights by operation of law whether they are named by the artist's will as heirs or not.

In contrast to other European countries such as France, where the law provides that third parties (including institutions and foundations) may inherit and be entitled to exercise the author's moral rights, in Italy such rights may only be exercised by relatives and descendants.[5] Thus, when an artist does not have any descendants and/or names a legal entity as his or her heir (for example, a foundation or an association), the named legal entity is not entitled to exercise any moral rights under Italian copyright law.

Despite this, an artist's foundation might be established with the scope of protecting the artist's legacy. Italian case law has recognized that artists' foundations are entitled to take legal action against any counterfeited or plagiarized works. But foundations do not have the "exclusive" right to claim or deny the authorship of the artist's work.[6] Instead, Italian artists' foundations are entitled to release authenticity certificates, whether they are established by the artist (for example, Fondazione Enrico Castellani) or by one of his relatives (Archivio Luciano Fabro, Fondazione Lucio Fontana, Fondazione Piero Manzoni, Associazione Paolo Scheggi, Archivio Mario Schifano). However, such certificates are considered mere opinions, even though the market attributes paramount importance to such opinions in order to establish the authenticity of an artwork.

Problems also arise under Italian law when there are competing heirs claiming ownership of a deceased artist's moral rights. According to established Italian case law, whenever there is more than one relative of the same degree of kinship, each said relative may separately exercise the right.[7] This can lead to controversies, since each of the relatives may take different legal actions in order to differently protect their ancestor's work (as has occurred in France for example, between members of Victor Vasarely's family, resulting in the judgment of the Paris Court of Appeal of March 24, 2005).

CERTIFICATES OF AUTHENTICITY AND THE EXPERT OPINION

Authenticity is key to all art transactions. Italian law states that any professional seller of an artwork must provide documentation attesting to the authenticity and provenance of the work up for sale or, at least, the likely attribution and provenance of the work to the purchaser.[8] A document attesting to the authenticity of an artwork is not necessarily a certificate of authenticity issued by the artist or the artist's foundation. It can simply be a certificate issued by a dealer or an "expert."[9]

With regard to modern and contemporary artworks, normally the market acknowledges who is an authoritative expert, including the artist, the artist's estate or foundation, or an expert on the artist's work. Without a certificate issued by the artist or the artist's foundation or, in case the latter decides not to issue any certificates, without the registration in the artist's archive or the listing in the artist's catalogue raisonné, it is unlikely that the artwork would be accepted on consignment by professional auctioneers or art dealers.[10] Furthermore, some artists' archives register artworks but do not issue authenticity certificates because they fear that such certificates may be counterfeited. In other words, artists' foundations and archives can be considered the gatekeepers of the market of the artworks of the deceased artist.

Without prejudice to the authentication rights of artists or their descendants, any art historian or expert has the right to express his or her opinion regarding the authenticity (or the attribution) of a work of art. This is because, under Italian law, any expert's statement is considered as an opinion protected by article 21 of the Italian Constitution, which recognizes the right of any person to freely express his or her opinion. If the right to authenticate is enshrined as a fundamental right in the Italian Constitution, the authenticating subject (such as an artist's foundation or archive) cannot be obliged to give an opinion, let alone to issue an authenticity certificate. Furthermore, under Italian law it would be challenging for an owner to take legal action against those (for example, a foundation or an archive) who, by expressing their opinion, deny the authenticity of a work or refuse to insert it in their archive.

For instance, on January 4, 2018, the Court of Milan ruled that the Fondazione Fontana was entitled to deny the authenticity of an artwork allegedly attributed to Fontana based on the report of a court-appointed expert witness report.[11] The expert witness had essentially based their negative opinion on connoisseurship, and the court entirely relied on this report.

The Court of Rome, in a case concerning Tano Festa's archive, ruled that the artist's descendants are not the only subjects entitled to give an opinion on the authenticity of the artist's works.[12] Consequently, any person may be an expert, with no prejudice to the right of the artist and, after his or her passing, of each next of kin to claim the paternity of the artwork, whether or not wrongfully attributed, or vice versa, to deny the attribution to the artist. The expert who is entrusted to carry out a valuation, attribution, or authentication of a work of art must operate under an obligation of due care and diligence in his authentication process. Conversely, an expert will only be liable for his or her opinion if it can be proven in court that the refusal to authenticate a work or insert it in the archive is affected by willful misconduct or gross negligence.

While giving their expert opinions, experts may both rely on traditional valuation methods (such as the historical context, stylistic analysis, and existing literature) and avail themselves of modern scientific techniques (including microscopic analysis, infrared reflectography, and infrared spectroscopy). Regardless of the means they use, experts are required to demonstrate that their opinion relies upon a solid methodology, otherwise the accuracy of such opinion may be challenged in court on the legal basis set out above.[13]

CASE STUDY 1: SCHIFANO

The Schifano Foundation was established in 1998 after the death of Mario Schifano (1934–1998) by Schifano's widow, Monica De Bei, and Monte Arte Titano, the artist's last entrusted art dealer, and since then the foundation has been involved in various legal cases. In *Monica De Bei, Giuseppe Schifano, Fondazione Schifano v. Anna Maria Marieni Governatori, Roberto Girardi*, the Italian court recognized the standing of the foundation (whose scope is to protect and enhance the artist's legacy) to take legal action against third parties, specifically, Anna Maria Marieni Governatori and Roberto Girardi, who had been carrying out the authentication and cataloguing of the artist's work without having been authorized by the descendant and the widow (Monica De Bei) of the artist.[14] Moreover, the court's judgment stated that this authentication activity was in conflict with the authorship rights granted to the artist and his heirs by Italian copyright law and, therefore, that such activity could only be exercised with the consent of the author or his heirs.

Schifano's legacy is one of the most controversial artistic legacies, since after the abovementioned case, the heirs left the foundation that they had set up together with Monte Titano Arte and established their own archive (Archivio Mario Schifano) in 2003. Subsequently, the heirs and the archive took legal action against the foundation. On the one hand, the court prevented the foundation from using the name of Mario Schifano, so as not to give the public the false impression that the foundation is entitled to protect the artist's legacy.[15] On the other hand, the court did not—and could not—prevent the foundation from continuing its activity of studying Schifano's work and giving its expertise on authenticity issues. Consequently, there are currently two legal entities that issue authenticity documentation regarding Schifano's work.

Even though they can both legitimately render opinions as to the authenticity of works by Mario Schifano, the market only recognizes the authenticity statements released by the archive, which was formed by the artist's wife and son. For example, there have been several cases of paintings attributed to Schifano by the foundation, which were subsequently not recognized as being authentic by the archive. These paintings are thus considered as counterfeits by the market. This has been to the detriment of all those collectors who purchased such paintings, which now have no value, and the collectors have no legal remedies against the archive. These cases are still pending.

CASE STUDY 2: ORIANI

An analysis of the concept of attribution, as opposed to authentication, is offered in the case *Oriani v. Centro d'Arte Mercurio*.[16] Mercurio was sued by the heirs of the Futurist artist Giuseppe Oriani (1909–1972). After being appointed by the artist to catalogue Oriani's works, Mecurio claimed on its website that it was the only entity authorized to issue authenticity certificates for Oriani's works. Oriani's heirs challenged this, and the court agreed. In its judgment, the court first opined that only the author is entitled to recognize or deny the authenticity of his or her works. Furthermore, the court remarked that an authenticity certificate—from a legal viewpoint—is nothing more than a mere expression of expertise. Therefore, the court upheld the heirs' request for damages against Mercurio, because the latter, by claiming that it was the only subject officially entitled to issue authenticity certificates, was negatively affecting the activity carried out by the artist's heirs in protecting Oriani's legacy.

It is worth highlighting that the court distinguished between "authentication" and "attribution" in its judgment: while authentication is a personal activity that may only be carried out by the author himself, attribution, even when made by the artist's heirs pursuant to Italian copyright law, has the legal value of expertise. Therefore, the court maintained that only those rights that do not implicate the direct and personal involvement of the author himself may be exercised by the author's heirs.

CASE STUDY 3: THE MANZONI ARCHIVE

The Piero Manzoni Archive has been involved in various legal cases.[17] The Manzoni Archive was set up in 1992 by the siblings of Piero Manzoni (1933–1963), who was one of the most prominent post-war Italian artists.[18] In *Elena Manzoni, Maria Melania Manzoni, Giuseppe Manzoni, Giacomo Maria Manzoni v. Giovanni Cervi*, a private collector named Giovanni Cervi filed an application for an authenticity certificate to the Manzoni Archive, which refused to issue the requested certificate. The archive considered the artwork to be a counterfeit, and Manzoni's relatives—who represented the archive—took legal action against Cervi in order to obtain a declaration by the court that the work was not authentic and to require its destruction.

In this case, the judge stated that Cervi, the defendant, as the owner of the painting and the subject who applied to obtain an authenticity certificate, had the burden to prove the authenticity of the work. This is contrary to the general rule under Italian civil procedure law, by which the plaintiff always has the burden to prove the grounds of his or her claims.[19] The judge did not consider the defendant's proof of authenticity to be sufficient. Accordingly, the work was held to be a counterfeit and its destruction was ordered. More specifically, the plaintiff did not give any evidence of the provenance of the artwork, and an authenticity certificate issued by a dealer was not considered sufficient to prove authenticity of the artwork. The court concluded that the destruction of the artwork was the only adequate measure to protect the descendants' moral rights in accordance with article 169 of Italian copyright law.

Other subsequent cases involving Manzoni's heirs confirmed the conclusion reached by the court in *Manzoni v. Cervi*: in both *Manzoni v. Tonin* and *Manzoni v. Gallo*, the judge declared the respective works not to be authentic because their respective owners did not provide sufficient evidence of their authenticity, and thus the heirs' right to deny the authenticity of such works prevailed.[20]

The cases discussed above demonstrate that authenticity issues can be very problematic when addressed by Italian courts, and that it is often difficult for a purchaser to have adequate certainty of the authenticity of the acquired artwork. The paradoxical result is that a court may decide in favor of a work's authenticity, contrary to the expertise of reliable experts or foundations, while in other cases, private collectors may not have protection against the artist's foundation's decision to deny the authenticity of his property (like in the Fondazione Fontana case) and as shown above the courts have ordered the destruction of the work (as in the Manzoni Archive case).

The above cases show that Italian copyright law was not drafted with a specific focus on the art sector and the result is that serious issues may arise when it must be decided who is entitled to authenticate a work of art. An improvement to the system could be to reform the law by giving to artists (normally, the most reliable authority to decide on the authentication of their works) the possibility to bequeath their authentication right to persons or entities that they consider reliable instead of providing that, upon the author's death, each next of kin enjoys moral rights. Descendants and next of kin frequently neither have an art history background, nor the experience or the knowledge of the artist's oeuvre to undertake such a delicate task.

Part Three: Legacy and Its Stewards

Approaches to Dealing with Artists' Estates

LORETTA WÜRTENBERGER AND KARL VON TROTT ZU SOLZ

Death can really make you look like a star.
—Andy Warhol

Most artists do not leave a will or consider what will happen to their work or legacy after death. If they do deal with death, they do so only, as the artist Jean Tinguely put it, "to fight against it."[1] Artists rarely make structural and strategic decisions for posterity, usually leaving these tasks to be addressed by others. In the void left by the absence of a will, the law says that an artist's descendants or loved ones must deal with the estate, which involves not solely the material distribution of assets but also the preserving and securing of a life's work that is of artistic and cultural value.

Occasionally artists have, during their lifetimes, specific ideas about what should happen to their estate and legacy after death. Erich Heckel (1883–1970) donated the majority of his work to public collections, and Franz West (1947–2012) established a private foundation just six days before his death that favored his family but prevented any access to his work and has caused lengthy litigation in the Austrian courts (see the discussion below). In the 1970s, emerging New York artist Jerry Wennstrom answered the question, "How will my work survive me?" rather dramatically: "Not at all!" He destroyed all his work. Franz Kafka had also once desired this fate for his unpublished manuscripts—a request that, fortunately, his publisher and close friend Max Brodt declined to execute after Kafka's death.

In most cases, however, nothing is arranged during the lifetime of the artist. The artist dies, and the work remains without guidance. It is then left to the artist's heirs to find a solution. Depending on the importance the artist had achieved before death, and the amount of interest on the part of the heirs and the art world, the work may stay where it is (for example, in a dusty attic), be added to private or public archives and collections, be shared among family members, or even remain untouched for years due to disputes. A good example is the case of Oskar Schlemmer. Because no curator or museum wanted to deal with the artist's unclear succession, or his very protective heir, Schlemmer's oeuvre was more or less disregarded for seventy years.

HOW CAN MY WORK SURVIVE ME?

The monetary value of most estates is not significant at the time of the artist's death, and in the vast majority of cases this will not change. The probability of the work of an artist becoming relevant only posthumously and consequently gaining in value, à la Vincent van Gogh, is in reality extremely small. Neither will its monetary or cultural value necessarily increase if the estate is left to a museum. On the contrary, when an estate gifts a number of works to a museum, only a fraction of them, if any at all, is likely to appear in exhibitions and publications. And museums may not even accept the work; although estates are still a cheap means for museums to expand their holdings, today's increasingly full repositories have made museums become far more selective. "The twentieth century left behind such a mass of artworks; the warehouses are full and the present pushes past eras into the background, sometimes even up against the wall," says Uwe Degreif, curator at the Museum Biberach, in Germany.[2]

Museums might be pleased to receive the gift of an estate if the artist is of international standing or particular local significance, but in most other cases, estate management is perceived as a burden. This is true even for a very large institution, as the case of Scott Burton (1939–1989) illustrates. In 1989 the American sculptor bequeathed his estate to the Museum of Modern Art (MoMA), in New York, saying that he "wanted his work in a public place as opposed to private gardens."[3] MoMa was not able to meet Burton's request because the museum was not prepared to manage an estate. With no one advocating for Burton's legacy, prices for his works steadily decreased. London gallerist Inigo Philbrick notes: "There needs [to be] someone in a position to say: 'I represent the estate and stand behind this work.'"[4]

If an artist would nevertheless like to bequeath work to a museum, it is only possible through individual solutions and so-called hybrid models. In a hybrid model, the estate is divided up into works that will enter the museum collection and salable works, and the estate-management work to be done by the museum is financed by the sale of works from the second category. If the right model is found, museums can be good partners for estates. For this reason, it is advisable for artists to contact potential institutions as early as possible, to assess the capacities of the institution. This contact will also aid in developing a structure that brings both sides together in a mutually beneficial arrangement.

The stewardship of an artist's legacy has always required, and still requires, the efforts of others: the artist's family, a gallery, a foundation, or a similar private administrator of the estate. How, and in what specific form, an artist's estate is handled will depend in part on the significance the artist had achieved while alive and on the financial resources that are available. In Europe, the two standard models for preserving an artist's legacy are an institution dedicated to the artist, in the form of an association or a foundation, which can be private or public, or the administration of the estate by the gallery that represented the artist.

LEGACY MANAGEMENT: EXPLOITATION OR APPRECIATION?

Regardless of the administrative and legal model selected to manage an artist's estate, there are always two objectives that have to be reconciled—maintaining the artist's legacy, and protecting the financial interests of the artist's heirs. The focus should be on preserving the artist's legacy for posterity; maintaining perceptions of the oeuvre's significance, or even helping it to enter into public discourse for the first time; and ideally fostering a long-term increase in the importance of the work in scholarly and critical contexts. Secondary to the main focus, and not necessarily in conflict with it, are the financial interests of the artist's heirs and the artist's interest in the financial security of the heirs. There are ways to combine the two interests—for example, by splitting assets between the heirs and a founded entity as the official and permanent point of contact for the estate work, or by managing the estate privately and devoting a fixed amount of revenue for the legacy work.

To achieve the best possible balance in pursuit of these two objectives, a number of fundamental questions must first be addressed: Should the decision of how to proceed with the estate be established during the artist's lifetime, or only posthumously? Should management of the estate continue indefinitely, or have a time limit? Is it sensible to separate management of the estate from other forms of representation? As is frequently the case, there is no perfect solution. The requirements for a suitable and efficient administration of an estate can be as diverse and different as the work of any artist. Nonetheless, the past has revealed certain circumstances that should definitely be avoided, as well as strategies that can successfully be employed today, when working with and for the work of a deceased artist.

Although an artist's will may cause jealousy or animosity among his or her descendants, even a rough plan for the distribution of assets is sometimes better than nothing; if there is a will, at least the artist has prevented the descendants from making erroneous decisions due to lack of knowledge or simply being overwhelmed. It is advisable for artists to approach this topic as early and precisely as possible to prevent families from justifiably questioning the artist's final decisions due to vague directions in the will or the circumstances of its genesis, as Henry Moore's daughter did in 1993 with regard to the ownership of "artist's copies," or the family of Franz West did more recently.[5]

The foundation model Franz West chose shortly before his death in

2012 immediately led to his family initiating legal proceedings due to doubts concerning his business acumen during the time he was establishing the foundation. "Deathbed decisions" like these are, in the literal sense of the term "last will," inevitably problematic. They can hardly be reviewed by external parties and always hold the negative connotation of exertion of influence from the outside. West's idea of appointing his long-standing office manager and closest employee as chair of the trustees, whether legally agreed when he was in full possession of his mental faculties or not, is still reasonable; probably no one knew his work better. At the same time, it has to be asked whether this specialist knowledge could have been employed in a different way, and a more neutral board of trustees appointed, as in the case of the American artist Mike Kelley (1954–2012), who selected two persons close to him—a former museum director and an art historian and expert on Kelley's work—to lead the foundation he established. In the meantime, the Austrian courts have ruled in favor of Franz West's family and concluded that the foundation was created without a proper contract.[6] Unless the foundation appeals the decision, the remaining art in the possession of the foundation and the proceeds from any works already sold will be turned over to West's two children and their legal guardian.

ADMINISTRATION VERSUS MANAGEMENT

It is important to examine the set of skills required to manage an estate. As a collection of artworks that must be catalogued, promoted, and sometimes sold, an artist's estate should be run by someone with curatorial expertise. And as an economic entity, an artist's estate should be financially viable. Those entrusted with running an artist's estate should thus possess both curatorial knowledge and managerial skills. They must be familiar with the artist's work, should be experienced with the upkeep and archiving of a collection, and should have museum contacts. They should additionally be adept at the development and implementation of strategic and financial models, and have a firm grasp of any related legal and tax issues—particularly if the estate is being managed in the form of a foundation. Reliable contacts in the art market are essential, as the majority of artists' foundations are financed by sales, and an increase in the value of holdings, including artwork and intellectual-property rights, is the most important component in the medium- and long-term financing of an estate. Finally, if the estate is run as a charitable foundation, those who run it must allocate resources effectively and sensibly, in the form of stipends, gifts, and the support of other charitable objectives.

In examining this range of skills, it quickly becomes clear that the conventional mode of managing an artist's estate, as it existed in the twentieth century, has become practically obsolete. Today, custodians of an artist's legacy are required to play a far more active role and embody multiple areas of expertise to survive in a bigger and much more professionalized art world. It is no longer sufficient for an artist's legacy to be managed only by family, or only by someone knowledgeable about the artist's work. Over the last twenty years, the cultural sector and the art market have changed as rapidly as the rest of the world, and with it so have the challenges facing the custodians of estates. The professionalism necessary to deal with such responsibilities requires people whose qualifications extend beyond the traditional skills of an art expert, and beyond merely being a member of the artist's family.

While the quip "Never believe the widow and don't listen to the children" is certainly an exaggeration, family members do usually need to be provided with commercial, legal, and specialist support. There are, however, examples of thoroughly satisfactory cases, ones in which the widow, children, or grandchildren possess a comprehensive expertise encompassing all the skills mentioned above. I am thinking, for example, of Sandy Rower, one of Alexander Calder's grandchildren, who manages the Calder Foundation in New York with great professionalism. The Judd Foundation has taken a very successful middle route; Donald Judd's two children, Rainer and Flavin Judd, head its board but are supported by four professional and independent advisers who are also members of the board. Such structures not only assemble the necessary specialist knowledge but also neutralize what is, frequently, the spouse and children's very emotional relationship to the deceased artist, and to the artist's work, which often hinders the objective and unemotional approach that is required.

In past decades, in addition to family members and acquaintances that were familiar with the field of art, custodians of an artist's legacy often also had suitable training, for example as lawyers or accountants. However, there is no guarantee that the designated caretakers, suitably educated or not, will always act in favor of the artist. What is in the artist's favor is in many cases unclear, which leaves room for disputes. For example, in 1965 David Smith (1906–1965) made his friend, the renowned art critic Clement Greenberg, the administrator of his estate and, as a result, an adversary of his descendants. Openly, but without the explicit right to do so, Greenberg removed white paint from six large-scale sculptures, to increase not only their artistic value, but presumably their market value too, using the justification that this was only an undercoat, and Smith had never wanted to leave them in this state anyway.[7] After Smith's daughters won the power struggle, they took over Greenberg's responsibilities.

The estates of Andy Warhol, Francis Bacon, and Robert Rauschenberg —all managed by friends and expert acquaintances—have been at the center of legal disputes relating to money and fees. This is probably also a consequence of the three being great favorites of the art market, awakening greediness everywhere, but at the same time arousing the state's and general public's attention and their ambitions to control the estates. This has led to many cases in which judges are given the responsibility of deciding what would be in the interest of the artist, and how the will and the articles of a foundation should be interpreted.

The Rauschenberg Foundation and three former trustees of the Robert Rauschenberg Irrevocable Trust played this all out, before the art-world public, through a legal dispute over appropriate compensation for the "extraordinary services" performed by the trustees. Opening a new chapter in the history of the art market, the trustees claimed fees of around $50 million from the foundation. The trustees asserted that they were responsible for a $1.6 billion increase in the value of the estate's assets between 2008, the year of Rauschenberg's death, and 2012, when they handed over the assets to the foundation. The district court in Florida awarded the trustees no less than $24.6 million. The foundation appealed against the decision, and the case was settled later on.

The perceived significance of Rauschenberg's (1925–2008) work, and therefore its monetary value, undoubtedly increased during the first four years after his death, which is at least partly due to the contribution of those Rauschenberg entrusted with his legacy for those years. They understood their task, which, simply stated, was to get the artist talked about and to keep the discussion going. This was made possible through publications, exhibitions in galleries and museums, and the placing of work in the right private and public collections. In 2012 alone, Rauschenberg's work appeared in more than twenty-five exhibitions in galleries, collections, and museums around the world. This is certainly easier to achieve for an artist of such caliber than for one of lesser standing.

In addition to knowledge of the work, the market, and the curatorial world, those managing an artist's legacy must also have the right network. It is frequently gallerists who offer these services. But in the last decade more and more professional agents have appeared on the scene to exclusively represent the interests of estates, working constructively with galleries, and letting them do what galleries do best—that is, sell art. All other responsibilities can then remain under the jurisdiction of the estate. Retaining its autonomy and flexibility, the estate is able to seek out the best gallery representation—for any given time and in each respective market. This could mean having different gallery representation in the United States and in the European or Asian markets. For example, after Rauschenberg's death in 2008, Gagosian Gallery was the sole representative of the estate, but in 2015 it lost this mandate to Pace Gallery, with its four locations in New York, London, Beijing, and Hong Kong, as well as Galeria Luisa Strina, in São Paulo, Brazil, and Galerie Thaddaeus Ropac, in Salzburg and Paris.[8]

KEY FACTORS: ACADEMIA, MUSEUMS, AND THE MARKET

The route to successful management of an artist's legacy is affected by three factors: academia, museums, and the market. The estate can deal most successfully with all three areas by promptly publishing a catalogue raisonné—a comprehensive list of works by the artist, with accompanying information about the exhibition and publication history of each work. After immediately checking the location of loans from the artist's own collection, the first step should be the creation of a professional record of all the artist's works. Very few artists and executors will be as fortunate as German artist Gerhard Richter (b.1932), whose complete works have been catalogued by one of his collectors during the artist's lifetime. Such stocktaking is painstaking and repetitive work, but it is the best way of thoroughly researching the oeuvre. A catalogue raisonné provides not only a structure for the future but, more importantly, a reliable basis for approaching the work.

The estate of Jean (Hans) Arp (1886–1966), which has been advised by the Institute for Artists' Estates since 2010, is a good example of how much a catalogue raisonné can help. Only a consistent approach to the inventory, the complete opening of the archives to independent researchers, and a review of the legitimacy of all the sculpture casts have led to a new start in the overall examination of Arp's oeuvre. Previously there had been doubts about the authenticity of some of his works due to the existence of posthumous and unauthorized casts. Today, due to new transparency, the market has regained trust in Arp's work, and the artist can take his rightful place among the twentieth century's most outstanding artists.

When the research is as comprehensive as it has been in the case of Arp, the catalogue raisonné can generally be considered complete. Exceptions include when a catalogue is later supplemented by the confirmation of legitimate casts or (apparently) obscure finds, which also should be in the catalogue. Upon the death of the artist, the process of production has ended. The most important factor in the appreciation of fine-art assets is the scarcity of the commodity. The size of the oeuvre and the details of the works of art such as title, dimensions, date, and materials will no longer change; only changes in the provenance of works will continue as the result of each transaction.

As an aside, it should be noted that the creation of a catalogue raisonné, which claims to be a complete a record of an artist's work, entails some risks due to the authentication it indirectly implies—a risk of which authors of the catalogue should at least be aware. This may begin with an inquiry as to whether a hitherto unrecorded work can legally be included in the catalogue, and end with the risk of litigation for possible damages, if the decision is unfavorable. This is a factor that should not be underestimated, particularly in the United States, where all parties are responsible for their own legal costs, and was apparently the main reason, according to rumors, why the Warhol Foundation's Authentication Board ceased its work in 2012.[9]

Once a catalogue raisonné has been published, it forms the basis for any engagement with the artist, not just for the foundation's management but for academic researchers as well. The management of the foundation should therefore be regarded as a service provider for academia, with the catalogue raisonné being the point of departure. Any academic involvement with the artist's work should receive the full support of the foundation; it not only strengthens general perceptions of the artist's work, but also maintains a lively discourse around the oeuvre. The custodians of an estate should therefore proactively seek academic contacts, and ideally suggest ideas for research papers, too. The quickest and most effective way of achieving this is by the awarding of grants. This need not be limited to just the most obvious art-historical context, but moreover may be a means of seeking out further scholarly links that are thematically appropriate to an artist's output, and which open up new perspectives on the oeuvre.

Academia and museums go hand in hand in this. Exhibitions and museum collections are key sites for reexamining a deceased artist's work, so that it remains lively and compelling, not only for the wider public but also for subsequent generations of artists. From the very beginning, artists' estates should focus on working with museums.

After reviewing the artist's work and producing a catalogue raisonné, it is advisable to start making selective gifts and loans to museums. This will not only fill gaps in the respective museum collection but at the same time promote the artist. However, if the estate's work involves pursuing objectives beyond merely distributing its holdings, such as promoting a self-determined legacy, then gifts like these should not exceed 10 to 15 percent of the artist's entire output, and the works and institutions should be selected with care.

The inventory of work is usually the predominant source of wealth for financing the estate's overall efforts in promoting the artist's memory. For an artist who does not enjoy the world renown of someone like Pablo Picasso, making a gift of the entire estate—even if over many years and to diverse institutions—will not necessarily lead to any increase in the work's significance, but could rather result in just a noble interment in the museum, as discussed above. For example, the artist David Park (1911–1960)—an outstanding representative of the Bay Area Figurative Movement, a dissenting counterpart to Abstract Expressionism—would today be known to a much wider public if his widow and her second husband had followed a different strategy. Initially they gifted parts of the estate to various regional museums over a number of years and then left the remainder to the Oakland Museum and the Santa Barbara Museum, both in California. Today, they may not have made the same decisions again and would probably have dispensed the collection more internationally.

The Rauschenberg Foundation, which recently launched its Gift/Purchase Program, provides a great model for how gifts can and should be made. Through the program, certain US institutions were given the option to purchase particular works at favorable prices. Six of the museums used this program to buy the artist's works. Even if it would appear that Rauschenberg had long ago reach the summit, and the power relations between the foundation and museums were apparently well balanced, this program concerned the availability of Rauschenberg's late work, from the 1970s, 80s, and 90s, which generally is not considered to be the most significant of his oeuvre. By granting favorable rights for acquisition of the late work, the foundation skillfully created incentives for museums, which could then select works strategically. The work was chosen based on geography and the existing inventory. Similar to the programs of the Warhol, Robert Motherwell, and Robert Mapplethorpe estates, the Rauschenberg Gift/Purchase Program allowed the already favorable purchase prices to be deferred over three years, during which time the museums could seek out donors or other sources of finance. These examples are meant to demonstrate the need for artists' estates to have individual strategies for museums. Along with long-term loans, where in contrast to gifts there is no transfer of ownership, this can also take the form of raising awareness through instigating, organizing, and funding exhibitions, and supporting exhibitions by way of encouraging curatorial access to the estate's archives and holdings. Merely waiting for loan requests will only suffice for a minority of estates.

Finally, the art market is the third column on which any successful estate will rest. This includes, as already mentioned, selecting the right gallery for the right market at the right time, but does not necessarily mean that the work should immediately be offered for sale. If at all financially feasible, merely exhibiting the work in a commercial space is enough to raise awareness. Art that does not find an audience, will not, as a rule, increase in either its significance or monetary value.

The work of pioneering art adviser Barry Rosen is a model for how independent estate management can best function. For the last twenty years he has represented estates as an independent consultant, including that of Eva Hesse (1936–1970), which he has decisively "built up." Following numerous publications and gallery exhibitions of Hesse's work in Germany, the United States, and France, as well as museum shows in San Francisco, São Paulo, London, and New Haven, Connecticut, Rosen decided in 2002, jointly with Hesse's sister, to work with the gallery Hauser & Wirth, which has since marketed the estate very successfully. In the meantime, Hauser & Wirth is also doing the same for Lee Lozano and Allan Kaprow, who are likewise represented by Rosen. Nevertheless, each estate's management is still essentially free to act autonomously—that is, to continue issuing publications and exhibit and sell works—if it so desires. In its function as a consultant to the gallery, the estate can control marketing, in the interest of the estate, while simultaneously supporting the gallery.

A further good example of successful placement at the upper end of the market is the late work of Willem de Kooning (1904–1997), who has already been mentioned. At the time of his death he was, without question, a star of the art world, but similar to Rauschenberg, the works that had made him were from the 1940s and 50s. The estate consisted mainly of works from the 80s. That he was already a great name, as well as the zeitgeist of the art market, certainly helped to make these works desirable, but exhibitions of the work in Bonn and New York in 1996, and again in 2011 at MoMA as part of his retrospective, were also helpful to an appreciation in value. Two years later, Gagosian, which had been commissioned to sell ten works from these later years, achieved proceeds of not less than $30 million.

ETERNITY AND THE COSTS; OR, COSTS FOR ETERNITY?

No matter who has been entrusted with these responsibilities, one thing remains clear: all this costs money. The administrative operation of an estate should be kept as lean as possible. Besides management costs, there are expenses involved in preventive conservation, which encompasses not only appropriate storage but also ongoing monitoring of the work. The condition of the inventory of artworks should be regularly examined, the risk regarding loans and transport should be analyzed, and protective measures should be continually improved.

Having clarified initial, possibly still unresolved, items of a financial nature, such as tax arrears or other liabilities, the administrators of an artist's estate must address long-term financial requirements. As far as is possible, the basic structural questions are best resolved during the artist's lifetime, as already mentioned above. The artist must be decisive and answer elementary questions: shall my loved ones benefit from the vestiges of my life's work? If yes, who, and in what way? How can I support the financial needs of my loved ones while also ensuring the posthumous stewardship of my oeuvre? Do I want an institutionalized legacy vehicle? Can I afford it? What will be the purpose of my estate, and will it change over time? Who will do the legacy work, and for how long? What are the assets that will create streams of revenue for the legacy work? And finally, what is the best legal and fiscal structure to reach these objectives?

If the artist does not want or would not be able to found a soundly based museum—which is almost always the case—then the financial stability and viability of the estate will rely on the sale of works of art. However, the consequence of this is that the monetary branch on which it all rests is being continually sawn away. The main prerequisite, therefore, is the establishing of sustainable resources that enable the proper preservation of the legacy, even once the majority of the tangible silverware has been sold.

On the other hand, the establishing of a model that is viable in perpetuity is not absolutely necessary, if there is any legal flexibility. An increasingly common form in the United States—for charitable organizations of all kinds—is the "sunset end" model, which will eventually arrive at a legally determined end. The managing institution will only exist until its task has been completed—a very sensible approach; sometimes there is even a definite deadline for its termination. What is the rationale for the existence of an artist's foundation once the work has already been examined academically and distributed, and no studio, museum, or family members require further financial support? The foundation's purpose as mere self-preservation is surely never in the artist's interest.

However, the preservation of an artist's legacy does not only rest on the conservation and marketing of physical products. This is just one aspect. An artist's foundation can continue to play an important role even after the liquidation of all assets. This may involve the promoting of younger artists, or supporting further publications on the oeuvre. A good example of this is the Henry Moore Foundation. For some time now, Moore's work has been housed in the world's museums and private collections; nevertheless, the foundation's activities, which started in 1977, continue. Beyond and above the conservation of Moore's own work, the foundation has also adopted the cause of sculpture in general, researching, supporting, and exhibiting it in all its conceivable aspects. This ranges from providing workshops for children to hosting live performances of experimental dance by Siobhan Davies. Thus the Moore Foundation has created a raison d'être reaching far beyond focusing solely on the legacy of the deceased artist, preventing eventual exhaustion. The administration of Warhol's (1928–1987) estate takes a different approach. For someone who was so decisively influential on the art of the twentieth century, and whose reception has exhausted every superlative, there is only one logical conclusion: a bare cupboard. Accordingly, the Warhol Foundation decided to sell all the works, making the proceeds available to nonprofit art projects and organizations. As a result, history will remember Warhol not only as a great artist but also as a great philanthropist. I think this would have pleased him.

Ultimately, it is the deceased—that is, the artist—and their stated or presumed wishes, and other aspects such as the size of the estate or the possible existence of family members in need of financial support, that decide how long work will continue to be done in the interest of the artist. The selection of appropriate personnel and devising of a concept should then be made on this basis. The decisive question for all the parties concerned should be: what would the artist have wanted? Those running an artist's estate must have adequate knowledge and staff, and the right motives. Do they have everything that the private and public art world demands today? Do they know and understand the art in question, and is that what they are working for, rather than primarily their own personal and financial success? If the right choices are made, perhaps Warhol's quote about death will ring true: "Death means a lot of money, honey. Death can really make you look like a star!"[10]

What's an Artist to Do?—
Artist-Endowed Foundations and Legacy Stewardship in the United States

CHRISTINE J. VINCENT

How can artists in the United States ensure the posthumous sustainability of their creative achievements? How can they be confident that once they are no longer living, their assets will be put to the uses they envision? In fact, there are no guarantees in life. But artists can make thoughtful and well-considered plans, and in so doing, they may be able to weight the scales of fate in their favor.

When charting a course for posthumous stewardship, artists must consider what type of entity will provide the best care for their works and the copyrights therein, attending to the broader scholarly, critical, market, and public understanding of their oeuvre. Three factors are key in this deliberation: the character of an artist's works in the context of the broader culture; the extent to which an oeuvre's cultural currency translates to economic value in the marketplace; and the abilities and intentions of the individuals who are available to oversee the artist's works and copyrights. Underpinning these factors is the question of structure: what legal form and tax status are best suited to serve the artist's intentions? To answer this question, artists must first decide if their aim is to benefit specific private individuals, such as family members, through a taxable, private entity, or to benefit the general public using a tax-exempt, charitable organization.[1]

When deciding who should care for their collected works and steward their creative legacy posthumously, artists in the United States have a number of options for both noncharitable and charitable entities. In decades past, many artists chose no specific legal form. They simply bequeathed their collected artworks to private individuals—heirs or other beneficiaries—to be managed to the best of those individuals' abilities and for their benefit, most often under the rubric "estate of artist x." Examples include John D. Graham, Florine Stettheimer, and Gene Davis, among many others. In some cases, such as those of Louise Nevelson, Brett Weston, and R. C. Gorman, following the artist's death the collected artworks have been sold en masse to third parties, such as art dealers and collectors, so that the artist's heirs are not involved in stewarding "the estate of artist x."

A more formal version of posthumous private ownership is a noncharitable trust—a legal entity established to own and administer the artist's works and/or copyrights for the benefit of specified private individuals, typically the artist's heirs, and administered by one or more trustees. Examples of noncharitable trusts include the Thomas Hart Benton and Rita P. Benton Testamentary Trust, Mondrian/Holtzman Trust, and Ansel Adams Publishing Rights Trust. A legal form that has gained popularity in recent years is the noncharitable limited liability company (LLC), a type of corporate entity with private ownership rights typically held by artists' heirs that provides a more flexible option than the trust form, with its requisite trustees. The estates of David Smith, Jean Charlot, and Ana Mendieta, among others, are structured as noncharitable LLCs. Regardless of the particular legal form of private ownership, none can claim status as a tax-exempt, charitable entity due to the presence of private, noncharitable interests.[2]

Beyond these noncharitable options, artists whose aim is to benefit the general public, as opposed to benefitting specified private individuals, may consider charitable versions of either the trust or corporate form. Once established under state law, a charitable trust or nonprofit corporation may then seek tax-exempt status from the Internal Revenue Service (IRS), which may recognize the trust or corporate entity as tax-exempt under Section 501(c)(3) of the Internal Revenue Code and categorize it with the tax status of either "private foundation" or "public charity," as defined by Congress in the Tax Reform Act of 1969.[3] Accordingly, tax-exempt charitable entities—both charitable trusts and nonprofit corporations—by definition are organized and operated exclusively to serve a public benefit, whether categorized with the tax status of private foundation or public charity.[4] The distinctions between these tax statuses are noted below.

Artists may use a tax-exempt, charitable entity for posthumous stewardship purposes in several ways. They may make their bequests to an established charitable entity, such as a museum, educational institution, community foundation, historic preservation organization, or multiartist fund. Examples include bequests made by Marisol (Maria Sol Escobar) to the Albright-Knox Art Gallery in Buffalo, New York; Roger Brown to the School of the Art Institute of Chicago, in Illinois; John Gutmann to the San Francisco Foundation and the Center for Creative Photography in Tucson, Arizona; Philip Johnson to the National Trust for Historic Preservation in Washington, DC; and Viola Frey to the Artists' Legacy Foundation in Oakland, California. Alternatively, artists may establish an independent charitable entity—typically a private foundation or, in some cases, a public charity—during their lifetime (inter vivos) or posthumously, under their estate plan (testamentary). Helen Frankenthaler, Keith Haring, Lee Krasner, Robert Mapplethorpe, Joan Mitchell, and Andy Warhol chose to establish private foundations. Sam Maloof, Clyfford Still, and Eric Carle established public charities, functioning as museums.

Whether formed as a charitable trust or nonprofit corporation, an entity with the tax status of public charity is defined as one that is supported by contributions from members of the general public. Likewise, whether formed as a charitable trust or nonprofit corporation, an entity with the tax status of private foundation is defined as one funded by a sole donor and their relations. Of note: "private foundation" is a legal term that was created by the Internal Revenue Code, as is "public charity"; however, a tax-exempt charitable entity, including a public charity, is free to use the word "foundation" in its title, regardless of its tax status.[5] The private foundation is the most highly regulated tax-exempt status in the United States, and also the one most commonly used by artists, thus it is given particular attention in this essay.[6]

ANTECEDENTS OF THE MODERN ARTIST-ENDOWED FOUNDATION

Before reflecting on the challenges artists face in creating viable tax-exempt charitable entities able to successfully steward their works and copyrights for public benefit, I will comment on the evolution in the way that artist-endowed foundations have been structured. For the purposes of this essay, an artist-endowed foundation is defined as a tax-exempt, private foundation, organized as either a charitable trust or a nonprofit corporation, that has been created or endowed by a visual artist, the artist's surviving spouse, or other heirs or beneficiaries, to own the artist's assets for use in furthering charitable and educational activities serving a public benefit.

Although the earliest artist-endowed foundations may have been endowed with cultural assets, including valuable artworks and aesthetically significant properties, they did not employ a business model based on the sale of artworks, but were supported instead by investments and revenues not related to art. Nor did they specify as a charitable purpose the responsibility of increasing understanding of and access to an artist's creative legacy for public benefit. This is exemplified by two antecedents of the modern artist-endowed foundation, the first found in Italy and the second in the United States.

The oldest identified artist-endowed foundation was created in Rome by the expatriate Bavarian artist Franz Ludwig Catel (1778–1856).[7] The Fondazione Catel, established in 1873 following the death of the artist's surviving spouse, was endowed with his assets, the most valuable being a real-estate portfolio assembled with proceeds from a successful career creating genre paintings of Italian country life, sold to members of the international upper class enjoying the Grand Tour. Now approaching 150 years, the Fondazione Catel has survived as an institution through world wars, foreign occupation, and political turmoil. It continues to house a study center and collection of the artist's works, which are valued now more for their historic note than artistic achievement. Consistent with Catel's philanthropic intentions, the foundation makes grants to assist the Italian and German poor in Rome, particularly artists, and sponsors exhibitions and awards for university students studying fine arts and architecture.[8]

Among the earliest artist-endowed foundations in the United States, the Louis Comfort Tiffany Foundation was created as a trust with charitable purposes in 1918, just two years after enactment of the modern federal estate tax and fifteen years prior to the artist's death. Louis Comfort Tiffany (1848–1933) endowed his foundation with $1 million (more than $14 million today) in support of its mission to operate his property Laurelton Hall, in Long Island, New York, as a residency program—a "school"—for young artists and designers.[9] The sprawling estate was outfitted with his collected design works, including now-iconic stained-glass windows, which he believed would inspire the program's residents. In one of the field's sadder stories, Tiffany lived to see much of his foundation's endowment, and a great deal of his own fortune, vanish following the 1929 stock market crash. Ultimately unable to afford its upkeep, the foundation's governing body sold Laurelton Hall for a nominal sum and auctioned Tiffany's collection, which had gone out of fashion, to generate only $100,000.[10] Celebrating its centennial in 2018, the foundation currently operates a grantmaking program with biennial awards to emerging artists and designers.[11]

These two examples offer a study in contrasts. Despite great market popularity during his lifetime, Catel's artistic reputation is now of minor note. Nonetheless, his foundation is an enduring philanthropic institution and remains true to his charitable intentions. In contrast, Tiffany's creative works have returned to high esteem in the eyes of collectors, curators, and the art market, while his foundation, although focused on the spirit of his charitable intentions, operates on a much less expansive basis than he had envisioned. Do these outcomes have anything to do with the caliber of the artists' creative achievements or the choices they made for the posthumous stewardship of their art assets? Or are these two stories simply a matter of historical events and inevitable economic cycles and artistic trends?

THE FIRST FOUNDATIONS SUSTAINED BY ART SALES

It was not until the 1950s and 1960s that there emerged the concept of an artist-endowed foundation as an economically self-sustaining entity based on sales from its art holdings. Even then, however, the goal of posthumously stewarding an artist's legacy for public benefit was not a specifically stated charitable purpose in the founding documents of these early artist-endowed foundations.

The Sansom Foundation, named for the Philadelphia street where William Glackens (1870–1938) spent his boyhood, was established in 1959 by the artist's son, his last survivor. Its founding mission was to assist the arts, education, and animal welfare, and it received the family's collected artworks to generate funds for those purposes.[12] This was the first foundation created to fund grants through sales of an artist's works. Alongside its grant program, the foundation made major gifts of artworks to support development of the William J. Glackens Collection and Study Center at Nova Southeastern University Art Museum, in Fort Lauderdale, Florida, which now comprises the definitive public collection of the artist's works.[13]

Almost a decade later, Charles Burchfield (1893–1967) created a foundation just prior to his death. The Charles E. Burchfield Foundation was established to steward the artist's collected works and make grants supporting the arts as well as community interests in the western New York region where he lived. This was the first foundation created by an artist to manage the posthumous disposition of his oeuvre as a charitable endeavor.[14] In addition to its philanthropy, the foundation lends works widely for exhibition and has made significant gifts of artworks to assist development of the Burchfield Penney Art Center at the State University New York at Buffalo, whose holdings now contain the largest public collection of the artist's works, including a re-creation of his studio.[15]

Approaching their sixth and fifth decades respectively, both of these foundations have sold artworks periodically since their inception and looked to this income to fund their grant programs, but they have eschewed directly operating archives and exhibition programs. In fact, neither has a staff. They work within the constraints of private foundation status at its most basic—the "nonoperating foundation." This type of foundation provides grants to support individuals or other tax-exempt charitable organizations and uses its assets, including artworks, as investment assets, intended to produce income to support its grant program. The value of these income assets is subject to the private foundation payout requirement, a provision of the Internal Revenue Code that stipulates private foundations must spend a specified amount annually on charitable purposes, which is calculated based on the net value of their investment assets, often adjusted for a blockage discount.[16]

Despite their nonoperating status, and as such being focused on grantmaking, the Sansom Foundation and Burchfield Foundation have made certain their artists' creative legacies are preserved and accessible for the public's benefit—Glackens as a crowd-pleasing American Impressionist and Burchfield as one of the twentieth century's most visionary artists. They have done this by supporting the creation of study centers independent of the respective foundations, ensuring that the artists' collected works and archives will continue to be available to the public and to scholars, educators, artists, and students. In both cases, this strategy has involved partnerships with emergent regional museums located far from the haute art world's urban centers.

LESSONS LEARNED ABOUT BEST PRACTICES

Although these early examples were marked by success, the following decades—1970s, 1980s, and 1990s—were a bumpy ride, with several high-profile artist-endowed foundations entangled in costly litigation that left lasting imprints on the field. Though concerned with different issues, the cases all demonstrated a lack of knowledge about best practices for artist-endowed foundations under private foundation law and also highlighted the complexities of utilizing nonoperating status for such a foundation.

The realization that placing a foundation's art dealer on its board can create a conflict of interest, and as such may provide opportunities for self-dealing, came courtesy of the Mark Rothko Foundation. Mark Rothko (1903–1970) established the foundation one year before his suicide and signed a will bequeathing it the artworks he owned. Not long after his death, it was revealed that the artist's accountant—who was his business adviser and art dealer, wrote his will, and subsequently served as one of three estate executors and the secretary/treasurer of the foundation—had sold the artist's works in bulk at a substantial discount to the gallery for which the accountant was a salaried officer.[17] This executor had also arranged for the amendment of the foundation's certificate of incorporation, worded originally to provide only for general "charitable" purposes, to specify a single purpose—the making of grants to mature artists.[18] It does not escape observation that this new purpose would help justify the sale of the artist's collection in order to provide sufficient liquid assets to fund grants that would be necessary to meet the private foundation payout requirement.[19]

Following these revelations, Rothko's estate and foundation were engulfed in charges of conflict of interest. In 1975 a New York State court ousted the executors, finding breach of fiduciary duties, directed the gallery to return all unsold works, and divided these among the artist's children and the foundation.[20] The foundation was reorganized with a new governing body and operated for fewer than ten years. It terminated by placing its art holdings in established public collections, with a major gift to the National Gallery of Art, in Washington, DC.[21]

Mark Rothko reportedly agonized in the last months of his life over the foundation's mission and whether it would maintain his artworks as a definitive collection and place selected works at museums over time, or sell them to fund grants to individual mature artists. Although these events stand as a nadir in the field's understanding of best practice, it would be hard to make the case that the Sturm und Drang that stained his foundation had much impact on the legacy of an artist now acknowledged as a defining practitioner of Abstract Expressionism.

The Joseph and Robert Cornell Memorial Foundation, established under the will of Joseph Cornell (1903–1972) and named to include his brother, who suffered from cerebral palsy and predeceased him, provided a different lesson. This was the recognition that some art assets—such as an artist's archive comprising ephemera, documents, photographs, source material, and unfinished artworks—may not have significant financial value despite having great cultural value. As such, an artist's archive may not be a good fit for a foundation with non-operating status in which assets are held purely to generate income. As documented in records held by the Smithsonian Archives of American Art, Joseph Cornell's executor, also a foundation trustee, initially planned to destroy the artist's archive, as it had no income-producing value, the foundation having been organized specifically to own the artist's completed artworks as investment assets.[22]

This disaster was averted when the artist's sister challenged that plan and claimed the archive as part of the artist's residuary estate, to which she held testamentary rights.[23] The artist's archive ultimately was placed at the Smithsonian Archives of American Art and the Smithsonian American Art Museum, spurring creation of the Joseph Cornell Study Center.[24] This is one situation in which our understanding of an artist's creative legacy would have been seriously disadvantaged were there to have been no challenge to the initial assumption as to which assets have utility for a foundation given its non-operating status.

Another situation involving the Cornell Foundation offers a paradoxical look at the matter of best practice. In 1994 the attorney general of New York State brought suit against the Joseph and Robert Cornell Memorial Foundation for failing to honor the artist's philanthropic intentions. As stated in his will, the artist desired that the foundation would not give his artwork to museums, but rather would sell his art and use the proceeds to make grants to programs serving humanitarian needs.[25] Yet the foundation had, since inception, exclusively made grants of artworks to museums in order to meet its payout requirement. The case was settled when the foundation agreed to make cash grants for humanitarian purposes at a financial level comparable to the value of its grants of art. Though it was not the artist's goal, by initially ignoring his philanthropic intentions, the foundation helped ensure his sustained visibility by placing his works in museum collections across the United States and internationally.[26]

A number of lessons on best practice were provided during the early years of the Andy Warhol Foundation for the Visual Arts, created under the will of Andy Warhol (1928–1987). The artist's executor chose to use nonoperating status for the foundation. As such, the foundation's assets, including artworks, would be held as investment assets, with the required annual payout calculated on the value of these assets, adjusted for a blockage discount. The foundation would meet its payout requirement through a grantmaking program with a mission to advance the visual arts—the charitable purpose mandated in the artist's will.[27] The artist's bequest was of a scale previously not received by any artist-endowed foundation and comprised primarily nonfinancial assets—the artist's own artworks, copyrights, and archive, as well as real estate, collectibles, works by other artists, and business interests. Contemplating the same "art rich and cash poor" dilemma as in the Rothko situation, the Warhol Foundation had to ramp up liquidity quickly in order to make sufficient grants to meet the payout requirement. Auctions and art sales began forthwith.

Like the Sansom and Burchfield Foundations, the Warhol Foundation committed a substantial collection of artworks to establish an independent public collection of the artist's works and archive—the Andy Warhol Museum, a division of Carnegie Museums of Pittsburgh.[28] On the one hand, this commitment, structured as a grant, helped to meet the foundation's payout requirement in the early years. But it also significantly reduced the number of the artist's works that could be sold to fund the foundation's grant program.

Even as the Warhol Foundation set up an unprecedented sales operation to begin liquidating its bequest, it also found itself fighting litigation brought by the Warhol estate's former legal counsel, whose compensation had been set based on the value of the estate's assets—an arrangement commonly applied for executors but highly unusual for estate counsel. This individual claimed the value of the art assets was much greater than what was asserted in an appraisal prepared for the estate, and as such he was due a much higher level of compensation. If successful, this litigation would have resulted in a nearly six-fold increase in the valuation of the foundation's assets, multiplying payout pressure substantially and compelling an even greater level of art sales at a pace that potentially would have undermined the market for the artist's works.[29] As it turned out, the Warhol Foundation ultimately prevailed, with the courts nullifying the asset-based compensation arrangement in favor of a service-based fee and affirming a value for the art assets that, though greater than claimed by the challenged appraisal, was far less than asserted by the unhappy former legal counsel.[30]

Almost thirty years on, the Warhol Foundation has weathered many other storms. Not the least of these was the early misstep, ultimately rectified, of permitting a member of the foundation's board to function as its art broker, leaving the foundation vulnerable to a public perception of conflict of interest and greatly distracting attention from its important charitable mission.[31] In the long view, however, by creating the Andy Warhol Museum, and operating a visual-arts grant program unmatched in scale among private foundations of any stripe, the Warhol Foundation can be judged as having served its artist's creative legacy while also being true to his philanthropic intentions. Nevertheless, the Warhol Foundation's complicated example convinced many attorneys advising prominent artists that nonoperating status—committed to payout calculated on the value of art assets and requiring substantial art sales be maintained to fund grantmaking, whatever the market's state—was far too risky for any successful artist's bequest comprising substantial collected works.

ADDITIONAL TAX STATUS OPTIONS

Even into the 1980s and 1990s, some artist-endowed foundations continued to be structured to use nonoperating status post-bequest. These include the Pollock-Krasner Foundation, created by the will of Lee Krasner (1908–1984) with a mission to provide financial assistance to individual visual artists of established ability and financial need, and the Renate, Hans, and Maria Hofmann Trust, established under the estate plan of Hans Hofmann (1880–1966) following the death of his surviving spouse in 1992, which makes grants to support programs of the German Catholic Church and to assist the arts, mental health, and social services.[32] By and large, however, the significant increase in the number of artist-endowed foundations has been marked by a concern to use a tax status that would better accommodate the special characteristics of these charitable entities, whose primary assets can serve both as investment assets as well as educational and cultural assets, and whose charitable purposes may be realized both through grantmaking and by directly conducting scholarly, educational, and charitable programs.

Thus, foundations created during an artist's lifetime—which as such do not hold the artist's artworks or copyrights due to the private foundation prohibition on self-dealing—typically utilize nonoperating status and focus on grantmaking, then subsequently convert post-bequest to the status that befits their charitable use assets and the programs related to those newly received assets, as discussed further below. Foundations created posthumously typically utilize the status preferred for their charitable use assets and related programs from the start.

Focused initially on grantmaking during the four years prior to the death of Josef Albers (1888–1976), the Josef and Anni Albers Foundation became the first artist-endowed foundation to claim "operating" status. As such, it directly maintains art collections, operates a study center with archive and library, and conducts related scholarly and educational programs, all with a mission to "further the revelation and evocation of vision through art," as specified by its founders.[33] Operating status, as claimed by the Albers Foundation, is now a clear favorite among attorneys advising prominent artists, and although they still comprise only one-quarter of all artist-endowed foundations, the number of foundations using this tax status is increasing.[34] In contrast to nonoperating status, in which a foundation typically is focused on grantmaking, the Internal Revenue Code defines a foundation with operating status as one that fulfills its charitable purposes by directly conducting programs serving those purposes, rather than making grants to other charitable entities to support their programs. As such, the value of assets utilized or held for use in the conduct of these direct charitable activities is not subject to the annual payout requirement.[35]

To be clear, operating status enables this favorable treatment of artworks' financial value only if the works are used directly, or held for use, in foundation-conducted programs, such as study centers, exhibition collections, scholarly projects, and the like, all of which can involve a substantial expense. Operating status has other limitations as well, most notably that the only type of grantmaking attributable to meeting the payout requirement is that which is integrated with the foundation's direct charitable activities.[36] Lastly, as an important note with respect to any type of foundation, charitable use assets, when consigned for sale, as would be the case of artworks consigned to an art dealer, convert to investment assets (those held for income), and in this "dual use" mode their value is subject to the payout requirement until they are no longer consigned for sale.[37]

Interestingly, the structuring of the Adolph and Esther Gottlieb Foundation, established following the death of Adolph Gottlieb (1903–1974), indicated that neither operating status nor nonoperating status, in its basic form, would suffice for some artist-endowed foundations, meaning a further iteration would be required. To this point, the Gottlieb Foundation utilized a hybrid arrangement. It maintained nonoperating status, which one might expect given that a program making grants to individual visual artists is one of its two charitable activities. However, the other of its two charitable activities is the direct operation of a program organizing exhibitions from its collection of the artist's works and lending these to museums.[38] Because the art collection is used directly by the foundation to accomplish a charitable purpose, the value of the artworks is exempt from the calculation of the foundation's annual payout requirement (except if the works were to be consigned for sale). Likewise, the expense of operating the collection and exhibition program is considered a charitable expenditure, attributable to the payout requirement, as are the expenses of operating the grant program.

This hybrid status—nonoperating status with charitable use assets—has become popular, particularly in cases of necessity where artists' charitable intentions cannot be entirely integrated with direct charitable activities based on the artists' works, thus ruling out operating status.[39] Examples include the Robert Mapplethorpe Foundation, Keith Haring Foundation, and Herb Ritts Foundation, each of which owns and directly manages archives and art collections, from which they loan works to exhibitions, while also making grants to concerns unrelated to those directly conducted programs, such as assisting HIV/AIDS research and services, as well as supporting the arts.[40]

Another tax status employed less frequently for artist-endowed foundations is that of "public charity," which, as noted above, is distinct from "private foundation" status in that tax-exempt organizations of this type are supported by contributions from members of the general public, as opposed to contributions from a sole donor and their relations.[41] In general, the Internal Revenue Code provides that donors to public charities receive more advantageous income-tax treatment for their contributions than do those who direct their gifts to private foundations, making public charity status optimal when fundraising is key.[42] The challenge is that qualifying as a public charity and retaining that status requires an organization to maintain a substantial level of annual support from members of the general public. The transition to public charity status typically becomes necessary when an artist-endowed foundation's charitable purpose—most often operation of a museum—exceeds the capacity of the artist's bequest to support it, making a broader resource base necessary.

For example, in 1968 Isamu Noguchi (1904–1988) created a small nonoperating foundation dedicated to funding artistic exchange between the United States and Japan. In 1980, eight years prior to the artist's death, the foundation was renamed as the Isamu Noguchi Foundation and converted to operating status, with the purpose of creating and maintaining a museum built around the artist's studio in Queens, New York, to house his collected works, which it ultimately received as his bequest. More than twenty years later, in 2004, the organization converted to public charity status as The Isamu Noguchi Foundation and Garden Museum (known as the Noguchi Museum), beginning a decade of significant capital fundraising activities.[43] Similarly, the Judd Foundation, established under the will of Donald Judd (1928–1994), maintains and operates the artist's permanently installed living and working spaces, libraries, and archives, housed in properties located in New York City and Marfa, Texas. Created initially with operating status, it converted to public charity status in 2013, concurrent with a major capital fundraising effort required to endow its programs and renovate its New York property, listed on the National Register of Historic Places.[44]

If artists and their advisers are confident that a sufficient level of public support can be secured, usually due to the artists' high profile and strong interest among donors, then a tax-exempt charitable entity is sometimes structured from the get-go with public charity status. The Sam and Alfreda Maloof Foundation for Arts and Crafts was established several years prior to the death of Sam Maloof (1916–2009) as an artist-endowed public charity to own and operate a museum comprising the artist's handcrafted home and furnishings, including his own sculptural furniture and an extensive collection of fine art and design works by other artists.[45]

Lastly, a few artist-endowed foundations are established with a special type of public charity status, as a "supporting organization."[46] Although a supporting organization is formed as and remains a distinct legal entity, its governance is integrated with or controlled by an extant public charity, such as a museum or educational institution, whose charitable purposes the supporting organization's activities support or carry out. The Internal Revenue Code provides that although a supporting organization is a public charity, it is not subject to the public charity requirement that a substantial level of public support be maintained, because the organization it supports already meets this rule. Further, because of its status as a public charity, a supporting organization is not subject to the private foundation rules, including the payout requirement or excise tax on net investment income, such as that generated by art sales. If all of this sounds appealing, there are indeed drawbacks. Supporting organizations cannot be controlled by, nor can they compensate, their substantial donors and related parties.

The John Cage Trust owns John Cage's musical compositions, copyrights, multimedia archive, and library, as well as a collection of his artworks, and makes these available to encourage broader understanding of his creative achievements through study, performance, publication, and exhibition. It was established following the death of John Cage (1912–1992) as a supporting organization of the Cunningham Dance Foundation, a public charity that terminated following the death in 2009 of the choreographer Merce Cunningham. Since 2013 the John Cage Trust has been classified as a supporting organization of Bard College, with activities supporting the college's Conservatory of Music.[47] The trustee/director of the John Cage Trust serves as a member of the Bard College faculty, and an officer of the college is a member of the trust's governing body.

ARTISTS' DIFFICULT CHOICES

Choosing among the legal forms and tax statuses that can be employed for an artist-endowed foundation is difficult enough. Yet artists face many additional decisions in the process of establishing and providing for a foundation that will steward a creative legacy by advancing the public's access to and understanding of the artist's works. There are five areas in particular that require artists to make well-informed determinations and choose the appropriate experts for advice: legal counsel, generally; estate-planning counsel and private foundation counsel, specifically; estate executors/trustees; the valuation of their artworks; and foundation governance.

The single most significant factor influencing the success of an artist-endowed foundation is the caliber of its legal counsel. The impact of knowledgeable and prudent counsel bears on an artist's estate planning, on foundation establishment, on the operation of a foundation during an artist's lifetime, and on the operation of a foundation following an artist's death. Artists and foundations must choose experienced, knowledgeable legal advisers who can navigate the complex rules and regulations applicable to organizations with private foundation status. For example, some artists who create foundations during their lifetime are not aware of the limitations federal and state laws impose on private foundations during their donors' lifetime. As a result, artists mistakenly assume that while they are living, their foundation will undertake activities with their artworks that are typical of posthumous artist-endowed foundations, such as owning, exhibiting, publishing about, and making gifts of the artist's works; conducting or supporting scholarship on the artist's oeuvre; or authenticating the artist's works. It is counsel's responsibility to educate their clients on the significantly risky error of this assumption in light of the prohibition on self-dealing for private foundations, as well as the prohibition on inurement and private benefit for charitable entities generally.

Unfortunately, this does not always happen. In 1992 the IRS retroactively revoked the tax-exempt status of an artist-endowed foundation, which was not named in the ruling. This action was based on findings that the artist who had created the foundation, ostensibly to assist up-and-coming artists in a particular field, had instead employed it to exhibit, publish about, and promote the artist's own work. The foundation terminated following the revocation. Its attorney was a member of its board.[48]

Artists must also acquire expert advice on planning their estates, and this is not always easy to find. The importance of working with expert estate-planning counsel, as opposed to a business accountant or art-law attorney alone, cannot be emphasized strongly enough. Sam Francis (1923–1994), for example, relied on his longtime accountant and business adviser, and not on expert estate-planning counsel; as a result, he failed to properly plan his estate. His executor ultimately was forced to sell a significant portion of the artist's works in order to pay millions of dollars in estate taxes and legal fees to settle the litigation among his heirs.[49] This left the Sam Francis Foundation with very modest assets to steward such a high-caliber creative legacy for public benefit.

Even prominent trust and estate counsel, however, can be unaware of the unique pitfalls facing visual artists. This is because they tend to be more familiar with planning the estates of art collectors, whose art holdings are diverse and limited to the artworks themselves, than planning the estates of artists, whose assets can include intellectual property, substantial bodies of work by the same artist, significant collections of unfinished works and archives, and in some cases, interests in creative businesses. For example, if flawed plans are made for an artist's intellectual property, including transferring it to a trust or corporate entity during the artist's lifetime, the result can be a tangle of conflicting interests among the foundation and the statutory heirs to the copyright termination rights, potentially undermining the artist's intentions for the foundation.[50] Likewise, many artists, on the advice of their accountants, incorporate their studio practice, placing their extant works and copyrights under the control of a corporation and becoming a compensated employee and shareholder of the ongoing business. Unfortunately, private foundations are prohibited from holding more than a small percentage of the ownership interest in a corporation, either on their own or in combination with their insiders. Not all estate planners are aware of this rule and unwinding this mistake can cost the foundation a great deal, either in significant tax payments incurred to release artworks from the corporation's ownership or in substantial legal fees paid to secure an IRS ruling that the corporation may be retained and operated as a business functionally related to the foundation's charitable purposes.[51]

In addition to making informed choices about legal counsel, estate-planning advice, and private foundation guidance, artists must choose wisely when selecting the estate executors and/or trustees who will implement the settlement of the artist's testamentary provisions and, as such, have a significant impact on an artist-endowed foundation's ability to steward the artist's creative legacy. Although there are numerous examples of successfully administered estates, some artists' estates have encountered major challenges during administration. Already mentioned is the problem of appointing a self-interested executor, as in the case of the Mark Rothko estate, or an executor unfamiliar with the cultural value versus the economic value of artists' assets, as with the Joseph Cornell estate. Another troubling example is the recent case of Robert Rauschenberg (1925–2008). The artist failed to specify any limit on compensation to the friends and business associates he appointed as trustees of the trust he created during his lifetime to realize his testamentary plans. The result was a $24.6 million charge when the trustees completed the transfer of the trust's assets to the foundation.[52]

Artists face further difficulties when assessing the value of their own works and answering the inevitable question: are my assets sufficient to create a viable foundation? Foundations are self-supporting entities and typically generate their resources from art sales, copyright licensing, and investment returns. A rule of thumb is that if the artist's studio practice did not support the artist during his or her lifetime—if a teaching salary or private income, for example, was a necessary supplement—then it is unlikely to support a foundation after the artist's death, in which case it will be necessary for the artist to provide other resources if the foundation is to succeed.

Some artists believe their artworks have significant financial value, and they are correct. Their misstep, however, is to hope that their foundation can navigate an orderly start-up with a bequest comprising solely artworks and other non-liquid assets. The Judd Foundation received an extraordinary bequest including artworks along with a variety of properties in New York and Texas housing installed spaces, archives, and libraries, but no financial assets. Consequently, it struggled financially for almost a decade. Donald Judd had been disinclined to sell his art during his lifetime, and the art market was uncertain of the posthumous value of his oeuvre when the foundation's governing body chose to undertake an unprecedented auction sale of a group of his works in 2006.[53] Contrary to predictions that a block sale would depress prices, this gutsy strategy worked. The market's appetite for the artist's works was strong, and the sale was a success, with the foundation's tax return reporting net proceeds of more than $26 million from the sale.[54]

Other artists hope their artworks have financial value sufficient to be the sole source of support for an artist-endowed foundation and unfortunately are not correct, at least initially. Despite national recognition early in the career of Jay DeFeo (1929–1989), her work had fallen into obscurity by the time of her death. Making a mistake of generosity not uncommon among artists, DeFeo bequeathed all of her modest financial assets to establish an award for Master of Fine Arts students at Mills College, in Oakland, California, where she had taught.[55] As a result, upon her death, the Jay DeFeo Trust (now The Jay DeFeo Foundation) received solely her artworks and archive. Happily, the foundation was blessed with a patient, talented director who understood the artist's high-caliber work and, despite minimal resources, doggedly charted DeFeo's reemergence over more than twenty-five years through carefully choreographed exhibitions, publications, and placement of works in public collections. The foundation now can claim appropriate recognition for this artist in the eyes of the art world and enhanced public access to her works.[56] Would that this result could be true for all artists whose works are undervalued at their death and committed to an artist-endowed foundation.

The fifth topic that bedevils artists in laying plans for a successful artist-endowed foundation is the choice of the individuals who will serve as members of the governing body charged to carry out the artist's intentions with respect to stewardship of artworks and fulfillment of philanthropic purposes. The chief challenge the artist faces is to appoint a set of individuals who will place the foundation's interests above their own personal interests and, as a group, provide the range of expertise required to navigate the complicated concerns of a private foundation endowed with artworks. The default strategy—appointing solely friends, associates, and family members—generally fails to provide the needed expertise. For example, the governing body of the Hon Chew Hee Estate Foundation, created in Hawaii following the death of Hon Chew Hee (1906–1993), comprised the artist's friends and associates. Unsure of a long-term strategy to manage the foundation's art assets, the board accepted an art dealer's offer to purchase the foundation's total art collection for a steeply discounted price. Alongside this possible waste of charitable assets, several board members also decided that the discounted prices set by the dealer's offer were appealing and themselves purchased works directly from the foundation based on that price. With only a few specific exceptions, transactions between a private foundation and its insiders are prohibited by law.[57] In a significantly lenient comment, the Hawaii Attorney General declined to censure the board, citing its acts as the result of ignorance and not malfeasance.[58]

As to the question of artists' family members serving as members of foundations' governing bodies, there are many examples that might be cited to illustrate the wisdom or the foolishness of an artist's decision to involve family members in this way. Three definitive things can be said on the topic, however: first, mere status as an artist's family member, absent other qualifications and relevant experience, is not sufficient for an individual to play a productive role as a member of a foundation's governing body; second, governing bodies comprising solely members of artists' families are likely to lack the range of necessary expertise; and third, if all members of a governing body are family members, it will lack the independent members required to implement procedures stipulated by law to manage conflicts of interest.[59]

THE ART MARKET, THE ESTATE TAX, AND STEWARDSHIP CHOICES

While many factors are spurring the increase in the number of artist-endowed foundations, the chief one is the intersection of the art market with artists' demographics. Even given the inevitable cycles in art prices over past decades, the global art market in the long view has risen substantially, making wealthy individuals of many living artists now in their later decades. This trend sharpens the question of posthumous stewardship of creative legacies and is likely to spur creation of many artist-endowed foundations, though not all of them will have the same characteristics and circumstances.

For example, more than half of artist-endowed foundations holding at least $1 million in assets are associated with artists who had no immediate survivors or were survived solely by a spouse.[60] Presumably, the motivation for these artists was to provide for the orderly stewardship of their creative works and copyrights as a charitable endeavor under a foundation's auspices, not to minimize estate tax on non-charitable bequests to descendants, of which there were none.[61] Thus, we can assume that many of the new artist-endowed foundations will be created by artists with no immediate heirs who will bequeath all of their assets to this tax-exempt charitable beneficiary, as did Robert Mapplethorpe, Andy Warhol, and Helen Frankenthaler, among numerous others. Many also will be created by artists survived solely by a spouse, who will enjoy the intervening arrangement evidenced almost a century and a half ago by the estate plan of Franz Ludwig Catel. In this current era, the surviving spouse will receive lifetime use of the artist's assets, free of federal estate tax under the federal estate tax marital exemption, with the artist-endowed foundation in the role of residual beneficiary, as were the foundations of Hans Hofmann and Esteban Vicente, among others. The Supreme Court's 2015 ruling in favor of marriage equality will likely increase substantially the number of foundations for whom there are such intervening interests in the artist's assets.

Lastly, some of the new foundations will be created by the type of artist that faces the greatest complications, that is, those with immediate heirs beyond a spouse—children. In a perfect world, artists in this situation would heed closely the precedent offered on this specific point by Robert Motherwell, Robert Rauschenberg, and Cy Twombly. Per their example, the artist's estate plan would provide that immediate heirs receive financial and other assets, and the foundation receive all of the artworks and copyrights, enabling a coherent, unified strategy of legacy stewardship by the foundation. This would also enable the children to participate as members of the foundation's governing body free of conflicts of interest related to the art. Unfortunately, this simple and clean arrangement can be expected to remain more an ideal and less a reality.

Today it is more likely that the works of an artist with lineal descendants will be divided between these noncharitable beneficiaries and the foundation. The typical arrangement is for the heirs to receive the greatest number of artworks on which the estate tax can be paid by the cash assets available to the estate or generated quickly through asset sales, while the artist-endowed foundation receives the remainder of the works, unburdened by the estate tax. This is a common tactic when an artist's assets are exclusively artworks and there is no other way to provide for the children, or when an artist's estate counsel promotes a view of estate planning that emphasizes maximum art bequests to heirs, unaware or unconcerned as to how this arrangement may hamper the stewardship role of the artist-endowed foundation.

Regrettably, when children who serve on the foundation's board own the artist's art, or are beneficiaries of a trust funded with the artist's art, the question of legacy stewardship by the foundation can be muddled by short-term strategies to avoid conflicts of interest and self-dealing risks, rather than focused clearly by an unhampered commitment to sharing the artist's creative achievements for public benefit. In December 2017 Congress approved the Tax Cuts and Jobs Act, significantly revising the federal tax code on several fronts. Among these, the legislation doubled the estate tax exemption for a period of eight years, raising it to $11 million per individual ($22 million per married couple with proper planning). Thus a significant number of artists will be able to plan for posthumous stewardship of their oeuvre using noncharitable options, as discussed previously or, if they do choose to create an artist-endowed foundation, do so as an affirmative choice to commit stewardship of their works to a public benefit mission, rather than as a compromising strategy to minimize the estate tax.

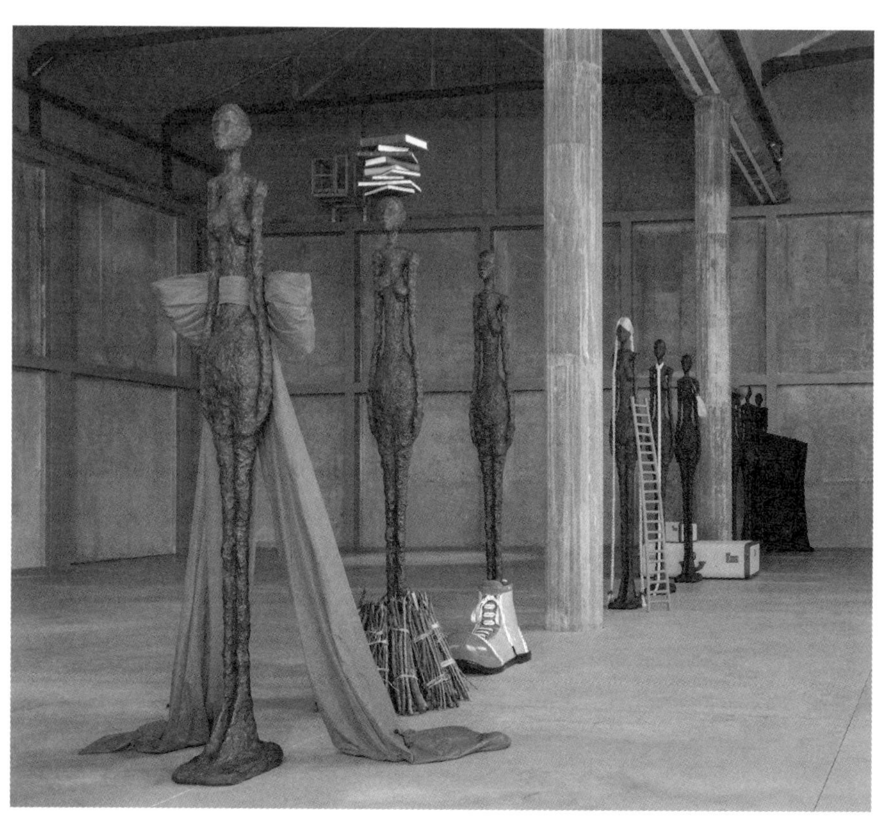

John Baldessari
The Giacometti Variations, 2010
Nine resin sculptures with objects, 450 × 60 × 50 cm (each)

Artists' Estates as Guardians of Artistic Legacy: Custodians or Gatekeepers?

DANIEL McCLEAN

As with many important reflections on artistic authorship, one turns to a work by Marcel Duchamp (1887–1968): the artist's remarkable tableau *Étant donnés: 1. La chute d'eau, 2. Le gaz d'éclairage* (1946–66), permanently installed inside the Philadelphia Museum of Art. Duchamp's enigmatic and erotic final work—which stages and allegorizes the act of looking (through a peep hole in a wooden door onto a landscape with a reclining female nude holding a gas lamp)—was planned secretly by the artist for over twenty years. However, it only came into being upon Duchamp's death, when it was posthumously installed in 1969 inside the Philadelphia Museum of Art in accordance with his "Manual of Instructions." With *Étant donnés*, Duchamp paradoxically created the truly "original" posthumous work, thereby symbolically cheating his own death. Duchamp's work presciently opens two lines of inquiry germane to our understanding of artistic authorship and legacy today: first, what is the status of the posthumous iteration of the work, and might a work executed by others posthumously have the same or even greater value than an (identical) work made by the artist during the artist's lifetime? And second, who are the guardians of the artist's work and authorship when the artist is no longer around, and in particular, who has the final say?

For Duchamp, as *Étant donnés* reflects, the long-term guardian of the artwork was the museum: his artwork exists in situ so long as the museum remains. However, although the Philadelphia Museum of Art was the recipient of Duchamp's final work, the task of executing it was entrusted by Duchamp not only to its curators but also to his heirs—his widow and son.[1] Unintentionally, perhaps, Duchamp's final work reveals the ongoing role of the artist's estate as a guardian of an artist's legacy alongside the museum.

ARTISTS' ESTATES AS GUARDIANS

Artists' estates are essentially all the assets bequeathed by the artist on death, including artworks. They are typically privately owned and run by the artist's heirs.[2] However, they may also take varied institutional forms or may be directly transferred to galleries or to museums. In some instances, as seen with wealthy artists' endowed private foundations or public charities (particularly in the United States), they are structured as not-for-profit legal entities with tax-exempt status run as trusts by boards of independent trustees, or in some cases as corporations. (In contrast to private estates, private foundations and public charities are state regulated and transparent to differing degrees.) Artists' foundations may have broad legacy aims beyond promoting the deceased artist's work; for example, the Robert Rauschenberg Foundation works to advance the visual arts through grants and artist residencies, and some, like the Robert Mapplethorpe Foundation, even have social goals, in their case to help find a cure for AIDS. I use the terms "artists' estates" collectively, to refer to all of the configurations mentioned to above.

In today's art world, artists' estates have come to assume increasing significance as guardians of artistic authorship and legacy, mediating between the art market (blue-chip contemporary art galleries compete aggressively to represent the estates of high-caliber artists), museums, and the domain of art-historical research and scholarship. Artists' estates have unique authority as guardians, often underscored by their mandate from the artist, as expressed in the artist's will, or through the creation of a foundation or charity while the artist was alive. An artist's estate owns not only the artworks and archival materials left by the artist but also the deceased artist's intellectual-property rights, which enables the estate to control in many ways how the artwork is exhibited, reproduced, and even, in some European civil-law countries, authenticated.[3] In addition, an artist's estate often has an unrivalled expertise in the deceased artist's work, making it the de facto authority for authentication.

Accordingly, artists' estates sometimes even have the authority to intervene inside the museum, to determine whether the artist's work may be exhibited, as revealed in the legal dispute between the Joseph Beuys estate and the Museum Schloss Moyland, in Bedburg-Hau, Germany.[4] At issue was the museum's display, in 2009, of a series of black-and-white photographs by Wolfgang Tischer—which the museum owned—documenting *The Silence of Marcel Duchamp Is Overrated* (1964), a performance by Joseph Beuys (1921–1986) that had been broadcast live on German television. The Beuys estate (run by Joseph Beuys's widow, Eva Beuys), which is the owner of the copyright of all of Beuys's works, objected through the German copyright-collecting society (VG Bild-Kunst) to the museum's display, complaining that Tischer's photographs infringed the artistic copyright subsisting in Beuys's performance by presenting an unauthorized "adaptation." In 2013, after protracted litigation, the case was settled in the museum's favor in the German Federal Supreme Court (the lower German courts had ruled in the estate's favor). The court held that though Beuys's performance was protected under German law as an "artistic work," it was unable to determine whether Tischer's photographs were infringing copies, because there was no existing independent recording of Beuys's performance to compare to Tischer's photographs.

CUSTODIANS OR GATEKEEPERS?

The litigation between the Beuys estate and the Museum Schloss Moyland reveals the problems that can arise when different legacy guardians (the estate and museum) come into conflict. It also reveals two contentious issues: what should be the scope of estates' responsibilities as guardians? And by what standards should estates operate?

Artists' estates perform a wide range of invaluable tasks, often under severe economic constraint: from conservation to archiving; from cataloguing to authentication; from working with galleries, museums, and collectors that are exhibiting the artist's work to instigating art-historical research and scholarship about the artist's oeuvre. Yet despite the valuable work that artists' estates do, there are some situations in which they overreach their authority as guardians. These instances of overreach are underscored, perhaps, by the lack of clear normative and professional shared standards among artists' estates, in contrast, for example, to those adopted by public museums (through documents such as the ICOM Code of Ethics for Museums, published by the International Council of Museums).[5]

Although guarding legacy can be a complex and difficult task, artists' estates work effectively as guardians of artistic authorship when they act as *custodians*, protecting the work yet encouraging dissemination, rather than as *gatekeepers*, restricting access to and use of the artist's work. The notion of custodianship, like stewardship, implies entrustment rather than mere ownership and suggests that legacy is something greater than the exercise of property rights. Interestingly, the definition of "legacy" as a noun connotes both bequeathed personal property and "something left or handed down," including having an immaterial impact on others.[6] Legacy requires being responsible not just to the intentions of the deceased artist, but also to other members of the artistic community, such as artists, curators, and scholars, as well as to the wider public and to society and culture at large. The issues of guardianship can be analyzed in relation to three crucial areas where artists' estates frequently act as guardians: (1) ownership of the artist's archive, (2) reproduction of the artwork, and (3) the authentication of artworks.

THE ARCHIVE

An artist's archive is critical to his or her legacy. It is an essential resource for scholars, curators, and artists who may wish to research the artist's biography, artworks, or exhibitions, and it enables scholars to write histories of the artist or any associated art movements, galleries, or museums. An artist's archive may also contain records that trace the ownership of the artist's work and enable its authentication. Artists including Lawrence Weiner and Carl Andre operate archival systems that register ownership and transfers in ownership of their works and thus facilitate their authentication. It is perhaps because the archive is so central to the mediation of artistic authorship that many contemporary artists, from Marcel Broodthaers onwards, have a self-reflexive fascination with it—what the art theorist Hal Foster terms the "archival impulse." Artists have imitated the archive's visual forms (vitrines) and typological arrangements (indexes) for ordering documents, records, and materials, as well as questioned its very structures of ownership and control.[7]

If an artist's legacy is to be sustained, the artist's archive should be open to the public (free of charge, where possible) to allow for research and critical interpretation, so that new perspectives can be formed on the artist over time, and his or her place in art history can be consolidated. There are many positive examples in which artists' estates and foundations have opened artists' archives for access to the public—thereby acting as custodians rather than as gatekeepers. Consider the archives of Donald Judd, run by the Judd Foundation, located in Marfa, Texas, along with Judd's permanently installed collection of artwork dispersed across different locations in the town; or the Andy Warhol archive, comprising thousands of artifacts, housed at the Andy Warhol Museum, in Pittsburgh. Yet there are also negative instances, in which artists' estates and foundations (as well as museums) have restricted access to artists' archives or charged exorbitant fees for reproducing the documents contained in them.

In her ongoing project the *Barragán Archives*, the artist Jill Magid (b.1973) interrogates the Barragan Foundation's control over the authorial legacy of the legendary Mexican modernist architect Luis Barragán (1906–1988).[8] Barragán's professional archive comprises thousands of original drawings by the architect, as well as his architectural models, photographs, and professional letters (Barragán created a separate personal archive of intimate letters and photographs). The archive controversially left Mexico in the early 1990s after Barragán's death. It was bizarrely inherited by the widow of Barragán's studio assistant, Raul Ferrera, to whom Barragán had bequeathed it and who committed suicide in 1993. It was then consigned by Ferrara's widow to a New York art dealer, and it was reportedly purchased for $3 million by Rolf Fehlbaum, the chairman and board director of Vitra, a Swiss corporation famous for manufacturing products of contemporary design. The archive was then allegedly gifted by Fehlbaum to his wife, the architecture critic Frederica Zanco, as a wedding present in 1995. The eponymous Barragan Foundation (a foundation not established by Barragán but by Zanco and closely aligned to the Vitra corporation) now controls the archive. The Barragan Foundation also acquired the copyright to Barragán's architectural works and models at some point during the late 1990s.

Magid initiated the project in 2013, when she made an official request to access Barragán's archive at the foundation's premises. She sent the request through the organizers of *Parcours*, a public-art project run by Art Basel, and the request was surprisingly declined. The foundation's refusal to allow Magid (and other scholars, as well as the public) access to the Barragán Archives and to reproduce photographic images of Barragán's architecture inspired her to embark upon a series of exhibitions reflecting on the physical and legal restrictions imposed by the foundation, and on what she describes as "the ownership of an artist's legacy by a corporation." While the acquisition of Barragán's archive by Felhbaum and Zanco may well have prevented it from being dispersed (which is laudable), the foundation's control over access to the archive and wider dissemination is, as Magid's project illuminates, problematic.

Throughout Magid's nuanced project, she has consciously worked within the legal limitations imposed by the foundation, displaying in exhibitions the restricted range of images and texts whose distribution has been authorized by the foundation, and framing them as readymades.

She uses these displays—which often include previously published books on the architect, such as *Luis Barragán: The Quiet Revolution by Federica Zanco* (published by the Vitra Design Museum, 2001)—to mark the archive's very absence, and the absence of images of Barragán's architecture save for those officially sanctioned by the foundation.

Magid's project has culminated in her spectacular and provocative *Proposal* (2016). The artist, with the consent and assistance of Barragán's relatives, disinterred Barragán's cremated ashes from a public crematorium in Mexico and sent them to a Swiss specialist diamond company to be compressed into a diamond, which was set into an engagement ring. Magid then sent the ring to Federica Zanco. Mirroring the alleged wedding gift of Barragán's archive from Rolf Fehlbaum to Federica Zanco in the mid-1990s, *Proposal* stages the potential negotiated return of the archive to Mexico (in exchange for the ring). The literal legacy of Barragán (the body of the artist) is metamorphosed into a diamond ring—a "tool for negotiation," in the artist's words—to facilitate dialogue between the foundation and the State of Mexico, and to encourage the "return" of the archive in a form to be determined, to Mexico, and with it the possibility of wider public access.

REPRODUCTION

An artist's estate is usually the beneficiary of the deceased artist's intellectual-property rights, which include copyright, moral rights of authorship, and in some countries (for example, within the European Union) the artist's resale royalty rights. In rare instances, the estate is also responsible for other intellectual-property rights, such as trademarks (most artists and estates do not trademark their names), which can control the use of the artist's name and signature. The family of Pablo Picasso famously licensed the artist's trademarked name and signature to the car manufacturer Citroën—a decision that reportedly divided the heirs.[9]

Copyright—which controls the copying, distribution of copies, public performance, and public communication of protected "works" (including artistic works)—can be licensed and commercially exploited as a property right by the artist's estate. It typically lasts, in many jurisdictions (including in the European Union and the United States), for the lifetime of the author plus seventy years. Accordingly, copyright is a valuable instrument for an artist's estate in controlling the public dissemination of the deceased artist's work, as well as a potentially valuable income stream, particularly for estates that may otherwise lack a substantial inventory of the artist's artworks to sell in the art market.

Used positively, artistic copyright can help to maintain the integrity of the artist's work and to prevent its misuse through unauthorized commercial reproduction. Copyright can, for example, stop the merchandising of an artist's work on products and in advertising that the artist might have found highly offensive and damaging to the work's meaning. In 2016 the estate of the LA graffiti artist Dash Snow (1981–2009) sued the US corporation McDonalds for copyright infringement, alleging that McDonalds had re-created Snow's graffiti in more than one hundred of its global locations, thereby wrongfully associating Snow with corporate culture and consumerism, which the artist had strenuously avoided when alive.[10]

Used negatively, however, copyright can restrict the circulation of images of the artist's work by museums, educational institutions, and publishers. It can also prevent other artists from building on the deceased artist's work through being copied, cited, and even contested, thus stopping the work entering an "artistic commonwealth" of shared images and forms, and conflicting with how the artist would have exercised this copyright as an author when alive.[11] Generally speaking, fine artists do not sue one another for copyright infringement—a notable exception being the litigation in 2014 between the artists Bridget Riley (b.1931) and Tobias Rehberger (b.1966) regarding the alleged infringement by Rehberger of the copyright subsisting in a Riley painting.[12]

The litigation between the Giacometti Foundation and John Baldessari/Fondazione Prada (2010–13) in the Milan courts illustrates how misguided an artist's estate can be when it seeks to use copyright law to prevent the copying by other artists of a deceased artist's work—particularly when that copied work is itself of iconic artistic and cultural significance and hence an invaluable reference point for other artists and culture at large.[13] In this case, the Giacometti Foundation sought a permanent injunction from the Italian court to prevent the exhibition of Baldessari's *Giacometti Variations* (2010), commissioned by Fondazione Prada, Milan. John Baldessari (b.1931) created without authorization nine enlarged figurines by Alberto Giacometti (1901–1966), each 4.5 meters tall and draped in garments and objects designed by Baldessari. The artist did this to comment ironically on the mutation of representations of the human figure within Western culture from the time of Giacometti (his figurines symbolizing post–World War II humanist notions of existential anxiety) to the present day (the age of postmodern consumerism and fashion). Ultimately, Baldessari and the Fondazione Prada were able to successfully contest the injunction under the fair-use/parody exception provided under Italian copyright law. The exhibition never reopened – the litigation took too long to be settled but Fondazione Prada exhibited the work in 2016.

By contrast, many artists' estates appreciate the importance for an artist's legacy of the work being copied, transformed, and even contested by other artists (though not used in commercial merchandising or in advertising). The Rauschenberg Foundation allows museums and educational institutions to reproduce images of work by Robert Rauschenberg (1925–2008) without paying fees or royalties, and they have given artists wide access to recycle and use Rauschenberg's works, not only appreciating the deceased artist's own reproduction and mixing of images borrowed from high and low culture but also mindful of the importance of such practices for the sustaining of Rauschenberg's legacy. In 2015, for example, the foundation gave the artist Rachel Harrison (b.1966) unfettered access to Rauschenberg's work to use as the basis of her exhibition at the Cleveland Museum of Art, *Gloria: Robert Rauschenberg and Rachel Harrison*, allowing her to juxtapose her own works next to Rauschenberg's.[14] The approach of the Rauschenberg Foundation should be applauded as a positive example of custodianship exercised by an artist's estate.

Other artists' estates have also enabled productive dialogues around the deceased artist's work. For example, the Henry Moore Foundation—dedicated to the legacy of British sculptor Henry Moore (1898–1986), but also to the support of sculpture and the visual arts in the United Kingdom—allowed the British artist Simon Starling (b.1967) to reproduce Moore's sculpture in several projects, including in Starling's memorable sculpture *Infestation Piece (Musselled Moore)* (2006–8).[15] Starling's sculpture is a slightly less-than-to-scale reproduction of Moore's sculpture *Warrior with Shield* (1953–54)—a version of which is owned by the Henry Moore Sculpture Centre at the Art Gallery of Ontario, in Toronto. Referring to this work and to Moore's historical connection with the city of Toronto, Starling submerged his reproduction in the icy waters of Lake Ontario for over a year before exhibiting it encrusted with mussels and shellfish in 2008 at the Power Plant, in Toronto.

AUTHENTICATION

Authentication is fundamental to protecting the integrity of an artist's work and to protecting its market over time. The forgery scandal engulfing the leading Korean Minimalist painter Lee Ufan (b.1936) in 2016 is a spectacular example of how doubts about the authenticity of an artist's work can undermine its integrity. In this case, the artist was alleged to have wrongly verified faked paintings as his own work to prop up his market, which led to numerous arrests in South Korea, including that of a prominent art dealer.[16] It is not clear what impact the scandal will have on Lee Ufan's market, but it is likely to be negative.

Central to the concept of authenticity are the notions of "original" expressive authorship and the auratic "uniqueness" of the object, as described by the German philosopher Walter Benjamin in his essay "Work of Art in the Age of Mechanical Reproduction" (1936). Authenticity also refers to an array of characteristics linked to the artwork's aesthetic "quality"—such as the work's age, condition, period, school, and style—that can be used to prove or certify authorship. Without these ascriptions of authorship and unique objecthood, the artwork loses its symbolic and monetary value. The two historical enemies of authenticity are the fake (the fraudulent copy) and the misattribution (the innocent copy), as they undermine the regime of original authorship. Authenticity is also undermined when a work is restored too many times, or restored in a way that changes the object substantially. With contemporary artworks, which are often executed in multiple form, and often fabricated by third parties on behalf of the artist and not by the artist, the question of authenticity has become even more elastic and challenging.

Artists' estates often play a critical role as guardians in the authentication of artworks, by family members and by foundations deciding whether or not artworks are original. This is done through the authentication of individual artworks via certification and the preparation of the artist's catalogue raisonné—a comprehensive catalogue of works by an artist, compiled by experts and usually arranged chronologically with date, medium, provenance, and exhibition history for each work. When an artwork is omitted from the catalogue raisonné, its exclusion undermines the status of its authorship among scholars and in the marketplace. If an individual artwork is specifically denied authenticity in the form of certification, then the result can be arguably even more damaging as it is likely to be very difficult for the owner to sell the artwork (or at least for a sum close to its true market value) without the issued certificate.

Yet if artists' estates are the de facto singular source of authority (and in some countries, the legal source of authority) for authenticating artworks, by what procedures and standards should they do this? The litigation between the art collector Joe Simon-Whelan and the Andy Warhol Foundation for the Visual Arts and its authentication body, the Andy Warhol Art Authentication Board (2007–9), reveals both the control that artists' estates can have in this arena and the legal risks that artists' estates run of being sued over questions of authentication by disgruntled owners.[17] It also reveals the problems caused when boards do not follow transparent and coherent criteria and board members are perceived to have conflicts of interest (principally as dealers in the artist's work they are authenticating).

Simon-Whelan owned a work allegedly by Andy Warhol (1928–1987). *Red Self-Portrait* (1965), one of an edition of ten works produced by Warhol's silkscreen factory, had once been sold by Christie's at auction in 1987 and authenticated prior to this sale as being a Warhol both by the foundation (Vincent Froment, a trustee, stamped the work with Warhol's signature!) and by Fred Hughes, the executor of Warhol's estate. Simon-Whelan purchased the work for $195,000 in 1989. In 2001 he submitted it to the authentication board. He had been encouraged to do so by Froment, the Warhol Foundation's exclusive sales agent and a member of the authentication board, who had formerly positively authenticated Simon-Whelan's work. Following Simon-Whelan's application, the board twice rejected the authenticity of the silkscreen, finally stamping "DENIED" in large uppercase letters on its back so as to permanently damage it. The board gave no initial explanation for its rejection, but subsequently, in 2004, explained its decision on the basis that Warhol had not been involved in any stage in overseeing the production of this series of works—a decision that, as Richard Dorment argued in a notable article in the *New York Review of Books*, would appear to be fundamentally flawed in terms of how Warhol worked as an artist and, importantly, perceived the authenticity of his *Red Self-Portrait* series.[18]

Angered by the board's rejection in 2007, Simon-Whelan spearheaded a class action against the board, the foundation, and other parties in New York Federal District Court on the basis of antitrust, fraud, and unjust-enrichment claims, also requesting a court declaration that the waiver of his rights to sue the board and foundation when signing up to the board's Submission Agreement was unenforceable. Simon-Whelan accused, inter alia, the foundation and board under sections 1 and 2 of the Sherman Antitrust Act of conspiring in restraint of trade to artificially restrict the supply of Warhol's work, thereby inflating the value of each work held by the foundation, and colluding to monopolize trade in Warhol's works. (The foundation funds its charitable activities by selling Warhol works, of which it owned a significant market share.) The accused parties achieved all this, Simon-Whelan claimed, through the board wrongfully denying the authenticity of genuine Warhol works, including his own *Red Self-Portrait*. In 2009 a US Federal Court rejected a motion brought by the foundation and board to dismiss Simon-Whelan's claim, allowing it to proceed on the fraud and unjust-enrichment claims, and in part on the antitrust claims. In particular, the court found that there was a plausible basis for Simon-Whelan to claim antitrust injury because the board prevented him from operating as a competitor in the market by denying the work's authenticity, although Simon-Whelan was not found to suffer injury through the alleged price-inflationary aspects of the conspiracy. Following the court's decision in 2009, the litigation was eventually settled when Simon-Whelan voluntarily abandoned his claim. By then, however, the foundation had incurred over $7 million in legal fees (which the foundation then sought to recover from its insurance company, Philadelphia Indemnity Insurance Company, leading to further litigation), and a dangerous precedent had been set. If Simon-Whelan could bring antitrust claims this far (anticompetitive claims, in this instance), so could other potential claimants.

In 2012 the Warhol Foundation closed the authentication board, ceasing its certification activities (though the foundation continues its comprehensive Warhol catalogue raisonné project to document and authenticate Warhol's works). Since then other artists' estates have also voluntarily ceased their authentication activities, including the respective authentication boards of the Alexander Calder, Keith Haring, and Roy Lichtenstein foundations and the heirs of Jean-Michel Basquiat. The voluntary dissolution of the Andy Warhol Art Authentication Board and other artists' authentication boards has arguably caused an authentication crisis in the blue-chip contemporary art market, particularly in the United States, where, unlike in Europe, artists' estates face heavy litigation costs that are generally nonrecoverable, even when claims are successfully defended by estates or foundations. Unfortunate owners who lack requisite certificates find it much harder to sell their works and to obtain a fair market value, even when they have strong evidence of the work's provenance and can point to its inclusion in the artist's catalogue raisonné or other important publications on the artist. Conversely, and paradoxically, the absence of certificates makes it easier for forgeries to enter the art market, as there are fewer barriers to scrutiny. The risks of relying on individual experts' opinions and the seller's representations as opposed to a certificate issued by an artist's sanctified authentication board is dramatically illustrated by the closure of New York's Knoedler Gallery in the wake of its forgery scandal in 2011.[19]

As Simon-Whelan's dispute with the Warhol Foundation and authentication board illustrates, some of these problems could seemingly have been overcome if there had been different standards of governance—that is, if artists' estates acted less as gatekeepers and more as true custodians. The US Federal Court found sufficiently "plausible" alleged facts that the Warhol authentication board lacked the required independence from the foundation (and contained members who were not even experts), and that the board's "policies" were arbitrary and inconsistent. For example, the board sometimes reversed its own prior authentication determinations and even occasionally refused to authenticate works that it had previously attempted to purchase. Compounding this was the board's lack of transparency: it refused to provide clear reasons or explanations for its decisions.

Some of these litigation risks might be mitigated if artists' authentication boards were run in the future by experts independent of the estate or the foundation. These experts could be appointed on a temporary and revolving basis to lessen the development of self-interested attachments. Above all, decision-making should be transparent and consistent. It is noteworthy that the art dealer Richard Polsky has recently created a substitute service for authenticating Andy Warhol's artwork and those of other artists.[20] Polsky proclaims to follow "transparent" and "fair" criteria and to explain how decisions are reached when works are reviewed, though it remains open as to whether his authentications will be followed by the market in practice.

To date, the authentication crisis shows no imminent signs of abating in the United States. There have, for example, been various aborted attempts to promote a New York state law that would protect art experts from litigation when offering authenticity opinions, though there is still hope the law might eventually pass.[21] The lawsuit brought in late 2016 in the New York state court by the Mayor Gallery, London, against the compilers of the Agnes Martin catalogue raisonné and other parties for refusing to positively authenticate thirteen "Agnes Martin" paintings formerly sold by the Mayor Gallery illustrates once again the litigation risks assumed by authentication boards when offering opinions.[22] In this case, the Mayor Gallery alleges that by wrongfully refusing to include these paintings in the catalogue raisonné, the defendants have rendered them valueless, subjecting the gallery to multiple refund claims from disaffected buyers. In doing so, the Mayor Gallery alleges the board committed various torts, including the tort of wrongful interference with prospective business relations. To succeed in its claim, the Mayor Gallery will need to establish "malice" on the part of the defendants, which is a difficult hurdle to surmount. However, as the Warhol litigation illustrates, just defending this type of litigation in the New York courts is likely to be expensive.

For this situation to change, there needs to be legislative reform, offering greater protection to experts, coupled with reform in the governance of some authentication boards, which effectively have a monopoly on determining authenticity in the art market. Whether this can be achieved remains to be seen.

FOLLOWING THE ARTIST'S INTENTIONS AFTER DEATH

The purpose of this essay is to open critical discussion about the role of artists' estates as guardians of artistic legacy—a task that is too often little addressed. Generally, as discussed, artists' estates provide an invaluable role as custodians of artistic legacy, as opposed to gatekeepers. Nor should we assume simplistically that museums by contrast automatically act as custodians of artistic legacy (a discussion that is beyond the scope of this text). However, there are situations in which the authority of artists' estates is overreached—an overreach perhaps rooted, in part, in the tension between artistic authorship as a bundle of property rights, exercised by third parties when the artist has died, and authorship as the deceased artist's immaterial, creative influence on the language of art and the culture at large. Authorship as property and authorship as legacy can come into conflict because property rights and intellectual-property rights may be exercised in ways that are incommensurate (as discussed above) with the dissemination and use of the artist's work and ideas within public culture.

Yet it should be recalled just how complex and difficult it can be for artists' estates to follow the intentions of the deceased artist and protect the integrity of the work. An artist's authorial legacy can assume myriad forms, both material and immaterial; ultimately, it requires an understanding of the artist's intentions behind the work. When artists do not leave specific instructions on how their estate is to be handled, as is often the case, artists' estates must grapple with a bewildering range of questions: did the artist intend this artifact to be an artwork or not? How did the artist intend the work to be conserved? How did the artist intend the artwork to be remade? And how did the artist intend for it to be viewed? Inherently demanding, these questions are further complicated by the nature of much contemporary artistic production, in which the artwork is often defined not by its "permanent" material form, but by its concept (for example, as written instructions that can be reenacted, as in Conceptual art and beyond); in which production or performance of the artwork is delegated by the artist to others (as in much post-Minimalist and Conceptual art, and so-called performative art); and in which the boundaries between the artwork and its environment (installation/relational aesthetics) and the artwork and its documentation (performance art) are often blurred.

Another controversy, interestingly also involving the legacy of Joseph Beuys, illuminates some of these difficulties. The Hessisches Landesmuseum Darmstadt, in Germany, houses Beuys's iconic seven-room installation *Block Beuys* (1970–86), which comprises more than two hundred and fifty objects. In 2009 the museum decided controversially to renovate the rooms housing Beuys's "total work" by removing the decaying beige jute wallpaper and gray carpet that had been in the room since the 1970s.[23] Beuys had been unclear as to whether the environmental "frame" surrounding his installation was intended to be part of the work or not; yet for many scholars and connoisseurs of Beuys, the museum's discolored walls and fading carpet were an integral and authentic part of Beuys's "entropic" installation, and their removal by the museum violated the work's integrity. This example highlights the difficult decisions artists' estates and museums both face when acting as guardians. On this occasion, the Beuys estate tacitly supported the museum's actions, though some commentators urged it to legally intervene to prevent it. But who is to say—given Beuys's own lack of guidance on this matter—who was right or not?

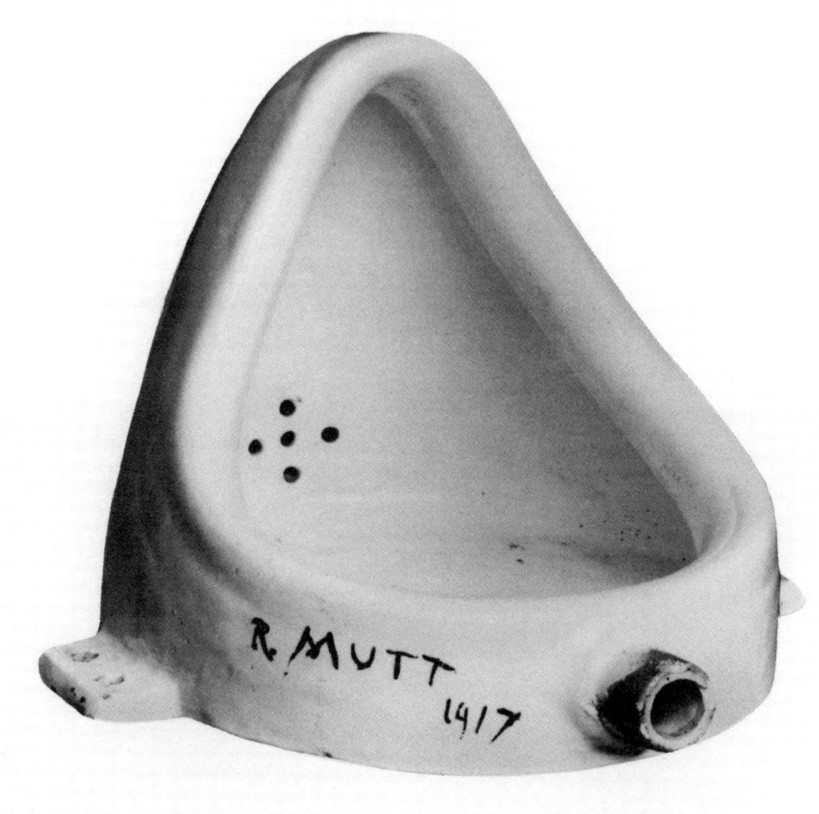

Marcel Duchamp
Fountain, 1917 original
Ceramic, 36 × 48 × 61 cm

Marcel Duchamp, *Fountain*, 1917: A Controversial History

DAWN ADES

It would have no doubt pleased Marcel Duchamp (1887–1968) to know that one hundred years after the emergence of his *Fountain* in 1917 it is still being talked about and causing controversy. He was interested in a future public, rather than the immediate one that "gives you success, and everything. Instead of that, I would rather wait for a public that will come fifty years—a hundred years—after my death."[1] The questions of authorship, artistic identity, and originality that Duchamp raised with his readymades are as pertinent as ever today. *Fountain* itself has been nominated the most important and influential work of the twentieth century (outflanking works by Pablo Picasso and Henri Matisse), its legacy inscribed in the found object, the Surrealist object, and the general use of readymade materials, as well as in its position as the first example of Conceptual art.

But recently there have been startling attempts to question Duchamp's responsibility for *Fountain* and to reattribute its authorship to Baroness Elsa von Freytag-Loringhoven. Under the title "Did Marcel Duchamp Steal Elsa's Urinal?" Julian Spalding and Glyn Thompson argue that "the founding object of Conceptualism was probably 'by a German baroness,' but this debate is rarely aired."[2] Their speculation is without any evidential foundation, and their call for museums to relabel *Fountain* as "a replica, appropriated by Marcel Duchamp, of an original by Baroness Elsa von Freytag-Loringhoven" is unacceptable. This wording moreover, as will be discussed, betrays a misunderstanding of the whole history of Duchamp's readymades, within which *Fountain* has a very specific and unique role, and their reception.

While one is sympathetic to the general issue of misattributed works and the tendency for women on the margins of the avant-garde to get written out altogether, this attempt to revoke Duchamp's authorship of *Fountain* and to thereby rewrite its history and, accordingly, the history of twentieth-century art is simply misguided. It is based on speculative and flawed arguments contained in Irene Gammel's biography *Baroness Elsa* (2002).[3] Welcome as a thorough reassessment of von Freytag-Loringhoven's strange life and involvement with the Munich and New York avant-gardes is (and Gammel does this well), it does not help the case to fabricate a role for her in the history of *Fountain*.

The trigger for Gammel's arguments about *Fountain* appears to be the reattribution of another object from the same period and from the same New York circles: a plumbing trap entitled *God* (1917). This object was traditionally ascribed to Morton Livingston Schamberg, but following research by Francis Naumann, it was newly credited to "Baroness Elsa von Freytag-Loringhoven with the collaboration of Morton Schamberg."[4] The evidence for this was an annotated catalogue of the Walter and Louise Arensberg collection prepared in the early 1950s, in which *God* is listed under Schamberg's name but with the added note: "This construction was made by both Schamberg and von Loringshoven [*sic*]."[5] The addition of the Baroness's name in this case made sense and clarified a puzzle. Although Schamberg was known for his precise machine paintings of abstracted mechanical objects, he produced nothing else like *God*, a plain piece of metal pipe. The Baroness, on the other hand, as Naumann says, "seemed to have been born with a natural penchant for the found object." Her studio "was crowded and reeking with the strange relics she had purloined over a period of years from the New York gutters, . . . old bits of ironware, automobile tires, gilded vegetables, a dozen starved dogs, celluloid paintings, ash cans, every conceivable horror, which to her tortured, yet highly sensitized perception, became objects of formal beauty."[6] Duchamp, though, was not a scavenger in this way. Each of the carefully limited number of readymades he chose was a mass-produced, manufactured object, anonymous and standardized. They are not curiosities, like found objects, and they do not have the aura of the handmade, though they often have a sensual connection to the body.

The nature of the collaboration that produced *God* is unknown; Schamberg photographed the object, perhaps collected and named by von Freytag-Loringhoven, in front of one of his machine paintings, and carefully dated it 1917. It could well have been a response to *Fountain*. However, the attempt to redirect authorship of *Fountain* to the Baroness does not stand up to analysis.

The first, fundamental, error in Gammel's account is her claim that *Fountain* was exhibited at the Independents exhibition, the "*pièce de resistance* of the 1917 exhibition of the American Society of Independent Artists, where it sat on a pedestal, turned upside down.... Thus displayed in April and May 1917, *Fountain*'s toilet aesthetics detonated the unity of the vanguard itself."[7] The object never was exhibited. The story of its non-exhibition but public life must first be told from a public perspective, for reasons that will become apparent.[8]

The context for *Fountain* was, indeed, the first exhibition of Independent Artists in New York. In 1916 the Society of Independent Artists was founded in New York largely through the support of Walter and Louise Arensberg, who were major collectors of modern art and, in particular, friends and patrons of Duchamp. The first Independents exhibition was planned for April 1917, and the widest possible participation was encouraged: an entry fee of one dollar and an annual membership fee of five dollars gained anyone the right to exhibit two works. There was no jury, as at the Paris Indépendants exhibitions. Over two thousand works were submitted, by both American and foreign artists, to what was by far the largest show of modern art to have taken place in America. The artist William Glackens was president of the board, Walter Pach was treasurer, and the directors included George Bellows, Katherine S. Dreier, Rockwell Kent, John Marin, Man Ray, Morton Schamberg, Joseph Stella, and Duchamp, famous in New York since the Armory Show of 1913, and the only European artist named as a director. In apparently enthusiastic welcome of this event, the first issue of a little magazine, *The Blind Man*, was published dated

April 10, 1917, the day of the opening of the Independents.[9] Texts by Duchamp's friend Henri-Pierre Roché (later famous as the author of *Jules et Jim*, 1953) celebrated the coming "artistic revolution"; Beatrice Wood, a young American actress, artist, and girlfriend of both Roché and Duchamp, contributed amusing pieces about her experience as picture hanger for the exhibition; and the poet Mina Loy wondered about the capacity of the public to be educated in artistic matters.

Shortly before the opening of the exhibition, a white porcelain urinal arrived at the exhibition venue, the Grand Central Palace, signed "R. Mutt." A meeting of the board was called, and the "Fountain" was voted down. The incident was widely reported in the press though Duchamp himself "went to considerable lengths to conceal the identity of R. Mutt."[10] A newspaper story on the decision stated that *Fountain* "will never become an attraction . . . of the improvised galleries of the Grand Central Palace, even if Mr. Duchamp goes to the length of withdrawing his own entry, 'Tulip Hysteria Co-ordinating,' in retaliation. 'The Fountain,' said the majority, 'may be a very useful article in its place, but its place is not an art exhibition, and it is, by no definition, a work of art.'"[11] Duchamp immediately resigned from the Independents board, as did Walter Arensberg. Duchamp had apparently not sent in a work himself. The work he was supposedly going to the lengths of withdrawing in protest at Mr. Mutt's exclusion, *Tulip Hysteria Co-ordinating*, never existed, and the title must have been a canard.

The second issue of the magazine *The Blind Man*, in May 1917, went to battle, trumpeting the case of *Fountain* and challenging the publicly quoted justification of the Independents board that it was not a "work of art." A photograph by Alfred Stieglitz, captioned "The Exhibit refused by the Independents: Fountain by R. Mutt," was reproduced full-page. This full-frontal photograph shows *Fountain* for what it is—a urinal placed on its back. Opposite this, the anonymous text "The Richard Mutt Case" laid out the arguments in favor of the "exhibit." This important text, the first public statement of the raison d'être of a readymade, was unsigned. "They say any artist paying six dollars may exhibit. Mr Richard Mutt sent in a fountain. Without discussion this article disappeared and never was exhibited."[12]

Following a neat defense against accusations that *Fountain* was either immoral, or just plagiarism ("a plain piece of plumbing"), the anonymous text continues: "Whether Mr Mutt with his own hands made the fountain or not has no importance. He CHOSE it. He took an ordinary article of life, placed it so that its useful significance disappeared under the new title and point of view—created a new thought for that object." The text concludes: "The only works of art America has given are her plumbing and her bridges." A longer text, this time signed, by Louise Norton, titled "Buddha of the Bathroom," meditates further on *Fountain* and its challenge to the notion of a work of art.[13]

GAMMEL'S ACCOUNT OF *FOUNTAIN*'S HISTORY

In the biography of the Baroness, Gammel's account of *Fountain*'s history is inaccurate from the start, and her speculations about its origins flawed. She says, as was noted above, that *Fountain* was exhibited, when in fact it was "suppressed" on the eve of the opening and never was exhibited.[14] This is a fundamental historical error. She has evidently assumed that Alfred Stieglitz's photograph was taken at the exhibition, whereas, as we shall see, it was taken in Stieglitz's studio. She seems not to be properly familiar with the controversy deliberately orchestrated in the two issues of *The Blind Man*, edited by Duchamp, Beatrice Wood, and Henri-Pierre Roché, which make it clear that the purpose of *Fountain* was to test the Independents' claim to accept and exhibit anything on payment of the fee, to reveal the limits of this claim, and to question the definition of art—something Duchamp consistently does in his *Notes*, for instance when he writes, "Can one make works which are not 'of art'?"[15]

The evidence of letters, memoirs, and hearsay, not at the time in the public domain, confirms the complexity of the episode and the secrecy with which Duchamp and his small group of co-conspirators operated. It is not certain when the identity of Mr. Mutt became public.

The link with Duchamp's resignation from the board of the Society of Independent Artists was not made immediately. The directors of the Independents were not aware of it, as a letter from one of Duchamp's most devoted supporters, Katherine Dreier, to Glackens on April 13 makes clear: she proposes that Duchamp be invited to give a lecture on his "Readymades" and Richard Mutt be asked to bring his "discarded object" and to explain his "theory of art." This letter was clearly written in good faith and on the assumption that there was indeed an artist called Richard Mutt.[16]

After being suppressed on the eve of the opening of the Independents, *Fountain* was rescued and taken to Stieglitz's studio. It seems that it had been hidden behind a partition, where it was found by Duchamp and possibly Man Ray.[17] Stieglitz, with some glee, wrote to Georgia O'Keeffe that he "had some fun in photographing.... There was a row at the *Independent*—a young woman (probably at Duchamp's instigation) sent a large porcelain urinal on a pedestal to the *Independent*. Duchamp, Marin, Covert, Arensberg wanted to show it. The rest of the committee wouldn't. So there is a row—a jury after all.... *The Blind Man* wants to use the matter for a number—a discussion of 'Art.'"[18] The photographer also wrote to the art critic Henry McBride on April 19, inviting him to come and see his photograph of the rejected object, and added, "The Fountain is here too." He had been asked to photograph it "at the request of Roché, Covert, Miss Wood, Duchamp & Co."[19] Stieglitz was proud of the result, as he wrote later on the same day to O'Keeffe: "The *Urinal* photograph is really quite a wonder. Everyone who has seen it thinks it beautiful. And it's true—it is.... It has an oriental look about it—a cross between a Buddha & a veiled woman."[20]

The only contemporary first-hand reference to the event by Duchamp himself is in a letter to his sister, Suzanne, from April 11, 1917, a day after the opening of the Independents (the exhibition opened to the public on April 10, with a preview on April 9).[21] In this now famous letter, Duchamp tells Suzanne that a female friend of his has sent a urinal in to the Independents exhibition under a masculine pseudonym: "Les Independents sont ouverts ici avec gros succès. Une de mes amies sous un pseudonyme masculin, Richard Mutt, avait envoyé une pissotière en porcelaine comme sculpture."[22]

Gammel not only misquotes the second sentence but omits the previous one, which explains the context. She "quotes" the letter as follows: "One of my female friends who had adopted the pseudonym Richard Mutt sent *me* [*sic*] a porcelain urinal as a sculpture."[23] But Duchamp's letter makes it clear that the urinal was *not* sent to him as a sculpture but was rather sent to or submitted to the Independents, in the category "sculpture." There is all the difference in the world between these two situations. It is simply sent—not made or chosen by the female friend—and to the Independents, not to Duchamp. In her translation, moreover, Gammel omits the "masculine" to qualify "pseudonym" from Duchamp's letter, and vainly pursues the proposition that *Fountain*'s signature was not only anonymous (a curious notion, an anonymous signature) but also androgynous. She sums up by claiming that a "great deal of circumstantial evidence suggests that if a female friend was involved, . . . the Baroness was probably that friend."[24] Duchamp did, significantly, have female accomplices in the *Fountain* episode, but they did not include the Baroness. Whether Duchamp had met von Freytag-Loringhoven at this stage is unknown. They certainly became acquainted after she moved to Greenwich Village in 1918, and she was to figure prominently in the little magazine edited by Duchamp and Man Ray, *New York Dada* (1921).[25] The contact telephone numbers in New York given by the artist Charles Demuth in a letter to the art critic Henry McBride, trying to drum up publicity for the affair, were those of Duchamp, and, for "Richard Mutte [*sic*]," that of Louise Norton, whose New York address has moreover been made out on the label attached to *Fountain* in Stieglitz's photograph.[26]

DUCHAMP'S MOTIVES

Apart from questioning what makes a work "of art," there were two main strands in Duchamp's motivation behind the *Fountain* project: a skeptical attitude to the idea of an "Independents" exhibition and its Paris precedents, and a recognition of the very interesting phenomenon of the New York avant-garde at the time—its highly feminized and even feminist character. Duchamp's dislike of organized, official art institutions, whether academic or modern, was deep-rooted and probably originated with his experience at the Paris Indépendants in 1912. His painting *Nude Descending a Staircase (No. 2)* had created such a scandal among the Cubist artists hanging their works in a special gallery at the exhibition that before the opening Albert Gleizes, leader of the Cubist group, asked Duchamp's brothers, the artists Jacques Villon and Raymond Duchamp-Villon, to request that he withdraw the painting. The problem was the combination of title and picture—how could a nude be *descending* the stairs?—and they politely suggested that he at least change the title. Rather than change anything Duchamp took his painting away. From that point on he determined never to be part of a group—"one can only count on oneself, alone."[27] He also decided not to be dependent on art for a living, as this would inevitably lead to repetition and compromise. In his letter to his sister Suzanne, Duchamp goes on to link the New York Independents to the long history of such exhibitions. "I handed in my resignation and it'll be a juicy piece of gossip in New York. I felt like organizing a special exhibition for things refused at the Independents but that would be a pleonasm! And the urinal would have been lonely."[28] Duchamp did effectively create a "salon de refusé" with *Fountain*, even if it was never exhibited. The first Independents exhibition in New York is now remembered for this one "refusal" rather than for any of the other more than two thousand works on show. The original *Salon des refusés* of 1863—the paintings rejected by the official Salon of the French Academy—marked the birth of modern art in France, with works by Edouard Manet, Paul Cézanne, and Gustave Courbet. The second

Salon des refusés, in 1883, launched the Impressionists, and in 1884 the first exhibition of the Société des Artistes Indépendants formalized the idea of "free" exhibitions for modern artists: "No Jury, No Prizes!" With *Fountain*, Duchamp effectively proved the New York Independents to be just as dependent on taste, fashion, and convention, and on what was acceptable as art, as Paris in 1912, where Duchamp had come up against the Cubists' rigid definition of "Cubist" painting.

The second motivation behind the work highlights Duchamp's response to the prominence of active, creative women with whom he mixed in the avant-garde circles in New York. He was already engaging in the complex gender games, culminating in his invention of a female alter ego, Rrose Sélavy, that are involved in the object itself. He was at this time in New York also working on his *Bride Stripped Bare* by *Her Bachelors, Even (The Large Glass)* (1915–23), which included the forms of the bachelors as "malic" (male-like) molds. The urinal could be seen as both archetypal male symbol and, as the recipient of male emissions, a female mold. In a note in the *Box of 1914*, Duchamp wrote: "One only has: for *female* the public urinal and one *lives* by it."[29] The object is feminized, given a "new thought," and has a pseudonymous male "maker." The *Fountain* incident as publicized in *The Blind Man* is the work of a collective with Beatrice Wood writing its justification and Duchamp's intellectual female friend Louise Norton its explanation. The second issue of *The Blind Man* had a remarkable number of contributions by women: not only from Wood and Norton but also from the artist Clara Tice, Duchamp's friend the musician and writer Gabrielle Buffet-Picabia (an article on Marie Laurencin), and the artist and writer Mina Loy (two texts—a critical commentary on Louis M. Eilshemius, the naive-academic painter much admired to most people's bafflement by Duchamp, and a comic compilation of overheard tidbits from social evenings at Walter and Louise Arensberg's apartment: "O Marcel . . . otherwise I also have been to Louise's").[30] These contributors had also been prominent in the little magazine *Rogue* (1915–16), which Louise Norton, a close friend of Duchamp and Roché, edited with her former husband, Allan Norton.[31] Described as the "Ford" or the "cigarette" of literature, *Rogue* published extreme modernist experiments in language, by Gertrude Stein and Mina Loy among others, including Duchamp's text "The," and had a nifty line in satirical illustrations. As "Dame Rogue," Louise Norton wrote the column "Philosophic Fashions," setting the tone for *Rogue*'s "jocular" feminism, frequently with a humorous glance at their magazine's near namesake, the fashion bible: "Forecast for 1916: shorter skirts and suffrage." The new woman was a free agent, smoked, made love freely, and refused to wear corsets. Mina Loy wrote a satirical article, "Consider Your Grandmother's Stays." In her sketches "Who's Who" in Manhattan, Clara Tice depicted the key women of the New York avant-garde, including Louise Norton, wearing nothing but a corset and a frilly skirt. Duchamp embraced this lively feminized avant-garde and co-opted it.

For Duchamp to conceal his identity as the author of *Fountain* for a time as part of a collaborative game makes sense; to claim, as Spalding and Thompson do, that he deliberately appropriated another person's readymade does not.[32] There is no doubt that *Fountain* raises interesting questions about authorship, and retains its controversial character. However, this should never be linked to doubt about Duchamp as its instigator.

Thing 000955 (Martha Graham's Choreographies)

AGENCY

In 1925, after completing her studies with Ruth St. Denis and Ted Shawn at the Denishawn School of Dancing and Related Arts in Los Angeles, Martha Graham (1894–1991) began to make dances. In 1926 she gave the first public performance of her dance *Chorale*, after which she formed an all-woman company named the Martha Graham Group. Later, when men were invited to join the group, she changed the name to the Martha Graham Dance Company.

In the late 1920s Graham developed her own system of dance exercises and movements focusing on contracted muscles and energy release. Around 1930, after teaching her work informally and as an instructor at various institutions, Graham also opened a school called the Martha Graham School of Dance. Graham ran both the dance company and the dance school.

In 1948 Graham founded and led a nonprofit corporation to support her work. Initially it was known as the Martha Graham Foundation for Contemporary Dance, but in 1968 the corporation was renamed the Martha Graham Center of Contemporary Dance.

In December 1956, on the advice of her tax accountant, Rubin Gorewitz, Graham also founded a second nonprofit corporation for the school. It was called the Martha Graham School of Contemporary Dance. In January 1957 Graham sold her sole proprietorship to the school and entered into a ten-year employment agreement with the school to serve as a program director. In June 1966 Graham's employment agreement was extended for another ten years. Graham's job title at the school later changed to artistic director. As artistic director, her responsibility was to create new dances, to maintain the repertory of dances, to rehearse with the company, and to supervise the school. Graham worked with both nonprofit corporations: the Martha Graham Center of Contemporary Dance and the Martha Graham School of Contemporary Dance. The center oversaw and funded the performances of the Martha Graham Dance Company, Graham's unincorporated performance group, and the dance company often used dancers from the school to participate in performances. The center operated as an umbrella organization, encompassing the teaching, choreographing, and performing of dances by the school and the dance company. In 1968 Graham assigned all performing rights of her choreographies to the center. Graham served as artistic director and board member of both the center and the school until her death.

Around 1967 Martha Graham, then in her seventies, became acquainted with a twenty-six-year-old freelance photographer named Ronald Protas. With Protas's support, she pulled herself out of a depression that had developed when she retired from dancing. Protas and Graham became close friends. In 1972 Protas became an employee of the Martha Graham Center of Contemporary Dance. Although he had no prior dance background, Graham increasingly trusted him to represent her in both personal and professional matters. By 1975 Protas had become executive director of the center and a board member of the center and the school. In 1980 he was given the title of co-associate artistic director. As Graham's health waned in the final years of her life, Protas became her spokesperson. On January 19, 1989, Graham wrote a will naming Protas her sole executor and legatee. She gave him her personal property, her residuary estate, her personal papers, the use of her name, and any rights or interests in dance works, musical scores, and scenery sets.

Martha Graham died in April 1991 and Protas succeeded her as artistic director of the center. As heir, Protas claimed ownership of the copyrights in all of Graham's seventy-one choreographies. In 1998 he placed all copyrights in the Martha Graham Trust, a revocable trust that he had created and of which he was trustee and sole beneficiary. The trust licensed many of the dances and sets. In 1998 the trust sold numerous books, musical scores, films, and tapes of performances and dance rehearsals and personal files relating to Graham's choreographies to the Library of Congress for $500,000. As a result, the relations between Protas and the dancers of the company deteriorated. Many dancers also disagreed with the way Protas directed the center.

On July 15, 1999, the center and the school proposed a ten-year license agreement with the Martha Graham Trust. Their principal motive was to persuade Protas to resign as artistic director. The license agreement purported to license the ballets, sets, and costumes. The trust would give the school an exclusive license to teach the Martha Graham technique and give the center a nonexclusive license to present live performances of Graham's dances; to use sets, costumes, and properties; to use Graham's images; and to use the Martha Graham trademark. The center in return would agree that Protas approves the selection of a new artistic director, that he stays a member of the board, that he gets paid a salary of $55,000 to $72,000 for ten years, and that they bill him as artistic consultant.

In 2000, when Protas and the center failed to find a mutually agreeable replacement for the artistic director, the board voted to remove Protas from the post. On May 25, 2000, Protas sent a letter to the center's board of directors, terminating the license agreement with the Martha Graham Trust. Shortly thereafter, the board voted to suspend operations due to severe financial difficulties. Meanwhile, Protas, acting through the trust, founded the Martha Graham School and Dance Foundation, also a not-for-profit corporation.

In July 2000 Protas began to register copyright in forty of Graham's choreographic works as unpublished works. He obtained certificates of registration for thirty of Graham's dances as unpublished works. By agreement with the trust, the Martha Graham School and Dance Foundation became the exclusive licensee in the United States for live performance of virtually all of Graham's dances and use of the Martha Graham trademarks.

In 2001, after receiving substantial funding, the center and the school reopened. The center applied for copyright registration of fifteen of Martha Graham's dances. In January 2001 the Martha Graham Center of Contemporary Dance also obtained registration certificates for initial and renewal terms for some of Graham's dances.

Protas sued the Martha Graham Center of Contemporary Dance and the Martha Graham School of Contemporary Dance for trademark and copyright infringement. He initiated a lawsuit to forbid the center and the school from using the Martha Graham trademark, from teaching the Martha Graham technique, and from performing all Graham's dances. He claimed that the trust owned all rights in the dances, that the Martha Graham School and Dance Foundation was the current and authorized licensee of such rights, and that any unauthorized use of these dances would constitute willful copyright infringement. But the Martha Graham Center claimed that the dances, sets, and costumes at issue belonged to the center either by virtue of the work-for-hire doctrine or Graham's assignments.

On August 7, 2001, the first court case, *Martha Graham School and Dance Foundation v. Martha Graham Center of Contemporary Dance*, took place at the District Court for the Southern District of New York. Judge Miriam Cedarbaum held that the Martha Graham Center of Contemporary Dance and the Martha Graham School of Contemporary Dance proved they were prior users of the trademarks and that Protas could not preclude the center and school's use of a name that they bought, used, and owned prior to Protas's registration of the trademark.[1] Protas appealed the decision. On July 2, 2002, the second court case took place at the United States Court of Appeals. The court concluded that Martha Graham's consent to the center and school's use of her name was not a license, but was an irrevocable assignment.

Protas then brought action against the center and the school to determine ownership of copyright in dances created by Graham and of related costumes and sets. On August 23, 2002, the third court case, *Martha Graham School and Dance Foundation v. Martha Graham Center of Contemporary Dance*, took place at the District Court for the Southern District of New York. Judge Miriam Cedarbaum held that:

What property did Martha Graham, the great dancer, choreographer, and teacher, own at the time of her death in 1991? That is the central question in the second phase of this lawsuit. The main dispute is with respect to ownership of copyright in the dances she created.... The parties agree that, during her lifetime, Graham created 70 dances that are fixed in a tangible medium of expression from which they can be reproduced. 34 of those 70 dances were created after 1956, during Graham's employment by [the Martha Graham Center of Contemporary Dance], and 36 were created prior to 1956....

During a bench trial held between April 22 and April 29, eighteen witnesses testified in the courtroom and designations from the deposition of one witness were submitted. This trial was an effort to recapture a history that partially predated the knowledge and memory of the living witnesses. Accordingly, the few ancient documents that were produced became very important guideposts....

I. The License Agreement...
This agreement is incomplete because no "Applicable Works Addendum" was ever finalized by Protas....

II. Significance of Publication...
The 1976 Act defines publication: *"Publication" is the distribution of copies or phonorecords of a work to the public by sale or other transfer of ownership, or by rental, lease, or lending. The offering to distribute copies or phonorecords to a group of persons for purposes of further distribution, public performance, or public display, constitutes publication. A public performance or display of a work does not of itself constitute publication....*

Accordingly, 26 of the [filmed] dances have been published.... With respect to published works, the affixation of adequate notice was the principal "statutory formality" required for copyright protection prior to March 1, 1989. On March 1, 1989, United States adherence to the Berne Convention abolished affixation of notice as a statutory requirement for securing copyright.... Proof of authorship may be sufficient to establish copyright ownership in an unpublished work....

III. Certificates of Copyright Registration . . .
Both sides have procured certificates of copyright in dances described in the applications as unpublished works. Protas has 30 such certificates, and [Martha Graham Center of Contemporary Dance] 12. . . . It is undisputed that the Copyright Office has no record of any copyright registration made prior to 2000 for any of the dances at issue. . . .
A preponderance of the credible evidence shows that 18 of the 30 dances registered by Protas as unpublished had been published at least seven years before the Copyright Office received any applications for copyright registration from him. . . . In 2001, the Center obtained certificates of copyright registration for 12 post-1956 works as unpublished works made for hire and certificates of copyright renewal for three published works made for hire. . . . Both Protas and the Center have obtained certificates of copyright registration for . . . [the same] eight dances. . . .
With respect to dances as to which there is no evidence of publication, [Protas] has obtained nine, and [Martha Graham Center] have obtained six, non-competing certificates of copyright registration. . . .

IV. Dances Created by Graham During the 35 Years that She Was Employed by [Martha Graham Center of Contemporary Dance] . . .
During the 35 years that Martha Graham was employed by the [Martha Graham Center of Contemporary Dance], she created 34 dances. . . .

In 1956, Graham entered into a ten-year employment agreement with the School for the position of Program Director. Her title of employment later changed to Artistic Director. . . . Graham remained a salaried employee of the Center until the time of her death in 1991. . . .

It is undisputed that Martha Graham was ultimately responsible for making all final artistic decisions relating to the dances. Nevertheless, a preponderance of the credible evidence shows that she created the dances as an employee. . . . [The Martha Graham Center of Contemporary Dance has] shown by a preponderance of the credible evidence that all of the 34 dances created by Martha Graham while she was employed by them between 1956 and her death in 1991 were works made for hire. . . .

V. Works Created by Graham prior to 1956 . . .
Of the 70 dances at issue, Graham created 36 prior to the time that she commenced her employment with the [Martha Graham Center of Contemporary Dance] in 1956. Of the 36 pre-1956 dances, 16 have been published. . . .

Copyrights secured before January 1, 1964 are governed by the stringent renewal requirements of the 1909 Act. . . . Under the renewal provisions of the 1909 Act, the copyright term of published works ended 28 years after the date of first publication with adequate notice unless copyright was renewed in the final year of copyright protection. . . . Of the 16 published dances created prior to 1956, ten were first published before January 1, 1964. . . . Since the Copyright Office has no record of any registration prior to 2000, the evidence is clear that any copyrights secured in those ten published works were not timely renewed. Accordingly, those ten works are in the public domain, even if they had been first published with adequate notice of copyright. . . .

A preponderance of the credible evidence shows that prior to 1956, Martha Graham was commissioned to create seven dances by a number of renowned musical and cultural organizations and that these dances were first performed between 1944 and 1953. . . . With respect to all of the commissioned works, no party has proved that Graham and the commissioning parties intended the copyright to be reserved to Graham. . . .

There is no writing in evidence in which Graham assigned copyright in the dances to the Center. . . . In January of 1957, Graham gave all her theatrical properties to the [Martha Graham Center of Contemporary Dance], but the document conveying these properties did not mention the copyright in the choreographic works. . . . A preponderance of the credible evidence shows that between January of 1957, but prior to 1965 or 1966, Graham assigned to the [Martha Graham Center of Contemporary Dance] copyright in 21 non-commissioned, pre-1956 works that were unpublished at that time. . . . Documentary evidence and the credible testimony of several witnesses show that throughout the 1960s, 1970s, and 1980s, the [Martha Graham Center of Contemporary Dance] consistently acted as the owners of the ballets created by Graham prior to 1956, and that Graham did not object to such actions by the [Martha Graham Center of Contemporary Dance]. . . .

Sixteen of the pre-1956 works have been published. As discussed above, ten of these works are in the public domain because of the failure to renew copyright timely, and two dances, *Herodiade* and *Cave of the Heart*, are commissioned works. The right to renew the copyright in *Seraphic Dialogue* has reverted to Protas. The remaining three works are *El Penitente* (published 1991), *Errand into the Maze* (published 1984), and *Diversion of Angels* (published 1976). [The Martha Graham Center of Contemporary Dance] copyright in *El Penitente* has been preserved because it was first published in 1991, after the permissive notice requirements of the Berne Convention Implementation Act took effect. With respect to the remaining two works, *Errand into the Maze* and *Diversion of Angels*, there is no evidence that copyright in these works was secured upon first publication by the affixation of the required notice of copyright.

VI. Sets and Costumes . . .
As discussed above, Graham transferred all of her then existing theatrical properties, costumes, and stage equipment to the [Martha Graham Center] in January of 1957. Accordingly, [Martha Graham Center of Contemporary Dance] own[s] all of that property.[2]

The court concluded that copyrights in a total of 45 dances belonged to the Martha Graham Center of Contemporary Dance.[3] The copyright in only one dance, *Seraphic Dialogue*, belonged to Protas. Neither side has established ownership in twenty-four dances. Of those twenty-four dances, ten works, two of which were commissioned, are in the public domain for lack of timely renewal.[4] And five dances belonged to commissioning parties who were not involved in the action.[5] The remaining nine dances have been published, but neither side has shown whether any of those dances were published with adequate notice of copyright.[6] The Martha Graham Center of Contemporary Dance was entitled to a declaration of ownership of all the remaining sets and costumes for the dances.

The same year, the center and the foundation both appealed this decision. On August 18, 2004, the court case *Martha Graham School and Dance Foundation v. Martha Graham Center of Contemporary Dance* took place at the United States Court of Appeals. Judge Jon Newman held that:

> The critical events span sixty-five years, many of the pertinent facts are obscured by inadequate recordkeeping, and the copyright issues require consideration of several provisions of both the 1909 and 1976 Copyright Acts. . . . Explicit federal copyright protection for choreography was not provided until the 1976 Act included choreographic works among the categories of works eligible for protection. . . . Under the 1909 Act, choreography could be registered, pursuant to regulations, as a species of dramatic composition. . . . Like other creative works, dances are available for statutory copyright if fixed in any tangible medium of expression.
>
> Under the 1909 Act, applicable to works created before January 1, 1978, state common-law copyright provided protection until first publication, and thereafter the work was entitled to an initial 28-year term of statutory copyright, provided that adequate statutory notice was given at publication, or appropriate registration and deposit were made. . . . In the absence of adequate statutory notice at publication, the work was injected into the public domain. If adequate statutory notice was given, then application for renewal made during the last year of the initial term would extend the copyright for a renewal term of 28 additional years.
>
> Under the 1976 Act, works that were created on or after January 1, 1978, acquired statutory copyright upon creation. . . . The copyright terms for works [registered between January 1, 1964 and December 31, 1977] in their initial 28-year term on January 1, 1978 . . . are automatically renewed for 67 years after the initial 28-year term ends.
>
> With respect to works for hire, the employer is legally regarded as the author, as distinguished from the creator of the work . . . A work

is made at the hiring party's instance and expense when the employer induces the creation of the work and has the right to direct and supervise the manner in which the work is carried out. . . . The concept of "work made for hire" . . . in the 1976 Act, . . . defines the phrase to mean *a work prepared by an employee within the scope of his or her employment or, for certain types of works, a work specially ordered or commissioned.*

As Graham's beneficiary, Protas inherited the copyrights in *Seraphic Dialogue* and *Acrobats of God*. The District Court correctly ruled that Protas owned the copyright in *Seraphic Dialogue*. However, the District Court erred in ruling that *Acrobats of God* belonged to the Center, and we therefore reverse the District Court's decision with respect to this work.[7]

The appeal court affirmed the district court for most issues in this case, but reversed the district court's determination of ownership of *Acrobats of God* because its renewal term belongs to Protas and vacated and remanded to the district court for determination of ownership with respect to seven dances created from 1956 through 1965, and two dances that were incorrectly deemed unpublished and for recalculation of the amount subject to the constructive trust.

On June 23, 2005, the partly remanded court case *Martha Graham School and Dance Foundation v. Martha Graham Center of Contemporary Dance* took place at the District Court for the Southern District of New York. The court answered the remaining questions of the court of appeals as follows. The dance *Tanagra* was in the public domain. There was no distinct dance within *Frescoes* and there is no dance called *Duets*. The copyright notice appearing at the end of the Kennedy Center Honors television broadcast was sufficient to preserve the copyright by the Martha Graham Center of Contemporary Dance in the excerpt from *Frescoes* that was published in the broadcast. And evidence showed that the common-law copyrights in the seven unpublished dances, created from 1956 through 1965, were also assigned to the center by Martha Graham.[8]

Although the dancers of Martha Graham's company were relieved by this decision, a fear rose in the dance community about the implications of this conclusion. On the one hand choreographers gained legal protection for their dances with the addition of choreographic works to the copyright act. On the other hand it became obvious that the enforcement of the copyright doctrine interfered strongly with long-held customs in the dance community. According to some customs, dances were preserved by "guardians" of a dance. They teach the integrity of a dance in person, which involves the adaption of movements in dialogue with the dancers. For many choreographers the fixation requirement of the copyright act is difficult to meet in dance.

A Brass-Plated Boxing Ring: Foundations, Artists' Estates, and Legacy

GABRIEL PÉREZ-BARREIRO

The foundation occupies a complex place in the artistic ecosystem. Neither fully public nor fully private, foundations are defined by their in-between status, as mediators between art and its many audiences. In exchange for fiscal benefits to the foundation's donors, formerly privately owned resources are made a little bit more public, in the name of maintaining and protecting a legacy that can be tangible (artworks, collections, and archives) or intangible (an artist's legacy, reputation, and intellectual property), and often a combination of both the tangible and intangible. While the very word "foundation" may bring to mind the brass-plated respectability of an academic institution, in fact foundations can be sites for considerable dispute and litigation, owning and controlling as they do resources that can have a dramatic effect on the market and on the field of art in general.

Foundations are established with as many different missions as there are artists and collectors. Among the various models we can find the jealously guarded collection (Barnes), the authenticator (Lygia Clark), the publisher of the catalogue raisonné (Dedalus), the defender of particular art-historical trends (Dia), the supporter of contemporary artistic creation and social activism (Warhol, Tremaine, Henry Moore, Rauschenberg), the advocate for art of a specific region (Fundación Cisneros, for Latin America), and many that combine different parts of these over time. Some choose to have associated museums, and others have no collections, or even dispose of their collections over time to help further their mission. What they all share is a mission to influence the professional field in one way or another, and they assert this influence by administering and controlling access to the resources under their control, through grant-giving, publishing, charging fees for reproduction of images, or allowing access to archives. Because foundations are usually created by individuals, and often retain a strong link to their founders, the vast majority differs from universities or museums, where the staffing is always fully professional, with tried and tested systems for entry and promotion. Foundations are often run by their founders and descendants, or, in the case of foundations that manage an artist's estate, the artist's family and friends. In the best cases, such as the Dia Art Foundation or the Andy Warhol Foundation for the Visual Arts, this allows for visionaries to take risks and establish values that the mainstream institutions have yet to realize, and thus make the whole system richer. In the worst cases, the families or descendants either do not understand or abuse their power, generating frustration and confusion all around. This is especially a problem when the foundation controls access to copyright, archives, or reproductions in a rapacious and blinkered manner, and thus can have a huge impact on what is studied and reproduced.

Within the complicated ecosystem of the art world, the foundation has been a unique platform for the circulation of ideas and ideals. Contemporary art is richer for the activities and support of the Warhol Foundation, the Henry Moore Foundation, and the Andrew W. Mellon Foundation; American art is better understood thanks to the Terra Foundation; we have a greater comprehension of globalized culture thanks to the Rockefeller and Ford Foundations. At their best, foundations provide support for novel ideas and research that can become transformative in the long term. This role as a catalyst for fresh thinking is an important annex to the academy or the museum, the traditional locations in which knowledge is generated. The foundation can create a community of thinkers who share common beliefs, and can support them and allow their voices to be heard. As the "venture capitalists" of new ideas, foundations have borne many fruits over time, and their support helps engender a diversity of voices within the art system as a whole. Foundations typically have no power to censure institutions, but they can offer incentives and stimuli through grants, publications, conferences, etc.

Foundations often suffer from the same ills as the United States Constitution. Once a set of intentions and principles is instituted and recorded at a particular point in history, who is to say how it should be interpreted over time? Was the right to own guns specific to late eighteenth-century militias, or should it be a defining characteristic of American life today? Similarly, when foundations are set up, it is with a specific goal in mind, yet even the most powerful foundation cannot slow down time. When Alfred Barnes began his foundation in 1922, it was to establish a pedagogical position free of the Philadelphia elite of the time, so he created all kinds of conditions that proved to be unworkable in our contemporary world, such as prohibiting the photographing of works in the collection in color. Foundations are caught in the tricky position of needing to preserve a set of intentions and at the same time to continue to interpret and refine those intentions to adapt to a changing world.

AUTHENTICATION

One area where foundations and artists' estates hold particular strength and power is in authentication, in determining if a specific work of art is indeed by the artist, or if it can be deemed a fake. The art world runs on authenticity opinions. Unless the provenance of an artwork is fully and independently documented, which is rare, someone has to weigh in on authenticity. In many instances, before a modern or contemporary artwork is offered for sale at auction or privately, the artist's estate or foundation is consulted, and without their approval the work will be withdrawn and will therefore be essentially unsellable. This opinion is what makes the difference between a multimillion-dollar artwork and the low cost of the materials used in its manufacture. This sphere is therefore where the stakes are highest and where passions run hottest. In theory, an artist's foundation is often the most qualified body to make these judgments (as it has trusted experts on the deceased artist's works, family heirs who are also knowledgeable, access to family archives, etc.)—a position that is often reinforced in law and in practice. But it is not always so. The descendants of an artist are certainly the legitimate heirs to the physical and intellectual property of their illustrious ancestors (at least for a fixed period, in the case of intellectual property), but does this always qualify them to make difficult judgments on art-historical grounds? Even when a foundation sets up a professional panel of art historians, there can be significant differences in how each member approaches the task of authentication, and this before the risks and complications of litigation are considered. In fact, in recent years, several foundations have closed their authentication boards in response to the mounting costs of legal defense, partly as a result of the growing value of the works themselves. The estates of Andy Warhol, Keith Haring, and Jean-Michel Basquiat no longer provide authentication services. In these cases, the decision was made consciously by the board, while in the case of the Brazilian artist Lygia Clark, the same decision was reached by default, as the result of internal conflict among the heirs.

The estate of Lygia Clark (1920–1988) was managed by her sons and grandchildren under the name "The World of Lygia Clark." The estate documented and certified the late artist's work, and maintained a database of her production. Because many of Clark's works were unsigned and manufactured by others, or are instructional, in the case of later works, this is by no means an easy task. To add to this problem, she conceived of many of her sculptural works as editions, but did not always realize the full number in her lifetime. None of these problems is unique to Clark, and many other estates suffer from similar concerns (for example, the Jean Arp Foundation has been actively trying to address issues of posthumous casts of the artist's work, sometimes compensating owners of works that were formerly sold by the estate in ways the estate now deems to be incorrect). The Clarks have become somewhat infamous, though, for taking legal action against exhibitions that include works that they have not certified (even when such works are widely accepted to be genuine).[1] They have also, supported by Brazil's aggressive authors' legislation (moral rights), taken action against the use of Clark's name in exhibitions or in projects that feature videos in which the artist is present, and even in instances where her work was not physically present.[2] Clark's importance to art history has been widely recognized; in 2014 the Museum of Modern Art (MoMA), New York, organized a major career survey, confirming her entry into the pantheon of modern art. Yet the difficulties of working with the estate are legendary; for example, my own organization, Fundación Cisneros, published dozens of books in which the Clark plates were left blank because the estate refused to authorize reproduction of then-uncertified works.[3] Within a few months of the MoMa show, and the artistic canonization of the artist's legacy, "The World of Lygia Clark" was no more, as one of the sons publicly withdrew his authorization, causing the organization to have no legal power, and leaving Clark certification and image releases in a limbo that continues at the time of writing.[4] It could be argued that, in this example, the success of the artist occurred in spite of, rather than in partnership with, the estate.

COPYRIGHT

The temptation of short-term fees over a longer-term more strategic use of intellectual-property rights, particularly copyright, can be seen in the case of another Brazilian modern artist: Alfredo Volpi (1896–1988). Volpi was an important painter in the history of Brazilian art, and his works sell in Brazil for high six-figure numbers (in US dollars), but he is virtually unknown around the world. Anyone trying to include his images in an international publication (which ostensibly would make his work better known and understood) will be presented with an invoice three or four times the value of an equivalent work by Pablo Picasso or Henri Matisse. As a result, Volpi continues to be relatively unfamiliar, and, even within Brazil, a major exhibition was canceled when the museum was unable to pay the astronomical fees for image rights.[5] In this instance, the estate is actively hindering a mission to increase recognition of the artist's works. In contrast, the foundation dedicated to the work of Brazilian painter Iberê Camargo (1914–1994) makes high-quality images available to scholars at no cost and encourages regular seminars and conferences on the artist's work and influence.

The contrast between the Volpi and Camargo estates points to the complexity in how estates can measure their rights against their obligations. Take publications, for example: the model of charging fees for image use is related to the copyright holders' right to participate in any potential commercial gains owing to the use of their property. With clearly commercial products and merchandise, this is easily defensible and calculable through flat fees or percentages. In the case of publications put out by not-for-profit institutions (the majority of art publishing), the publication is actually designed to lose money and is therefore supported by grants that make possible its production. In these instances, the argument for image fees is less clear-cut. Yet many estates feel that they should not be in the position of providing something for free to an organization that may be wealthier than theirs, and that often has a powerful name attached to it. Today image fees are a huge burden for academics looking to get published, as publishers have passed the onus of clearing reproduction rights on to the author, especially for academic journals and books. What we see is a tension between a funder who wants to make information circulate, and an estate that wants the same but feels it needs to be compensated for doing so and, in charging, may make the project unviable. Sometimes the issue is not even the expense, as the copyright holder may object to the curatorial framework or interpretation being presented and thus withhold image rights.[6] The lawyer for the Volpi estate has even gone on record to state that they maintain a list of curators and critics with whom they refuse to work.[7]

In the art world, it is difficult to distinguish between for-profit and not-for-profit publishing. Very few books actually make any money, and when they are published by museums, any profits are simply ploughed back into the institution to support the extremely expensive infrastructure that makes such projects possible. To add insult to injury, the books that advance new knowledge and present lesser-known artists are often the ones most heavily penalized by less-professional estates. To reproduce a work by Matisse or Picasso is simply a question of filling out a form with the professional agencies that represent those estates and that have no stake in trying to control the content of the publication beyond charging their fees. When authors have to deal with the descendants of a lesser-known artist, they may find an enthusiastic partner, or resistance, distrust, unrealistic expectations, unreasonable demands, and so on. This suggests that greater professionalization of artists' estates would be a good thing, but of course with that comes greater expenses, bureaucracy, and, as we saw in the case of Lygia Clark, not necessarily better practices.

So is there a way out of this catch-22? I would suggest that artists' estates are different from mission-led foundations. Authorization of copyright is a right enshrined in law, and by definition there is no way to circumvent it legally. Foundations that are set up to advance a field of research, or to promote a specific kind of artistic practice or scholarship, can basically cause no harm. If a scholar does not agree with the particular perspective being proposed by a foundation, they can argue against it, or simply ignore it. In the case of artists' rights, that option does not exist. Those rights are legally enforceable, and the heirs of an artist could legally muffle dissenting voices and exercise a form of censorship of free speech by withholding image rights. While fair-use guidelines do exist, most publishers and museums tend to be conservative and are afraid of alienating an artist's estate or facing litigation. The right to enforce copyright violations is given by law, and the law is given by the state. I believe it would be acceptable for the state to grant estates this right on the condition that it is applied reasonably, with suitable checks and balances. If estates were given a formal structure and guidelines for how to grant and charge for rights, incorporating suitable safeguards for fair use and not-for-profit activities, the state could guarantee the income to which the heirs are entitled, while curtailing the currently unlimited power they have over legitimate research and cultural activities. If we understand copyright to be a protection that allows for profit to accrue to the inventor, we should be able to codify this in a way that makes sense for all sides, and that allows for proportionate profit-sharing. Artists' estates essentially have a monopoly over artists' rights, and experience has proven time and again that, as with all monopolies, abuse can happen.

THE RECONSTRUCTED AND RE-PERFORMED ARTWORK

Another area where artists' estates have huge power is in dealing with the physical traces of an artist's career. Art changes over time: physically it decays, the effects of time can radically alter its appearance, and certain key elements in its context can shift. For example, while Brazilian artist Hélio Oiticica (1937–1980) made his *Parangolé* works (1964–79) from poor and unstable materials, to be worn as capes on the bodies of dancers in the Rio de Janeiro shantytowns, today that specific interaction between the object and its performer is lost to us. So how does the work exist today? As the remnants of the original object, carefully conserved in a vitrine? Reconstructed and presented on the wall? Reconstructed for use with museum docents so that people can experience them, even if in an environment very different from its first one? Or is the contemporary documentation of the original dancers the best way to understand their initial use and context? Each of these choices creates a complex set of questions about authorship and authenticity, intention and physicality, or, once again, the tangible and the intangible. In a booming art market, the pressure to make an artwork "ownable" is huge, as collectors and museums recognize the great historical importance of works like the *Parangolés* and wish to incorporate them into their collections. In most instances, the artist's estate makes the final determination on what may circulate and what may not. In cases like those of the Clark or Oiticica estates, the family charges a fee for approved replicas, which generally cannot be traded as original artworks but do provide a solution for temporary exhibitions.

A similar set of issues can arise with performance works, or with works that are editioned at a later date. In an unregulated market, artists can "reissue" works, or create editions that were not part of the original intent of the work. With the current rise of interest in Conceptual art from Latin America, a number of living (older) artists, whose work was not traded or collected at the time it was produced, find themselves with various forms of evidence (negatives, records of destroyed works, etc.) and pressure from the market to offer sellable artworks. To give an example, the Argentinian Conceptual artist Marta Minujín (b.1943) made many of the key Conceptual works of her generation, the majority of which were ephemeral objects or performance works. Anyone wanting to collect her work now is offered a bewildering range of items, from VHS videos to architectural plans to printed ephemera. Without a coherent way of codifying the material presence of these works, the likelihood is that after her death disputes will emerge about what constitutes the "authentic" work—a situation aggravated by the fact they were sold in her lifetime and therefore in good faith. This confusing scenario is repeated for artists whose work is predominantly project based or ephemeral. Can the objects circulating in the market be presented as the actual artwork, or are they mere souvenirs? What constitutes the artwork, and, crucially, who gets to make that decision?

In these cases, a well-run estate can be helpful in setting the rules and conditions under which the work can circulate and trade. For example, the foundation of Félix González-Torres (1957–1996), which was created in the artist's lifetime with the close collaboration of his dealer Andrea Rosen, has regulated the very challenging work of this artist, with the result that his production is reliably catalogued and also reaches high market prices and institutional credibility. The work of cataloguing an artist's production, and then being able to mediate between that original production and the art market, is a key function of the artist's estate. For the collector it is extremely important to know precisely what is being sold. Is it an edition? How many more are there? Where are they? Are there similar works elsewhere? Without this information, it is virtually impossible to make an informed decision. The larger galleries will often take on this role, assigning researchers to each artist they represent and controlling the circulation of works in the marketplace. But in the case of Latin America, for instance, there are no comparable institutions able to commit the resources to this important work. As a result, the only Latin American artists who have been able to penetrate systematically the global market (and as a result into museum collections) are those who have a major international gallery behind them.

Artworks represent artistic legacy in a tangible way, yet their status can often be complicated and contentious. The market demands products, but it also requires that those products be reliable and regulated to some extent. Artists' foundations and well-run estates can act as useful mediators between the artist and the market. However, if they are afraid of offering authentication services, or are themselves taking sides in academic disputes, their credibility is limited. It is quite possible that within a generation a new technology will emerge that will help to document artworks as they are made, and it is arguable that the proliferation of digital images and records will make it much easier in the future to determine the life of a particular object and the conditions under which it was produced.

MARKETS, ESTATES, AND LEGACY

As the art market continues to boom, museums are flooded with visitors, and more people study art history, the pressure to create reliable systems of authentication is growing exponentially. For contemporary art this is less of an issue, as works are documented and traded almost as soon as they are made, but for artworks older than a decade or so, we have few ways of knowing if they are genuine, or if an object was ever intended to be seen or traded a particular way. So while there is a growing need for reliable mediators between art and its market, we see many estates and foundations fleeing from the risky business of authentication, and many academics refusing to go on the record with their opinions for risk of litigation. At the same time, one of the traditional functions (and income streams) of artists' estates—copyright licensing—is under threat from the ubiquity of images on the internet.

Given all this, it would appear that it is time to rethink artists' estates, to provide a framework in which they could return to authentication by having a form of indemnity and protection against legal action in exchange for a more transparent and rigorous methodology, including opportunities for appeal. Authentication boards should have a built-in rotation of members to allow dissenting voices to be heard, and to avoid the appearance of conflicts of interest. At the level of intellectual property, a set of guidelines could be developed that better define fair use and the public interest served by not-for-profit institutions.[8]

As wealth continues to accumulate at the top of the system, and art becomes an asset class, we are likely to see more foundations emerging over the coming years. Where those foundations are created to advance a certain view on art or culture, or promote an artist's legacy, their appearance will only make the entire system richer and more diverse. Where they are set up exclusively as vehicles to avoid tax, the state should step in, and already is, to question their public benefit.[9]

Art has always been a complex articulator between the private and the public. The foundation, along with the museum, is one of the prime agents in this conversation, and as such should be judged both in terms of its service to the art it represents and also to the public, and neither to the exclusion of the other.

Appendix; or, Some Adjectival Notes on Authorship and Legacy

GILANE TAWADROS

When it comes to safeguarding an artist's legacy, the cacophony of competing claims about the artist's intent often appears far removed from the artist's expressed intention. In an effort to assert authority over an artist's legacy, the dissonant voices of curators, friends, commercial representatives, and family members compete to ventriloquize the artist's original intent in ways that sometimes reveal more about those left behind to enact the artist's will than the artist him- or herself. At a time when the commercial value of works of art continues to break ever-greater records, it seems paradoxical that the voice and volition of the individual artist is becoming increasingly marginalized in the art world. Yet it is precisely the rising value of artworks in an expanded, global marketplace that makes questions of authorship and legacy not only legal and moral questions but also ones that impact upon the sustainability of artists' livelihoods. In an economic context in which artworks can accumulate value far more rapidly than other classes of assets, artists frequently find themselves negotiating in a progressively complex environment, in which they risk losing control of their own work and intentions. One would assume that these risks would be significantly lower and even negligible while artists are alive and present to assert their authorship and articulate their desires, but this is not the case. In numerous contexts, artists are being challenged by situations that undermine the integrity of their practice.

ARTISTS CANNOT BE RELIED UPON TO KNOW THEIR OWN WORK

At a panel discussion at Prince Philip House in London in 2015, the American painter Eric Fischl (b.1948) described his visit to a Swiss auction house. An enthusiastic auctioneer informed Fischl with a great deal of excitement that the London branch of the auction house was preparing to sell one of his drawings. When Fischl was shown a reproduction of the work presented for sale, he unequivocally rejected authorship of the drawing, which he said had not, and could never have, been made by him. The drawing was very similar to a well-known painting by Fischl, but as he pointed out, he never made drawings "after" his own paintings, and his preparatory drawings were always very different from the finished painting. After a very brief silence, the auctioneer, undeterred by the artist's response, asked Fischl how he (the auctioneer) could be sure that he (Fischl) had not indeed made the work: might he perhaps have made the work and given it as a gift to a lover from whom he was now estranged and, consequently, was now disowning the artwork and his former lover at the same time? According to the auctioneer, the artist could not be depended upon to be a reliable source of authentication for his own work. (More recently, the British painter Peter Doig was similarly challenged to authenticate a painting that he had not painted.) The subject of the Fischl panel discussion was the significant problem of fakes and forgeries in the art world: if the artist could not assert his authorship of works unchallenged while he was still alive, reflected Fischl, how could his estate possibly do better when he was dead?

WHO NEEDS THE ARTIST ANYWAY?

The Absence of the Artist is the title of a 1968 photographic work by the British Conceptual artist Keith Arnatt (1930–2008). A banal white sign is nailed to a brick wall. The black, hand-painted lettering reads: "The

Absence of the Artist." Presumably it was the artist—whoever he or she is—who painted the sign, in which case, is this actually a painting by the artist who was there—he/she painted the sign and fixed it to the wall—but is no longer present? The work makes you think about the artist who is not there, about what they have done and what being an artist means. Is this all there is to being an artist: declare yourself to be one, make something, hang it on a wall, then walk away, leaving it for others to view, contemplate, and find their own meaning and resonance in what you have done?

The theme of the absent/disappearing artist is one that recurs in a number of works made by Arnatt between 1967 and 1972. In *Self-Burial* (1969), Arnatt pictures himself gradually disappearing beneath a mound of earth until he is (apparently) completely buried beneath the ground, with only a faint disturbance of earth marking the spot. Similarly, in *Portrait of the Artist as a Shadow of His Former Self* (1969–72), the disembodied shadow of the artist is imprinted on a pavement and adjacent wall like a shroud etched into the urban landscape, somehow material and de-material at the same time.

In 1970 Arnatt took even further the conceit of the withdrawal of the artist. With *Is It Possible to Do Nothing as My Contribution to This Exhibition?* (1970), the artist proposed, for an exhibition at Camden Arts Centre, in London, that he do nothing. His proposal to do nothing, reproduced only as a text in the exhibition catalogue, is the artwork: a permanent statement of intent to make no contribution, "paradoxically immortalising the artist's desire to contribute nothing, to forgo the making of an artwork, and simply to disappear."[1]

DYING IS NOT ENOUGH TO GUARANTEE IMMORTALITY.

In the late 1980s and early 1990s, London's Goldsmiths College was a ferment of artistic talent that blossomed into not only the hugely successful and celebrated group of artists now known as the YBAs, or Young British Artists, but also many others who are lesser known, unrecognized, or barely remembered. One of those artists was a brilliant young Asian called Hamad Butt (1962–1994), who tragically died of AIDS in 1994, at a time when being diagnosed as HIV-positive was an automatic death sentence. Butt's interests ranged widely across alchemy, science fiction, and popular culture, among other things, and his artistic practice meditated on themes of death, danger, and disease. He died just as his star was in the ascendant, having been included in the exhibition *Rites of Passage: Art for the End of the Century*, curated by Stuart Morgan and Frances Morris, at the Tate Gallery, in London. At the time of Butt's death, Stephen Foster, director of the John Hansard Gallery, in Southampton, was preparing an exhibition of his work and an accompanying publication, which he and I edited together and published posthumously under the Iniva (Institute of International Visual Art) imprint. Before he died, the artist had set out his vision for the book, defining it in careful detail, including the front and back covers, which were to be holograms (at that time a new and ground-breaking technique for producing 3-D images). After his death, we tried to enact Butt's ideas for the book but encountered a number of barriers, including the cost of producing the multiple holograms of a particular scene from the Bollywood movie *Pakeezah* (Kamal Amrohi, 1972), in which the heroine dances on broken glass, and of the fictional character Davros, creator of the Daleks in *Doctor Who*, the long-running science-fiction television series.[2] The fact that the designer of Davros and the Daleks had refused permission to furnish us with the rights to reproduce his designs on the cover of Butt's monograph was an exquisite twist of irony. While at art school, Butt had made a work that was breathtaking in its originality and portent, and in its material evocation of death and decay. Another student at the same art school produced a work that was extremely similar to Butt's original. In apparent fury at this blatant plagiarism, Butt destroyed his own work. A few, but not many, artists, curators, and critics remember Hamad Butt and his extraordinary work. The other student is now a commercially successful artist.

MAKING YOUR MARK ON AN INSTITUTION = MAKING YOUR MARK ON HISTORY

Shibboleth (2007–8), by Doris Salcedo (b.1958), effected a rupture in the physical fabric of the Turbine Hall of Tate Modern, in London—a fissure that cut through the floor of the space, revealing a fault line in the very foundation of the museum and, hence, in the history of modernity. The word *shibboleth* refers to a story in the Bible that describes how the Ephraimites, attempting to flee across the River Jordan, were stopped by their enemies, the Gileadites. The Ephraimite dialect did not include a *sh* sound, and those who could not say the word *shibboleth* were captured and executed. Salcedo speaks about the piece in terms of a disruption in the physical space of the museum, but also an interruption of the post-war consensus of European culture, which celebrates the triumph of democracy and the resolution of conflict. In an interview at the Tate, she explained:

> *Shibboleth* is a piece that refers to dangers at crossing borders or to being rejected in the moment of crossing borders.... This piece is trying to introduce into the Turbine Hall another perspective.... The presence of the immigrant is always unwelcome, the presence of the immigrant is seen as jeopardizing the culture of Europe. Europe has been seen as a homogenous society, a democratic society that has learnt through centuries of development, has learnt to resolve issues through dialogue. And if that is the case, then where do we place these outbreaks of racial hatred?... So once the show is over,... the piece will be sealed, the piece will remain under the floor and it will be sealed. So a permanent scar will always be in the Turbine Hall as a memory and as a commemoration of all these lives that we don't recognize, that for us are like ghosts anyway. So in that way, the memory of the piece and the presence of the people that we don't want to look at, the presence of this life that we don't want to acknowledge, will have pretty much the same character, just a vague memory.[3]

In stark contrast to the fleeting temporality of Arnatt's performances and the lightness of the permanent residues and marks left behind by the artist's actions, Salcedo's *Shibboleth* creates a permanent, physical scar in the fabric of the institutional space, which may be forgotten like the memory of the artist and the artist's intention, but can never be completely erased.

THERE IS MORE TO LEGACY THAN BRICKS AND MORTAR

Donald Rodney (1961–1998) was another British artist who died prematurely. A prominent member of the Black Art Group in the 1980s, Rodney died of sickle cell anemia in 1998. A number of works made toward the end of the artist's life meditate on the fragility of the human body and identity and anticipated his physical absence from the world. *In the House of My Father* (1996–97) is a photographic work that incorporates a sculptural piece, *My Mother, My Father, My Sister, My Brother* (1996–97), which takes the form of a tiny house, fabricated from fragments of the artist's own skin, removed during one of many operations he underwent in his battle with sickle cell disease. In the photograph, the house is delicately balanced in the palm of the artist's outstretched hand. The work speaks to the precarious nature of legacies that are often fragile and transient. Who wishes or is able to take up the mantle of an artist's legacy, particularly when that artist dies before their position within the art-historical canon has been admitted, let alone consolidated?

In the aftermath of an artist's death, the questions around artistic legacy become submerged beneath a tide of grief, administrative paperwork, legal processes, and mounds of banal everyday stuff. Somewhere in the midst of all that will be the artist's works: wrapped works recently returned from an exhibition, older works in the farthest corners of the studio that even the artist may have forgotten, and works in progress, started but not yet finished, which others now contemplate completing. Unfinished and unrealized projects present particular dilemmas. Should an attempt be made to complete or realize these works in the absence of the artist? How can one be sure if the artist intended to make these works, or whether those projects were set aside purposefully alongside other ideas never to be implemented? And if the works are realized, what is their status? Can they ever be judged as "authentic" artworks, or will they always be facsimiles—unsigned/unattributed works with an equivocal status?

In 1988 the magazine *20/20* prematurely announced Rodney's demise. The artist was dying from the slow degenerative disease he had had since childhood but was not yet dead. Mike Phillips and Geoff Cox, two of Rodney's collaborators, wrote later of the artist's final days:

> Rodney's body had, for many years, existed in a close symbiotic relationship with medical technology that has kept him alive. On a regular basis his body was invaded by steel devices to drain internal juices, only to be replaced and replenished by sanitised fluid. Enclosed bone structures were excavated and replaced by metal and plastic, a continual process of scarring and restructuring. And left behind: a data trail of information; photographs, X-ray's, scans, measurements, data, scars, and imprints. It is rare to find such a perfect, detailed body documentary.[4]

This body of medical data was to be integrated with Donald Rodney's personality and working process, synthesized from interviews with the artist, to create AUTOICON, one of a number of projects that Rodney was working on at the time of his death. A "rule based montage machine," AUTOICON would be powered to carry on generating works of art after the artist's death.

Rodney's last exhibition, *9 Nights in El Dorado*, took place at the South London Gallery in 1997, curated by David Thorpe and prepared by the artist from his hospital bed in King's College Hospital in south London. In the last few years before his death, Rodney had drawn a group of close friends and artists into a collective—affectionately dubbed "Donald Rodney plc"—to realize his abundant flow of ideas, translating them from his numerous sketchbooks effectively into artworks. One of the works in the show—*Psalms* (1998)—was an unoccupied electric wheelchair moving around the exhibition space, between the viewers and the artworks, apparently of its own volition. Unable to attend his own exhibition openings, the autonomous wheelchair attended in Rodney's place. This uncanny apparatus would start up, move, stop, turn, start up again, moving in a different direction. Donald Rodney's absent presence haunted the exhibition, continuously present and absent at the same time.

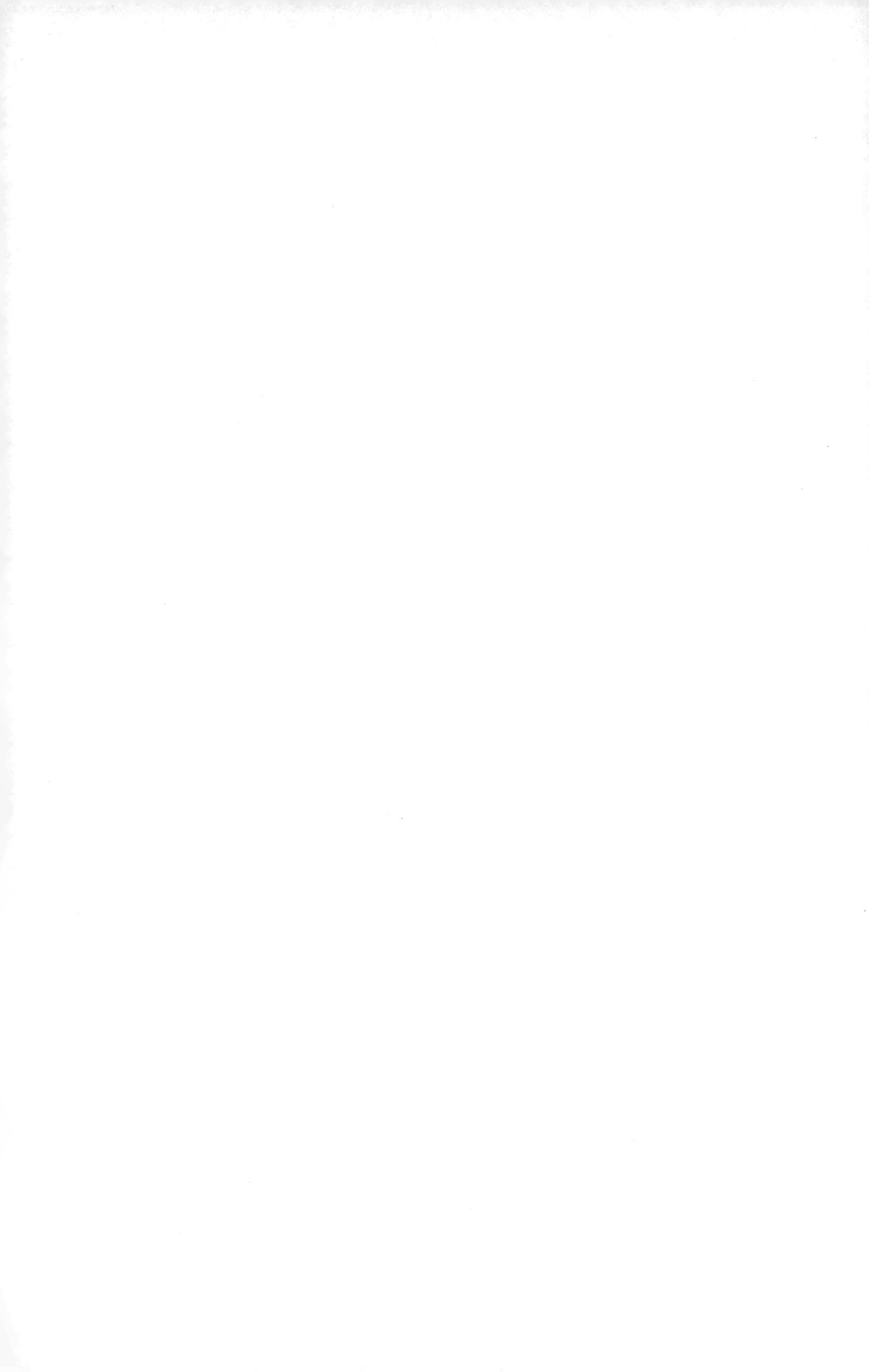

NOTES

Introduction

DANIEL MCCLEAN

1 See "Verdict and Settlement Summary, Disputed Painting Results in Defense Judgment," *Fletcher v. Doig*, no. 1:13-cv-03270 (N.D. Ill. August 23, 2016), and Daniel McClean, "It's Not Mine," *ArtReview* 67, no. 10 (October 2016): 51–52.

2 Henri Neuendorf, "Collectors Alarmed as Gerhard Richter Disowns Early Works from West German Period," *Artnet News*, July 21, 2015, https://news.artnet.com/art-world/gerhard-richter-omits-art-from-catalogue-318665. See Suzanne Pagé et al., *Gerhard Richter: Catalogue Raisonné 1962–1993*, 3 vols. (Ostfildern, Germany: Hatje Cantz, 1993), and the artist's website, www.gerhard-richter.com, on which the catalogue of his works is continuously updated.

3 See Christian Viveros-Fauné, "Up for Grabs; or, Artistic Authorship in the Age of the Flipper: *Kreuk v. Vō*," in this volume.

4 Nate Freeman, "Jute-Sack Case Heats Up: Ibrahim Mahama Countersues Simchowitz, Ellis King," *Artnews*, March 31, 2016, http://www.artnews.com/2016/03/31/jute-sack-case-heats-up-ibrahim-mahama-countersues-simchowitz-ellis-king/.

5 See Martha Buskirk, "Retraction," in this volume.

6 For a discussion of the growth and excesses of the high end of the global art market and with it the rise of legal conflicts, see Georgina Adam, *Dark Side of the Boom: The Excesses of the Art Market in the 21st Century* (London: Lund Humphries, 2017), especially chapter 1, "Supply," 39–49, and chapter 8, "The Dark Side," 167–95.

7 The practice of galleries "blacklisting" collectors who breach resale prohibitions is seen in the legal dispute between the collector Craig Robins and the David Zwirner Gallery, *Robins v. Zwirner et al.*, 713 F.Supp.2d 367 (S.D.N.Y 2010). See also Alexandra Peers, "Lawsuit Goes to the Heart of the Gossipy, High-Stakes Art World," *Observer*, April 7, 2010, http://observer.com/2010/04/lawsuit-goes-to-the-heart-of-the-gossipy-highstakes-art-world/.

8 See Joan Kee, "Artists' Rights," in this volume.

9 Alexander Alberro, "The Artist's Reserved Rights Transfer and Sale Agreement," in *Conceptual Art and the Politics of Publicity* (Cambridge, MA: MIT Press, 2003), 163–70.

10 Hans Haacke, interview by Maria Eichhorn, in Maria Eichhorn, *The Artist's Contract* (Cologne: Walther König, 2009), 67–77.

11 Resale Rights Directive, or Directive 2001/84/EC.

12 Visual Artists Rights Act of 1990 (VARA), 17 U.S.C. § 106A.

13 *Massachusetts Museum of Contemporary Art Found., Inc. v. Büchel*, 593 F.3d 38 (1d Cir. 2010).

14 See Donn Zaretsky, "Training Ground for Moral Rights: *MASS MoCA v. Christoph Büchel*," in this volume.

15 See Martha Buskirk, "Retraction," in this volume, and Julia Halperin, "Art Dealers Strike Back at Cady Noland in an Increasingly Philosophical Legal Dispute about a Restored Sculpture," *Artnet News*, April 5, 2018, https://news.artnet.com/art-world/noland-log-cabin-lawsuit-1259900.

16 See John C. Welchman, "Timeless/Authorless," in this volume.

17 See Lisa Rosendahl, "The Author Stripped Bare by Its Employees: Artistic Authorship in the Twenty-First Century and Beyond," in this volume.

18 *Cariou v. Prince*, 714 F.3d 694 (2d Cir. 2013).

19 See Nate Harrison, "Authoring Contradictions: Modern Appropriation Art and Postmodern Copyright Law in *Cariou v. Prince*," in this volume.

20 See Shane Burke, "Score, Performance, and the Posthumous Conductor," in this volume, and Guy Brett, "Hélio Oiticica: A Principle of Renewal," originally written for *Inherent Vice: The Replica and Its Implications in Modern Sculpture Workshop*, Tate Modern, London, October 18–19, 2007, revised and reprinted in this volume.

21 For a discussion of Rodin's industrialized sculptural production, see Penelope Curtis, "Demonstrable Legacy; or, What Sculptors Leave Behind," in this volume.

22 Rosalind E. Krauss, "The Originality of the Avant Garde," in *The Originality of the Avant Garde and Other Modernist Myths* (Cambridge, MA: MIT Press, 1986), 1.

23 See "French Court Delivers Verdict on Rodin Case," *Artnet News*, December 2, 2014, https://news.artnet.com/art-world/french-court-delivers-verdict-on-rodin-case-185341. The French criminal court declined jurisdiction to hear the case.

24 See Georgina Adam, "Artists' Legacies, Authentication, and the Art Market: Not Always a Happy Ménage," in this volume, especially her discussion of the role of artists' authentication committees in the section "Authentication, Foundations, and Market Manipulation?"

25 *Sobel v. Eggleston*, no. 12 Civ. 2551 (DAB) (S.D.N.Y. March 28, 2013). See also, Irina Tarsis, "Sobel v. Eggleston Limited Edition Is No Limit to Subsequent Editions," Center for Art Law Blog, April 15, 2013, https://itsartlaw.com/2013/04/15/in-sobel-v-eggleston-limited-edition-is-no-limit-to-subsequent-editions.

26 Daniel McClean, "Authenticity In Art and Law: A Question of Attribution or Authorization?" in *In Deed: Certificates of Authenticity in Art*, ed. Susan Hapgood and Cornelia Lauf (Amsterdam: Roma Publication, 2011), 88–96.

27 *Steinkamp v. Hoffman Gallery et al.*, 2012, WL1941149 (N.Y. Sup.).

28 See Alessandra Donati, "From the Object to the Archive: Guaranteeing Authorship and Ownership in Contemporary Art," in this volume.

29 See Ronald D. Spencer, "The Risk of Legal Liability for Attributions of Visual Art," in *The Expert versus the Object: Judging Fakes and False Attributions in the Arts* (New York: Oxford University Press 2004), 143–87.

30 *Joe Simon-Whelan v. Andy Warhol Foundation for the Visual Arts, Inc., et al.*, no. 07 Civ. 6423 (LTS) (S.D.N.Y. May 26, 2009). See also Judith Bresler, "Brave New Art Market: Unsilencing the Authenticators," and Daniel McClean, "Artists' Estates as Guardians of Artistic Legacy: Custodians or Gatekeepers?," both in this volume.

31 Richard Dorment, "What Is an Andy Warhol?" *New York Review of Books*, October 22, 2009, http://www.nybooks.com/articles/2009/10/22/what-is-an-andy-warhol/.

32 *Cramer v. Calder Foundation et al.*, no. 14-cv-1375, *complaint filed*, 2014 WL 790727 (S.D.N.Y. Feb. 28, 2014). See Irina Tarsis, "The Shifting Sands of Art Authentication: As Calder Foundation Finds Itself in Court again Who Will Have the Last Word in Authentication?" Center for Art Law Blog, April 23, 2014, https://itsartlaw.com/2014/04/23/shifty-art-authentication/.

33 See Giuseppe Calabi, "Authentication and the Italian Art Market," in this volume.

34 See Corinne Hershkovitch, "Artistic Authorship, Legacy, and Expert Liability in the French Art Market," and Georgina Adam, "Artists' Legacies, Authentication, and the Art Market," both in this volume.

35 See Adam, "Artists' Legacies, Authentication, and the Art Market," in this volume.

36 See Bresler, "Brave New Art Market," in this volume.
37 See McClean, "Artists' Estates as Guardians of Artistic Legacy," and Loretta Würtenberger and Karl von Trott, "Approaches to Dealing with Artists' Estates," both in this volume.
38 See Sarah Hanson, "The Great Artists Estates Race," in *Art Newspaper*, May 16, 2017, https://www.theartnewspaper.com/news/the-great-artists-estates-race. Leading international art galleries, including Gagosian, David Zwirner, and Hauser & Wirth, compete to globally represent artists' estates. For example, the estate of Félix González Torres is now represented by David Zwirner (2017), and the estates of August Sander and Eduardo Chillida by Hauser & Wirth (2017). See also Dushko Petrovich, "The Living Dead: Why Are Curators Putting Deceased Artists in Contemporary Art Shows?" *Artnews*, December 14, 2015, http://www.artnews.com/2015/12/14/the-living-dead-why-are-curators-putting-deceased-artists-in-contemporary-art-shows/.
39 Examples include the Institute of Artists Estates, established in Berlin, Germany, in 2016, and Art Legacy Planning, in New York, 2017.
40 See Würtenberger and von Trott, "Approaches to Dealing with Artists' Estates," especially the section "Legacy Management: Exploitation or Appreciation?" in this volume.
41 Milton Esterow, "The Battle for Picasso's Multi-Billion-Dollar Empire," *Vanity Fair*, March 7, 2016, https://www.vanityfair.com/culture/2016/03/picasso-multi-billion-dollar-empire-battle.
42 See Christine Vincent, "What's an Artist to Do?—Artist-Endowed Foundations and Legacy Stewardship in the United States," in this volume.
43 *Matter of Rothko*, 43 N.Y.2d 305, N.Y. Court of Appeals (1977). See also Judith H. Dobryznski, "A Betrayal the Art World Can't Forget: The Battle for Rothko's Estate Altered Lives and Reputations," *New York Times*, November 2, 1998, https://www.nytimes.com/1998/11/02/arts/betrayal-art-world-can-t-forget-battle-for-rothko-s-estate-altered-lives.html.
44 Bernard Reis.
45 The Mark Rothko Foundation created by the artist prior to his death was also a plaintiff in the litigation as represented by the Attorney General. Of the 2,000 Rothko works returned, half of these were distributed to the Foundation and half to the Rothko heirs.
46 See Agency, "Thing 000955 (Martha Graham's Choreographies)," in this volume, which discusses the posthumous dispute over copyright ownership of Martha Graham's (1894–1991) seventy-one choreographies, and hence over Graham's artistic legacy when she died.
47 Henri Neuendorf, "Franz West Archive Wins Back Rights to Images and Furniture," *Artnet News*, May 4, 2016, https://news.artnet.com/market/franz-west-archive-wins-rights-foundation-487703, and Henri Neuendorf, "Austrian Supreme Court Accuses Franz West Private Foundation of Embezzlement," June 14, 2016, https://news.artnet.com/market/franz-west-private-foundation-embezzlement-517316.
48 See Gabriel Pérez-Barreiro, "A Brass-Plated Boxing Ring: Foundations, Artists' Estates, and Legacy," in this volume.
49 See the website of the Chinati Foundation, https://chinati.org.
50 See GilaneTawadros, "Appendix; or, Some Adjectival Notes on Authorship and Legacy" and Dawn Ades, "Marcel Duchamp, *Fountain*, 1917: A Controversial History," both in this volume. Ades criticizes the contentious reattribution

of authorship of Duchamp's seminal readymade *Fountain* (1917) to Baroness Elsa von Freytag-Loringhoven.

51 The landmark *Documenta 11* (2002), Kassel, Germany, directed by Nigerian curator Okuwi Enwezor, is often celebrated as being the first global, postcolonial exhibition.

52 See Adam, "The Dark Side," 190–92.

53 *Greenberg Gallery, Inc. v. Bauman*, 817 F. Supp. 167 (D.D.C. 1993).

54 Ronald D. Spencer, "The Calder Case," in *The Expert versus the Object*, 196–97.

Part One: Authorship and Artists' Rights

JOAN KEE
Artists' Rights in the United States; or, A Remembrance of Claims Occasionally Checked

1 Julia Bryan-Wilson, *Art Workers: Radical Practice in the Vietnam War Era* (Berkeley: University of California Press, 2009), 13.

2 The higher Italian court found for de Chirico, claiming that he could intervene in the exhibition because an "artist lives in the work." The higher court overturned this judgment on the grounds that moral rights did not explicitly grant artists the right to withdraw their works from an exhibition. John Henry Merryman, "The Refrigerator of Bernard Buffet," 27 *Hastings Law Journal* 1022 (May 1976).

3 See, for example, Michelle O'Malley, *The Business of Art: Contracts and the Commissioning Process in Renaissance Italy* (New Haven: Yale University Press, 2005).

4 A related right was to show work in the way artists, not institutions, wanted. This was a key reason behind the establishment of numerous, if short-lived, alternative art spaces in early 1970s' New York. See Jacki Apple, ed., *Alternatives in Retrospect: An Historical Overview, 1969–1975* (New York: New Museum, 1981).

5 "AWC Open Hearing," January 1969, quoted in Andrea Fraser, *Museum Highlights: The Writings of Andrea Fraser*, ed. Alexander Alberro (Cambridge, MA: MIT Press, 2005), 60.

6 Bryan-Wilson, *Art Workers*, 15.

7 "Carl Andre," *Avalanche* 1 (Fall 1970): 26 (caps in original).

8 Edward Kienholz, "Contract for Purchase of a Concept Tableau," *Work from the 1960s by Edward Kienholz* (Washington, DC: Washington Gallery of Modern Art, 1967), 36.

9 Transcript of "Recent New York Artists," *60 Minutes*, September 19, 1993, Hirshhorn Museum and Sculpture Garden, Dept. of Public Programs/ Curatorial Division, Exhibition Records, 1988–1999, accession 00-024, box 1.

10 In 1972 legal scholar John Henry Merryman first offered his course on "Art and the Law" at Stanford Law School in California. He recalled how his colleagues ridiculed the course, suggesting that "Astrology and the Law" also be included among the curricular offerings. J. H. Merryman, "Art and the Law: Part I, A Course in Art and the Law," *Art Journal* 34, no. 4 (Summer 1975): 332.

11 Even more astonishing was the price for *Thaw*, a painting Scull purchased from Rauschenberg for $900 and later sold for $85,000.

12 "People," *Time*, October 29, 1973. Jerry Ordover expressed a similar kind of indignation in *Factor v. Stella*, when the buyer held the artist accountable for his work not fetching a high enough price at auction even though the buyer purchased the work directly from Stella at a much lower price. Jerry Ordover to Irwin Spiegel, April 9, 1975, Archives of

American Art, Frank Stella Papers, series 1(5), box 2. Compare Scull with Holly and Horace Solomon, who were deeply involved in the operation of 98 Greene Street, one of New York's first important alternative spaces for art and who saw their collecting as a way of helping artists "live a dignified life." Apple, *Alternatives in Retrospect*, 28.

13 For a brief history of art funds from the 1970s to the present, see Noah Horowitz, *Art of the Deal: Contemporary Art in a Global Financial Market* (Princeton: Princeton University Press, 2014), 143–87.

14 In 1974 the painter Judy Pendleton helped found the Artists Rights Association, an organization dedicated to securing artists' resale rights. See Grace Glueck, "Artists Seek Royalties in Painting Sales," *New York Times*, March 12, 1974.

15 The Society of Artists cited the example of Jean-François Millet, whose painting *The Angelus* (1859) sold for $160 during his lifetime and for $160,000 twenty years after his death. "Painters Seek New Rights," *New York Times*, March 7, 1909. For more on Grant Wood, see Sylvia Hochfield, "Artists Rights: Pros and Cons," *Artnews* 74 (May 1975): 20.

16 The efficacy of this Act is questionable, not only because of the difficulty of enforcement but also on grounds of legality. In *Estate of Robert Graham v. Sotheby's, Inc.*, 860 F. Supp. 2d 1117 (C.D. Cal. 2012), the District Court for the Central District of California held that the Act violated the Commerce Clause of the US Constitution, which forbids states from burdening interstate commerce. Upon its review of the decision in 2015, the Ninth Circuit stated that the Act would only apply to sales of works taking place within California. The decision of the Ninth Circuit is reprinted in full at http://cdn.ca9.uscourts.gov/datastore/opinions/2015/05/05/12-56067.pdf.

17 Lawrence Scott Bauman, interview by John Henry Merryman, "Legal Control of the Fabrication and Marketing of Fake Paintings," 24 *Stanford Law Review* 935 (1972). Bauman proposed the creation of an art registry that would house certificates of authenticity as a means of combating what by the early 1970s had been the rampant circulation of forgeries. Ibid., 939.

18 Maria Eichhorn, *The Artist's Contract* (Cologne: Walther König, 2009), 232.

19 Robert Projansky, "The Perilous World of Art Law," *Juris Doctor* (June 1974): 15.

20 Seth Siegelaub to Jerry Ordover, February 5, 1970, The Museum of Modern Art Archives, New York, Seth Siegelaub Papers, Gift of Seth Siegelaub and the Stichting Egress Foundation, Amsterdam, I. D.27.

21 For a discussion of this imbalance of power as exemplified in the contracts issued by corporations and signed by the participants of LACMA's Art and Technology Program, see Christopher De Fay, "Art, Enterprise and Collaboration: Richard Serra, Robert Irwin, James Turrell, and Claes Oldenburg at the Art and Technology Program of the Los Angeles County Museum of Art, 1967–1971" (Ph.D. diss., University of Michigan, 2005), 225–72.

22 Jurgen Arnold, "Art and Justice: An Eternal Satire," in *Legal/Illegal: Art beyond Law*, ed. Hans Winkler (Berlin: NGBK, 2004), 61.

23 Ibid. On Toche's legal tribulations see Annette Kuhn, "Culture Shock," *Village Voice*, August 4, 1975.

24 For a comprehensive examination and collection of documents related to the Brancusi case, see Margit Rowell, ed., *Brancusi v. United States: The Historic Trial, 1928* (Paris: Adam Biro, 1999).

25 A rare exception was the Tax Reform Act of 1976, which permitted an artist to deduct his or her rent or studio-related

maintenance costs. The effect of US tax law on artists merits special attention. Rubin Gorewitz, who oversaw accounting for more than six hundred artists, including Rauschenberg, was especially vocal on the need to reform tax laws having an "iniquitous" effect on artists. An example was to bring about reform that would allow artists to donate their works and deduct from their taxes the full market value of their donations. "Group Portrait with Accountant," *Esquire*, November 1974, 124.

26 *Crimi v. Rutgers Presbyterian Church*, 89 N.Y.S. 2d 813 (Sup. Ct. 1949).

27 Seth Siegelaub, "Artists' Reserved Rights Transfer and Sale Agreement," *Studio International* 181, no. 932 (April 1971): 144.

28 Seth Siegelaub, "The Artist's Reserved Rights Transfer and Sale Agreement," *Leonardo* 6 (1973): 347.

29 Michel Claura to Seth Siegelaub, December 12, 1971, MoMA Archives, New York, Siegelaub, I.A.92. According to Claura, Yvon Lambert had a collector who said, "If you want me to sign this contract, I won't buy you anything more [*sic*]."

30 Roger Rocklles, "Artists Decide They Should Share Profits on Resale of Paintings," *Wall Street Journal*, February 11, 1974.

31 John Henry Merryman and Albert E. Elsen, *Law, Ethics and the Visual Arts* (New York: Matthew Bender, 1979), 37.

32 Robert Rie to Siegelaub, February 5, 1971, MoMA Archives, New York, Siegelaub, I.A.99.

33 Laurace James wrote of the Jurrist contract, a modification of "The Artist's Reserved Rights Transfer and Sale Agreement," in Laurace James, "Artists, Dealers and Economics at A.I.R. April 7th," *Women Artists Newsletter* 1, no. 1 (April 1975). Developed by a young attorney, Charles Jurrist, the agreement sought a 15 percent royalty for the artist only on the first resale of the work. It also barred artists from duplicating their work and from expanding the size of an edition. Carl M. and Carol G. Colonna, "An Economic and Legal Assessment of Recent Visual Artists' Reversion Rights Agreements in the United States," *Journal of Cultural Economics* 6, no. 2 (December 1982): 80. Jurrist himself left what he described as a "repressive" legal field in the early 1970s to become a dance critic for the *New York Daily News*. See "Charles Jurrist," *Orlando Sentinel*, July 1, 1991.

34 Leslie Satin, "The $100 Gallery," *Women Artists News* 4, no. 3 (Summer 1978): 13. Of the purchase price, 80 percent would go to the artist, with the remaining 20 percent going to the gallery. Located at 319 Greenwich Street in New York, the $100 Gallery sold works from a range of artists, including Louise Lawler, Sol LeWitt, and Carl Andre.

35 Athena Tacha, "The Vagaries of VARA: Can the Law Save Your Art?" (College Art Association Annual Conference, Philadelphia, February 2002).

36 Ibid.

37 Timothy Cone, "A Case for Contracts," *Arts Magazine* 65 (November 1990): 27.

38 Ibid.

39 On the removal of *Shinto*, see Grace Glueck, "Bank Cuts Up a Noguchi Sculpture and Stores It," *New York Times*, April 19, 1980.

40 Cone, "A Case for Contracts," 37.

41 For a critical exploration of the issues involved, see Harriet Senie, *The Tilted Arc Controversy: Dangerous Precedent?* (Minneapolis: University of Minnesota Press, 2002); and Clara Weyergraf-Serra and Martha Buskirk, *The Destruction of Tilted Arc: Documents* (Cambridge, MA: MIT Press, 1991).

42 See Title 17, Section 106A, of the United States Code, https://www.law.cornell.edu/uscode/text/17/106A.

43 Justin Hughes, "Symposium II Art and the Law: Suppression and Liberty, the

Line Between Work and Framework, Text and Context," *Cardozo Arts and Entertainment Journal* 19 (2001): 21.

44 The first criminal trial of an art museum on the grounds of content, the Mapplethorpe case began when the Contemporary Arts Center in Cincinnati exhibited photographs showing explicit sexual activity. See *City of Cincinnati v. Contemporary Arts Center*, 57 Ohio Misc.2d 15 (1990). The "NEA Four," so named after the abbreviation used for the National Endowment for the Arts, brought their case to the US Supreme Court. See *National Endowment for the Arts v. Finley*, 524 U.S. 569 (1998). Although the artists eventually prevailed, their victory was bittersweet as Congress eliminated individual NEA grants for artists in 1994, a major setback in what, since the early 1970s, had been an unprecedented level of US governmental support of the arts. The photographer Sally Mann, too, was repeatedly tried and found guilty in the court of public opinion; see Richard Woodward, "The Disturbing Photographs of Sally Mann," *New York Times Magazine*, September 27, 1992, 35.

45 Committee for the *Real Estate Show*, "Manifesto, or Statement of Intent," 1980, http://www.abcnorio.org/about/history/res_manifesto.html.

46 Originally reproduced on greeting cards and postcards, the photograph appealed to Koons, who had the depiction made into a sculpture. Although Koons pleaded that his use was a case of "fair use," the Second Circuit ruled in Rogers's favor. See *Rogers v. Koons*, 960 F.2d 301 (2d Cir. 1992). The same court would find in favor of the alleged infringer almost a quarter of a century later.

47 *Blanch v. Koons*, 467 F.3d 244 (2d Cir. 2006).

48 *Cariou v. Prince*, 714 F.3d 694 (2d Cir. 2013). In 2008 Prince used photographs taken by Cariou for his *Canal Zone* series. In 2009 Cariou sued Prince, his gallery, his gallerist, and the catalogue publisher on copyright-infringement grounds. Although he initially won his suit, the Second Circuit reversed the decision. For an incisive discussion about the future of fair use in cases involving contemporary artworks, see Amy Adler, "Fair Use and the Future of Art," 91 *New York University Law Review* 559 (June 2016).

49 *Massachusetts Museum of Contemporary Art Foundation v. Büchel*, 593 F.3d 38 (1st. Cir. 2010). Yet the court also held fast to VARA's limitations, claiming that an artist is barred from claiming statutory damages even if his or her right of attribution has been violated.

50 Hans Haacke, "The Constituency," *Tracks: A Journal of Artists' Writings* 3, no. 3 (Fall 1977): 104.

51 This marks the third iteration of the Bill, first introduced in 2011 by Jerrold Nadler, US Congressman from New York. This and two previous versions failed to become law. See American Royalties Too Act 2015, H.R. 1881, 114th Cong. (2015), https://www.govtrack.us/congress/bills/114/hr1881.

52 For an analysis of whether fair use is a privilege reserved only for the privileged, including a discussion of the Richard Prince case, see Andrew Gilden and Timothy Greene, "Fair Use for the Rich and Fabulous," 80 *University of Chicago Law Review* 88 (July 2013).

DONN ZARETSKY
Training Ground for Moral Rights: MASS MoCA v. Christoph Büchel

1 *Massachusetts Museum of Contemporary Art Foundation Inc. v. Buchel*, 565 F. Supp. 2d 245, 249 (D. Mass. 2008). I will refer to this as the District Court Decision.
2 Quoted in Geoff Edgers, "Dismantled," *Boston Globe*, October 21, 2007, http://archive.boston.com/ae/theater_arts/articles/2007/10/21/dismantled/?page=full.
3 *Massachusetts Museum of Contemporary Art Foundation Inc. v. Buchel*, 593 F.3d 38, 45 (1st Cir. 2010). I will refer to this as the Appellate Decision.
4 District Court Decision, 254.
5 The museum placed yellow tarpaulins over the unfinished work, but the parties differed on whether this "actually concealed all of the individual components and vital design elements of 'Training Ground,' or whether the tarpaulins simply 'hid . . . an elephant behind a napkin,' effectively inviting individuals to peek behind the cloth coverings and view the unfinished work." Charles Giuliano, "Christoph Buchel's Tarp Art at Mass MoCA," *Berkshire Fine Arts*, July 31, 2007, http://www.berkshirefinearts.com/07-31-2007_christoph-buchel-s-tarp-art-at-mass-moca.htm, quoted in Appellate Decision, 46.
6 Appellate Decision, 49 (citations omitted).
7 District Court Decision, 258.
8 Ibid., 260 (emphasis added).
9 Ibid.
10 Roberta Smith, "Is It Art Yet? And Who Decides?" *New York Times*, September 16, 2007, http://www.nytimes.com/2007/09/16/arts/design/16robe.html.
11 Appellate Decision, 51 (citations omitted, emphasis in original).
12 Ibid., 51–52.
13 Ibid., 52.
14 The effect of the appellate court decision was to reverse the District Court's grant of summary judgment in favor of the museum and remand the case for further proceedings. The parties reached a settlement soon thereafter. See also the email cited in note 4.
15 Appellate Decision, 62.

MARTHA BUSKIRK
Retraction

1 In his classic essay on the author function, Michel Foucault emphasizes the potential distinctions in terms of function between the proper name associated with authorship and the individual thus named, as well as the challenge of establishing what should be defined as the author's work from within a larger continuum that might range from working notes to laundry lists and other traces. See Foucault, "What is an Author?" (1969), in *Language, Counter-Memory, Practice: Selected Essays and Interviews by Michel Foucault*, ed. and trans. Donald F. Bouchard and Sherry Simon (Ithaca, NY: Cornell University Press, 1977), 113–38.
2 Quoted by Richard Dorment, "What Is an Andy Warhol?," *New York Review of Books*, October 22, 2009, http://www.nybooks.com/articles/archives/2009/oct/22/what-is-an-andy-warhol/. This was the first in an extended set of articles and rebuttals in the *New York Review of Books* discussing the lawsuit brought by Joe Simon-Whelan, owner of a different self-portrait from the same series, against the authentication board in 2009.
3 Email from Jonathan Halpern (Noland's lawyer) to Jonathan Olsoff (North American General Counsel of Sotheby's), November 9, 2011 (following up on a briefer statement in a November 8 email

that the work should be withdrawn). Included as exhibit 7, "Motion of Defendant Sotheby's to Dismiss Plaintiff's Complaint and for Summary Judgment," March 27, 2012, *Marc Jancou Fine Art Ltd., doing business as Marc Jancou Contemporary v. Sotheby's, Inc. and Cady Noland*, no. 650316/2012 (N.Y. Sup. Ct. February 1, 2012).

4 Ibid.

5 For background on this action, see Julia Bryan-Wilson, "From Artists to Art Workers," in *Art Workers: Radical Practice in the Vietnam War Era* (Berkeley, CA: University of California Press, 2009), 13–39.

6 See Greg Allen, "An Anthology of Cady Noland Disclaimers," *greg.org*, June 13, 2015, and updated on an ongoing basis, http://greg.org/archive/2015/06/13/an_anthology_of_cady_noland_disclaimers.html.

7 The final price for *Oozewald*, including buyer's premium, was $6,578,500. Kusama's *White No. 28* (1960), from her *Infinity Net* series, sold at Christie's for $7,109,000 in November 2014. The fact that Noland's related *Bluewald* (1989) sold for $9,797,000 at a May 2015 Christie's auction was, however, somewhat eclipsed by the record $179,365,000 paid for Pablo Picasso's *Les femmes d'Alger* (1955) at the same auction.

8 The price paid by Jancou in 2011 was part of the information revealed in conjunction with the Sotheby's counterclaim. Faxed correspondence between Christie's and Noland also indicated a more direct communication link—and the fact that Christie's had consulted with Noland much earlier in the consignment process meant that the lot was withdrawn well before their catalogue was printed.

9 The condition report from Christian Scheidemann was included as exhibit 10 accompanying Sotheby's Motion to Dismiss.

10 Discussion of the stand appears in email correspondence from Noland's lawyer included as exhibit 6 accompanying Sotheby's Motion to Dismiss. For Sotheby's catalogue information regarding *Oozewald*, see Sotheby's, New York, *Contemporary Art Evening Auction*, sale cat. (November 9, 2011), lot 7, http://www.sothebys.com/en/auctions/ecatalogue/2011/contemporary-art-evening-sale-n08791/lot.7.html.

11 Judge Ellen M. Coin, "Decision and Order," November 13, 2012, *Marc Jancou Fine Art Ltd. v. Sotheby's Inc. and Cady Noland*.

12 Schnader Harrison Segal & Lewis LLP for Cady Noland, "Answer to Amended Complaint with Counter-Claim(s)," *Marc Jancou Fine Art Ltd. v. Sotheby's Inc.*, May 11, 2012.

13 For a comparison between Robert Morris's ironic gesture, with his "Statement of Esthetic Withdrawal," and Donald Judd's entirely serious denunciation, via a 1990 *Art in America* advertisement, of a refabrication that was authorized by Giuseppe Panza, see Martha Buskirk, *The Contingent Object of Contemporary Art* (Cambridge, MA: MIT Press, 2003), 1–6.

14 See Michael Lobel, *Fugitive Artist: The Early Work of Richard Prince, 1974–77* (Purchase: Neuberger Museum of Art, Purchase College, State University of New York, Purchase, 2007).

15 Dietmar Elger, "Key to Catalogue Entries," in *Félix González-Torres: Catalogue Raisonné*, ed. Dietmar Elger (Ostfildern-Ruit, Germany: Cantz, 1997), 14.

16 See, for example, Tim Ackermann, "Das Bild, das Gerhard Richter nicht schätzt," *Die Welt*, December 1, 2012, http://www.welt.de/print/die_welt/kultur/article111739673/Das-Bild-das-Gerhard-Richter-nicht-schaetzt.html.

17 Sarah Thornton, *33 Artists in 3 Acts* (New York: W. W. Norton and Company, 2014),

327. Unlike other chapters in the book, the one on Noland does not include a reproduction of the artist's work on the facing page, and it carries the following disclaimer: "Ms. Noland would like it to be known that she has not approved this chapter" (325).

18 Steven Parrino, "Paranoia Americana: The New Work of Cady Noland" (2001), *Afterall* 11 (Spring/Summer 2005): 8. However, there is an untitled work dated 2008 in the Walker Art Center's online collection catalogue that it listed as "Gift of the artist and Helen van der Miej-Tcheng, by exchange, 2009"; see Cady Noland, *Untitled*, 2008, Walker Art Center, accessed September 29, 2017, http://www.walkerart.org/collections/artworks/untitled-285. Greg Allen speculates that this new work was traded for a work called *Cowboy Blank* (1990), made of aluminum and rope, listed as a 2005 gift from van der Miej-Tcheng in the Walker's 2006 annual report, which no longer appears to be in the collection. See Allen, "Wait, What Cady Noland, 2008?" *greg.org*, November 10, 2014, http://greg.org/archive/2014/11/10/wait_what_cady_noland_2008.html.

19 Number 8 from the edition of 20 of Cady Noland's *Four in One Sculpture* (1998), made of painted wood and plastic, sold at Christie's in 2013 for $68,750, and number 5 from the edition, sold at Christie's in 2008 for $61,000. Both listings indicate that the work was accompanied by extra sawhorses. See Christie's, *New York, Post-War and Contemporary Afternoon Session*, sale cat. (May 16, 2013), lot 462, http://www.christies.com/LotFinder/lot_details.aspx?intObjectID=5680313; and Christie's, New York, *Post-War and Contemporary First Open*, sale cat. (April 1, 2008), lot 24, http://www.christies.com/LotFinder/lot_details.aspx?intObjectID=5050406.

20 The Salvage Art Institute's 2012 *No Longer Art* exhibition provided a striking example of works written off as total losses by the AXA insurance company. See Salvage Art Institute, accessed September 29, 2017, http://salvageartinstitute.org/); and Jeffrey Weiss, "Things Not Necessarily Meant to Be Viewed as Art," *Artforum* 51, no. 7 (March 2013): 221–29. For a general discussion of status shifts, see Martha Buskirk, "When Is the Work of Art," in *Creative Enterprise: Contemporary Art between Museum and Marketplace* (New York: Continuum, 2012), 147–200.

21 See Clara Weyergraf-Serra and Martha Buskirk, eds., *The Destruction of Tilted Arc: Documents* (Cambridge, MA: MIT Press, 1991), as well as Buskirk, *The Contingent Object*, 48–51.

22 The case concerned a painting sold at Sotheby's London in 2006 by Lancelot Thwaytes, which was thought at the time to be a copy of Caravaggio's *Cardsharps* (ca. 1594). In 2007 a Caravaggio expert declared that the work was another version rather than a copy, and Thwaytes subsequently sued Sotheby's for negligence. For a full discussion of the lawsuit, see Bendor Grovsvenor, "'Caravaggio' Lawsuit Dismissed by High Court," *Art Newspaper*, March 1, 2015, http://old.theartnewspaper.com/news/art-market/caravaggio-lawsuit-dismissed-by-high-court/.

23 See Buskirk, *The Contingent Object*, 1–6, 33–55.

24 *Mueller v. Michael Janssen Gallery Pte. Ltd. et al.* (Scott C. Mueller against Michael Janssen, Wilhelm Schurmann and Marisa Newman Projects, LLC), no. 1:2015cv04827 (S. D. N.Y. June 22, 2015). In the accompanying Schedule A, a document titled "Artwork Description and Provenance" indicates that the work consists of "a log cabin façade fabricated to the Artist's specifications, and American flag, metal rings, and paper

construction plans." However, it also states: "All components other than the wood and hardware that comprise the log cabin façade are original to the artwork"—a qualification that excludes most of the work's original components.

25 Decision by Naomi Reice Buchwald, signed December 1, 2016, ibid.

26 *Cady Noland v. Galerie Michael Janssen, Michael Janssen, Wilhelm Schurmann, KOW, and Chris D'Amelio*, no. 1:17-cv-05452-JPO (S.D.N.Y. July 18, 2017). According to Noland's complaint, the defendants "conspired to infringe Noland's copyright by making or authorizing others to make an exact reproduction of *Log Cabin* without Plaintiff's knowledge." In addition, the suit claimed infringement on Noland's moral rights under VARA and/or the New York Artists Authorship Rights Act, with jurisdiction for the latter asserted on the basis of business conducted by the various named parties in New York State. Despite the references to VARA, the fact that *Log Cabin* dates to 1990, and appears to have been sold the same year it was made, would situate it before the June 1, 1991, effective date for VARA.

27 Arjun Appadurai, "Introduction: Commodities and the Politics of Value," in *The Social Life of Things: Commodities in Cultural Perspective*, ed. Arjun Appadurai (Cambridge and New York: Cambridge University Press, 1986), 4, 13, 15.

CHRISTIAN VIVEROS-FAUNÉ

Up for Grabs; or, Artistic Authorship in the Age of the Flipper: Kreuk v. Vō

1 Anna Altman, "Buy, Sell, Hang on Your Wall," *Bloomberg Businessweek*, November 12, 2015, https://www.bloomberg.com/news/articles/2015-11-12/artrank-gives-art-the-stock-market-treatment.

2 Ibid.

3 Mark C. Taylor, "Is Modern Finance Ruining Modern Art, Part 1," *Bloomberg View*, January 30, 2012, https://www.bloomberg.com/view/articles/2012-01-30/is-modern-finance-ruining-modern-art-part-1-commentary-by-mark-taylor.

4 Mark C. Taylor, *Refiguring the Spiritual: Beuys, Barney, Turrell, Goldsworthy* (New York: Columbia University Press, 2012), 1.

5 Eilene Zimmerman, "The Risks and Rewards of Short-Termism," *New York Times*, November 4, 2015, https://www.nytimes.com/2015/11/05/business/dealbook/the-risks-and-rewards-of-short-termism.html?mcubz=0.

6 Jeff Rabin, "The Art Fund Landscape," Art Investment Council Conference (Armory Art Fair, New York, March 9, 2012).

7 Rebecca Hawkins, "Artvest: Renaissance Advisors," *Private Art Investor*, May 19, 2015, http://www.privateartinvestor.com/art-business/artvest-renaissance-advisors/.

8 These are not sales in which either the artist or his primary gallery benefitted, but instead constitute sales of artwork by third parties in the secondary market.

9 Greg Allen, "The Power of Kreuk Compels You! The Trials of Danh Vo," *ARTnews*, September 24, 1915, http://www.artnews.com/2015/09/24/the-power-of-kreuk-compels-you/.

10 Ibid.

11 Doreen Carvajal, "Danh Vo and Bert Kreuk's Legal Battle Pits Artist against Collector," *New York Times*, July 13, 2015, https://www.nytimes.com/2015/07/14/arts/design/danh-vo-and-bert-kreuks-legal-battle-pits-artist-against-collector.html.

12 Ibid.

13 Greg Allen, "The Power of Kreuk Compels You!"

14 Marta Gnyp, "Protect Me from What I Want: Kreuk versus Vo," trans. Marta

Gnyp, *Die Welt am Sonntag*, August 2, 2015, http://www.martagnyp.com/articles/protect-me-from-what-i-want.php.

15 Ibid.

16 "Danh Võ Tells Collector Bert Kreuk to 'Shove It' in Stunning Private Letter after Contentious Court Ruling," *Artnet News*, July 16, 2015, https://news.artnet.com/art-world/danh-vo-tells-bert-kreuk-to-shove-it-317385.

17 Ibid.

18 Doreen Carvajal, "Danh Vo and Bert Kreuk's Legal Battle Pits Artist Against Collector."

19 Ibid.

20 Dushko Petrovich, "Peter Doig Wins Bizarre Authentication Trial," *Artnet News*, August 23, 2016, https://news.artnet.com/art-world/peter-doig-trial-verdict-618932.

NATE HARRISON

Authoring Contradictions: Modern Appropriation Art and Postmodern Copyright Law in Cariou v. Prince

1 Transcribed in Greg Allen, ed., *The Deposition of Richard Prince* (Zurich: Bookhorse, 2012), 218.

2 See John C. Welchman, *Art after Appropriation: Essays on Art in the 1990s* (Amsterdam: G+B Arts International, 2001).

3 Leo Steinberg, "The Glorious Company," in *Art about Art*, ed. Jean Lipman and Richard Marshall (New York: E. P. Dutton and Whitney Museum of American Art, 1978), 25. Thank you to Natilee Harren for pointing me to this essay. See also Douglas Crimp, "Pictures," *October* 8 (Spring 1979): 75–88.

4 Linda Hutcheon, *A Theory of Parody: The Teachings of Twentieth-Century Art Forms* (Urbana and Chicago: University of Illinois Press, 1985), 85 (emphasis in original).

5 See *Cariou v. Prince*, 784 F.Supp. 2d 337 (S.D.N.Y. 2011), https://scholar.google.com/scholar_case?case=18222445238017802130&hl=en&as_sdt=6&as_vis=1&oi=scholarr; and *Cariou v. Prince*, 714 F.3d 694, 712 (2d Cir. 2013), https://scholar.google.com/scholar_case?case=com/5845890683658306826&hl=en&as_sdt=6&as_vis=1&oi=scholarr.

6 "Joint Brief and Special Appendix for Defendants-Appellants," *Cariou v. Prince* (2013), http://docs.justia.com/cases/federal/appellate-courts/ca2/11-1197/100/0.pdf?ts=1350506951, 24.

7 Patrick Cariou, *Yes Rasta* (New York: powerHouse Books, 2000).

8 See Title 17 U.S.C. § 107, https://www.copyright.gov/title17/92chap1.html#107.

9 Pierre N. Leval, "Toward a Fair Use Standard," 103 *Harvard Law Review* 1105 (1990), http://docs.law.gwu.edu/facweb/claw/levalfrustd.htm.

10 *Campbell v. Acuff-Rose Music* (92-1292), 510 U.S. 569 (1994), https://www.law.cornell.edu/supct/html/92-1292.ZS.html.

11 See *Mattel Inc. v. Walking Mountain Productions*, 353 F.3d 792 (9th Cir. 2003), http://scholar.google.com/scholar_case?case=7581792703482092445...ttel+v.+WALKING+MOUNTAIN+PRODUCTIONS&hl=en&as_sdt=2,5&as_vis=1; and *Blanch v. Koons*, 467 F.3d 244 (2nd Cir. 2006), https://cyber.harvard.edu/people/tfisher/IP/2006%20Blanch%20Abridged.pdf.

12 "Memorandum of Law in Support of Defendants' Joint Motion for Summary Judgment," *Cariou v. Prince* (2011), https://www.scribd.com/document/328321103/Cariou-v-Prince, 5.

13 "Joint Brief and Special Appendix for Defendants-Appellants," 30–31.

14 Ibid., 15.

15 Parody's requirement that an original's source and context be familiar (if only to be ridiculed through an appropriating artistic gesture) is illustrated in the notorious case *Rogers v. Koons*, which is

discussed briefly in following paragraphs. In their rulings, the courts concluded that Rogers's photograph was not well known enough for viewers to understand Koons's appropriating work as a parody.

16 See *Rogers v. Koons*, 960 F.2d 301 (2nd Cir. 1992), http://ncac.org/resource/rogers-v-koons.

17 "Memorandum of Law in Support of Defendants' Joint Motion for Summary Judgment," 1–6.

18 Allen, *The Deposition of Richard Prince*, 192.

19 See Title 17, Section 101, United States Code, https://www.copyright.gov/title17/92chap1.html#101. US copyright law defines "derivative works" as translations, abridgments, and other forms that recast, transform, or adapt their sources. The law's use of the word "transform" in this context is problematized by the rhetoric of the "transformative" in fair-use defenses. It would seem "transformed" works, which do not, on their surface, add meaning (such as a translation), infringe copyright, while "transformative" works, produced specifically to offer new meanings of existing materials, do not.

20 *Cariou v. Prince* (2011).

21 Hal Foster, *Recodings: Art, Spectacle, Cultural Politics* (Port Townsend, WA: Bay Press, 1985), 128.

22 As art collector Adam Lindemann stated in an interview with Cariou: "It irks him that the images were used out of context, 'he (Prince) made them look like zombies, it's a racist piece of art.'" Adam Lindemann, "My Artwork Formerly Known as Prince," *Observer*, March 29, 2011, http://observer.com/2011/03/my-artwork-formerly-known-as-prince/.

23 Here the charge of "appropriator" could be leveled at both Cariou and Prince. Both occupy the clichéd position of the privileged, Anglo-European creative subject attempting to represent "the other." Here I would simply, if crudely, state that there is something embarrassing about two white men arguing over whose representations of black men are the more sincere or "artistic" expressions.

24 *Bleistein v. Donaldson Lithographing Co.*, 188 U.S. 239 (1903), http://scholar.google.com/scholar_case?case=3277054592305773876&q=bleistein+v.+donaldson&hl=en&as_sdt=2,33. Of course, the ways in which courts have evaluated works of art, parsing the subjective from the objective, have themselves changed over time. Such a historical analysis would require an essay unto itself.

25 "Joint Brief and Special Appendix for Defendants-Appellants," 39–40.

26 Ibid., 41–51.

27 *Cariou v. Prince* (2013).

28 Leval, "Toward a Fair Use Standard," 1111.

29 *Cariou v. Prince* (2013) (emphasis added).

30 Ibid.

31 Randy Kennedy, "Richard Prince Settles Copyright Suit with Patrick Cariou over Photographs," *New York Times*, March 18, 2014, http://artsbeat.blogs.nytimes.com/2014/03/18/richard-prince-settles-copyright-suit-with-patrick-cariou-over-photographs/?rref=collection%2Ftimestopic%2FPrince%2C%20Richard&action=click&contentCollection=timestopics®ion=stream&module=stream_unit&version=latest&contentPlacement=10&pgtype=collection&_r=0. How the court arrived at a fair-use ruling for all but five of the paintings remains unclear, but highlights one of the difficulties of the "reasonable observer" standard as it relates to subjective judgments of taste.

32 Laura Heymann, "Everything Is Transformative: Fair Use and Reader Response," 31 *Columbia Journal of Law and the Arts* 445, 449–50 (2008).

33 See Andrew Gilden and Timothy Greene, "Fair Use for the Rich and Famous?" 80 *The University of Chicago Law Review* 88

(2013), http://lawreview.uchicago.edu/page/fair-use-rich-and-fabulous.

34 I am not aware of any art historian or critic who has explicitly dismissed Prince's recent works as banal or derivative. However, it is not difficult to imagine certain academics and other intellectuals, especially those critical of the collusion between corporate interests, the art market, and spectacle culture generally, who would testify against Prince's brand of appropriation.

JOHN C. WELCHMAN
Timeless/Authorless

The epigraph at the head of this essay can be found in Mike Kelley, "The Complex," in *Mike Kelley: Educational Complex Onwards (1995–2008)*, ed. Anne Pontégnie, exh. cat. (Zurich: JRP | Ringier, 2009), 72.

1 Kelley's annotation to a diagrammatic drawing associated with *My Space* (1979).

2 With the exception of three essays in the exhibition catalogue *Mike Kelley: Catholic Tastes*, there is, as yet, little detailed research on Kelley's performances. See Timothy Martin, "Janitor in a Drum: Excerpts from a Performance History"; Howard Singerman, "Charting *Monkey Island* with Levi-Strauss and Freud"; and Colin Gardener, "Let It Bleed: *The Sublime* and *Plato's Cave, Rothko's Chapel, Lincoln's Profile*," in *Mike Kelley: Catholic Tastes*, ed. Elizabeth Sussman, exh. cat. (New York: Whitney Museum, 1993), 56–88, 89–110, 112–34. See also John C. Welchman, "Mike Kelley: Work," in *Mike Kelley*, exh. cat. (Munich: Prestel, 2013), on which I draw in this and the following paragraph.

3 I address Kelley's refutation of standardization in John C. Welchman, "Stopgap Measures: Reading Mike Kelley's Writings," in *The Space of Reading*, ed. Christina Barton, Natasha Conland, and Wystan Curnow, special issue, *Reading Room: A Journal of Art and Culture*, no. 5 (2012): 50, 54, 56, 61, 65.

4 On the role of photography in Kelley's work, see John C. Welchman, "History and Time in the American Vernacular: Mike Kelley's Work with Photography," in *Imaging History: Photography After the Fact*, Lieven Gevaert Series, vol. 12, ed. Bruno Vandermeulen and Danny Veys (Brussels: ASA, 2011), 107–12; and Welchman, "Documents, Dreams and Fantasies: Passages through the Involuntary from Photography to Sculpture in the Work of Mike Kelley," in *Found Sculpture and Photograph from Surrealism to Contemporary Art*, ed. Anna Dezeuze and Julia Kelley (Farnham, England: Ashgate, 2013), 137–56.

5 Head text for Mike Kelley, "Some Aesthetic High Points," in *Minor Histories: Statements, Conversations, Proposals* (Cambridge, MA: MIT Press, 2004), 40. The piece was first published in William S. Bartman and Miyoshi Barosh, eds., *Mike Kelley* (Los Angeles: A.R.T. Press, 1991), 54–59.

6 On Kelley's writings and his work as a writer, see my introductions to *Foul Perfection: Essays and Criticism*, ed. John C. Welchman (Cambridge, MA: MIT Press, 2003), ix–xx, and Kelley, *Minor Histories*, xiv–xxvi; and my related and updated "Stopgap Measures: Reading Mike Kelley's Writings," in *The Space of Reading*, 48–69. There are few sustained discussions of wider questions relating to Kelley's ideas and practices of authorship, although a recent Master's thesis makes some useful contributions, see Elizabeth Hirsch, "Origination Narratives in the Work of Mike Kelley" (Master's thesis, Art History, Hunter College, City University of New York, 2013).

7 On the "author function," see Michel Foucault, "What Is an Author?" in *Language, Counter-Memory, Practice: Selected Essays and Interviews by Michel Foucault*, ed. Donald F. Bouchard, trans. Donald F. Bouchard and Sherry Simon (Ithaca, NY: Cornell University Press, 1977), 113–38.

8 This description of *Timeless/Authorless* draws on my head text in *Minor Histories*, 274–76; and on my essay "Mike Kelley and the Comedic," in *Mike Kelley*, ed. Ann Goldstein, Eva Meyer-Hermann, and Lisa Gabrielle Mark, exh. cat. (Munich: Prestel, 2013), 332–44.

9 Renee Fredrickson, author of *Repressed Memories: A Journey to Recovery from Sexual Abuse* (New York: Simon and Schuster, 1992), and Ellen Bass and Laura Davis, authors of *The Courage to Heal: A Guide for Women Survivors of Child Sexual Abuse* (New York: HarperCollins, 1988), are some of the best-known champions of the recovered-memory movement. Works that dispute their claims include: Richard Ofshe and Ethan Watters, *Making Monsters: False Memories, Psychotherapy, and Sexual Hysteria* (New York: Charles Scribner, 1994); Elizabeth Loftus and Katherine Ketcham, *The Myth of Repressed Memory: False Memories and Allegations of Sexual Abuse* (New York: St. Martin's Press, 1994); Mark Pendergrast, *Victims of Memory: Incest Accusations and Shattered Lives* (Hinesburg, VT: Upper Access Books, 1995); and Kathryn Lyon, *Witch Hunt: A True Story of Social Hysteria and Abused Justice* (New York: Avon Books, 1998).

10 Kelley's texts "Goin' Home, Goin' Home" (1995) and *Missing Time, Works on Paper 1974–1976, Reconsidered* (1995) are collected in *Minor Histories*, 72–80, 60–70.

11 Three of the narratives were published as "Bee, Gang, P Eye," along with writings by twenty-three other LA-based artists, critics, and writers, in *Asteroid Impaired: Righteous American Fiction*, vol. 1, ed. Alexis Hall, Catherine Sullivan, and Benjamin Weissman (Pasadena, CA: Art Center College of Design, n.d.); "Recovered Memory 1" was also published as a facsimile of the original photo-texts, *Timeless/Authorless* 4, 7 and 11, under the banner title of *The Westland Eagle*, *The Ann Arbor News*, and *The Wayne Eagle*, in *Mike Kelley* (London: Phaidon, 1999), 134–37.

12 Kelley, "Isabelle Graw in conversation with Mike Kelley," *Mike Kelley* (London: Phaidon, 1999), 19.

13 The allusion here is to *Family Tyranny (Modeling and Molding)* (1987, 8:08 mins., color, sound) and *Cultural Soup* (1987, 6:55 mins., color, sound), videos made by Paul McCarthy with Mike Kelley in a six-hour session in a public-access television studio, for which McCarthy "built a rough set approximating the type seen in television situation comedies." See Kelley, *Minor Histories*, 194.

14 Kelley, "*Timeless/Authorless: Four Recovered Memories*," in *Minor Histories*, 281–82.

15 Ibid., 282.

16 Thomas Fuchs, "Temporality and Identity in Borderline Personality Disorder," *Psychopathology* 40 (2007): 379–80, available on the website of Universitäts Klinikum, Heidelberg, https://www.klinikum.uni-heidelberg.de/fileadmin/zpm/psychatrie/fuchs/Fragmented-Selves.pdf.

17 Ibid., 379–80.

18 Ibid., 381.

19 Mike Kelley, "The Complex," 72.

20 Kelley, interview by Hans Ulrich Obrist (unedited, unpublished transcript), 2005. Thanks to Hans Ulrich Obrist for sharing the interview.

21 These arguments and their contexts are developed more fully in John C. Welchman, "Fête Accompli," in *Mike Kelley: Day Is Done* (New York: Gagosian Gallery, 2007).

22 Mike Kelley, "Kandors," in *Mike Kelley: Kandors*, ed. Rafael Jablonka (Munich: Hirmer, 2010), 53.

23 Ibid., 53–54.
24 Ibid.
25 Ibid., 54.
26 Ibid.
27 Kelley, "The Poetry of Form" (1996), in *Minor Histories*, 96.
28 Ibid., 96. Kelley tested his hypothesis that "in many cases, one person, one author, was responsible for the names" by writing "to the companies and inquir[ing] about their titling process." He discovered that "one person was generally responsible for naming the colors. In a few instances, professionals had been employed to perform this task, but more often the colors were named by someone from the company itself, who worked in another capacity and simply had a knack for naming. This led me to look for other examples that illustrated an auteur theory of naming. I wanted to stress the naming process, as in some Conceptual Art, as a primary aesthetic characteristic, and to find examples of things that, in and of themselves, were uninteresting unless they were singled out with 'aesthetic' titles"; ibid., 97.
29 The first iteration of *The Uncanny* was an "exhibition within the exhibition" curated in 1993 by Kelley for *Sonsbeek 93* at the Gemeentemuseum, Arnhem, the Netherlands. *The Uncanny* was restaged in 2004 at Tate Liverpool and at Museum Moderner Kunst Stiftung Ludwig, Vienna, with a new catalogue; see Mike Kelley, *The Uncanny*, exh. cat. (Cologne: Walther König, 2004). Kelley showed many of the same artists from 1993, but added works by Nancy Grossman, Damien Hirst, Sarah Lucas, Ron Mueck, Malcolm Poynter, Marc Quinn, and others.
30 Jack Burnham, *Beyond Modern Sculpture: The Effects of Science and Technology on the Sculpture of This Century* (New York: Braziller, 1968), 185, cited by Mike Kelley as a head text in "Playing with Dead Things: On the Uncanny," in Welchman, *Foul Perfection*, 72. I make this observation in my essay "On the Uncanny in Visual Culture," in Kelley, *The Uncanny*, 43–44.
31 Mike Kelley, "Presenting the Preservationist Journal of Hick Erotic Folklore," in *Sex to Sexty: The Most Vulgar Magazine Ever Made!*, ed. Dian Hanson (Los Angeles: Taschen, 2008), 20–21.
32 Ibid.
33 Mike Kelley, interview by John C. Welchman, "Qualities, Being Hidden: John C. Welchman Interviews Mike Kelley about Interviewing," in *Mike Kelley: Interviews, Conversations, Chit-Chat*, ed. John C. Welchman (Zurich: JPR|Ringier, 2006), 35–36.
34 Ibid., 34.
35 Jamie, Kelley argued, attempts "to cut down on the exploitation side and get to a kind of documentary—a kind of subculture documentation—that's also more collapsed with their own subjectivity"; ibid., 27.
36 Ibid., 33.

LISA ROSENDAHL

The Author Stripped Bare by Its Employees: Artistic Authorship in the Twenty-First Century and Beyond

1 Michel Foucault, "What Is an Author?" in *Language, Counter-Memory, Practice: Selected Essays and Interviews by Michel Foucault*, ed. Donald F. Bouchard, trans. Donald F. Bouchard and Sherry Simon (Ithaca, NY: Cornell University Press, 1977), 113–38.
2 Cornelia Klinger, "Autonomy-Authenticity-Alterity: On the Aesthetic Ideology of Modernity," in *Modernologies: Contemporary Artists Researching Modernity and Modernism*, exh. cat. (Barcelona: Museu d'Art Contemporani de Barcelona, 2009), 29.

3 Ibid., 30.
4 "1. The artist may construct the work 2. The work may be fabricated 3. The work need not be built." Lawrence Weiner, "Statement of Intent," 1968. First published in *January 5–31, 1969*, exh. cat. (New York: Seth Siegelaub, 1969), n.p.
5 Sol LeWitt, "Paragraphs on Conceptual Art," *Artforum* 5, no. 10 (Summer 1967): 79–83.
6 Alain Badiou, *Saint Paul: The Foundation of Universalism*, trans. Ray Brassier (Stanford, CA: Stanford University Press, 2003), 10.
7 See, for example, John Cage's work *4.33*, performed at the Maverick Concert Hall, in Woodstock, New York, in 1952.
8 *Collins*, s.v. "flux" and "corporation," accessed May 30, 2017, https://www.collinsdictionary.com/dictionary/english/flux, and https://www.collinsdictionary.com/dictionary/english/corporation.
9 Bennett Simpson, "Techniques of Today: Bernadette Corporation," *Artforum* (September 2004): 8. Available on the Bernadette Corporation website, http://www.bernadettecorporation.com/introduction.htm.
10 Bernadette Corporation, preface to *Reena Spaulings* (New York: Semiotext(e), 2004), n.p.
11 Reena Spaulings, quoted in McKenzie Wark, "Indestructible Life: A Review of Bernadette Corporation, *Reena Spaulings*," February 2005, http://amsterdam.nettime.org/Lists-Archives/nettime-l-0502/msg00025.html.
12 Galerie Chantal Crousel, "Claire Fontaine," accessed July 18, 2017, https://www.crousel.com/home/artists/Claire%20Fontaine/bio.
13 Claire Fontaine, interview by John Kelsey, accessed July 18, 2017, http://brocblegen.com/collection/Artists/Claire%20Fontaine/Interview%20with%20John%20Kelsey.pdf.
14 Alexi Kukuljevic, "More or Less Art, More or Less a Commodity, More or Less an Object, More or Less a Subject—The Readymade and the Artist," in *The Art of the Concept*, ed. Nathan Brown and Peter Milat, *Frakcija*, no. 64/65 (2013): 62–70. Available on Alexi Kukuljevic's website, http://www.alexikukuljevic.com/pdf/more_or_less.pdf.
15 Alexander Provan, introduction to *Headless* (New York: Triple Canopy, Sternberg Press, and Tensta Konsthall, 2015), 13.
16 Emma Smith, *The Practice of Place* (London: Bedford Press, 2015), 81.

Part Two: The Artwork, Aura, and Authentication

PENELOPE CURTIS
Demonstrable Legacy; or, What Sculptors Leave Behind

1 "Proces des faux Rodin," 8th chambre correctionnelle de la Seine, dossier 5.044 et seq., Archives du Musée Rodin, Paris.

2 See Anna McNally, "Gabo Cataloguing Project at the Tate Archive," *Tate Papers*, no. 8 (Autumn 2007), http://www.tate.org.uk/research/publications/tate-papers/08/gabo-cataloguing-project-at-the-tate-archive, along with other papers on *Inherent Vice* in the same issue.

3 Over 50,000 items make up the main Gabo archive (TGA 9313), which was given to the Tate by the artist and his family and includes correspondence, diaries, writings, drawings, press cuttings, and photographs. Another archive (TGA 9314) includes prints. Additional archives are held at the Beinecke Rare Book and Manuscript Library at Yale University, in New Haven, Connecticut, and the Berlinische Galerie.

4 A good example of this problematic area arose when the artist Charlotte Moth wished to redisplay the project she had made based on the Barbara Hepworth photographs she had found in the Tate Archive. See her consecutive shows at Tate Britain in 2015 and the Kunstmuseum Liechtenstein in 2016.

5 See Penelope Curtis, "Standing Sculpture at the Turn of the Century: Exchange Values and Metamorphoses," in *The Human Factor: The Figure in Contemporary Sculpture*, ed. Ralph Rugoff (London: Hayward Gallery, 2014), 20–25, for which the right to reproduce this image was refused. See also the project around the same Caro piece by Henrik Olesen in Thomas Demand's exhibition *Stolen Image* (2016) at Fondazione Prada, in Milan.

6 Compare the consecutive reconstructions, first in the exhibition *Modern British Sculpture* (2011) at the Royal Academy, in London, and then in *Richard Hamilton* (2014) at Tate Modern. In a number of ways the Royal Academy exhibition of twentieth-century British sculpture, which I curated with Keith Wilson, explored the line of legacy, or influence, from one artist to another; we selected particular works and responses to them, rather than particular artists. It suggested the slow-motion relay. This made the narrative both more specific and less conventional, even if some of the names are frequently linked. Moore's name is often put next to that of Caro, but his work more rarely. This is also the case, to greater and lesser degrees, with Hamilton and Pasmore to Caro; Carl Andre to Richard Long; Hirst to Schwitters, Andre, and Jeff Koons.

7 A salutary story here is that of the Fondation Giacometti vis-à-vis the Fondazione Prada, in relation to John Baldessari's *Giacometti Variations* (2010). Commissioned by the Fondazione Prada, the work included nine enlarged copies of Giacometti's standing figures. The Fondation Giacometti had refused permission to duplicate Giacometti's sculptures, but Baldessari completed and showed the work anyway, and the exhibition was closed temporarily while the two parties argued their case in the Milan courts. In the end, the court allowed the work to be shown under the fair-use/parody exception in Italian copyright law.

ALESSANDRA DONATI
From the Object to the Archive: Guaranteeing Authorship and Ownership in Contemporary Art

1 For more on "dematerialization," see Lucy R. Lippard, *Six Years: The Dematerialization of the Art Object from 1966 to 1972* (Berkeley: University of California Press, 1973). On installation work, see Vivian van Saaze, *Installation Art and the Museum: Presentation and Conservation of Changing Artworks* (Amsterdam: Amsterdam University Press, 2013); Juliane Rebentisch, *Aesthetics of Installation Art*, trans. Daniel Hendrickson with Gerrit Jackson (Berlin: Sternberg Press, 2012); Martha Buskirk, *Creative Enterprise: Contemporary Art between Museum and Marketplace* (London: Continuum, 2012); and Tatja Scholte and Glenn Wharton, eds., *Inside Installation: Theory and Practice in the Care of Complex Artwork* (Amsterdam: Amsterdam University Press 2011).

2 See Jean-Marc Poinsot, *Quand l'oeuvre a lieu: L'art exposé et ses récits autorisés* (Villeurbanne, France: Art Edition, 1999), 16; Ijsbrand C. M. Hummelen, *Conception, Creation and Re-creation: Embodied Knowledge and the Preservation of Contemporary Art*, in *Theory and Practice* in *Conservation, A Tribute to Cesare Brandi*, ed. José Delgado Rodrigues and Jão Manuel Mimoso (Lisbon, National Laboratory of Civil Engineering, 2006); and Nathalie Heinich, *Le paradigme de l'art contemporain: Structures d'une révolution artistique* (Paris: Éditions Gallimard, 2014).

3 Antonio Rava, "Il restauro dell'arte contemporanea come testimonianza del cambiamento," *Kermess* 100 (forthcoming), author's translation,

4 See Ben Kinmont, *Prospectus, 1988–2010* (Sebastopol, CA: Antinomian Press, 2011); see also the interactive constructions by Rasheed Araeen, *Zero to Inifinity* (1968–2007); those by Charlotte Posenenske, *Square Tubes (series D)* (1967); or the sculptures by Lygia Clark that the public can shape, for example *Poetic Shelter* (1960).

5 See Martha Buskirk, *The Contingent Object of Contemporary Art* (Cambridge, MA: MIT Press, 2005).

6 In addition to installations that may be reactivated and, often, modified for exhibition purposes, one could also mention, selecting from many possible examples, the light bulbs for Dan Flavin's artwork, that always need to come from the same source (hence the Dan Flavin Foundation acquired the factory that produces them); the artwork *Untitled (Scultura che mangia)* (1968), by Giovanni Anselmo, which requires daily replacement of fresh salad in order to remain in existence; the complex conservation of works by Adrián Villar Rojas or by John Bock; or works by Ben Kinmont, which must continue to be modified according to the artist's indications even after his death.

7 Carolyn Christov-Bakargiev, "The Dance Was Very Frenetic, Lively, Rattling, Clanging, Rolling Contorted, and Lasted for a Long Time," in *The Books of Books, dOCUMENTA (13), Catalog 1/3*, ed. Katrin Saurlander (Ostfildern, Germany: Hatje Cantz, 2012), 30, 35.

8 For example, note the difficult conservation of Cady Noland's works, in particular the case of *Log Cabin Blank with Screw Eyes and Cafe Door* (1990), a work purchased in 2014 by collector Scott Mueller through the Galerie Michael Janssen, which underwent restoration treatment without the artist's consent and is subject of a complicated legal battle that is still awaiting a solution; or the case of her work *Cowboys Milking* (1990), for which Noland disavowed authorship after finding the work damaged when it went up for auction in 2011, and which ended with the

withdrawal of the work from auction and the ruling in *Jancou v. Sotheby's*, 650316/2012 (N.Y. Sup. Ct. June 27, 2013).

9 For more on "scripta," see Anne Bénichou, ed., *Ouvrir le document* (Dijon, France: Les Presses du Réel, 2010). See also Heinich, *Le paradigme de l'art contemporain*, and Jackie Heuman, ed., *From Marble to Chocolate: The Conservation of Modern Sculpture* (London: Archetype, 1995).

10 Daniel McClean, "The Artist's Contract/ From the Contract of Aesthetics to the Aesthetics of the Contract," *Mousse Magazine*, no. 25 (September–October 2010), http://moussemagazine.it/daniel-mcclean-the-artists-contract-2010; Daniel McClean, "Authenticity in Art |and Law: A Question of Attribution or Authorisation?" in *In Deed: Certificates of Authenticity in Art*, ed. Susan Hapgood and Cornelia Lauf, exh. cat. (Amsterdam: Roma Publication, 2011), 87; on comparative perspective, see Alessandra Donati, *Law and art: Diritto civile e arte contemporanea* (Milan: Giuffrè, 2012); see also Judith Ickowitcz, *Le droit après la dématérialisation de l'oeuvre d'art* (Dijon, France: Les Presses du Réel, 2013).

11 Glenn Wharton, "The Challenges of Conserving Contemporary Art," in *Collecting the New: Museums and Contemporary Art*, ed. Bruce Altshuler (Princeton: Princeton University Press, 2006), 164–78, http://glennwharton.net/wp-content/uploads/2015/07/Wharton-Challenges-Conserving-Contemporary-Art.pdf.

12 For example, Jana Sterbak's work *I Want You to Feel the Way I Do (the Dress)*, 1984, purchased in 1986 by the National Gallery of Canada, undergoes successive variations for exhibitions, each time agreed on with the artist and documented by the museum, leading over time to loss of reference to the work's initial form. At a certain point, the artist recognizes as original one of the subsequent variations of the work, thus considering the original version purchased by the museum no longer relevant and requiring the museum to withdraw from circulation any photographic copies of it. "Si les oeuvres peuvent changer tout en étant encore considérées comme authentiques, ce n'est qu'à la condition de pouvoir retourner aux versions antérieures pas le biais d'une documentation augmentée et adaptée,": Alain Depocas, "Documenter les pratiques artistiques utilisant la technologie: Des modèles à développer," in *Ouvrir le document*, ed. Anne Bénichou (Dijon, France: Les Presses du Réel, 2010), 349, and in particular 352.

13 See, for example, the recent case *Cady Noland v. Michael Janssen Gallery Pte., Ltd. et al.*, no. 1:17-cv-05452 (S.D.N.Y. July 18, 2017).

14 For example, Title 17 U.S.C. § 102(a) protects only "original works of authorship fixed in any tangible medium of expression, now known or later developed, from which they can be perceived, reproduced, or otherwise communicated, either directly or with the aid of a machine or device." See *Kelley v. Chicago Park District*, no. 04 C 07715, 2008 WL 4449886 (N.D. Ill. September 29, 2008). See also, a case from the UK, *Merchandising Corp. of America Inc. and Others v. Harpbond Ltd. and Others*, [1983] F.S.R. 32; and Megan Carpenter and Steven Hetcher, "Function over Form: Bringing the Fixation Requirement into the Modern Era," *Fordham Law Review* 82 (2014): 2221–71, http://ir.lawnet.fordham.edu/flr/vol82/iss5/11.

15 But, conversely, see Cour de Cassation [Cass.], 1e civ., November 13, 2008, no. 06-19.021 (Arrêt Paradis); *VG Bild-Kunst v. Museum Schloss Moyländer*, 2010 District Court of Dusseldorf, Chamber: 12 Civil

Division, Application Number: 12 O 255/09, final reversed by BGH, May 16, 2013, Az. I ZR 28/12. See also Henry Lydiate, "What Is Art? A Brief Review of International Judicial Interpretations of Art in the Light of the UK Supreme Court's 2011 Judgment in the *Star Wars* Case: Lucasfilm Limited v. Ainsworth," *Journal of International Media and Entertainment Law* 4, no. 2 (2012–13): 111–47.

16 See Alessandra Donati, "Autenticità, authenticité, authenticity dell'opera d'arte: Diritto mercato e prassi virtuose," *Rivista di diritto civile* 61, no. 4 (2015): 987.

17 Nadia Walravens, "The Concept of Originality and Contemporary Art," in *Dear Images: Art, Copyright, and Culture*, ed. Daniel McClean and Karsten Schubert (London: Ridinghouse, 2002), 171.

18 McClean, "The Artist's Contract."

19 An important example of management and collection of artwork-plans is the Panza Collection Initiative, a research project organized by the Solomon R. Guggenheim Museum in 2010 to further explore questions related to the authenticity of works by some of the most important Conceptual artists collected by Panza di Biumo. See "About the Collection: Panza Collection," Solomon R. Guggenheim Museum, accessed March 3, 2017, http://www.guggenheim.org/new-york/collections/about-the-collection/the-panza-collection-initiative.

20 The material importance of the certificate was legally reinforced in *Steinkamp v. Hoffman*, no. 651770 (N.Y. Sup. Ct. May 22, 2012).

21 On the case sited above, in which a collector sued his gallery for allegedly losing the certificate of authority to a LeWitt wall drawing, see Adam Klasfeld, "Collector Says Gallery Lost Key to Minimal Art," *Courthouse News Service*, May 25, 2012, https://www.courthousenews.com/collector-says-gallery-lost-key-to-minimal-art/; and Henry Lydiate, "Authenticating Sol LeWitt," *Art Monthly* 358 (July–August 2012): 41.

22 Buren's *avertissement* explicitly states that a new certificate must be registered with each transfer of ownership. For González-Torres, see the correspondence between Cornelia Lauf and John Connelly, the Director of the Félix González-Torres Foundation, published in Hapgood and Lauf, *In Deed*, n.p. Connelly states, "Each time a manifestable work is purchased it was Félix's intention that a certificate be issued in the name of the new owner. If it is a work that was previously owned the old certificate is voided and attached to the new one creating a beautiful history of the work's ownership as well as a record of the certificate's evolution in time."

23 Daniel McClean, "The Artist's Contract."

24 See Swiss Federal Tribunal September 16, 2008, 5A 279, http://www.juricaf.org/arret/SUISSE-TRIBUNALFEDERALSUISSE-20080916-5A2792008.

25 Daniel McClean, "Free Sol LeWitt: Superflex's Copy Machine," in *Free Sol LeWitt*, ed. Christiane Berndes et al. (Eindhoven, Netherlands: Van Abbemuseum, 2010), 38. See also John Roberts, *The Intangibilities of Form: Skill and Deskilling in Art after the Readymade* (New York: Verso, 2007), 215.

26 Christiane Berndes, foreword to Berndes et al., *Free Sol LeWitt*, 6.

27 Sol LeWitt, "Paragraphs on Conceptual Art," *Art Forum* 5, no. 10 (June 1967): 79.

28 Christiane Berndes, "Discussion between Christiane Berndes, Charles Esche, Daniel McClean and Superflex," in Berndes et al., *Free Sol LeWitt*, 54.

29 Sol LeWitt, "Comments on an Advertisement," *Flash Art*, no. 41 (1973): 97.

30 Walter Benjamin, "The Work of Art in the Age of Mechanical Reproduction,"

in *The Work of Art in the Age of Mechanical Reproduction and Other Writings on Media*, ed. Michael W. Jennings, Brigid Doherty, and Thomas Y. Levin (Cambridge, MA: Belknap Press of Harvard University Press, 2008), 24 (first published 1936).

31 See, for example, the big archive of artists' archives owned by the Museo di Arte Moderna e Contemporanea di Trento e Roverto (Mart), http://www.mart.tn.it/archivio and http://www.mart.tn.it/fondi, or the artists' archives at Galleria d'Arte Moderna, in Turin. In other countries, as well, the museum has become the conservator of archives. Recently the Whitney Museum of American Art, New York, acquired the archives of Edward Hopper, and the Getty Museum, LA, acquired the important archive of curator Harald Szeemann.

32 Alexander Alberro, "Reconsidering Conceptual Art, 1966–1977," in *Conceptual Art: A Critical Anthology*, ed. Alexander Alberro and Blake Stimson (Cambridge, MA: MIT Press, 1999), xxiii.

33 See Susan Hapgood and Cornelia Lauf, "Doodles, Deeds, and Claims," in *In Deed*, 80, where the authors describe how a certificate is granted by Lawrence Weiner and sent to Jerald Ordover, his lawyer and long-time archive manager; and Alexander Alberro, *Conceptual Art and the Politics of Publicity* (Cambridge, MA: MIT Press, 2000), 124. See also Nadia Walravens, *L'œuvre d'art en droit d'auteur: Formes et originalité des œuvres d'art contemporaines* (Paris: Economica, 2005), 293; Giuseppe Panza di Biumo, *Ricordi di un collezionista* (Milan: Jaca Book, 2006), 115.

34 The full text of the *avertissement* is published at: https://danielburen.com/pages/archives/bibliographie_texts/text:6. See also Donati, *Law and Art*, 72; Ickowitcz, *Le droit après la dématérialisation de l'œuvre d'art*, 557; and Sophie Gayet, "Les avertissements de Daniel Buren: La menace du faux, "*La voix du régard*, no. 14 (2001): 66.

35 The English translation of Buren's *avertissement* is published in Hapgood and Lauf, *In Deed*, n.p.

36 Ibid.

37 Daniel Buren, interview by Maria Eichhorn, in Maria Eichhorn, *The Artist's Contract* (Cologne, Germany: Walther König, 2009), 87.

38 Section f of the *avertissement*: "Tout manquement aux clauses du présent avertissement entraîne immédiatement et automatiquement l'interdiction absolue d'attribuer l'œuvre qui y est décrite à Daniel Buren." (Any failure to observe the clause of this notice will immediately and automatically prohibit the owner of the work from attributing that work to Daniel Buren). The English translation of *avertissement* is published in Hapgood and Lauf, *In Deed*, n.p.

39 See Seth Siegelaub, *The Artist's Reserved Rights Transfer and Sale Agreement* (1971), reproduced in *Studio International* (April 1971): 142; Eichhorn, *The Artist's Contract*, 66; and Alberro, *Conceptual Art and the Politics of Publicity*. See also Alessandra Donati, *I contratti degli artisti: Nuovi modelli di trattativa* (Turin, Italy: Giappichelli, 2012), 29.

40 See Ben Kinmont, *Project Series: Archive Contracts* (Paris: Antinomian Press, 2005).

41 Jacques Derrida, *Mal d'archive* (Paris: Editions Galilée 1995, 2008); see also *Erinnerungsräume: Formen und Wandlungen des kulturellen Gedächtnisses* (Munich: C.H. Beck, 1999), 343.

42 Interesting considerations in *Thome v. Alexander & Louisa Calder Found.*, 70 A.D.3d 88, 95 (N.Y. App. Div. 2009), and in the appeal, 933 N.E.2d 216 (N.Y. 2010), where the court found that exclusion of the sculpture from Alexander Calder's catalogue raisonné rendered the work fundamentally unmarketable.

43 This practice is followed by the main international art fairs: TEFAF (the European Fine Art Fair) in Maastricht, the Netherlands, only accepts works for the Modern Art section if they are supported by "references to catalogues raisonées or certificates/authentications from the accepted authorities on each artist."

44 See Cour de Cassation [Cass.], January 22, 2014, no. 12-35264, *Recueil Dalloz* (February 6, 2014), 276, on the Jean Metzinger case. The French Court of Cassation overturned a ruling at appeal that had ordered an artist's archive to pay damages (€30,000) because the archive managers had refused to include the work, purchased by a collector and already certified as authentic in court, in the catalogue raisonné. The first instance ruling had ordered the archive to issue the certificate and include the work in the catalogue raisonné; the court of appeal, after quantifying the damage suffered, had allowed the respondent the alternative of not having to pay damages on condition that the certificate of authenticity be issued and the work be included in the catalogue raisonné. At Cassation, the second instance ruling was partially overturned; with an *arrêt de principe* with regard to article 10 of the Convention of Human Rights, the court held that the principle of freedom of expression "est un droit dont l'exercice ne revêt un caractère abusif que dans les cas spécialement déterminés par la loi" and that therefore in the absence of specific regulations in the area, there are no grounds to impose any obligation or performance on the author of the catalogue raisonné.

45 See the website of the Associazione Italiana degli Archivi d'Artista (AitArt), accessed March 3, 2017, http://www.aitart.it.

46 See, among others, Jean Aittouares, "Les risques de démembrement des droits de l'auteur décédé," in *Actes du collogue: La transmission successorale du droit d'auteur, Questions d'actualité et difficultés pratiques*, ed. Tristan Azzi (Lyon, France: Institut Art et Droit, 2014), 7.

47 However, there is some change: to identify and protect this sometimes weak figure in the certification process the State of New York has approved, for now in the Senate only, a reform of the Arts and Cultural Affairs Law (S1229A-2015).

48 Marilena Pirrelli, "La corsa ai lasciti degli artisti e la riforma dell'authenticator," *Il Sole 24 Ore*, October 24, 2015, 27.

49 See Loretta Würtenberger, *The Artist's Estates: A Handbook for Artists, Executors, and Heirs* (Berlin: Hatje Cantz, 2016), and her important work in supporting the management of artists' estates through the Institute of Artists' Estates, http://www.artists-estates.com/en/.

50 Alice Gregory, "The Architect Who became a Diamond," *New Yorker*, August 1, 2016, http://www.newyorker.com/magazine/2016/08/01/how-luis-barragan-became-a-diamond.

51 Randy Kennedy, "Tug of War Stretches Architect's Legacy: Luis Barragán Homage Tweaks Vitra, the Copyright Owners," *New York Times*, November 3, 2013, http://www.nytimes.com/2013/11/04/arts/design/luis-barragan-homage-tweaks-vitra-the-copyright-owners.html.

52 Jill Magid, "Atlas of Intimacy: Jill Magid with Jarrett Earnest," *Brooklyn Rail*, October 3, 2013, http://brooklynrail.org/2013/10/art/atlas-of-intimacyjill-magid-with-jarrett-earnest.

SHANE BURKE
Score, Performance, and the Posthumous Conductor

I would like to thank Daniel McClean, Jonathan Griffiths, and Marta Iljadica for their very helpful comments during the preparation of this essay. All errors or omissions are my own. I am grateful also to John Hogan, John ffrench, and Daniel McClean for their participation in the interviews that form the basis for this essay.

1 See Rorty's seminal 1967 anthology, Richard Rorty, ed., *The Linguistic Turn: Recent Essays in Philosophical Method* (Chicago: University of Chicago Press, 1967).
2 Tony Godfrey, *Conceptual Art* (London: Phaidon, 1998), 163.
3 Benjamin H. D. Buchloh, "Conceptual Art 1962–69: From the Aesthetics of Administration to the Critique of Institutions," *October* 55 (Winter 1990): 117.
4 Ibid., 119.
5 For a discussion of the relationship between art and property, see Marta Iljadica, "Land and Ornament" (paper submitted to the Modern Studies in Property Law publication workshop, University of Cambridge, April 10, 2017).
6 Félix González-Torres followed a similar trajectory as the complexity of his directions in certificates of authenticity increased in his later work. David Deitcher, "Contradictions and Containment," in *Félix González-Torres*, ed. Julie Ault (New York and Göttingen, Germany: Steidldangin, 2006), 321.
7 LeWitt famously wrote, "The idea becomes the machine that makes the art." Sol LeWitt, "Paragraphs on Conceptual Art," *Artforum* 5, no. 10 (June 1967): 79.
8 Martha Buskirk, *The Contingent Object of Contemporary Art* (Cambridge, MA: MIT Press, 2003), 24.
9 See, for example, Hans Ulrich Obrist, ed., *Do It: The Compendium (New York: Independent Curators International*, 2013), 17. See also Buskirk, *The Contingent Object of Contemporary Art*, 44.
10 In 1982 Flavin stated, "Only I know the work as it ought to be. All posthumous interpretations are less. I know this. So I would rather see it all disappear into the wind. Take it all away." Dan Flavin, in an interview with Tiffany Bell, quoted in Greg Allen, "The Dark Side of Success," *New York Times*, January 2, 2005, http://www.nytimes.com/2005/01/02/arts/design/the-dark-side-of-success.html.
11 See, for example, *Feist Publications v. Rural Telephone Service*, 499 U.S. 340 (1991), 345.
12 See, for example, the judgment of the Court of Justice of the European Union in *Eva-Maria Painer v. Standard Verlags GmbH and Others*, Case C-145/10, [2012] E.C.D.R. (6) 89 (E.C.J., Third Chamber).
13 Daniel McClean, "Piracy and Authorship in Contemporary Art and the Artistic Commonwealth," in *Copyright and Piracy: An Interdisciplinary Critique*, ed. Lionel Bently, Jennifer Davis, and Jane C. Ginsburg (Cambridge: Cambridge University Press, 2010), 320.
14 For a discussion on certification and authenticity, see Laura A. Heymann, "Dialogues of Authenticity," in *Thinking and Rethinking Intellectual Property*, ed. Austin Sarat, special issue, *Studies in Law, Politics and Society* 67 (2015): 25. See also Martha Buskirk, "Public Experience/Private Authority," 26 *Cornell Journal of Law and Public Policy* 469 (Spring 2017).
15 John Hogan, the Mary Jo and Ted Shen Installation Director and Archivist for Sol LeWitt Wall Drawings, Yale University Art Gallery, interview with the author, New Haven, CT, and London, February 5, 2015. Martha Buskirk has spoken about the certificate of authenticity in terms of "a behind-the-scenes

license, or even contractual agreement, to reinterpret certain aspects of the work." Martha Buskirk, "Public Experience/Private Authority," 480.

16 David Booton, "Framing Pictures: Defining Art in UK Copyright Law," 1 *Intellectual Property Quarterly* 38, 47 (2003).

17 Certificates of authenticity may not always be viewed by the courts as a contract. See, for example, *Tovar v. Indiana*, no. 1:2012cv06104 (S.D.N.Y., January 17, 2013). For a discussion of the legal standing of certificates of authenticity, see Joan Kee, "Félix González-Torres on Contracts," 26 *Cornell Journal of Law and Public Policy* 517 (Spring 2017).

18 The Berne Convention (1886, latest revision Paris 1971) both initially and throughout its various revisions leaves the expression "author" as undefined despite the fact of the frequent use of the term in its text. This is equally true of the Universal Copyright Convention (UCC) of 1952.

19 The definition of ideas has been problematic in relation to copyright protection, particularly in light of the gradual development of protection against nonliteral copying. For a formulation of the doctrine in the United Kingdom, see the judgment of Lord Hoffmann in *Designer's Guild v. Williams*, [2000] 1 W.L.R. 2416, 2423.

20 David Booton, "Framing Pictures," 43. It would have to be acknowledged, however, that the recent jurisprudence of the Court of Justice of the European Union has led to a questioning of whether the "closed list" system is still tenable considering current EU law. See, for example, the judgment of Justice Arnold in *SAS Institute v. World Programming Ltd.*, [2013] EWHC 69 (Ch) [27]. Whether such an approach would still be appropriate in view of the possible outcomes of any Brexit agreement with the European Union remains a moot point.

21 Copyright Designs and Patents Act of 1988 (CDPA), § 17(3).

22 CDPA § 17(2).

23 For an exploration of the criteria for "sufficiently objectively similar," see *Francis Day and Hunter v. Bron*, [1963] Ch. 587, 614. For cases specifically concerning literary instructions, see also *Brigid Foley Ltd. v. Elliot*, [1982] R.P.C. 433, 434; and *Plix Products Limited v. Frank Michael Winstone (Merchants)*, [1986] F.S.R. 63, 89–90.

24 *Interlego v. Tyco Industries*, [1988] R.P.C. 343, 374. It is the case that this approach may no longer be tenable under EU law. See Lionel Bently and Brad Sherman, *Intellectual Property Law*, 4th ed. (Oxford: Oxford University Press, 2014), 106.

25 See, for example, CDPA § 3(2); Jonathan Griffiths, "Copyright's Imperfect Republic and the Artistic Commonwealth," in Bently, Davis, and Ginsburg, *Copyright and Piracy: An Interdisciplinary Critique*, 340, 345. See also Ysolde Gendreau, "The Criterion of Fixation in Copyright Law," 159 *Revue internationale du droit d'auteur* 110, 146. Booton also argues that the fundamental distinction between notational forms and artistic works would need to be maintained in order to preserve the approach to definition of protectable artistic works in the statutory regime since 1956. He highlights the fact that after the 1956 UK Copyright Act, the designation of plans, and by way of analogy engineering drawings, as artistic works, is anomalous as these works are not examples of "drawing" but are in fact notational in character while the likes of painting or sketches are not. See David Booton, "Framing Pictures," 40.

26 See, for example, *Abraham Moon v. Thornber*, [2012] EWPCC 37.

27 Cited in David Booton, "Framing Pictures," 47.

28 Ibid.
29 Ibid., 48.
30 Ibid.
31 See, for example, *Lerose Ltd v. Hawick Jersey International Ltd.*, [1973] F.S.R. 15 (knitting instructions); and *Vermaat v. Boncrest Ltd.*, [2001] F.D.R. 43 (bed-linen patterns).
32 *Abraham Moon v. Thornber.*
33 *Abraham Moon v. Thornber*, [102].
34 In doing so, the court did not engage with the possibilities afforded by more recent judgments concerning artistic works that allow for an approach informed by the intention of the artist and, at least implicitly, institutional validation by the art world. See, for example, the High Court judgment of Justice Anthony Mann in *Lucasfilm v. Ainsworth*, [2008] EWHC 1878 (Ch) [118].
35 *Abraham Moon v. Thornber*, [107].
36 *Walt Disney Productions v. the Air Pirates et al.*, 581 F. 2d 751, 755 (9th Cir. 1978); see Tony R. Martino, "'Popeye the Sailor'... Man of Letters: The Copyright Protection of Literary Characters" 10(3) *European Intellectual Property Review* 78 (1988); see also the Canadian decision in *Anne of Green Gables Licensing Authority Inc. v. Avonlea Traditions Inc.*, (2000) 4 C.P.R. (4th), 289 (Ont. S.C.J.).
37 See, for example, the judgment of Judge Posner in *Gaiman v. McFarlane*, 360 F. 3d 644, 660 (7th Cir. 2004).
38 Generally on this issue, see Lionel Bently and Laura Biron, "Discontinuities between Legal Conceptions of Authorship and Social Practices: What, If Anything, Is to Be Done?" in *The Work of Authorship*, ed. Mireille van Eechoud (Amsterdam: Amsterdam University Press, 2014).
39 For a discussion on joint authorship and contemporary art in the United States and United Kingdom, see Laura Biron and Elena Cooper, "Authorship, Aesthetics and the Artworld: Reforming Copyright's Joint Authorship Doctrine" 53(1) *Law and Philosophy* 55 (2016). For a discussion of similar indeterminacy issues in the instructions of Félix González-Torres, see Joan Kee, "Félix González-Torres on Contracts," 517–18.
40 *Levy v. Rutley*, [1871] LR 6 CP 523, 529.
41 *Beckingham v. Hodgens*, [2003] EWCA Civ. 143 [51]; cf. Lior Zemer, "Is Intention to Co-author an Uncertain Realm of Policy?" 30(4) *Columbia Journal of Law and the Arts* 611, 617 (2007).
42 *Ray v. Classic FM*, [1998] F.S.R. 622, 636.
43 Bently and Biron, "Discontinuities between Legal Conceptions of Authorship and Social Practices," 237.
44 Ibid., citing *Tate v. Thomas*, [1921] 1 Ch. 503, 510–11; and *Hadley v. Kemp*, [1999] E.M.L.R. 589, 643–644.
45 CDPA § 9(1).
46 John Hogan, interview, February 5, 2015.
47 Ibid.
48 Bently and Biron, "Discontinuities between Legal Conceptions of Authorship and Social Practices," 247.
49 Ibid., 248.
50 John Hogan, interview, February 5, 2015.
51 Ibid.
52 Ibid.
53 Ibid.
54 Ibid.
55 John ffrench, Director of Visual Resources, Yale University Art Gallery, interview with the author, New Haven, CT, December 11, 2014.
56 A number of potential legal remedies could be available to purchasers facing threat of an effective withdrawal of authorship. For example, under the head of product disparagement and business defamation, see *Hahn v. Duveen*, 133 Misc. 871, 234 N.Y.S. 185 (Sup. Ct. 1929); *Tovar v. Indiana*; or breach of contract or breach of express warranty. On the latter see specific state statues that grant assurances to buyers of art in relation to its authenticity that extend beyond those relating to other goods as contained in

the Uniform Commercial Code (UCC), for example, the 1968 enacted New York Arts and Cultural Affairs Law § 13.01.

57 Daniel McClean, interview with the author, London, August 21, 2014.

58 While generally seen as a creature of the civil-law tradition, there was historically occasional support expressed for such rights in the common-law courts. See *Millar v. Taylor*, [1769] 4 Burrow 2303, 98 ER 201, where Lord Mansfield expressed support for rights akin to those of paternity, integrity, and retraction were voiced.

59 For a discussion of the general issues surrounding the exercise of moral rights postmortem in the Australian context, see Jani McCutcheon, "Death Rights: Legal Personal Representatives of Deceased Authors and the Posthumous Exercise of Moral Rights," 3 *Intellectual Property Quarterly* 242 (2015).

60 See, for example, CDPA, chapter 4.

61 *Kelley v. Chicago Park District*, 635 F. 3d 290, 300 (7th Cir. 2011).

62 CDPA § 86(1).

63 Ibid., § 86(2).

64 See, for example, ibid., § 95.

65 Ibid., § 106A(a)(1)(B), and § 106A(a)(2).

66 Ibid., § 106A(d).

67 See Title 17 U.S.C. § 106A(d)(1).

68 Eric J. Schwartz, "United States," in *International Copyright Law and Practice*, vol. 2, ed. Paul Edward Geller and Lionel Bently (New York: Matthew Bender, 2015), § 7[1][a] USA, 125n5. See Title 17 U.S.C. § 301(f)(1), (2)(A), (2)(C).

69 See Cal. Civ. Code § 987(g)(1), and § 987(d). There have also been indications from the courts that New York's Artists' Authorship Rights Act may, despite indications in the text to the contrary, contain rights therein that may be exercisable postmortem. See, for example, *Board of Managers of Soho International Arts Condominium v. City of New York*, U.S. Dist. Lexis 10221, 45 (S.D.N.Y. 2003).

70 CDPA § 80(3); see also, for example, the Intellectual Property Code 1992, France, art. L.132-22: "An entertainment promoter shall ensure that public performance takes place under technical conditions that guarantee respect for the author's intellectual and moral rights." See also the French case of *Lindon et SACD La Compagnie Brut de Beton et Boussagol*, T.G.I. Paris, 3e ch., October 15, 1992, 155 *Revue internationale du droit d'auteur* 255 (1993), in which the use of female actors in a production of Samuel Beckett's *Waiting for Godot*, where the author specified that male actors must be used, was held to be a breach of the author's moral rights postmortem.

71 Elizabeth Adeney, *The Moral Rights of Authors and Performers: An International and Comparative Analysis* (Oxford: Oxford University Press, 2006), 192–93.

72 *Lacordaire v. Marle*, Lyon, July 17, 1845, cited in Maria Mercedes Frabboni, "France," in *Moral Rights*, ed. Gillian Davies and Kevin Garnett (London: Sweet and Maxwell, 2010), 118. The right is statutorily provided for in the Intellectual Property Code 1992, France, art. L121-2.

73 Cass. civ., March 14, 1900, DP 1900, 1, 497.

74 Adeney, *The Moral Rights of Authors and Performers*, 194–95.

75 Intellectual Property Code 1992, France, art. L.121-2.

76 Adeney, *The Moral Rights of Authors and Performers*, 203.

77 Maria Mercedes Frabboni, "France," 391. See *Consort Hugo v. Sté Éditions Plon*, Tribunaux de grande instance [TGI], Paris, 1e ch., September 12, 2001, 191 *Revue internationale du droit d'auteur* 321 (January 2002).

78 Adolf Dietz, "Germany," in Davies and Garnett, *Moral Rights*, 423.

79 Intellectual Property Code 1992, France, art. L.121-4.

80 Andre Lucas, "Moral Rights in France Toward a Pragmatic Approach," accessed

July 31, 2017, http://www.blaca.org/Moral%20right%20in%20France%20by%20Professor%20Andre%20Lucas.pdf. Lucas notes that the one case concerning this right that did reach the Cours de Cassation was dismissed as an abuse of that right. See *Raymond Chiavarino v. Sté SPE*, Cour de Cassation [Cass.], 1e civ., May 14, 1991, 151 *Revue internationale du droit d'auteur* 272 (January 1992). See also in relation to the same point in the context of German law in Dietz, "Germany," 424.

81 Adeney, *The Moral Rights of Authors and Performers*, 204.

82 For example, the California Art Preservation Act places great emphasis on the preservation of art for the benefit of the general public. See Joseph Zuber, "The Visual Artists Rights Act of 1990: What It Does, and What It Preempts," 23 *Pacific Law Journal* 445, 449 (1991–1992). See also VARA, § 106 A(a)(3)(b), with its provisions against destruction of works of "recognized stature."

83 See Jane Ginsburg, "Moral Rights in the Common Law System," 1(4) *Entertainment Law Review* 121 [1990]; and Gerald Dworkin, "The Moral Right of the Author: Moral Rights and the Common Law Countries" 19 *Columbia Journal of Law and the Arts* 229 (1994–1995).

84 Buchloh, "Conceptual Art 1962–69," 128; and see Walter Benjamin, *The Work of Art in the Age of Mechanical Reproduction*, trans. J. A. Underwood (London: Penguin, 2008).

85 On Félix González-Torres, see Martha Buskirk, "Public Experience/Private Authority," 469; and Joan Kee, "Félix González-Torres on Contracts," 517. On Tino Sehgal, see Mary Richards, "This Progressive Production: Agency, Durability and Keeping It Contemporary," *Performance Research: A Journal of the Performing Arts* 17, no. 5 (2012): 71.

86 John Hogan, interview, February 5, 2015.

87 John ffrench, interview, December 11, 2014.

GUY BRETT
Hélio Oiticica: A Principle of Renewal

An earlier version of this text was written as a short discussion document for *Inherent Vice: The Replica and Its Implications in Modern Sculpture Workshop*, held at Tate Modern, London, October 18–19, 2007. I would like to acknowledge the help I have received from Luciano Figueiredo, artist and former director of the Centro Cultural Hélio Oiticica, in Rio de Janeiro. He was one of the original group of Friends of Hélio Oiticica assembled after the artist's death in 1980 to care for his work and legacy. Luciano has been close to all decisions regarding making replicas of Oiticica's existing works or objects, and constructing works from the artist's notes and plans. I am equally grateful to Ariane Figureido, who looks after the archive of the Projeto Hélio Oiticica, the estate's collection of work and documentation housed in the family house in Jardim Botanico, in Rio de Janeiro, and who actually made the replicas of Oiticica's *Parangolé* capes. The replicas have "stood in" for some of the originals—now in precarious condition—in exhibitions that have permitted the public to wear and explore the works. For my original paper I drew on my email correspondence with both Luciano and Ariane, and I remain deeply grateful to them for their collaboration.

1 Hélio Oiticica, from textual notes on the work *Contra-Bólide (Devolver a Terra à Terra)*, published in Guy Brett, ed., *Hélio Oiticica*, exh. cat. (Rotterdam, Netherlands: Witte de With Center for Contemporary Art, 1992), 236.

2 Hélio Oiticica to Paulo Bruscky, July 12, 1979, published in Paulo Kuszynski, *HO* (São Paulo: Escritorio de Arte, 2006), n.p.

3 See Brett, *Hélio Oiticica*. The exhibition began in 1992 at the Witte de With Center

for Contemporary Art, Rotterdam, and traveled over the course of two years to the Galerie Nationale du Jeu de Paume, Paris; the Fundació Antoni Tàpies, Barcelona; the Centro de Arte Moderna da Fundação Calouste Gulbenkian, Lisbon; and the Walker Art Center, Minneapolis.

4 Helio Oiticica to Guy Brett, quoted in Luciano Figueiredo and Guy Brett, eds., *Oiticica in London* (London: Tate, 2007), 16.

5 The artist's brothers, Claudio and Cesar, founded the Projecto Hélio Oiticica a year later for the preservation and care of the estate in collaboration with a volunteer force of the artist's friends. It is housed in their family home in Jardim Botanico, Rio de Janeiro, which has been converted into a store and study center.

6 Luciano Figueiredo, email message to author, October 2007. Luciano Figueiredo is one of the original group of "Friends of Hélio Oiticica," who assembled after the artist's death in 1980 to care for his work and legacy. Luciano has been closely involved in all decisions regarding the production of replicas of Oiticica's existing works and of constructing works from his notes and plans. In this essay, I draw on emails Luciano and Ariane Figueiredo sent me in September and October 2007.

7 Ibid.

8 Ariane Figueiredo, email message to author, October 2007.

9 Guy Brett et al., *Hélio Oiticica*, exh. cat. (Paris: Jeu de Paume, 1992), 194.

10 Noam Chomsky, *9-11* (New York: Seven Stories Press, 2002), 74.

11 Luciano Figueiredo, email message to author, October 2007.

GEORGINA ADAM

Artists' Legacies, Authentication, and the Art Market: Not Always a Happy Ménage

1 "The Artist-Endowed Foundation Field: Scope, Scale, and Development," in *The Artist as Philanthropist: Strengthening the Next Generation of Artist-Endowed Foundations* (Washington, DC: The Aspen Institute, 2010), 1: 23, https://assets.aspeninstitute.org/content/uploads/2010/11/AEF_V1b.pdf.

2 Hannah Furness, "Caravaggio in Court: Sotheby's Wins Case after '£10m' Painting Sold for £42,000," *Daily Telegraph*, January 16, 2016, http://www.telegraph.co.uk/news/uknews/law-and-order/11349854/Caravaggio-in-court-Sothebys-wins-case-after-10m-painting-sold-for-42000.html.

3 Anita Singh, "Russian Oligarch Wins £1.7m Refund from Christie's after Auction House Sold Him 'Fake' Painting," *Daily Telegraph*, July 27, 2012, http://www.telegraph.co.uk/culture/art/artsales/9432441/Russian-oligarch-wins-1.7m-refund-from-Christies-after-auction-house-sold-him-fake-painting.html.

4 Emmanuel David, *Le metier de marchand de tableaux: Entretiens avec Hervé Le Boterf* (Paris: Editions France-Empire, 1978), cited in François Duret-Robert, *Marchands d'art et faiseurs d'or* (Paris: Belfond, 1991), 207.

5 Lucinda Bredin, "Judge Forces Purchaser of Chagall to Pay Up," *Art Newspaper*, January 5, 1992.

6 See *The Keith Haring Foundation, Inc. v. Colored Thumb Corp, et al.*, no. 1:13-cv-20830-MGC (S.D. Fla. March 8, 2013).

7 *Bilinski et al. v. The Keith Haring Foundation, Inc. et al.*, no. 1:14-cv-01085 (S.D.N.Y. February 21, 2014).

8 Ibid.

9 "Opinion and Order," March 6, 2015, ibid.

10 Nicholas O'Donnell, "Authentication Lawsuit against Keith Haring Foundation Is Dismissed," *Art Law Report* (blog), March 11, 2015, http://blog.sandw.com/artlawreport/2015/03/11/authentication-lawsuit-against-keith-haring-foundation-is-dismissed/.

11 Christie's, New York, *Looking Forward to the Past*, sale cat. (May 11, 2015), lot 29A, http://www.christies.com/lotfinder/Lot/alberto-giacometti-1901-1966-lhomme-au-doigt-5895983-details.aspx .

12 For an in-depth analysis of the Giacometti story, see Marc Spiegler, "The Giacometti Legacy: A Struggle for Control," *Artnews* 103, no. 9 (October 2004): 168–77.

13 Anonymous source, conversation with the author.

14 Spiegler, "The Giacometti Legacy: A Struggle for Control," 174.

15 Farah Nayeri, "Reviving Giacometti's Legacy," *New York Times*, April 16, 2015, http://www.nytimes.com/2015/04/16/arts/international/reviving-giacomettis-legacy.html.

16 Christie's, London, *The Art of the Surreal Evening Sale*, sale cat. (February 4, 2015), lot 125, http://www.christies.com/lotfinder/sculptures-statues-figures/alberto-giacometti-homme-5869333-details.aspx.

17 Roseline Letternon, "Catalogue raisonné: L'art, l'argent et la liberté d'expression," *Contrepoints*, August 7, 2014, https://www.contrepoints.org/2014/08/07/176133-catalogue-raisonne-lart-largent-et-la-liberte-dexpression.

18 Meryle Secrest, *Modigliani: A Life* (New York: Knopf, 2001), 308.

19 Ibid.

20 Marc Spiegler, "Modigliani: The Experts Battle," *Artnews* 103, no. 1 (January 2004): 127.

21 Secrest, *Modigliani*, 334.

22 Philip Hook, interview with author, London, April 2015.

23 Sotheby's, London, "Contemporary Art Evening Auction Including Property from the Sammlung Lenz Schönberg," sale cat. (February 10, 2010), lot 37, http://www.sothebys.com/en/auctions/ecatalogue/lot.37.html/2010/contemporary-art-evening-auction-including-property-from-the-sammlung-lenz-schnberg-l10020.

24 Charlotte Burns, "Heirs of Brazil's Leading Artist at War over Estate," *Art Newspaper*, July 1, 2015, http://theartnewspaper.com/market/art-market-news/heirs-of-brazil-s-leading-artist-at-war-over-estate.

25 Ibid.

26 "Les faits de contrefaçon reprochés à la petite-nièce de Claudel jugés prescrits," *L'express*, December 19, 2014, http://www.lexpress.fr/actualites/1/societe/la-petite-niece-de-camille-claudel-attend-son-jugement-pour-contrefacon_1634256.html (author's translation).

27 Ibid.

28 See Alain Servais, "Video Market: The Right Time to Rethink the Structure," *Texts to the World* 19 (n.d.), http://sammlung-haus-n.de/pdf/heft_19.pdf; and Peter Fischli and David Weiss, *Making Things Go / Sketch / The Way Things Go*, 2007, Artspace, accessed November 9, 2017, http://www.artspace.com/peter_fischli_david_weiss/making_things_go_way_things_go.

JUDITH BRESLER
Brave New Art Market: Unsilencing the Authenticators

1 *Travis v. Sotheby Parke Bernet, Inc.*, no. 4290/79, slip op. (N.Y. Sup. Ct. November 11, 1982).

2 Martin Bailey, "Van Gogh Museum Rejects Artist's 'Lost Sketchbook,'" *Art Newspaper*, November 16, 2016, https://

fineartbiblio.com/news/39341/van-gogh-museum-rejects-artist-s-lost-sketchbook.

3 Nina Siegal, "A Dubious Old Master Unnerves the Artworld," *New York Times*, October 26, 2016, https://www.nytimes.com/2016/10/27/arts/design/a-dubious-old-master-unnerves-the-art-world.html.

4 See generally Ralph Lerner and Judith Bresler, *Art Law: The Guide for Collectors, Investors, Dealers and Artists*, 4th ed. (New York: Practicing law Institute, 2012), 1: 491–562.

5 *Kirby v. Wildenstein*, 784 F. Supp.1112 (S.D.N.Y. 1992), http://law.justia.com/cases/federal/district-courts/FSupp/784/1112/1907567/.

6 *Ravenna v. Christie's, Inc.*, no. 121367-00 (N.Y. Sup. Ct., N.Y. County, Masr. 22, 2001), *aff'd*, 289 A.D.2d 15, 734 N.Y.S.2d 21 (1st dep't 2001).

7 *Kramer v. Pollock-Krasner Foundation*, 890 F. Supp. 250 (S.D.N.Y. 1995), http://law.justia.com/cases/federal/district-courts/FSupp/890/250/1410901/.

8 Andy Warhol Art Authentication Board, Inc., "Authentication Procedure: Statement from the Board of Directors," www.warholfoundation.org/legacy/authentication_procedure.html.

9 *Simon-Whelan v. Andy Warhol Foundation for the Visual Arts, Inc., et al.*, no. 07 Civ. 6423 (LTS) (S.D.N.Y. 2007); 2007 US Dist. Ct. Motions LEXIS 76423; 2007 US Dist. Ct. Motions LEXIS 88832, at *8 (November 30, 2007), http://dockets.justia.com/docket/new-york/nysdce/1:2007cv06423/310072.

10 One such notable controversy was six wooden Brillo boxes in the Andy Warhol collection at Moderna Museet, a museum in Stockholm, which were determined to be fakes, having been made in 1990, three years after Warhol had died. In a letter to the Warhol Authentication Board, the museum director, Lars Nittve, noted that the boxes had not been authorized by Warhol and "should be removed from the official list of Andy Warhol Brillo Boxes." Apparently, a former director of the Swedish museum had Swedish carpenters build 105 copies of the box for a 1990 exhibition in Russia. Purportedly, that former museum director, who died in 2006, sold a number of the copies with certificates falsely indicating that the boxes were made for a 1968 Warhol exhibition in Stockholm. "Swedish Warhols Are Fake," *New York Times*, November 17, 2007, www.nytimes.com/2007/11/17/arts/design/17arts-SWEDISHWARHO_BRF.html.

11 Laura Gilbert and Bill Glass, "Ann Freedman, Former Knoedler Director, Settles Final Lawsuit," *Art Newspaper*, September 11, 2017, http://theartnewspaper.com/news/ann-freedman-former-knoedler-director-settles-final-lawsuit.

12 Patricia Cohen, "Selling a Fake Painting Takes More Than a Good Artist," *New York Times*, May 2, 2014. https://www.nytimes.com/2014/05/03/arts/design/selling-a-fake-painting-takes-more-than-a-good-artist.html.

13 Ibid.

14 For some informative reading relating to the Knoedler forgeries, see Michael Shnayerson, "A Question of Provenance," *Vanity Fair*, April 23, 2012, www.vanityfair.com/unchanged/2012/05/knoedler-gallery-forgery-scandal-investigation; Dayla Alberge, "A Sense of Betrayal and Suspicion Grips the Art World," *Financial Times*, March 27, 2014, www.ft.com/cms/s/1662d400-ae60-11e3-aaa6-00144feab7de; Julia Halperin, "Everything You Ever Wanted to Know about the Knoedler Forgery Debacle but Were Afraid to Ask," *Blouin Artinfo*, December 6, 2011, www.blouinartinfo.com/news/story/753301/everything-you-ever-wanted-to-know-about-the-knoedler-forgery.

15 Gilbert and Glass, "Ann Freedman,

Former Knoedler Director, Settles Final Lawsuit."

16 Ibid.

17 "Collectors, Artists, and Lawyers: Fear of Litigation Is Hobbling the Art Market," *Economist*, November 24, 2012, http://www.economist.com/news/business/21567074-fear-litigation-hobbling-art-market-collectors-artists-and-lawyers.

18 *Andy Warhol Foundation for Visual Arts, Inc. v. Philadelphia Indem. Ins. Co.*, 2012 NY Slip Op. 5228(U), http://law.justia.com/cases/new-york/other-courts/2012-ny-slip-op-52228-u.html.

19 Mary Elizabeth Williams, "Update: Warhol Foundation Wins $6.6 Million Insurance Payment after Six Years," *Center for Art Law*, June 20, 2013, https://itsartlaw.com/2013/06/30/update-warhol-foundation-wins-6-6-million-insurance-payment-after-six-years/.

20 Michael Fahlund, "Professional Liability Insurance for Art Authenticators," *CAA News Today*, March 8, 2012, www.collegeart.org/news/2012/03/08/professional-liability-insurance-for-art-authenticators/.

21 Visual art multiples, defined in Section 11.01(20) of the New York Arts and Cultural Affairs Law, include most prints, photographs, negatives, sculpture, and similar art objects produced in more than one copy and that are the subject of a transaction in New York State.

22 The particularity requirement set forth in the proposed Section 15.12 to the New York Arts and Cultural Affairs Law parallels similar requirements in Rule 3016 of New York's Civil Practice Law and Rules, and in Rule 9(b) of the Federal Rules of Civil Procedure.

CORINNE HERSHKOVITCH
Artistic Authorship, Legacy, and Expert Liability in the French Art Market

1 Cour d'Appel [CA], Versailles, January 12, 2010, no. 05/9374.

2 Cour d'Appel [CA], Paris, October 12, 2012, no. 11/11725.

3 Law no. 2000-642 (July 10, 2000) created the status of "vetted expert" to regulate the profession, but few experts went through the vetting process, and the status was revoked in 2011.

4 Artists' moral rights in France are defined by articles L. 121-1, L. 121-2, and L. 121-4 of the Intellectual Property Code. They encompass the right of attribution (or right to be credited as the work's author), right of integrity (right not to have the work distorted or damaged), right of disclosure, and right of withdrawal. These rights are perpetual, inalienable, and imprescriptible and are transferrable upon death, to the author's inheritors (article L. 121-1 of the above-mentioned code). Moral rights in France are much stronger than in the United States. In the United States, the VARA grants two rights to authors of visual works: the right of attribution and the right of integrity. However, these rights end with the author's death.

5 See Cour d'Appel de Paris, accessed November 24, 2017, http://www.ca-paris.justice.fr/index.php?rubrique=12177&article=21914, for a definition: "Court experts are professionals of all specialties who devote some of their activity to the service of Justice. These professionals are included in a list produced by the appeal court, after a careful examination of their candidature. They are appointed by the appeal court and the courts within its jurisdiction, in the context of disputes" (author's translation).

6 See decree no. 81-255, March 3, 1981, article 1: "Habitual or occasional vendors

of works of art or collectable objects, or their representatives, together with public or ministerial officers and persons authorized to conduct public auctions must, if the purchaser so requests, give them an invoice, acquittance, sales receipt or extract from the report of the public sale containing the specifications they have claimed concerning the nature, composition, origin and age of the object sold" (author's translation).

7 Article 1382 of the French Civil Code: "Every act whatever of man that causes damage to another, obliges him by whose fault it occurred to repair it" (author's translation).

8 Article 1110, paragraph 1, of the French Civil Code: "Error is a cause of nullity of an agreement only when it bears on the very substance of the thing that is the object of the agreement" (author's translation).

9 Article L. 321-17 of the French Commercial Code: "The operators conducting voluntary sales of movables by public auction mentioned in article L. 321-4 and public or ministerial officials authorized to conduct judicial and voluntary sales, and likewise experts who assist in the description, presentation, and valuation of assets assume liability when movables are sold by public auction, pursuant to the rules applicable to such valuations and sales. Clauses that seek to avoid or limit their liability are prohibited and deemed to be unwritten.

Actions for civil liability brought on the occasion of valuations and voluntary and judicial sales of movables at public auction are subject to limitation five years after the auction or valuation. This period of limitation must be mentioned given in the advertisement set out in article L. 321-11" (author's translation).

10 Article L. 321-30, paragraph 2, of the French Commercial Code: "[The expert] is held jointly liable with the auction organiser for all that relates to his activity" (author's translation).

11 See Paris Appeal Court, Division 1, Section A, March 22, 2005 no. 04/05000, Gaz. Pal. 2005, somm. 2270: "Whereas the discussion by (Mr X) in relation to his capacity of expert is in vain, since there is no regulation of this activity applicable in this case, and a person who certifies without reserve the authenticity of a work of art, whether or not they claim to be an expert, assumes liability on the basis of this assertion alone" (author's translation).

12 Cour de Cassation [Cass.], civ., October 8, 1986, no. 85-14201.

13 See Cour de Cassation [Cass.], 1e civ., March 13, 2008, no. 07-13024 (author's translation); and Cour de Cassation [Cass.], 1e civ., December 1, 2011, no. 09-67316.

14 Cour de Cassation [Cass.], 1e civ., March 13, 2008, no. 07-13024.

15 Cour d'Appel [CA], Versailles, December 3, 2015, no.13/06134.

16 Tribunal of Grande Instance [TGI], Nanterre, May 24, 2011, no. 11/03520.

17 See Tribunal of Grande Instance [TGI], Nanterre, May 24, 2013, no. 11/ 03520; and Cour d'Appel [CA], Versailles, December 3, 2015, no. 13/06134.

18 Tribunal of Grande Instance [TGI], Paris, Division 3, Section 3, May 27, 2011, no. 09/10051.

19 Cour d'Appel [CA], Paris, Unit 5, Division 2, October 12, 2012, no. 11/11725.

20 Ibid.

21 Cour de Cassation [Cass.], 1e civ., January 22, 2014, no. 12-35.264, Dalloz 2014, 276.

22 Christophe Caron, "La liberté d'expression de l'auteur d'un catalogue raisonné," *Communication commerce électronique* no. 3 (March 2014) (author's translation).

23 See "Declaration of Human and Civic Rights of 26 August 1789," Constitutional Council, accessed November 24, 2017,

http://www.conseil-constitutionnel.fr/conseil-constitutionnel/root/bank_mm/anglais/cst2.pdf, article 11: "The free communication of ideas and of opinions is one of the most precious rights of man. Any citizen may therefore speak, write and publish freely, except what is tantamount to the abuse of this liberty in the cases determined by Law."

24 Article 1382 of the French Civil Code: "Every act whatever of man that causes damage to another, obliges him by whose fault it occurred to repair it."

25 Cour d'Appel [CA], Versailles, Division 3, October 29, 2015, no. 14/02561.

GIUSEPPE CALABI

Authentication and the Italian Art Market

1 Berne Convention 1888, art. 6-bis, para. 1.

2 Italian law no. 633, April 22, 1941, art. 20–24.

3 The right of attribution affords to the author four separate but related forms of protection: first, it is the author's right to be identified as the creator of a work. If an author so desires, his or her name must appear on all copies, as well as on the advertising and other publicity for the work. Second, authors can reveal themselves as the authors of their works, especially when such works were made available to the public as anonymous or under a pseudonym. Third, an author has the right to claim his or her authorship of a work and prevent others from usurping his or her creation by indicating another person as the author. Finally, an author can prevent others from wrongfully attributing to him/her a work that he or she did not create. This right protects the author from false attribution of authorship. Furthermore, it also gives the author the right not to claim authorship of the work. Authors may choose to remain anonymous or use pseudonyms instead of their real names. However, this right does not necessarily entitle such authors to prevent a third party from disclosing the author's real name. Right of authorship also implies the author's right to identify any plagiarism and to have a plagiarized work destroyed or removed from the market.

4 Certain judgments upheld the right of the author to challenge the following: the distribution of live recorded performances with imperfections; the deterioration of a painting due to the owner's negligence. See Court of Milan, July 6, 2004, in 24 *Annali Italiani del diritto d'autore* 522 (2005); and Court of Milan, January 20, 2005, in 24 *Annali Italiani del diritto d'autore*, 614 (2005). On the contrary, courts did not recognize the violation of the author's moral rights in the following cases: the incorrect photographic reproduction of a painting, when such alteration is minor; the realization of an architecture work different from the original project when there is no loss of reputation of the architect. See Court of Milan, May 29, 2006, in 28 *Annali Italiani del diritto d'autore* 478 (2009); and Court of Cassation, Italy, October 18, 1991, no. 11043, in *Foro It.*, 1992, I, p. 2480.

5 See Intellectual Property Code 1992, France, art. L.121-1.

6 See below the *Fondazione Schifano* case (Court of Milan, July 1, 2004, in 24 *Annali Italiani del diritto d'autore* 512 (2005)).

7 Court of Milan, October 17, 1963, in 87(2) *Foro Italiano* 388 (1964).

8 Italian Copyright Law, Legislative Decree no. 42, January 22, 2004, art. 64.

9 In the case of disputes regarding the authenticity of an artwork, the judge may appoint an expert witness in order to obtain an authenticity expertise. Italian courts have an official list of

expert witnesses, but expert witnesses frequently do not have a specific knowledge of the artist whose work is in dispute.

10 Catalogues raisonnés may also need to be updated. For example, the catalogue raisonné of Modigliani by Ambrogio Ceroni was published in 1972. A new catalogue raisonné by Marc Restellini is underway. Restellini's catalogue is expected to include more than one hundred works in addition to those published in the Ceroni catalogue.

11 Court of Milan, January 4, 2018, unpublished.

12 Court of Rome, February 16, 2010, no. 3425, in 1 *Sezioni Specializzate Proprietà Intellettuale* 184 (2010).

13 Italian law does not provide for any formal requirements for an authenticity certificate in order to be considered valid, as it only refers to a generic "documentation" or "declaration," which the professional seller shall give to the purchaser; see Italian Copyright Law, art. 64.

14 *Monica De Bei, Marco Giuseppe Schifano, Fondazione Mario Schifano v. Fondazione MS-Multistudio*, Court of Rome, no. 11051/2006, and subsequently, Rome Court of Appeal, June 8, 2010 no. 3657.

15 *Gabriele Oriani, ASBL Pippo Oriani v. Giuseppe Mercurio, Centro d'Arte Mercurio s.r.l.*, Court of Milan, December 13, 2004, in 24 *Annali Italiani del diritto d'autore* 595 (2005).

16 See *Elena Manzoni, Maria Melania Manzoni, Giuseppe Manzoni, Giacomo Maria Manzoni v. Giovanni Cervi*, Court of Milan, November 25, 2004, in 24 *Annali Italiani del diritto d'autore* 583 (2005); and *Elena Manzoni, Maria Melania Manzoni, Giuseppe Manzoni v. Gian Guido Scarampella, Corrado Rota*, Court of Milan, October 17, 2007, in 27 *Annali Italiani del diritto d'autore* 781 (2008).

17 The Archivio Piero Manzoni was transformed into a private foundation in 2009.

18 See Italian Civil Code, art. 2697, and Italian Civil Procedure Code, art. 115.

19 See *Manzoni v. Tonin*, Court of Milan, January 18, 2006, in 27 *Annali Italiani del diritto d'autore* 550 (2008); *Manzoni v. Gallo*, and Court of Milan, June 19, 2006, in 26 *Annali Italiani del diritto d'autore* 911 (2007).

Part Three: Legacy and Its Stewards

LORETTA WÜRTENBERGER AND KARL VON TROTT ZU SOLZ
Approaches to Dealing with Artists' Estates

1 Bek Reinhard, "Die kunsttechnologische Erfassung der Maschinenskulpturen Jean Tinguelys," *Zeitschrift für schweizerische Archäologie und Kunstgeschichte* 62 (2005): 251, quote translated by Karl von Trott.
2 Uwe Degreif, "Künstlernachlässe sind Särge de luxe," interview by Franz-Josef Sladeczek, *Einsichten* 1 (July 2013), http://www.artexperts.ch/fileadmin/user_upload/Publikationen/Artikel_Interview_UweDegreif.pdf .
3 Julia Halperin, "MoMA Struggles to Fulfil Sculptor's Last Wishes," *Art Newspaper*, June 2, 2015, http://theartnewspaper.com/market/art-market-news/moma-struggles-to-fulfil-sculptor-s-last-wishes/.
4 Ibid.
5 See Marianne Macdonald, "Henry Moore's Daughter Sues over Artworks: High Court Case Will Clarify Rights to 'Artist's Copy,'" *Independent*, October 12, 1993, http://www.independent.co.uk/news/uk/henry-moores-daughter-sues-over-artworks-high-court-case-will-clarify-rights-to-artists-copy-1510448.html; and Henri Neuendorf, "Austrian Supreme Court Accuses Franz West Private Foundation of Embezzlement," *Artnet News*, June 14, 2016, https://news.artnet.com/market/franz-west-private-foundation-embezzlement-517316.
6 Rachel Corbett, "Austrian Court Rules in Favour of Franz West's Family in Legal Battle over Estate," *Art Newspaper*, June 27, 2017, http://theartnewspaper.com/news/news/austrian-court-rules-in-favour-of-franz-west-s-family-in-legal-battle-over-estate/.
7 Abigail Cain, "Why Clement Greenberg Defaced David Smith's Sculptures," *Artsy*, June 7, 2017, https://www.artsy.net/article/artsy-editorial-clement-greenberg-defaced-david-smiths-sculptures.
8 Ryan Steadman, "Rauschenberg Now Repped by Triplet of Three Blue-Chip Global Galleries," *Observer*, April 17, 2015, http://observer.com/2015/04/rauschenberg-foundation-now-repped-by-triplet-of-blue-chip-global-galleries/.
9 By 2012 the board had spent around $7 million on legal fees to fight litigation initiated by collectors whose works were denied authentication by the board. See Stephanie Cash, "Warhol Board Quits the Authentication Game," *Art in America*, October 20, 2011, http://www.artinamericamagazine.com/news-features/news/warhol-board-quits-the-authentication-game.
10 "I Wanted to Paint Nothing," *Adbusters* 80 (November/December 2008), http://www.adbusters.org/article/i-wanted-to-paint-nothing.

CHRISTINE J. VINCENT
What's an Artist to Do?—Artist-Endowed Foundations and Legacy Stewardship in the United States

1 Stephen K. Urice, "Creativity and Generosity: Considerations in Establishing an Artist-Endowed Foundation," in *The Artist as Philanthropist: Strengthening the Next Generation of Artist-Endowed Foundations* (Washington, DC: The Aspen Institute, 2010), 2:271–92.
2 An exception is a noncharitable trust that has a charitable interest, such as a charitable remainder trust or charitable lead trust, with tax exemption attributable to the charitable interest.
3 Thomas A. Troyer, "The 1969 Private

Foundation Law: Historical Perspectives on Its Origins and Underpinnings," 27 *Exempt Organization Tax Review* 52 (January 2000).

4 Frances R. Hill, "Public Benefit and Exemption: The Public Benefit Requirement as a Practical Aid in Designing, Organizing, and Operating Artist-Endowed Foundations," in *The Artist as Philanthropist*, 2:347–68.

5 Stephen K. Urice, "Creativity and Generosity," in *The Artist as Philanthropist*, 2:271–92.

6 This article is intended for a general readership, but it does necessarily reference important aspects of federal and state regulation applicable to artist-endowed foundations. Relevant sources for these references are cited in endnotes. For a full discussion of this topic, readers should refer to "Part B: Considerations in Foundation Practice," in *The Artist as Philanthropist*, 2:3–256; and *The Artist as Philanthropist: Strengthening the Next Generation of Artist-Endowed Foundations, A Study of the Emerging Artist-Endowed Foundation Field in the U.S.*, Study Report Supplement 2013 (Washington, DC: The Aspen Institute, 2013), both available at www.aspeninstitute.org/aefi.

7 Andreas Stolzenburg, *Franz Ludwig Catel (1778–1856): Paesaggista e pittore di genere* (Rome: Artemide, 2007).

8 "La Fondazione," Fondazione Franz Ludwig Catel, accessed August 15, 2017, www.fondazionecatel.it/arte/pio-istituto-catel/.

9 Jennifer Perry Thalheimer, "For the Advancement of Art: The Louis Comfort Tiffany Foundation," in *Louis Comfort Tiffany and Laurelton Hall: An Artist's Country Estate*, ed. Alice Cooney Frelinghuysen and Elizabeth Hutchinson, exh. cat. (New York: Metropolitan Museum of Art, 2006), 203–15.

10 Ibid.

11 "About the Foundation," The Louis Comfort Tiffany Foundation, accessed August 15, 2017, http://louiscomfort tiffanyfoundation.org/about.html.

12 Jorge H. Santis, "The Glackens Collection," in *William Glackens*, ed. William H. Gerdts (New York: Abbeville Press, 1996), 175–95.

13 "Glackens Study Center," NSU Art Museum Fort Lauderdale, accessed August 15, 2017, http://nsuartmuseum.org/collection-2/glackens-study-center/.

14 C. Arthur Burchfield, preface to *Charles Burchfield's Journals: The Poetry of Place*, ed. J. Benjamin Townsend (Albany, NY: State University of New York Press, 1993), xv.

15 "Charles E. Burchfield," Burchfield-Penney Art Center at SUNY Buffalo State, accessed August 15, 2017, www.burchfieldpenney.org/collection/charles-e-burchfield/.

16 A blockage discount is a reduction to the fair market valuation of similar assets held in bulk, such as an artist's collected works, to reflect the extent to which the selling price would be depressed were the assets to be sold at one time.

17 Gustave Harrow, "Reflections on Estate of Rothko: The Role of the Legal Advisor in Relation to the Artist," 26 *Cleveland State Law Review* 573 (1977).

18 Ibid.

19 The private foundation rules, including a mandated payout requirement calculated based on the value of noncharitable assets and an excise tax on net investment income, were established when Congress adopted the Tax Reform Act of 1969, which became effective as of tax year 1970, the year of Rothko's death.

20 Harrow, "Reflections on Estate of Rothko."

21 Donald M. Blinken, *Eliminating the Obstacles between the Painter and the Observer: The Mark Rothko Foundation,*

1976–1986 (New York: Mark Rothko Foundation, 1986).

22 "Joseph Cornell Estate Papers, circa 1911, 1944–1986," Smithsonian Archives of American Art, accessed August 15, 2017, http://www.aaa.si.edu/collections/joseph-cornell-papers-5790/series-10.

23 Ibid.

24 "Joseph Cornell Study Center," Smithsonian American Art Museum, accessed August 15, 2017, www.americanart.si.edu/research/cornell.

25 Carol Vogel, "Foundation Is Accused of Ignoring Artist's Will," *New York Times*, July 26, 1994, http://www.nytimes.com/1994/07/26/arts/foundation-is-accused-of-ignoring-artist-s-will.html.

26 The Joseph and Robert Cornell Memorial Foundation, accessed August 15, 2017, www.cornellmemorialfoundation.org.

27 "Foundation Past and Present: Creative Impact," The Andy Warhol Foundation for the Visual Arts, accessed August 15, 2017, www.warholfoundation.org/foundation/index.html.

28 Callie Angell et al., *The Andy Warhol Museum* (Pittsburgh: Andy Warhol Museum, 1994).

29 Carol Vogel, "Still Arguing the Value of Warhol's Estate," *New York Times*, June 16, 1992, http://www.nytimes.com/1992/06/16/news/still-arguing-the-value-of-warhol-s-estate.html.

30 Carol Vogel, "Lawyer for Warhol Estate Must Repay $1.35 Million," *New York Times*, February 9, 1996, http://www.nytimes.com/1996/02/09/arts/lawyer-for-warhol-estate-must-repay-1.35-million.html.

31 Vogcl, "Still Arguing the Value of Warhol's Estate."

32 See "About the Foundation," The Pollock-Krasner Foundation, accessed August 15, 2017, www.pkf.org/about/#overview; and "Mission of the Trust," Renate, Hans and Maria Hofmann Trust, accessed August 15, 2017, http://www.hanshofmann.org/thetrust/.

33 "Mission," Josef and Anni Albers Foundation, accessed August 15, 2017, www.albersfoundation.org/about-us/mission/.

34 *The Artist as Philanthropist*, Study Report Supplement 2013, 7.

35 Both nonoperating and operating foundations meet a payout requirement. Nonoperating foundations meet a simple requirement to expend for charitable purposes a defined amount calculated on the value of noncharitable use assets. Operating foundations meet a set of financial tests designed to confirm that expenditures are made to directly conduct programs accomplishing their charitable purposes, and the majority of assets are being used directly for such programs. See "Considerations in Foundation Planning," in *The Artist as Philanthropist*, 2:27–52.

36 Ibid.

37 Frances R. Hill and Douglas M. Mancino, *Taxation of Exempt Organizations* (Valhalla, NY: Thomson/RIA, 2002–8), 11-4–11-18.

38 "About the Foundation," Adolph and Esther Gottlieb Foundation, accessed August 15, 2017, www.gotliebfoundation.org/about/.

39 "Considerations in Foundation Planning," in *The Artist as Philanthropist*, 2:27–52.

40 See "Foundation," Robert Mapplethorpe Foundation, www.mapplehtorpe.org/foundation/; and "About the Keith Haring Foundation," Keith Haring Foundation, www.haring.com/kh_foundation/; and "The Foundation," Herb Ritts Foundation, www.herbritts.com/#/about/foundation/, all accessed August 15, 2017.

41 "Considerations in Foundation Planning," in *The Artist as Philanthropist*, 2:27–52.

42 "Other Philanthropic Forms Used by Artists," in *The Artist as Philanthropist*, 1:37–42.

43 "Timeline," The Isamu Noguchi Foundation and Garden Museum, accessed August 15, 2017, www.noguchi.org/noguchi/timeline.
44 "101 Spring Street: Restoration," accessed August 15, 2017, Judd Foundation, www.juddfoundation.org/the-restoration/.
45 "History of the Maloof Foundation," Sam and Alfreda Maloof Foundation for Arts and Crafts, accessed August 15, 2017, www.malooffoundation.org/mission-statement.
46 "Other Philanthropic Forms Used by Artists," in *The Artist as Philanthropist*, 1:37–42.
47 "About the John Cage Trust," John Cage Trust, accessed August 15, 2017, www.johncage.org/about.html.
48 Marion Fremont-Smith, "Federal and State Laws Regulating Conflict of Interest and Their Application to Artist-Endowed Foundations," in *The Artist as Philanthropist*, 2:311–46.
49 Frederick M. Nicholas, "Artists Beware," in *Foundation Management: Innovation and Responsibility at Home and Abroad*, ed. Frank L. Ellsworth and Joe Lumarda (Hoboken, NJ: John Wiley and Sons, 2003), 295–98.
50 Lee-Ford Tritt, "Statutory Copyright Terminations and Artist-Endowed Foundations," in *The Artist as Philanthropist*, Study Report Supplement 2013, 169–84.
51 Jill S. Manny, "Artist-Endowed Foundations Holding Stock in Artists' Corporations," in *The Artist as Philanthropist*, Study Report Supplement 2013, 161–68.
52 Philip Boroff, "Judge Awards Three Pals of Robert Rauschenberg $25 Million," *Artnet News*, August 3, 2014, https://news.artnet.com/art-world/judge-awards-three-pals-of-robert-rauschenberg-25-million-71989.
53 Roberta Smith, "Christie's Presale Show: Light and Space Enough to Really See Judd," *New York Times*, April 24, 2006, http://www.nytimes.com/2006/04/24/arts/design/christies-presaleshow-light-and-space-enough-to-really-see.html.
54 Judd Foundation, Form 990-PF, 2006.
55 Judith Dunham, "*The Rose* Chronology," in *Jay DeFeo and "The Rose,"* ed. Jane Green and Leah Levy (Berkeley: University of California Press, 2003), 155–68.
56 The Jay DeFeo Foundation, accessed August 15, 2017, www.jaydefeo.org.
57 Fremont-Smith, "Federal and State Laws Regulating Conflict of Interest," in *The Artist as Philanthropist*, 2:311–46.
58 Rob Perez, "Insider Purchase of Artwork Challenged," *Honolulu Star-Bulletin*, March 6, 2005, http://archives.starbulletin.com/2005/03/06/news/story3.html.
59 Fremont-Smith, "Federal and State Laws Regulating Conflict of Interest," in *The Artist as Philanthropist*, 2:311–46.
60 "Internal Influences: Artists' Demographics and Characteristics," in *The Artist as Philanthropist*, 1:53–60.
61 "External Influences: Public Tax Policy," in *The Artist as Philanthropist*, 1:61–70.

DANIEL McCLEAN
Artists' Estates as Guardians of Artistic Legacy: Custodians or Gatekeepers?

1 See Philadelphia Museum of Art, *Marcel Duchamp: "Étant donnés,"* August 15–November 29, 2009, http://www.philamuseum.org/exhibitions/324.html.
2 For a full account on the legal structure of artists' estates, see Loretta Würtenberger, *The Artist's Estate: A Handbook for Artists, Executors, and Heirs* (Berlin: Hatje Cantz, 2016). See especially chapter 3, "Types of Estate Administration: Between Attics, Museum Plans, and Other Desires for Perpetuity."
3 In France, for example, the "droit moral"

holder has the right to authenticate works by that artist (which is often bequeathed by the artist to his or her heirs). See Judith Prowda, "Expert Opinions," in *Visual Arts and the Law: A Handbook for Professionals* (Surrey, UK: Lund Humphries, 2013), 203–19.

4 See "Beuys-Witwe unterlieght vor BGH," *Handelsblatt*, May 16, 2013, http://www.handelsblatt.com/panorama/kultur-kunstmarkt/streit-um-fotoserie-beuys-witwe-unterliegt-vor-bgh/8220192.html.

5 See, for example, Principle 2, "Museums that Maintain Collections Hold Them in Trust for the Benefit of Society and its Development." *ICOM Code of Ethics for Museums* (International Council of Museums, 2013), 3, http://icom.museum/fileadmin/user_upload/pdf/Codes/code_ethics2013_eng.pdf.

6 *Oxford Dictionaries*, s.v. "legacy," accessed July 20, 2017, https://en.oxforddictionaries.com/definition/legacy.

7 See Hal Foster, "An Archival Impulse," *October* 110 (Fall 2004): 3–22.

8 The author of this essay has been the legal adviser to the artist Jill Magid for this project and has discussed it in Daniel McClean, "Jill Magid and Luis Barragán's Legacy," in *The Proposal: Jill Magid*, Critical Spatial Practice 8, ed. Nikolaus Hirsch et al. (Berlin: Sternberg Press, 2016).

9 See Alan Riding, "A Family Feud over a Picasso (on Wheels): A New Car's Logo Divides the Heirs of a Lucrative Name," *New York Times*, April 19, 1999, http://www.nytimes.com/1999/04/19/arts/family-feud-over-picasso-wheels-new-car-s-logo-divides-heirs-lucrative-name.html.

10 See Alyssa Buffenstein, "Dash Snow's Family Sues McDonald's for Copyright Infringement," *Artnet News*, October 5, 2016, https://news.artnet.com/art-world/dash-snows-family-sues-mcdonalds-copyright-infringement-685901.

11 See Daniel McClean, "Piracy and Authorship in Contemporary Art and the Artistic Commonwealth," in *Copyright and Piracy: An Interdisciplinary Critique*, ed. Lionel Bently, Jennifer Davis, Jane C. Ginsburg (Cambridge: Cambridge University Press, 2010), 311–39.

12 See "Riley v. Rehberger Copyright Lawsuit Settled," *Clanco*, January 22, 2014, http://clancco.com/wp/2014/01/painting-installation-checkerboard-art-law/.

13 Civil Court of Milan, no. 79957/2010, judgment of July 14, 2011.

14 See Cleveland Museum of Art, *Gloria: Robert Rauschenberg and Rachel Harrison*, July 1–October 25, 2015, https://www.clevelandart.org/events/exhibitions/gloria-robert-rauschenberg-rachel-harrison.

15 See "The Power Plant," *Simon Starling: Cuttings (Supplement)*, March 1–May 11, 2008, http://www.thepowerplant.org/Exhibitions/2008/2008_Spring/Cuttings-(Supplement).aspx.

16 See Nathalie Eggs and Victoria Stapley-Brown, "Forgery Scandal Surrounding Lee Ufan's Work Grows in Korea with Three Arrests," *Art Newspaper*, November 21, 2016, http://theartnewspaper.com/news/forgery-scandal-surrounding-lee-ufan-s-work-grows-in-korea-with-three-arrests/.

17 See *Simon-Whelan v. The Andy Warhol Foundation for the Visual Arts, Inc., et al.*, No. 07 Civ. 6423 (LTS) (S.D.N.Y. May 26, 2009).

18 Richard Dorment, "What Is an Andy Warhol?" *New York Review of Books*, October 22, 2009, http://www.nybooks.com/articles/2009/10/22/what-is-an-andy-warhol/.

19 See M. H. Miller, "The Big Fake: Behind the Scenes of Knoedler Gallery's Downfall," *Artnews*, April 25, 2016, http://www.artnews.com/2016/04/25/the-big-fake-behind-the-scenes-of-knoedler-gallerys-downfall/.

20 See Richard Polsky Art Authentication, http://richardpolskyart.com.

21 Since early 2015, the New York State Legislature has considered legislation limiting the legal liability of authenticators offering opinions. Though passed by the Senate, this legislation has not been passed by the Assembly. See, Assembly Bill A1018, relating to the authenticity, attribution, and authorship of fine works of art, https://www.nysenate.gov/legislation/bills/2015/a1018/amendment/original.

22 *Mayor Gallery Ltd. v. Agnes Martin Catalogue Raisonné LLC, et al.*, no. 655489 (Sup. Ct. N.Y. October 17, 2016).

23 See Tacita Dean, *Darmstädter Werkblock* (Göttingen, Germany: Steidl, 2008).

DAWN ADES
Marcel Duchamp, Fountain*, 1917: A Controversial History*

1 Marcel Duchamp, "Interview with James Johnson Sweeney" (1955), in *Wisdom: Conversations with the Elder Wise Men of Our Day*, ed. James Nelson (New York: W. W. Norton & Co., 1958), 94.

2 Julian Spalding and Glyn Thompson, "Did Marcel Duchamp Steal Elsa's Urinal?" *Art Newspaper*, November 3, 2014, http://old.theartnewspaper.com/articles/Did-Marcel-Duchamp-steal-Elsas-urinal/36155.

3 Irene Gammel, *Baroness Elsa: Gender, Dada, and Everyday Modernity, A Cultural Biography* (Cambridge, MA: MIT Press, 2002).

4 Francis Naumann, *New York Dada, 1915–1923* (New York: Abrams, 1994), 172. The Philadelphia Museum of Art catalogue now lists it as by "Morton Livingstone Schamberg (American, 1881–1918) and Elsa von Freytag-Loringhoven (German, 1874–1927)."

5 Naumann, *New York Dada*, 128, 234.

6 Recollections of Theresa Bernstein, quoted in ibid, 170. The Baroness also nourished an unrequited passion for Duchamp, for whom she composed a poem—"Marcel, Marcel, I love you like hell, Marcel"—and constructed a portrait, an assemblage of various objects including feathers and a coiled spring in a wineglass. Two bust-length photographs of her naked were reproduced in the single issue of *New York Dada* (1921), compiled by Duchamp and Man Ray, who also filmed her shaving her pubic hair.

7 Gammel, *Baroness Elsa*, 223.

8 For a full account, see William A. Camfield, *Marcel Duchamp: Fountain* (Houston: The Menil Collection, 1989).

9 "Little magazine" is the term widely used for the relatively modest, often ephemeral, swiftly and cheaply produced magazines put out by Dada and other avant-garde movements.

10 Camfield 1989, 22.

11 Anonymous review, "His Art Too Crude for Independents," *New York Herald*, April 14, 1917, 6, quoted in ibid., 26.

12 "The Richard Mutt Case," *The Blind Man*, no. 2 (May 1917): n.p. The text was written by Beatrice Wood, as she explains in her autobiography, *I Shock Myself: The Autobiography of Beatrice Wood* (San Francisco: Chronicle Books, 1985), 31. It was probably shown to and approved by Duchamp. See also Naumann, *New York Dada*.

13 Louise Norton, "Buddha of the Bathroom," *The Blind Man*, no. 2 (May 1917): n.p.

14 "Suppressed" is Duchamp's term; see Pierre Cabanne, *Entretiens avec Marcel Duchamp* (Paris: Editions Pierre Belfond, 1967), 98.

15 Marcel Duchamp, *A l'infinitif*, trans. Jackie Matisse, Richard Hamilton, and Ecke Bonk (Paris: The Typosophic Society, 1999), 1.

16 Camfield, 31.
17 See ibid., 33.
18 Alfred Stieglitz to Georgia O'Keeffe, April 19, 1917, in *My Faraway One: Selected Letters of Georgia O'Keeffe and Alfred Stieglitz, Volume 1, 1915–1933*, ed. Sarah Greenough (New Haven, CT: Yale University Press, 2011), 135.
19 Alfred Stieglitz to Henry McBride, April 19, 1917, Papers of Henry McBride, quoted in Naumann, *New York Dada*, 184.
20 Alfred Stieglitz to Georgia O'Keeffe, April 19, 1917, in *My Faraway One*, 135.
21 Marcel Duchamp to Suzanne Duchamp, April 11, 1917, in *Affectionately, Marcel: The Selected Correspondence of Marcel Duchamp*, ed. Francis M. Naumann and Hector Obalk, trans. Jill Taylor (Ghent, Belgium: Ludion Press, 2000), 47. The complete letter reads:

> Les Independents sont ouverts ici avec gros succès.
> Une de mes amies sous un pseudonyme masculin, Richard Mutt, avait envoyé une pissotière en porcelaine comme sculpture;
> Ce n'était pas du tout indécent. Aucune raison pour la refuser. Le comité a décidé de refuser d'exposer cette chose. J'ai donné ma démission et c'est un potin qui aura sa valeur dans New York.
> J'avais envie de faire une ex position speciale des refusés aux Indépendants— mais ce serait un pleonasme! Et la pissotière aurait été lonely . . .

22 Ibid., 47.
23 Gammel, 224.
24 Ibid., 227.
25 See note 5 above. In 1917 the Baroness was living in Philadelphia, and newspaper reports of the *Fountain* scandal identified Mutt as a Philadelphian. Gammel uses this to support her argument. However, the newspaper reports were almost certainly based on information put out by the *Blind Man* camp, possibly inspired by the fact that the Mott Iron Works, of New Jersey, source of the urinal, as Duchamp later claimed, had showrooms in Philadelphia as well as New York.
26 Naumann, *New York Dada*, 185.
27 Cabanne, *Entretiens avec Marcel Duchamp*, 52 (author's translation).
28 Marcel Duchamp to Suzanne Duchamp, April 11, 1917.
29 *The Writings of Marcel Duchamp*, ed. Michel Sanouillet and Elmer Peterson (New York: Oxford University Press, 1973), 23.
30 Two short enigmatic texts in the second issue of *The Blind Man* signed "S. T. E. K." might be by another female member of the Arensberg circle, Sophie Treadwell, whose role in the assisted readymade *A bruit secret* (With Secret Noise, 1916) is discussed in Molly Nesbit and Naomi Sawelson-Gorse, "Concept of Nothing: New Notes by Marcel Duchamp and Walter Arensberg," in *The Duchamp Effect*, ed. Martha Buskirk and Mignon Nixon (Cambridge, MA: MIT Press, 1996), 165, published in French in *Étant donné*, no. 1 (1999): 76.
31 See Jay Bochner, "The Marriage of *Rogue* and *The Soil*," in *Little Magazines and Modernism: New Approaches*, ed. Suzanne W. Churchill and Adam McKible (Burlington, VT: Ashgate, 2008); see also *Three New York Dadas and the Blind Man: Marcel Duchamp, Henri-Pierre Roché, and Beatrice Wood*, introduction by Dawn Ades, trans. Chris Allan (London: Atlas, 2013).
32 Gammel makes further highly speculative arguments, including a claim that there was a connection between Mutt and Philadelphia, where von Freytag-Loringhoven was temporarily based; the Philadelphia connection appeared in the press, probably fed by bulletins from Wood and Norton, etc. This could have been an in-joke in the Arensberg circle:

Mina Loy's compilation of overheard fragments of conversation included the following potentially snobbish remark: "Are you an American representative? I am sorry—You are Pennsylvania I am Boston." Other claims, such as that the so-called religious subtext to the *Fountain*, are not compatible with Duchamp are absurd. Gammel asserts that the "intriguing religious twist" in the transformation of *Fountain* into a Madonna in the Stieglitz photograph is "not commensurate with Duchamp's work," but is a "signature trait" of von Freytag-Loringhoven. This is to overlook a host of subtle religious/iconoclastic allusions in Duchamp's *Large Glass* (1915–23) and its related notes, for a start.

AGENCY
Thing 000955 (Martha Graham's Choreographies)

1 *Martha Graham School and Dance Foundation v. Martha Graham Center of Contemporary Dance*, 153 F. Supp. 2d 512 (S.D.N.Y. 2001).
2 *Martha Graham School and Dance Foundation v. Martha Graham Center of Contemporary Dance*, 224 F. Supp. 2d 567 (S.D.N.Y. 2002).
3 The forty-five dances were: *Tanagra, Three Gopi Maidens, Harlequinade, Primitive Mysteries, Serenade, Satyric Festival Song, Dream, Saraband, Imperial Gesture, Deep Song, Every Soul Is a Circus, El Penitente, Letter to the World, Punch and the Judy, Salem Shore, Deaths and Entrances, Eye of Anguish, Ardent Song, Embattled Garden, Episodes: Part I, Acrobats of God, Phaedra, Secular Games, Legend of Judith, The Witch of Endor, Part Real–Part Dream, Cortege of Eagles, Plain of Prayer, Mendicants of Evening, Jacob's Ladder, Lucifer, The Scarlet Letter, O Thou Desire Who Art About to Sing, Shadows, The Owl and the Pussycat, Ecuatorial, Frescoes, Judith (created in 1980), Andromache's Lament, Phaedra's Dream, Song, Tangled Night, Persephone, Maple Leaf Rag*, and *The Eyes of the Goddess*.
4 The ten works in the public domain are: *Flute of Krishna, Heretic, Lamentation, Celebration, Frontier, Panorama, Chronicle/ Steps in the Street, American Document, Appalachian Spring*, and *Night Journey*.
5 The five commissioned dances are: *Herodiade, Dark Meadow, Cave of the Heart, Judith (I)*, and *Canticle for Innocent Comedians*.
6 The nine dances are: *Errand into the Maze, Diversion of Angels, Clytemnestra, Circe, Adorations, Acts of Light, The Rite of Spring, Temptations of the Moon*, and *Night Chant*.
7 *Martha Graham School and Dance Foundation v. Martha Graham Center of Contemporary Dance*, 380 F.3d 624 (2d Cir. 2004).
8 *Martha Graham School and Dance Foundation v. Martha Graham Center of Contemporary Dance*, 374 F. Supp. 2d 355, 363 (S.D.N.Y. 2005). The seven unpublished dances in question were: *Embattled Garden, Episodes: Part I, Phaedra, Secular Games, Legend of Judith, The Witch of Endor*, and *Part Real–Part Dream*.

GABRIEL PÉREZ-BARREIRO
A Brass-Plated Boxing Ring: Foundations, Artists' Estates, and Legacy

1 For example, in 2014 the Clark foundation demanded the closure of the exhibition *Lygia Clark: Todo que é concreto se desmancha no ar* at the Museu de Arte Contemporânea, in Niteroi, Brazil, which included many works from the museum's collection that are widely considered to be genuine, albeit not certified by the foundation. See Luiza Franco, "Herdeiros de Lygia Clark exigem fim de mostra no Rio," *Folha de S.Paulo*, March 12, 2014, http://www1.

folha.uol.com.br/ilustrada/2014/12/1556465-herdeiros-de-lygia-clark-exigem-fim-de-mostra-no-rio.shtml.

2 In 2010, the Clark foundation demanded that the Centro Cultural Banco do Nordeste, in Fortaleza, Brazil, withdraw Clark's name from the title and labels of *Lygia Clark: Da obra ao acontecimento*, an exhibition produced in honor of Clark that included no actual works by her, but rather a series of recorded interviews about her influence. See Fabio Cypriano, "Lygia Clark à distância," *Folha de S. Paulo*, June 4, 2010, http://www1.folha.uol.com.br/fsp/ilustrad/fq0406201009.htm; and Ana Cecília Soares, "Herdeiros X artistas," *Diário do Nordeste*, July 24, 2010, http://diariodonordeste.verdesmares.com.br/cadernos/caderno-3/herdeiros-x-artistas-1.379193.

3 See, for example, Gabriel Pérez-Barreiro, ed., *The Geometry of Hope: Latin American Abstract Art from the Patricia Phelps de Cisneros Collection*, exh. cat. (Austin, Texas: Blanton Museum of Art, 2007), 164–65, 193–94.

4 See Charlotte Burns, "Heirs of Brazil's Leading Artist at War over Estate," *The Art Newspaper*, July 1, 2015, http://theartnewspaper.com/market/art-market-news/heirs-of-brazil-s-leading-artist-at-war-over-estate/.

5 See Vanda Klabin, "O Caso Volpi," DASartes, April 10, 2010, http://dasartes.com.br/materias/o-caso-volpi/. The article points out that the estate demanded a fee of R$150,000 (approximately US$70,000 at the time) to reproduce sixty-one works in the catalogue.

6 For example, in 2007, as curator of the 6th Mercosul Biennial, in Porto Alegre, Brazil, I organized an exhibition of prints by Swedish-Brazilian artist Öyvind Fahlström. The artist's widow and executor of the estate wanted to be credited as cocurator, and when this was not granted, she refused to authorize the images. As a result, the catalogue was published with no images.

7 Suzana Velasco, "Familia de Volpi cobra R$100 mil por imagens do artista e impede catálogo," *O Globo*, June 16, 2009, http://www.canalcontemporaneo.art.br/brasa/archives/002290.html.

8 The recent College Art Association *Code of Best Practices in Fair Use for the Visual Arts* (2015) is a great step in this direction.

9 In 2016, the Senate Finance Committee launched an investigation into eleven private museums and foundations to test if they provided enough public benefit to justify their tax-free status.

GILANE TAWADROS

Appendix; or, Some Adjectival Notes on Authorship and Legacy

1 Sprüth Magers, *Keith Arnatt, Absence of the Artist*, exhibition press release, London, September 2015, http://www.spruethmagers.com/exhibitions/390.

2 Stephen Foster and Gilane Tawadros, eds., *Familiars: Hamad Butt* (London: Iniva in association with John Hansard Gallery, 1996).

3 Doris Salcedo, interview for *TateShots*, October 1, 2007, www.tate.org.uk/context-comment/video/tateshots-doris-salcedo.

4 Mike Phillips and Geoff Cox, "Donald Rodney—Autoicon. The Death of an Artist," in *Emergent Futures: Art, Interactivity and New Media*, ed. Angela Molina and Kepa Landa (Valencia, Spain: Alfons el Magnanim, 2000), accessed online at http://i-dat.org/wp-content/uploads/2000/05/Rodney.pdf.

CONTRIBUTORS

DANIEL MCCLEAN
is an international art lawyer, writer, and independent curator. He is a partner at the law firm Cypress LLP, in Los Angeles, and consultant to the London-based law firm Howard Kennedy LLP. He has commissioned and edited numerous interdisciplinary publications on art law, including *Dear Images: Art, Copyright and Culture* (2002) and *The Trials of Art* (2007), both published by Ridinghouse.

GEORGINA ADAM
has spent more than thirty years writing about the art market and the arts in general. She is art market editor-at-large for the *Art Newspaper* and a contributor to the *Financial Times*, as well as a lecturer and moderator. She is the author of *Big Bucks: The Explosion of the Art Market in the 21st Century* (2014) and *Dark Side of the Boom: The Excesses of the Art Market in the 21st Century* (2017).

DAWN ADES
is Professor Emerita of the History and Theory of Art at the University of Essex, Professor of the History of Art at the Royal Academy, a former trustee of Tate (1995–2005) and of the National Gallery (2000–2005), and a Fellow at the British Academy. Her books include *Photo-montage* (1976/81), *Salvador Dalí* (1982), *André Masson* (1994), *Siron Franco* (1996), *Marcel Duchamp* (with Neil Cox and David Hopkins, 2000), and *Writings on Art and Anti-Art* (2015). She has organized many exhibitions in the UK and internationally, including *Dada and Surrealism Reviewed* (1978); *Art in Latin America: The Modern Era, 1820–1980* (1989); *Salvador Dalí: The Centenary Exhibition* (2004); *Undercover Surrealism: Georges Bataille and Documents* (2006); *Close-Up: Proximity and Defamiliar-isation in Art, Photography and Film* (2008); and *The Colour of My Dreams: The Surrealist Revolution in Art* (2011). She was Associate Curator for *Manifesta 9* in 2012. She recently devised the exhibition *Dalí/ Duchamp* (2017–18) with William Jeffett, curator at the Dalí Museum in Saint Petersburg, Florida.

AGENCY
is a Brussels-based international initiative that was founded in 1992 by Kobe Matthys. Agency constitutes a growing "list of things" that resist the radical split between the classifications of nature and culture. This list is mostly derived from juridical cases and controversies involving intellectual property (copyrights, patents, trade marks, etc.), from the start of the enclosures of the commons in the seventeenth century to today, and from various territories of world-integrated capitalism. The colonial concept of intellectual property relies upon the fundamental assumption of the split between culture and nature and consequently between expressions and ideas, creations and facts, subjects and objects, humans and nonhumans, originality and tradition, individuals and collectives, mind and body. Each "thing," or controversy, included on the list witnesses a resistance and a hesitation in terms of these divisions. Agency calls these "things" forth from its list via varying "assemblies" inside exhibitions, performances, publications. Each assembly speculates around possible inclusions. Agency looks at the operative consequences of the apparatus of intellectual property for an ecology of diverse art practices and aims at generating their singular modes of existence.

JUDITH BRESLER
is coauthor of the acclaimed treatise *Art Law: The Guide for Collectors, Investors, Dealers and Artists*, now in its fourth edition, counsel to the international law firm Withers Worldwide, a distinguished lecturer, and a prominent art attorney. She is an adjunct professor at New York Law School, and was on the adjunct faculty of the University of Pennsylvania Law School. She has served as General Counsel to the Appraisers Association of America (AAA); a member of the AAA Advisory Panel; a board member at the New York Law School; a board member at the Philadelphia Volunteer Lawyers for the Arts; Co-Chair of the Authenticity Subcommittee at the New York City Bar Art Law Committee; Chair of the NY State Bar Association, Entertainment Art and Sports Law Section (EASL); and Chair of the EASL's Art Law Committee. She publishes extensively on all aspects of the art market.

GUY BRETT
is a London-based art critic, curator, and lecturer on art. He has published widely in the international art press and has contributed monographic essays to many artists' catalogues. Among his books are *Carnival of Perception* (2004) and *Through Our Own Eyes: Popular Art and Modern History* (1986). Brett has curated a number of influential exhibitions, including *Georges Vantongerloo: A Longing for Infinity* (Museo Nacional de Arte Reina Sofía, Madrid, 2009), *Cildo Meireles* (co-curated with Vicente Todolí, Tate Modern, London, 2008), *Force Fields: Phases of the Kinetic* (Museu d'Art Contemporani de Barcelona and Hayward Gallery, London, 2000), *Transcontinental: Nine Latin American Artists* (Ikon Gallery, Birmingham/Cornerhouse, Manchester, 1990), and *Hélio Oiticica* (Whitechapel Gallery, London, 1969).

SHANE BURKE
is a lecturer in intellectual-property law at Cardiff University. His research interests lie in the area of intellectual property and legal regulation of the arts. His doctoral research at Queen Mary University of London was titled "Dematerialisation and Dissonance: Conceptual Art Practices, Art World Strategies, and the Role of Copyright Law." This interdisciplinary study, which focuses on the UK and US legal regimes, examines the nature of Conceptual art, the implications of its privileging of ideas over form, the role of documentation in the artistic process, judicial strategies for the definition of art, and the art-world realities that safeguard artists' interests, often in lieu of legal protections.

MARTHA BUSKIRK
is Professor of art history and criticism at Montserrat College of Art, in Beverly, Massachusetts. She is author of *Creative Enterprise: Contemporary Art between Museum and Marketplace* (2012) and *The Contingent Object of Contemporary Art* (2003), and she is coeditor of *The Duchamp Effect* (with Mignon Nixon, 1996) and *The Destruction of Tilted Arc: Documents* (with Clara Weyergraf-Serra, 1990). She is also author of numerous essays and articles that have appeared in *Artforum*, *October*, *Art in America*, and other venues. Her current research, supported by a 2015 Guggenheim Fellowship and a 2016 Clark Art Institute Fellowship, examines the interplay between artistic authorship and legal definitions of intellectual property.

GIUSEPPE CALABI
is senior partner at CBM & Partners, a law firm based in Milan. He has successfully developed the art law practice, in which his firm is widely

recognized as a leader both nationwide and internationally. He is currently a member of a government-appointed working group in charge of drafting a reform of the artwork export license regime in Italy. He is the Senior Vice-Chair of the Art, Cultural Institutions, and Heritage Law Committee of the International Bar Association (IBA). He is also a member of the Harvard Law School Leadership Council of Europe, the Copyright Commission of the Italian Publishers Association, and the Advisory Committee of the Italian Communication Authority (AGCOM) on online copyright infringement. He has published many articles and essays on art law.

PENELOPE CURTIS
is Director of the Calouste Gulbenkian Museum, in Lisbon. She was previously Director of Tate Britain, in London, and the Henry Moore Institute, in Leeds. She is known for her writing on modern and contemporary sculpture, and for her exhibitions, which work across chronologies and media. Her monographs include *Sculpture 1900–1945: After Rodin* (1999), *Patio and Pavilion: The Place of Sculpture in Modern Architecture* (2007), and *Sculpture: Vertical, Horizontal, Closed, Open* (2017). Recently she was the cocurator of *Modern British Sculpture* at the Royal Academy (2011) and *Barbara Hepworth: Sculpture for a Modern World* at Tate Britain (2015).

ALESSANDRA DONATI
is Professor of Comparative Contract Law at the University of Milano-Bicocca, and Professor of Art Law in the Master in Contemporary Art Markets program at the New Academy of Fine Arts (NABA), Milan. She is also a practicing lawyer. In 2015 she was honored as the Jacques Derrida / Law and Culture International Chair of Philosophy at the University of Turin. She serves as the Chair of the Scientific Committee of the Italian Association of Artists' Archives (AitArt) and is a member of the board of Careof, an organization that supports contemporary art research. She is the director of the Comparative Art Law series published by ESI and a member of the editorial board for the journal *Art and Law* (Brill). She has authored many articles and monographs on art law, including *Law and Art: Diritto civile e arte contemporanea* (2012), *I contratti degli artisti* (2012), and *Autenticità, authenticité, authenticity: Archivi d'artista e autenticità dell'opera* (2015).

NATE HARRISON
is an artist and writer working at the intersection of intellectual property, cultural production, and the formation of creative processes in modern media. His work has been exhibited at the Whitney Museum of American Art, New York; the Centre Georges Pompidou, Paris; and the Kunstverein, Hamburg, among others. He has several publications current and forthcoming and has also lectured at a variety of institutions, including Experience Music Project, Seattle; the Art and Law Program, New York; and SOMA Summer, Mexico City. He received the Videonale Prize from the Kunstmuseum Bonn, as well as the Hannah Arendt Prize in Critical Theory and Creative Research from Pacific Northwest College of Art, Portland, Oregon. He earned his doctorate from the University of California, San Diego, and is completing a book on contemporary appropriation art and intellectual property law. He chairs the Media Arts Department at the School of the Museum of Fine Arts at Tufts University, Boston.

CORINNE HERSHKOVITCH
is a lawyer and a member of the Paris Bar since 1992. She specializes in intellectual-property and art law. She deals with provenance, appraisal, attribution, authenticity, ownership, cross-border movement of art, recovery of lost or misappropriated art, and cultural heritage. She has been involved in many cases concerning looted art since 1996 and has a strong expertise in the restitution and repatriation of cultural heritage. She has lectured in art law at the University Lyon III, Institut National du Patrimoine, and Université Paris II Panthéon-Assas.

JOAN KEE
is Associate Professor of the History of Art at the University of Michigan. A former attorney, she has published frequently on the subject of law and contemporary art in such publications as *Law and Literature*, *American Art*, the *Cornell Journal of Law and Public Policy*, and the *Journal of Law, Culture and the Humanities*. Her book on the complexity of relationships between art and law, *Models of Integrity: Art and Law in Post-Sixties America*, is forthcoming from the University of California Press in 2019. A related project discusses how methods of interpretation employed in the discipline of art history might be adapted for legal cases requiring close visual analysis.

GABRIEL PÉREZ-BARREIRO
is Director and Chief Curator of the Colección Patricia Phelps de Cisneros, and Curator of the 33rd Bienal de São Paulo (2018). From 2002 to 2008 he was Curator of Latin American Art at the Blanton Museum of Art at the University of Texas, Austin. In 2007 he was Chief Curator of the 6th Mercosur Biennial, in Porto Alegre, Brazil. He holds a Ph.D. in Art History and Theory from the University of Essex, and an M.A. in Art History and Latin American Studies from the University of Aberdeen.

LISA ROSENDAHL
is a curator and writer based in Berlin. She has been a curator at Statens Konstråd (Public Art Agency Sweden) since 2014. From 2011 to 2013 she was the Director of Iaspis, the Swedish Arts Grants Committee's international program for visual art, architecture, and design. She has also served as Director of the Baltic Art Center (BAC), in Visby, Sweden, and Director of Exhibitions at the Lisson Gallery, London. She has curated exhibitions at Moderna Museet, Stockholm; Kunsthall Charlottenborg, Copenhagen; and the Institute of International Visual Arts (INIVA), London. She writes and lectures extensively on contemporary art and was a coeditor of *Work, Work, Work: A Reader on Art and Labour* (2012).

GILANE TAWADROS
is the Chief Executive of the Design and Artists Copyright Society (DACS), a nonprofit visual-artists rights-management organization in the UK. She was the founding director of the Institute of International Visual Arts (INIVA), in London, and has curated numerous exhibitions, nationally and internationally. In 2012 she was the first art historian to be appointed as the Blanche, Edith, and Irving Laurie New Jersey Chair in Women's Studies at Rutgers University. She has written extensively on contemporary art. Her books include *Changing States: Contemporary Art and Ideas in an Era of Globalisation* (2004) and *Life Is More Important than Art* (2007). An anthology of her writings, *The Sphinx Contemplating Napoleon: Global Perspectives on Contemporary Art and Difference*, is due to be published in 2018.

CHRISTIAN VIVEROS-FAUNÉ
is a New York–based writer and curator, and a former art dealer and fair director. He was awarded a Creative Capital | Warhol Foundation Arts Writers Grant in 2010, was named critic-in-residence at the Bronx Museum of the Arts in 2011, and has been a lecturer at Yale University, Pratt Institute, and Holland's Gerrit Rietveld Academie. He currently writes criticism for the *Village Voice* and *ArtReview*, and he is working on several museum exhibitions in the United States and Latin America, as well as a book about art and politics.

KARL VON TROTT ZU SOLZ
is director of Fine Art Partners in Berlin and consultant at the Institute for Artists' Estates. With Loretta Würtenberger he authored the book *The Artist's Estate: A Handbook for Artists, Executors, and Heirs* (2016). He studied law in Freiburg, Munich, and Berlin and earned a Masters in Art Business at Sotheby's Institute of Art, in New York. Before joining Fine Art Partners, he was founder and managing director of an online marketplace for art and antique dealers.

CHRISTINE J. VINCENT
is Project Director of the Aspen Institute Artist-Endowed Foundations Initiative/ AEFI. She was Deputy Director for Media, Arts, and Culture at the Ford Foundation, as well as a former president of Maine College of Art. Her essay in this volume draws on research conducted for AEFI's principal research initiative, the National Study of Artist-Endowed Foundations, with findings available at www.aspeninstitute.org/aefi.

JOHN C. WELCHMAN
is a professor of art history at the University of California, San Diego. His books include *Modernism Relocated* (1995), *Art after Appropriation* (2001), and *Past Realization: Essays on Contemporary European Art* (2016), the first volume of his collected writings. He coauthored the books *Dada and Surrealist Word-Image* (1987), *Mike Kelley* (1999), and *Kwang-Young Chung* (2014), and edited *Rethinking Borders* (1996), *Institutional Critique and After* (2006), *The Aesthetics of Risk* (2008), *Black Sphinx: On the Comedic in Modern Art* (2010), and the following volumes of writings by Mike Kelley: *Foul Perfection: Essays and Criticism* (2003), *Minor Histories* (2004) and *Mike Kelley: Interviews, Conversations, and Chit-Chat, 1988–2004* (2005).

LORETTA WÜRTENBERGER
is the founder of the Institute for Artists' Estates and editor of the book *The Artist's Estate: A Handbook for Artists, Executors, and Heirs*, published by Hatje Cantz in 2016. She has been working with artists' estates for many years, including those of Jean (Hans) Arp, Sophie Täuber-Arp, and Keith Arnatt. After studying law, philosophy, and art history, she earned her doctorate in international copyright and patent law at the Max Planck Institute, Munich. She is a partner at Fine Art Partners and a founder of the Contemporary Arts Alliance Berlin.

DONN ZARETSKY
is a partner at John Silberman Associates PC, in New York, and an adjunct professor at NYU Law School, where he teaches a seminar in Advanced Topics in Art Law. He is the author of the *Art Law Blog* (www.theartlawblog.blogspot.com), and his writings on art law have also appeared in the *Art Newspaper* and *Art and Auction*, among other places. He represented Christoph Büchel in his dispute with the Massachusetts Museum of Contemporary Art (MASS MoCA).

PHOTO CREDITS

© Association Marcel Duchamp/ADAGP, Paris and DACS, London 2018: p.302
© The estate of Sol LeWitt; image: Mondadori Portfolio/Electa/Lucio Rossi/ Bridgeman Images © ARS, NY and DACS, London 2018: frontispiece
© Courtesy Fondazione Prada, Milano; photo credit: Attilio Maranzano: p.284
© Mike Kelley Foundation for the Arts. All Rights Reserved/DACS, London/VAGA, NY 2018: p.96
© Myandywarhol.com: p.186
© PACER Court Records: p.54
© Richard Prince; photo credit: Rob McKeever: p.82
© Courtesy Simon Starling and Casey Kaplan, New York; photo credit: Steve Payne: p.130

Published in 2018 by Ridinghouse
46 Lexington Street
London W1F 0LP
United Kingdom
ridinghouse.co.uk

Distributed in the UK and Europe by
Cornerhouse Publications
c/o Home
2 Tony Wilson Place
Manchester M15 4FN
United Kingdom
cornerhousepublications.org

Distributed in rest of world by
ARTBOOK | D.A.P.
75 Broad Street, Suite 630
New York, New York 10004
artbook.com

Special thanks are due to Zsofia Jilling,
Sophie Kullmann, and Mark Thomson

British Library Cataloguing-in-Publication Data
A full catalogue record of this book is available from the British Library.

ISBN 978 1 909932 45 6

Copyedited by Zsofia Jilling
Proofreading by Sophie Kullmann

Designed by Mark Thomson

Printed in Estonia by Tallinna Raamatutrükikoja OÜ

frontispiece:
Sol LeWitt
Wall Drawing #528/G, 2005
Private collection

Ridinghouse